The Romance of
Innocent Sexuality

The Romance of
Innocent Sexuality

by GEOFFREY REES

 CASCADE *Books* · Eugene, Oregon

THE ROMANCE OF INNOCENT SEXUALITY

Cascade Books
An Imprint of Wipf and Stock Publishers
199 W. 8th Ave., Suite 3
Eugene, OR 97401

www.wipfandstock.com

ISBN 13: 978-1-60608-661-2

Cataloging-in-Publication data:

Rees, Geoffrey.

The romance of innocent sexuality / Geoffrey Rees.

xvi + 304 p. ; 23 cm. — Includes bibliographical references and index(es).

ISBN 13: 978-1-60608-661-2

1. Sex—Religious aspects—Christianity. 2. Augustine, Saint, Bishop of Hippo. 3. Sin, Original—History of doctrine—Early church, ca. 30–600. 4. Homosexuality—Religious aspects—Christianity. I. Title.

BT708 .R43 2011

Manufactured in the U.S.A.

Contents

Preface

I only desire one favour; that no part of this discourse may be judged of by itself and independently of the rest; for I am sensible I have not disposed my materials to abide the test of a captious controversy, but of a sober and even forgiving examination; that they are not armed at all points for battle; but dressed to visit those who are willing to give a peaceful entrance to truth.[1]

THE FOLLOWING WORK WAS written primarily in the private and leafy quiet of New Haven, Connecticut, but it begins in a noonday public encounter on lower Broadway. Adrift and barely employed in New York City, I was living alone in a studio apartment in the East Village, in the home stretch of what had been a difficult decade. At the time I was an avid collector of cookbooks, and mornings at home writing and editing were often followed by a walk that terminated in the cooking section of the Strand Bookstore. Tucked against the wall to the left about a quarter of the way back from the street entrance, the cookbooks were my diamond field, a refuge where I could lose myself in the search for some culinary treasure. Mostly I was scrounging in the dirt. Occasionally I walked away with a gem—*James's Beard's American Cookery*, Paula Peck's *The Art of Fine Baking*, Maida Heatter's *Book of Great Cookies*. In those days I kept a pile of cookbooks on my bedside table. On my pillow at night I recited Rose Levy Beranbaum's formula for Neoclassical Buttercream. Many nights I went to sleep excited to wake up the next morning with

---

1. Burke, *Philosophical Inquiry*, 50.

Marion Cunningham's *The Breakfast Book* beside me. Frequently also I thumbed through a copy of the New English Bible, in my drowsy wandering returning always to reading Psalm 13.

Entering the Strand off Broadway, it happened that the most direct access to the cookbooks was through the religion section, and one day, en route to my fix of food in print, the glint of white lettering against the maroon spine of a paperback caught my eye. Without thinking I stopped, reached overhead, and pulled the book from the shelf. Standing in view of the cashiers and the plate glass windows and the stalls beyond them turning onto Twelfth Street and the intermittent canary flurry of taxis speeding downtown, I began reading. Immediately time slowed, or rather expanded through a power I had associated with books in childhood. I was mesmerized, riveted to the spot. I knew that other persons had already journeyed through these pages, but still each word seemed vivid and distinct as if it had been addressed to me alone, had been waiting for me, and we were rejoicing at our happy discovery of each other through the shock of mutual recognition, but also were a little embarrassed, a sense of shared indecency binding us together even more tightly. The book was *Augustine of Hippo*, the author Peter Brown, and before I left the store I had finished the first chapter with the indelible impression that I had just discovered an ancient world so vivid and real and new that already it was exercising its power to transform my own.

Over the next couple of weeks I devoured Brown's book, but my pace altered when I subsequently turned to reading *Confessions*. For several months I savored R. S. Pine-Coffin's wonderfully mournful translation. It consumed an hour of each afternoon. I was so overwhelmed by the searching intensity of Augustine's questions that I could only read a few pages at a time. I call them Augustine's questions, but they seemed my own also. They promised definition and organization to a host of inchoate thoughts that had occupied my mind for as long as I could remember. It was through these months living with *Confessions* that religious ethics emerged to my view as a rubric of study under which my eclectic interests and disjointed education began to appear as a possible coherent trajectory with a future also. After a lot of reflection, weighing doubts that persist to the present, and at an age when many persons are already completing their doctorates I found myself at the public library on Second Avenue scanning the pages of Peterson's Guide to Graduate

Schools and wondering how I would explain to my family and friends that I was seriously considering attending Divinity School.

As I look back now in order to encourage my readers to look forward into this book, I realize also that in my turn to the study of theology and ethics I was honoring an earlier public encounter that had joined reading and friendship. Almost ten years previous I had been serving time as an undergraduate at the University of Chicago. One afternoon I was crossing the lobby of the Regenstein library—always a crowded gossipy space, especially in the dead of winter—when my friend Joseph—he was a student at the now defunct Graduate Library School—hailed me with excitement. With his arms crossed and his lips pursed, Joseph stood staring at me, fixing me to the spot with his wide-open brown eyes even as he was also batting his lacy black lashes at me, deliberately making a spectacle of ourselves. I must, he insisted, proceed directly to the fourth floor and read an excerpt, just published in the magazine *October*, from a remarkable new book on relations between men in the classical world. Then he batted his lashes some more, daring me to defy him. Moved by his fervor, charmed by his flirting, a little bit intimated by his schoolmarm severity (he was a born librarian, as passionately interested in the history of the papacy as he was horrified at the innovation of open stacks), I did as told and crept back upstairs where I remained reading until dusk. The excerpted chapter, it turns out, was from Michel Foucault's *The Uses of Pleasure*, and I left the library with the indelible impression that the actual event of sexual activity is the least interesting—to the point of even being boring—aspect of any sexual relationship.

It was only much later, at the mid point of graduate school as I was preparing a question on same-sex marriage for my comprehensive exams, that I was able to appreciate more fully Joseph's enthusiasm that afternoon and also my debt to his instruction. In preparing to write the exam I was continually puzzled by the vehemence of the arguments for and against same-sex marriage. Honestly it was and remains a question about which I care relatively little, so much so that I consider it almost unjustifiable how other persons spend so much psychic energy and political capital fighting for or against measures to recognize same-sex marriage when so many injustices in the world persist unrecognized. Not that I don't consider the unequal distribution of privileges and benefits associated with marriage a significant problem of justice, only that I consider the insistent bundling of them with marriage—in the provision of health care, for example—a frustration to their redress. It was out of that frustration that the question I had thought I was addressing began to dissolve, liberating in a way my inquiry from considerations of same-sex marriage in itself (as if it has any intrinsic qualities to assess) to the passions surrounding it, more specifically to the self-interest of those passions and their theological and political implications. Instead of asking about same-sex marriage, I would ask about the functions of the discourse surrounding same-sex marriage. I would ask about what people are doing when they argue about same-sex marriage. And in doing so I recalled the memory of Joseph's friendship as my own introduction to the dictum that the personal is political, about which he was adamant.

From that subtle shift in focus a boring question became a consuming question that resonated with my insatiable appetite for nineteenth-century fiction. Youthful readings of Dickens and Henry James and Proust in recent years had grown into an obsession of sorts with such unduly neglected authors as Fanny Trollope, Charles Reade, Mrs. Henry Wood, and Eliza Lynn Linton among many others, nourished by the bounty of musty leather-bound volumes ripe for the picking in the stacks of Sterling Memorial Library. All of which added up to the realization that the most novel aspect of debates surrounding same-sex marriage was their indebtedness to the tradition of novels in which marriage is at once idealized and challenged as a means of completion of one's sexed self, such completion itself imagined as necessary to the possibility of encounter between self and God. The question that subsequently emerged was twofold. How does alienation from God as a result of sin become narrated as alienation from God as a result of incompletion of one's sex? And how is it possible to engage theological debates about sexuality without contributing to their narrations of sexed identity achieving its completion in marriage?

It is these two questions that *The Romance of Innocent Sexuality* strives to address. Complicated as the argument gets, the bottom line is simple: sin, not innocence. Rather than attempt to discern whose sexual desires and relationships are innocent and whose not, a more responsible sexual ethics—and more constructive also—starts with acceptance of responsibility by each person individually for the universal ruin of humankind in a single inheritable original sin that is meaningfully and appropriately associated with sexuality. Stated more practically, the best way to show that what appears like irresolvable disagreement about issues of sexual morality is in fact a function of the nearness to crowding against each other of the standpoints of all the participants, is to pull the rug out from under everyone all at once. Easier said than done, though to the extent possible a proof I believe of my own longstanding conviction that innocence is overrated.

In light of these few remarks it will hardly appear a coincidence that my work is written through readings of writers who were themselves passionate readers. I have found a lot of pleasure in my readings, in the discovery of unexpected consonances among seemingly irreconcilable texts. I hope that my readers will share in some of that pleasure, will find some pleasure in their own indulgence of reading as imaginative play. Wide as the range of readings is, however, they are organized by interpretations of Augustine and Foucault, as they became organized in turn by acceptance of the literal sense of Scripture and the meaningfulness of the association of original sin with sexuality. Some comments on the hermeneutical starting points, and also on the status of theology as a cultural activity, should therefore help to orient readers towards the interdisciplinary, constructive, and exploratory qualities of the argument.

In writing of Augustine I have tried to follow the rule that he himself recommends to his readers as part of his discussion of the hermeneutics of charity in Book 12 of *Confessions*. Here Augustine insists that love of God and neighbor are the rule of interpretation. Here he insists, against the privatizing desires characteristic of sin, that the insights of interpretation are public property. And here he insists that the end of interpretation is the concord of the interpreting community. Most significant for my purposes, Augustine actually posits the future of his own writings in light of this hermeneutics:

> Certainly, to make a bold declaration from my heart, if I myself were to be writing something at this supreme level of authority I would choose to write so that my words would sound out with whatever diverse truth in these matters each reader was able to grasp, rather than to give a quite explicit statement of a single true view of this question in such a way as to exclude other views— provided there was no false doctrine to offend me.[2]

My own readings of Augustine all proceed in a way out of this bold declaration. They eschew claims to advanced expertise on Augustine and the classical world, but they do seek truth while also seeking to avoid the

2. Augustine *Confessions* 12.31.42 (Chadwick, 271).

offense he warns against. The doctrine around which they are structured is that most insistently identified with Augustine himself in its most defamed aspect: the doctrine of original sin as a literal inheritance of all humanity that begins in the singular disobedience of the two created human beings from whom all others human beings are descended. A great value I believe of original sin as a hermeneutical principle alongside love is that it pushes the reader to engage the "diverse truth" in "excluded other views," because it pushes the reader to recognize her own implication in the dynamics of exclusion that inescapably shape all reading practices. I recognize accordingly that *The Romance of Innocent Sexuality* is riddled with such exclusion. I cannot proceed otherwise, and I acknowledge that such exclusion is regrettable but also, crucially, that it is enabling.

Although my readings of Foucault focus almost entirely on the first volume of *The History of Sexuality*, they are shaped by the numerous essays and interviews from the latter years of his life, where he reflected most self-consciously on the political and practical as well intellectual import of his writings. It is during this final phase that Foucault breaks his silence and begins to affirm the possibilities of human freedom, to advocate resistance to oppressive and stultifying disciplines and technologies, and to explore the ideals of aesthetic/ascetic self-creation. This phase of Foucault's career culminates, for me, in his striking summary statement regarding the status of the first volume in relation to his subsequent work:

> This book does not have the function of a proof. It exists as a sort of prelude, to explore the keyboard, sketch out the themes, and see how people react, what will be criticized, what will be misunderstood, and what will cause resentment—it was in some sense to give the other volumes access to these reactions that I wrote this one first. As to the problem of fiction, it seems to me to be a very important one; I am well aware that I have never written anything but fictions. I do not mean to say, however, that truth is therefore absent. It seems to me that the possibility exists for fiction to function in truth, for a fictional discourse to induce effects of truth, and for bringing it about that a true discourse engenders or "manufactures" something that does not as yet exist, that is, "fictions" it. One "fictions" history on the basis of a political reality that makes it true, one "fictions" a politics not yet in existence on the basis of a historical truth.[3]

3. Foucault, *Power/Knowledge*, 193.

The language and idea of fiction as activity and accomplishment is the starting point of my constructive reading of the *History*. Following Foucault's own evaluation I use his book as a resource in an attempt to fiction a history of the fiction of sex on the basis of the contemporary political reality of debates about sexed identity finding its fulfillment in marriage. And to fiction a sexual politics not yet in existence on the basis of the historical truth of original sin. The possibility of a more just future political reality of personal identity is thus a function of present imagination's capacity to fiction it. In the meantime the story of same-sex marriage remains inseparable from the story of any marriage.

As a moderately observant Reform Jewish writer who dares to wade deep into contemporary Christian theological debates about sexuality and same-sex marriage, and even more daring perhaps, to propound an orthodox Christian doctrine, I find some support for my boldness in the conceptualization of theology as a cultural activity developed by Katherine Tanner. In her book *Theories of Culture* Tanner elaborates a framework that not only makes room for non-Christians to engage the doctrinal resources of Christian theology, but actually suggests that such non-Christian engagement with traditional doctrine demands serious attention from Christians themselves. Theology as a practice, Tanner explains, cannot wall itself off by specific defensible boundaries. Theological reflection is not finally bounded by any absolute cultural boundaries at all. Instead the boundaries are porous, shifting, indeterminate, so that theology is better described as a practice that arises at and across multiple boundaries. Just as Christian theological reflection potentially engages any aspect of the entirety of cultural resources that are its own context, so too the particular doctrinal resources of Christian theology are a constituent ingredient of that context. The following vision of theological imagination in practice emerges:

> What has just been said against putative constraints on theological creativity suggests something about the nature of theological creativity. It does not seem to amount to any "pure," freewheeling expression of creative drives. It seems, instead, to be the creativity of a postmodern "bricoleur"—the creativity, that is, of someone who works with an always potentially disordered heap of already existing materials, pulling them apart and putting them back together again, tinkering with their shapes, twisting them this way

and that. It is a creativity expressed through the modification and extension of materials already on the ground.[4]

I do not believe that Christian theology (nor any other tradition-dependent attempt to understand human beings in relation to their creator; the only kind of attempt humanly possible) has ever been an exclusive province of Christians, in the sense that its materials are always also the "materials already on the ground" of its cultural context. There has never been, I hope will never be, a world that is not plural. As a practical matter I therefore consider that the possibility of prophetic critique of culture includes within itself the possibility of critique by culture of its prophetic detractors.

In turning to the doctrine of original sin as an especially significant cultural-theological resource for analysis of a large array of additional "already existing materials," I further believe that I am honoring the Christian tradition even as I don't claim a place for myself exactly within it. In the process I am crossing, perhaps confounding, academic disciplinary boundaries. The interdisciplinarity of my project I consider a correlate of its theological presuppositions. As an exercise of theological creativity the arguments advanced throughout *The Romance of Innocent Sexuality* are more or less equal parts textual, cultural, critical, and historical. Readers who assert some enforceable boundary markers, whether disciplinary, doctrinal, political, across which the investigations presumably don't move—for example by insisting on the insufficiency of Augustine's and Foucault's texts in translation to support the themes of the book—are in a curious way therefore making the argument for the importance of those themes. At least they are retreating into the fortress of academic criticism just at the points where I wish to draw them out, invoking truth to hide from the powers of fiction that render diverse effects of truth possible.

In choosing to address such expansive topics as sexuality and same-sex marriage and the doctrine of original sin and the relation of fiction to narration of truths about self through figures each of whom are the focus of specialized study—Augustine, Foucault, Dickens, and numerous lesser lights—I am well aware how exposed I am on all sides to this kind of criticism. It has never seemed possible to me to keep fully abreast of the wealth of scholarship that continues to appear on any one of these

4. Tanner, *Theories*, 166.

topics or persons, let alone some combination of them. At least it has never seemed possible to do so and also sleep, watch movies, travel, bake Danish pastry, maintain relationships with friends and family, and most of all move on to new work. In the face of such a daunting task I have instead struggled to master some of the discipline of scaling back, of restraint in reference, of marshalling no more primary and especially secondary resources than are necessary to establish the plausibility, the viability, of the arguments at hand. It honestly took a lot of concentration to ignore as much as I know that I have, never mind to remain ignorant of so much more that I don't know. But then my aim has never been to intervene in one specialized discourse, but to generate a conversation across disciplines. My aim has been to write a book that others will find generally interesting, challenging, illuminating if also sometimes maddening, and perhaps occasionally even beautiful.

Among the numerous friends, colleagues, family, teachers, students —often in combination—whom it is a pleasure to thank personally for their assistance and support in realizing this work to its end, as well as the anonymous reviewers who have commented on the manuscript during its journey towards publication, three person I wish to acknowledge publicly and apart.

Throughout my years at Yale Divinity School and then Yale Graduate School and beyond, Gene Outka has been an unflappable mentor. He has never been anything less than genuinely encouraging that I pursue my own path intellectually even as he was continually opening that path to view for me. I cannot recall a single instance in which he has ever told me what to think, or what not to think. Instead he has always modeled for me how to think more clearly and carefully. It was in a pair of seminars he offered, the first on "Agape and Special Relations," the second on "Ethics and Human Nature," that I began to discern the intellectual footings of this work. From those seminars to the present I have always found my own close readings exceeded by his close readings of them in turn. His writings I consider a model of analytic nuance which I continue to strive to match in my own. And from his restrained and honest criticism and praise I have learned the pedagogical value of a single word well placed, a brief question inscribed in the margin, a polite demurral, all the slender but powerful instruments in the art of caring criticism as an incitement to my own students, if they only knew.

Of the persons I met when I was exploring making the transition to the study of theology and ethics, it was Margaret Farley who made all the difference. I had visited a number of professors at various schools, explaining my interests. At the end of each introduction I would ask: Does that make any sense to you? Each time my question was answered by a pause just a bit too long, and then a politely distancing statement like, "Have you looked at any of Martha Nussbaum's recent work?" or "Problems of personal identity are definitely important for ethics" followed by uncomfortable questions about my education and its notable lacunae. My last visit was to New Haven, on a muggy November day too warm. The night before I had been jumped on the street walking home from a movie in the rain (the only incident of its kind in my life). Sitting in her office at Yale Divinity School with a black eye enthusing over the vision of Eve in Charlotte Bronte's *Shirley* I must have looked a bit of a maniac, yet when I reached the end of my introduction and asked my question, the pause that followed was different. And then Margaret Farley said, the sincerity in her voice unmistakable: "Absolutely. I think it would be fascinating to work with you." Really that honest vote of confidence, that willingness to hear me out in the present, was a turning point, one that I return to regularly in thinking about my obligation to attend to my students whose attention I ask in turn. She has since modeled for me the indivisibility of the intellectual and the practical in ethics. Her genius in holding them together without compromising either continues to shape my own practice in the classroom and beyond.

Finally, I am very grateful to have worked with Charlie Collier at Cascade Books. On a gloomy January morning in the basement of the Hyatt Regency on Wacker in Chicago, my frustrations all too apparent and tinged with darker sentiments, he patiently heard me out. Good as his word at the time, he embraced my manuscript quickly and enthusiastically. He is a generous, sharp, and sure editorial guide. It is a great relief in multiple senses to turn over this work to him.

The Valorization of Sex in Death

The Faustian pact, whose temptation has been instilled in us by the deployment of sexuality, is now as follows: to exchange life in its entirety for sex itself, for the truth and sovereignty of sex. Sex is worth dying for. It is in this (strictly historical) sense that sex is indeed imbued with the death instinct. When a long while ago the West discovered love, it bestowed on it a value high enough to make death acceptable; nowadays it is sex that claims this equivalence, the highest of all. And while the deployment of sexuality permits the techniques of power to invest life, the fictitious point of sex, itself marked by that deployment, exerts enough charm on everyone for them to accept hearing the grumble of death within it.[1]

Mature Humor and Charitable Anger

SO MUCH HAS BEEN published in recent decades on theology and sexuality it seems foolhardy to attempt yet another contribution to the topic. The foolhardiness consists most of all in imagining that it is possible to articulate anything fresh or new. Still it should at least be possible to refresh some old wisdom and to present it in a renewed light. Even granting that such accomplishment is possible, however, it seems foolhardy to imagine that anyone might be able to listen above the din

1. Foucault, *History of Sexuality*, 1:156. Subsequent citations are parenthetical and refer to volume 1 of *The History of Sexuality*.

of a conversation that is already so over-crowded and overwrought. Nor does it seem likely that anyone who might bother to listen will stay tuned long enough to allow the possible insights of another voice on the subject. As if these obstacles are not discouraging enough, to write about theology and sexuality is also to expose oneself to a multiplicity of unwelcome interpretation. This is because the conversation is so discordant, marked more by the collision than intersection of divergent theoretical, methodological, and political approaches. To write about theology and sexuality is to invite ascription to oneself of all sorts of hopes, attachments, desires, and dreads that one is unlikely to wish to recognize as one's own.

Given these hazards of irrelevance, neglect, misinterpretation, and exposure, a sense of humor in a general way seems indispensable to participation in this conversation almost as a matter of survival. Yet in the place of humor a magisterial tone reigns supreme, as if it were the only means available to maintain one's dignity against the indignity of having to speak at all about such matters. Enjoining perhaps so much seriousness, the imperative of having always to keep a straight face, is that a bit of abjection, and the humorous wisdom to own its satisfactions, promises to accomplish more than just soften the edge of so much writing on theology and sexuality. To lack a sense of humor when writing about theology and sexuality is obligatory for so many because it is to lack the self-deprecating playfulness that makes discovery of the greater meaningfulness of such writing possible. Without a sense of the absurdities, the ironies, the vulnerabilities, and also the longings, the beauties, the fantasms, and the delights of sexual desire and relationship; without the capacity to relish some old-fashioned gossip and rumor-mongering; without the fearlessness of appearing abased; without the willingness to allow appetites and pleasures and bad smells and awkward postures; without the courage to look into the mirror and own that the strange animal with a forlorn gaze staring back at you, is *you*, the desire to engage this conversation looks less like a desire to think critically about sexed identity and more like a desire to enforce some impossible regimen of self-understanding. The absence of a general sense of humor consequently helps to explain why so much of what passes for writing about theology and sexuality is more screed than inquiry, more polemic than reflection, more shouting at than conversing with.

If humor is what is needed to break through the multiple barriers constraining theological discourse of sexuality, the writings of Saint

Augustine seem an unlikely resource to accomplish the task, least of all
the association of sexuality with a literally inheritable original sin. Unless
one takes the very suggestion itself as a joke. What could be funny, after
all, in the idea of an original sin in which all subsequent generations of
human beings fully and responsibly participate? For which all humanity
is justly punished by death? And which is transmitted through the biology of sexual reproduction? Not without apparent cause has Augustine
often been characterized (and then blamed too) as the greatest exponent
of human shame at the irrepressible stirrings of sexual desire:

> For after their disobedience to God's instructions, the first hu-
> man beings were deprived of God's favour; and immediately they
> were embarrassed by the nakedness of their bodies. They even
> used fig leaves, which were perhaps the first things they could lay
> hands on in their confusion, to cover their *pudenda*, the "organs
> of shame." The organs were the same as they were before, but
> previously there was no shame attaching to them. Thus they felt
> a novel disturbance in their disobedient flesh, as a punishment
> which answered to their own disobedience.[2]

   As Augustinian as Augustine gets, any humor in his account of how
humanity's collective fall from grace in the fact of an original disobedience by Adam and Even in Eden concentrates in a "novel disturbance"
of the "organs of shame" at first glance only looks possible at Augustine's
expense. As if he is unwittingly acknowledging the spontaneous delight
of a "matinee" and wondering at its exclusion from paradise. As if, in
his confused haste to lay his hand on some rhetorical "fig leaves," he has
been caught *in flagrante delicto* of the suggestiveness of his own words,
betraying his phallogocentric obsessiveness, his concern for the loss of
"God's favour" so intensely focused on his own erection that he cannot
comprehend that Eve does not have and never did have a disobedient
and offending penis, so that Augustine and all men bear a double burden of guilt for themselves and for those defective men with whom they
beget more misbegotten generations of human beings. Except that in a
felicitous word choice Augustine's translator hints that a more literally
novel disturbance will eventually prove the potency of words to shape the
experience of disobedient flesh.
   The case against any humorous appeal to the Augustinian association
of sexuality and sin only looks worse when one considers how passionately

2. Augustine *City of God* 13.13 (Bettenson, 52).

writings on theology and sexuality are energized by some combination of anger and fear. Adding sin to the conversation only seems to intensify the stakes, since so much of the anger and fear of theological discourse of sexuality concentrates in the contest to establish the innocence and guilt of the participants in the conversation through articulation of permissible and forbidden forms of sexual desire and relationship. Sin only figures negatively, as something other people do. It is only valued as the means for distinguishing the innocence of one's own desire and behavior. Hardly anyone seems willing to stand accused of sin, or to remain silent in the face of accusation of sin, let alone willing to embrace sin. Instead, accusation of sin is typically met by accusation of the sinfulness of the accusation of sin, enjoining a cycle of recrimination that ceaselessly undermines potential grounds for reconciliation. Defense against any imputation of sin, not confession of sin, is the default stance adopted by most writers. To suggest then that the inherent sinfulness of all sexuality is the most responsible and conciliatory starting point possible for a theological sexual ethics is only a little less incendiary than walking into a hydrogen factory with a blowtorch. It is also to offer oneself as a common target to forces that otherwise can agree on nothing, not even to disagree.

The promise for theological investigation, admittedly risky, of confession of the inherent sinfulness of all human sexuality is that it offends equally. It succeeds by pleasing no one. It comprehends the entire landscape of theological discourse of sexuality and places at its center not the morality of any particular sexual activity but instead the morality of the activity of the discourse itself. The ethics of sexual relationship and the ethics of the conduct of debates in sexual ethics become one continuous project, so that writings on sexuality and theology become subject to critique as a kind of fig leaves for which all the parties involved are reaching in haste to cover over the shame of their own sin. The nakedness of the body, implied in even the most elliptical discussion of sexual relationship, is only an index, Augustine explains, of the nakedness that all this writing attempts to cover over and that ensues from the original disobedience of Adam and Eve: "And so 'they recognized that they were naked'—stripped, that is, of the grace that prevented their bodily nakedness from causing them any embarrassment, as it did when the law of sin made war against their mind."[3] The embarrassment and shame of original sin turns out not to concern one's present body exactly, so much as it concerns a loss of

3. Ibid., 14.17 (Bettenson, 578–79).

experience of embodied completion that haunts human memory. What is embarrassing and shameful is the exposure of one's lack of grace. The association of sexuality and sin consequently seems even less amenable to humor because so profoundly obscene, more obscene than any image of individual or joined naked human bodies could be, projecting as it does an ultimate exposure of culpable human selves to each other in the starkest possible light of God's harsh judgment. An exposure that no amount of words or cloth or fig leaves can ever wholly cover over. Elaboration of the enduring meaningfulness of the association of sexuality and sin in a literal interpretation of original sin therefore requires recognition of the common exposure that joins all of humanity in a single fallen community. It also requires recognition, both by writer and reader, of the inevitable defensiveness, the ineluctable reaching for some sort of covering garment, which characterizes theological discourse of sexuality, and which thereby also signifies the potency of the association of sexuality and sin.[4]

To counter this defensiveness it is not only not possible, but also not desirable, to try to overcome directly or entirely the instinctive desire of the fallen self to hide one's sinfulness. To seek to do so would be Satanic shamelessness, since the very impulse to shame and embarrassment that persists after the Fall attests to the grace that remains of the grace that was stripped away. Every confused and hasty reach for whatever garment is at hand is a testament of memory to the one lost garment and thus an acknowledgment that the self apart from God is unbearably, impossibly naked, more flayed alive than naked, having lost the distinctive envelope of self that renders any person wholly recognizable to self and to others. To marshal this defensiveness in the service of open theological inquiry therefore requires more than a general sense of humor, but also a version of the psychodynamic of humor detailed by Sigmund Freud in the concluding section of his work *Jokes and Their Relation to the Unconscious.*[5]

4. For a helpful sketch of three "trajectories" of interpretation of the doctrine see Kelsey, "Whatever Happened?" The interpretation of sin developed throughout these pages fits roughly into the trajectory Kelsey labels "theological anthropology," especially as it addresses "a condition of human subjects in which they are estranged from themselves, others, and God..." which in turn entails "an analysis of what a subject is" (172). But it also necessarily engages the additional trajectory whereby sin is defined as "unjust societal self-contradiction" (175). I leave it to others to develop the implications that follow for the third trajectory, which treats sin as "willful disrelatedness to the risen Lord present here and now" (177).

5. In these comments I am following the lead of Moretti, *Way of the World*, 221–23. Whereas Moretti, in discussion of George Eliot, explicates humor as a maturity of

All forms of the comic, Freud argues, are "means of obtaining pleasure in spite of the distressing affects that interfere with it," but "humor" is distinguished from the prior categories of "jokes" and the "comic," because unlike the latter two, the pleasure of humor is not derived at any one else's expense. Freud explains: "Humour is the most easily satisfied among the species of the comic. It completes its course within a single person; another person's participation adds nothing new to it."[6]

Ultimately the distinction between humor as intra-psychic and inter-psychic requires qualification, but it nevertheless points to the way in which the humor denoted by the former term manifests a kind of emotional maturity that the humor denoted by the latter term does not. With regard to this maturity one need not accept the total model of psychic economy underlying Freud's definition of "defensive processes" in order to appreciate the value of humor as a means of enabling the mature individual to integrate uncomfortable truths into self-understanding:

> We can gain some information about humorous displacement if we look at it in the light of a defensive process. Defensive processes are the psychical correlatives of the flight reflex and perform the task of preventing the generation of unpleasure from internal sources. In fulfilling this task they serve mental events as an automatic regulation, which in the end, incidentally, turns out to be detrimental and has to be subjected to conscious thinking . . . Humour can be regarded as the highest of these defensive processes. It scorns to withdraw the ideational content bearing the distressing affect from conscious attention as repression does, and thus surmounts the automatism of defence. It brings this about by finding a means of withdrawing the energy from the release of unpleasure that is already in preparation and of transforming it, by discharge, into pleasure.[7]

Contrary to the Freudian model of intra-psychic energies, and the ejaculatory pleasure those energies presumably economize through mechanisms of "repression" and "discharge," the current argument proceeds on the assumption that no such interior economy, separable from the inter-

---

"awareness" that is opposed to "actions," I affirm humor as a starting point of engagement in the methodology of theological sexual ethics as a matter of social justice. For a comparable invocation of the comic as a basis of democratic social criticism, see West, *Prophesy Deliverance!* 8–10.

6. Freud, *Jokes*, 284.

7. Ibid., 289–90.

personal context of its actual production as psychology, is discernible. And that literature, and theological writings considered as a kind of literature, are integral to that productive context. Yet this counter-Freudian assumption only underscores the importance of humor as a defensive process that is also a disposition of interpersonal relationship.

Humor enables the possibility of "conscious attention," not to some "distressing affect" that is an object of repression arising from "internal sources," but to the interpersonal generation of both "distressing affects" and the "defensive processes" of relationality that serve as "automatic regulation" of the experience of those affects. Humor consequently enables the mature individual not to blame others for the discovery of distressing truths about the self as those truths are revealed through self-conscious attendance to one's affective response to other persons' insistent embodiment. A humorous disposition toward the narrative presentation of other persons' sexed selves enables a renewal of self-knowledge in knowledge of others. It opens the reader to a hermeneutic of reverence even toward those points of view, those traditions, those political, theological, and methodological commitments, that one finds most offensive, as they provide the occasion to take offense and thereby achieve "conscious thinking" that is not otherwise possible.[8]

With this more technical definition of humor at hand, enriched possibilities emerge for a mature reading of Augustine on the doctrine of original sin and its relevance for theological discourse of sexuality. An alarming power of the association of sexuality and sin is the ironclad enclosure it accomplishes of the particular sinning self within the universal scope of one single original sin. Instead of dismissing as offensive the meaningful possibility that anyone can justly inherit sin, the challenge becomes in humor to think more openly the place of oneself in the procreative dynamic that sinful sexuality describes:

> Human nature then is, without any doubt, ashamed about lust, and rightly ashamed. For in its own disobedience, which subjected the sexual organs solely to its own impulses and snatched them from the will's authority, we see a proof of the retribution imposed on man for that first disobedience. And it was entirely fitting that this retribution should show itself in that part which effects the procreation of the very nature that was changed for the

---

8. For recent reflections on the productive political dimensions of shame, see Stockton, *Beautiful Bottom*, and Halperin and Traub, *Gay Shame*.

worse through that first great sin. This offence was committed when all mankind existed in one man, and it brought universal ruin on mankind; and no one can be rescued from the toils of that offence, which was punished by God's justice, unless the sin is expiated in each man singly by the grace of God.[9]

If lust is shameful, it is not necessarily because it proves the disobedience of the body to the governance of the will's authority so much as because it proves the place of every human being within the chain of human relationship formed in sexual reproduction. Every individual after Adam and Eve is both created *and* born. Lust merely describes the movement by which the shame of sin, the exposure of the fallen self, proceeds from the created pair of originally sinning human beings to all their subsequent generations. The nakedness of the first sinners is no different than the nakedness of all other sinners. It is one common and complete disgrace from which there is no place to hide oneself. If theological debates in sexual ethics—unlike debates about other issues—are so impassioned, so heated, so bitter, perhaps it is because the activity of the sexual organs (sexual reproduction) defines the terms by which anyone ever enters into theological debate in the first place. And if the justice of an inheritable sin offends reason, it only makes sense also that reason focuses its protest on the supposed culprits, seeks to exculpate them from the stated charges.

Here it is important to emphasize however that sexual reproduction is no more than a potent figure for the mystery of the transmission of sin. And also that finitude *per se* is no more than a red herring in the search for a solution of that mystery. Just as no technological solution to the perpetuation of sin exists, so also the "original" aspect of original sin entails that any means devised by the human species to reproduce itself also always involves the transmission and perpetuation of sin.[10] A cloned human being, for example, would be no less in need singly of the expiation of sin that God's grace alone provides than a person conceived in vitro than a person conceived through artificial insemination than a person conceived through intercourse out of wedlock than a person conceived through intercourse between married sexual partners, so that it looks implausible to claim that sexual reproduction describes anything

---

9. Augustine *City of God* 14.20 (Bettenson 581).

10. See Gardella, *Innocent Ecstasy*, for compelling history of American Christian sexual ethics as the pursuit of a cure for original sin through more hygienic sexual reproduction.

essential about the persons who result. While good reasons may exist to value certain contexts of relationship as preferable for the conceiving and rearing of children, and even to refrain from certain forms of assisted reproduction, the variety of contexts and means of procreation turns out to be instructive by calling to mind that the result of ordinary sexual reproduction by married partners of opposite sexes is always, in Augustine's famous words, "So tiny a child, so great a sinner."[11] A sinful human being, that is, as culpably enmeshed as every other person in the total ruin of original sin.[12] If therefore the lust that Augustine identifies with sexual reproduction is wrongfully localized in the "sexual organs," it is only because they are wrongfully imagined as somehow bearing more of the brunt of sin's force. Or put another way, the procreation of the nature deformed comprehensively by original sin doesn't proceed through any specific part of the human body, but through the organizing intelligence of human beings whether they procreate or not, as the emerging prospect of procreation with only the most minimal involvement of the sexual organs discloses. Only it takes some humor, especially given the cultural associations of childhood with innocence, and a particular form of marital relationship as curator of that innocence, to accept as implication of the Augustinian association of sexuality and sin—and by extension the identification of the shame of sin with sexual reproduction—that to bear a child—by whatever means and in whatever context—is to enlarge the community of responsibility for sin.[13] And that not having children whether by choice or chance does not exculpate oneself from the responsibility for sin defining that expanding community.

It is sorely tempting also, given that the perpetuation of the species commanded by God also entails the perpetuation of the sinful individuals who comprise the species, to confuse the constraints of finitude with

11. Augustine *Confessions* 1.12.19 (Chadwick, 15).

12. These comments are only the beginning of the story. Advances in artificial intelligence, for example, join questions about "what a subject is" with questions about any individual's responsibility for original sin. Will a cyborg or an android reproduce sinful human nature?

13. The many criticisms of contemporary parenting as overly-plotted, as inhospitable to unexpected difference, has a queer potential that their proponents might not likely recognize or welcome. Compare for example the invocation of the "Word born in Bethlehem" at the conclusion of Hall, *Conceiving Parenthood*, 399 with Kiki and Herb's rendition of "What Child is This?"on their album "Do You Hear What We Hear?" In the twentieth century the history of Protestantism and parenthood and the history of camp are closely linked.

the constraints of sin.[14] The imperfectability associated with the former then suggests a possible escape from assumption of responsibility for the imperfectability associated with the latter.[15] Whereas sin is one's fault, finitude is one's fate. And when the failings, limitations, the incapacities of sin are matters of fate, then the inevitability of sin can serve as an excuse for sin. For how can anyone be blamed for their failings when they are acting with freedom and responsibility under the only conditions within which anyone can act with freedom and responsibility?[16] Yet Augustine insists otherwise, insists that human beings were created to live in the goodness of the time that is itself a creation of God.[17] And that the finitude of self, the limitation of self in time, and of all creation for that matter, is properly a cause for joyous celebration, though always relative to the much greater joy to be anticipated when time ends and the self finds its eternal rest in God.[18] Finitude, the termination of personal existence in time, which is anticipated with hope, must be carefully distinguished from death, the termination of personal existence in time, which is anticipated with dread. At stake in this distinction is the acceptance of responsibility for the punishment of sin, acceptance that is of divine justice: "There is no need then, in the matter of our sins and faults,

14. Perhaps the most famous example of this confusion is from Descartes in the *Meditations*, when he explains his propensity to go wrong morally in relation to his propensity to go wrong in his understanding, and explains both as a function of his intermediate nature as something between perfect being and non-being. So the solution to sin, in a couple of sentences, is to constrain one's will within the certainty attainable by one's intellect: "It must be simply this: the scope of the will is wider than that of the intellect; but instead of restricting it within the same limits, I extend its use to matters which I do not understand. Since the will is indifferent in such cases, it easily turns aside from what is true and good, and this is the source of my error and sin" (Descartes, *Writings*, 2:40–41). When these implications were pointed out to Descartes, he quickly issued a disclaimer (Descartes, *Writings*, 2:11, 106, 151, 172).

15. Wetzel, *Augustine*, 76–98 shows how Augustine himself had to work through the temptation to consider existence in time as a cause of sin for which one could not be justly held accountable.

16. It is notable that Kant in the *Critique of Practical Reason* argues that the immortality of the soul is a necessary postulate of morality, necessary it seems to obviate any transposition of blame for one's lack of moral improvement from oneself to the sensual conditions of one's moral agency.

17. Augustine *Confessions* 11.13.15–16, and 11.28.38 (Chadwick, 229–30, 243) and *City of God* 11.4–6 and 12.16 (Bettenson, 432–36, 490–93).

18. Augustine *Confessions* 13.35.50–13.38.53 (Chadwick, 304–5).

to do our Creator the injustice of laying the blame on the nature of the flesh which is good, in its own kind and on its own level."[19]

The difficulty in surrendering the necessity of this need is especially telling given how often sexual reproduction is extolled as a defense against the fact of mortality, even when it is apparently framed as an acceptance of mortality.[20] A rather hard joke on humanity after the Fall is that the disobedience of original sin and its punishment in death makes impossible perfectly faithful obedience to the divine command to be fruitful and multiply. The latter now always involves a prideful refusal of the punishment of sin because also a literal bodying forth of that punishment. One result is that the reproduction celebrated as a triumph over finitude is inevitably laden with violence toward the children it bears as evidence of the sin over which only God triumphs, so that mature humor is also required to begin to honor children by recognizing clearly of each one: "So tiny a child, so great a sinner." Recognition of the sinfulness of even the tiniest child, enabled by acceptance of the literal inheritability of sin, then becomes a hallmark of faithful parenting and a commitment to relieve children of some of the impossible burden of innocence—to be explicated at length in subsequent chapters—ascribed to them. It also affirms that the hostility directed toward children as the visible reminders of one's responsibility for sin generates an obligation to recognize and care for all sinners, and not just the cutest among them.

As much as caring better for children is advanced by the mature humorous recognition that even the tiniest child is a sinner, such recognition is only one instance of a more general possibility of a theological ethics that relinquishes simple claims to innocence in favor of responsible acknowledgment of the sinfulness of sexuality. Humor proves indispensable to a mature theological discourse of sexuality in that it promotes a disposition of charitable solidarity with and hospitality toward all members of the single community of fallen humanity, since every person is by definition an equal participant in the common inheritance of sin that begins with one original act of disobedience. A literal interpretation of the doctrine of original sin thereby weakens the

19. Augustine *City of God* 14.5 (Bettenson, 554).

20. For a withering critique of the typical association of immortality with sexual difference proven in procreation, see Edelman, *No Future*, 60–66. Edelman's queer polemic against reproductive futurism is potent, yet it shows how refusal of that futurism can't help but also refuse responsibility for sin. In other words, choosing not to procreate, as much as failing to procreate, doesn't make one less culpable for the community of sin that persists.

hold of the fantasy that human beings through particular forms of sexual relationship—usually, but not necessarily, marriage—can create for themselves privileged spaces of redemptive divine encounter. It renders cognizable as fantasy all claims that the shame of sin can be proportioned differentially, that any such thing as a person exists who hasn't already sinned and suffered the shame of its consequences. Humorous critique of the injustices that follow from a wrongfully conceived innocence will therefore be necessary for explication and exemplification of the reverence for others—not blame—that characterizes a mature response to the discovery of self through conscious thinking that other persons' uncomfortably sexed presence make possible. Such discovery is only likely to proceed, however, when humor subsumes the anger and fear that are its psychic correlates, and that focus so potently in discussions of children's sexed bodies on the one hand, and their parents' maritally sexed bodies on the other hand. The goal through humor is to transform fear into hospitality and refocus the remainder of anger in constructive criticism of the dynamic that obstructs that very transformation.

As Freud describes it, the relation of humor to anger is one of strict economy: "And indeed the small contributions of humour that we produce ourselves are as a rule made at the cost of anger—instead of getting angry."[21] Yet much reason does exist for anger when engaging contemporary disputes in sexual ethics, and it would be irresponsible to pretend otherwise, as if anger and humor were mutually exclusive or the only viable alternative to anger were a dismissive irony, what one might call a mature pagan humor that seeks no better for itself and others. As a function of interpersonal relations it is therefore more apt to describe faithful humor less as a direct substitute for anger and more as a means of discerning appropriate and inappropriate objects of anger, as a means of cultivating a charitable anger that does seek better for itself and others. Charitable anger in this way makes possible a version of the forgiveness as action described by Hannah Arendt, when she writes:

> In contrast to revenge, which is the natural, automatic reaction
> to transgression and which can be expected and even calculated,
> the act of forgiving can never be predicted; it is the only reaction
> that acts in an unexpected way and thus retains, though being a
> reaction, something of the original character of action. Forgiving,
> in other words, is the only reaction which does not merely re-act

21. Freud, *Jokes*, 287.

but acts anew and unexpectedly, unconditioned by the act which provoked it and therefore freeing from its consequences both the one who forgives and the one who is forgiven. The freedom contained in Jesus' teaching of forgiveness is the freedom from vengeance, which incloses both doer and sufferer in the relentless automatism of the action process, which by itself need never come to an end.[22]

Whereas Arendt posits forgiveness as initiating action that is "unconditioned by the act that provokes it," charitable anger seeks to act "anew" by accepting that charity and anger among fallen humanity are not separable, that anger is incited ideally by care, in multiple senses of that term, so that one need not cease to be angry in order to forgive. But one does need to direct one's anger in the service of a forward-looking freedom and strive not to allow the possibilities of charitable anger to become obstructed by anger that is focused on refutation of purportedly unjust accusations of sin. Then it remains caught in the "relentless automatism" of vengeance. Charitable anger instead must focus on the claims of innocence from sin that necessitate accusations of sin. Forgiveness, put another way, is most forgiving when it frees human beings to redress concretely the wrongs requiring forgiveness in the first place.

Once one admits the inherent sinfulness of all human sexuality, the subsumption of anger into humor liberates charitable anger for the service of justice by allowing one to distinguish between more and less justified anger; between anger that wrongfully defends against any and all accusation of sin and anger that rightfully defends against the harms that ensue from failures to own responsibility for sin. Not defense against every accusation of sinful sexuality, but defense of those who are wronged by the interpersonal dynamics that are a generative source of ascriptions to some of innocent sexuality and to others of sinful sexuality, then emerges as an important theme of a theological ethics. The title of this book, *The Romance of Innocent Sexuality*, is thus a descriptive summary in shorthand of these dynamics.

It is also important to emphasize the appropriateness of charitable anger to critique of the romance of innocent sexuality because it would be a grievous mistake to conclude from the requirement of humor that theological discourse on sexuality is not serious business, that it is not replete with a vengefulness that exacts a deadly toll. At best Michel

---

22. Arendt, *Human Condition*, 241.

Foucault is only half kidding when he writes that "The Faustian pact, whose temptation has been instilled in us by the deployment of sexuality, is now as follows: to exchange life in its entirety for sex itself, for the truth and sovereignty of sex. Sex is worth dying for."[23] Although it is not clear what Foucault considers anyone is giving up in making this Faustian pact, his invocation of an alchemist and doctor of theology who yearns so passionately—lusts really—for knowledge that he is willing to sell his already sinful soul to the devil; forsake, that is, the promise of redemption of his soul by God—bespeaks to his theologically minded readers a real alternative. But only when one begins to question the "truth and sovereignty of sex." That truth and that sovereignty, Foucault indicates, are neither exactly, so that to commit oneself to them is to commit oneself in the end to the painful discovery of the truth and sovereignty of the God one forsakes in making that pact in the first place. In Marlowe's version of the legend, for example, Faustus ironically acknowledges that the punishment of sin in death is a kind of relationship with God. So he begins his quest with dismissal of the doctrine of original sin and in a fateful pun bids "Divinity, adieu!"[24] Yet there is no leave-taking of God, only variations in address to God, as Faustus discovers at the end, when he does achieve a kind of ultimate knowledge for which he was seeking.

As for Foucault, in his exclamation that "sex is worth dying for" he articulates a reason to engage theological discourse of sexuality with extreme seriousness, not because one unquestioningly accepts this valuation of the worth of sex as an *a priori* condition, but because one recognizes its pervasiveness, its mortal consequences, and in charitable anger seeks to initiate new action that works to mitigate them. If, therefore, sex is worth dying for, it is only because this worth is bestowed in a process—the romance of innocent sexuality—that implicitly acknowledges the punishment of the original sin that it elides. The very valorization of sex in death indicates that something is profoundly sinfully the matter. Trading on the wages of sin, theological discourse of sexuality contributes to the culpable investment of sex with an unjustifiable worth. The call to account of theology is further impelled as Foucault continues:

> It is in this (strictly historical) sense that sex is indeed imbued with the death instinct. When a long while ago the West discovered love, it bestowed on it a value high enough to make death

23. Foucault, *History of Sexuality*, 156.
24. Marlowe, *Doctor Faustus*, 1.1.50 (141).

acceptable; nowadays it is sex that claims this equivalence, the highest of all. And while the deployment of sexuality permits the techniques of power to invest life, the fictitious point of sex, itself marked by that deployment, exerts enough charm on everyone for them to accept hearing the grumble of death within it.[25]

Though offered in parentheses, the qualification "strictly historical" is hardly parenthetical. On the contrary, it designates the ground of possibility of investigation by allowing that the "death instinct"—the instinct, from the inclusive perspective of a literally inheritable original sin, that every self has of the punishment of sin—is only contingently identified with sex. Once upon a time it was "love." In the future some other term will just as surely achieve this "equivalence, the highest of all." For as long as human beings perdure short of the end of time they will seek to displace onto an imagined organizing part of themselves the total judgment of themselves that began at the moment in time of that single original Fall from grace and thus seek to displace other persons' gaze from the awful nakedness of the common disgrace that remains. From a biblical perspective what is truly "strictly historical" is the fact of sin and the ensuing instinct of fallen humanity to valorize its punishment as a means of avoiding acceptance of the punishment. Some imaginary aspect of self then becomes worth dying for, because it allows the self to cling to the fantasy of its self-coherence after the Fall, to persist in its sinful fantasy that it is possible to clothe oneself properly after the Fall. To the extent that theological writers, among others, contribute to the investment of sex with a worth—"life in its entirety"—that is unnecessary and unjustifiable, a basis for critique of their writings is now identified.

This critique is a necessary prelude to constructive imagination of theologically meaningful self-identification. It engages seriously the claim that Foucault "opens up ways to 'think differently' about religion as the 'spiritual' and 'religious' are collapsed, or 'dispersed,' into a new set of force relations. This new set of force relations brings the body and sexuality into a new space of government, both of self and others, where new relationships and new modes of being can be established."[26] The possibility of a change in government follows from the description of "sex" as a "fictitious point." Sex is not to be sought in itself—a delusional enterprise—but in the narrative contexts through which it becomes apparent. Sex is thus a *fiction*

25. Foucault, *History of Sexuality*, 156.
26. Carrette, *Foucault*, 143.

with a *point*. Exploration of the continuities between the conventions for narration of sex in theological writings and traditions of popular fiction are therefore necessary in order to appreciate how fully theological texts, as much as their novelistic counterparts, are concerned to tell a common story about sex, to render accessible and intelligible this fictitious point, even as this same common story serves to obscure the discovery that whatever reality sex possesses is not grounded in some obvious truth of the human body, but arises as human imagination seeks to ascribe to itself a wholeness of identity organized through the body. The body, accordingly, receives its sex from the imagination, so that the reality sex bespeaks most of all is the novel disturbance of human imagination by sin. As a result, to say that sex is worth dying for is not to ascribe some inviolable value to the body, but to ascribe a negotiable value to a fantasied identity. To say that sex is worth dying for is to say that a particular formation of human imaginative capacity is experienced as profoundly indicative of the truth of one's embodied existence, and thereby receives an inordinate valuation. The alternative to the romance of innocent sexuality (the government whose authority is in question) emerges through alternative readings of the narratives organizing the experience of one's sex as the wholeness of one's identity.

From the description of sex as a fictitious point, especially for development of a theology of original sin, it also follows that to be willing to die for sex—to be willing to "exchange life in its entirety for sex itself"—is both to be willing to die for a kind of nothingness, and to be willing to die for the narrative coherence structured around that nothingness. The distinctive contribution of a theory of sexuality to critique of the romance of innocent sexuality is the conceptualization it makes possible of that narrative coherence. The theology of original sin makes its own distinctive contribution by illuminating the significance of that nothingness, that it is an indicative lack. Theology and theory of sexuality working together then make it possible critically to question the worth ascribed to sex. They illuminate that worth as an effect of fallen human avoidance of responsibility for original sin. In the process, mature humor turns out to be as necessary for thinking about God as for thinking about sexuality, because the truth that emerges in thinking theologically about sexuality undermines cherished forms of self-understanding. The worth ascribed to sex, realized in the exchange of life for sex, denotes something other than a truth of sexed embodiment as an explanatory force that generates and organizes personal identity. Sex considered in itself denotes nothing either essential or necessary about the self. Yet the worth ascribed to sex, as manifest in theological discourse of sexuality, does revolve about some necessity of human existence. Ideals of sexed identity, once imagined as God-given, now become uncomfortably recognizable as sinful human fantasies, as culpably implicated in the romance of innocent sexuality.

Finally, to say that the death instinct associated with sex is strictly historical, and that sex is a fictitious point, is not to deny the reality of either, but to ascribe to them a particular kind of reality.[27] It is precisely because they are at once real and unnecessary in their particularity that investigation of their lethal dynamics is enriched by a theology of original sin. Such a theology explicates how this death instinct can be organized around and energized by a fictitious point. Mature humor and charitable anger are most of all crucial to this project because they enable one to envision an altered self that need not unselfconsciously resist the disarmament of the deadly point of the fiction of sex. Humor orients engagement in theological discourse of sexuality that is non-defensive, so that such discourse can become the means of working out strategies for the successful disruption of the status quo investment of sex with the worth of death. And charitable anger in a vital imperative seeks disruption of a status quo that enforces mortal harms on actual persons as tangible proofs of the worth of sex. These proofs are false, but deadly. Refutation of the romance of innocent sexuality consequently requires careful investigation of how the valorization of sex in death is only a concentrated instance of a more general problem of human imagination of self in relation to God.

Theology and Sexuality as Doxa and Discourse

Before proceeding with that investigation, some comments on the use of the term "discourse" in relation to the terms "sexuality" and "theology" will help underscore the importance of both mature humor and charitable anger to a constructively critical theological sexual ethics. Two of the most influential expositors of a concept of discourse have been Foucault and Pierre Bourdieu.[28] Complicating the notion of referential signification, Foucault writes of discourse as:

27. The fiction of sex operates on something like the "infrasensible" plane described by Connolly, *Why*, 40.

28. For useful direction to the basic texts of each, see Bell, *Ritual Theory*, 55 n. 5.

A task that consists of not—of no longer—treating discourses as groups of signs (signifying elements referring to contents or representations) but as practices that systematically form the objects of which they speak. Of course, discourses are composed of signs; but what they do is more than use these signs to designate things. It is this *more* that renders them irreducible to the language (*langue*) and to speech. It is this "more" that we must reveal and describe.[29]

Contrary to the claims of some of his critics, Foucault does not deny the possibility of any empirical knowledge of the human body. Instead he urges that such knowledge formation is never innocent, because it is always also *doing* something else, what he designates as the "more" of discourse. Rather than characterize Foucault's vision of discourse as nihilistic, as reducing all "things" to "signs to designate things," it is therefore more apt to characterize his vision as comprehensive, since it ascribes to the processes of knowledge formation more than those processes themselves acknowledge.[30]

To clarify further: to say that discourses "systematically form the objects of which they speak" is to denote the formation of an additional species of objects—objects that are the productions of discourse—and not necessarily to deny the prior existence of other objects. But it is systematically to render the latter objects intelligible only in relation to the former objects.[31] Sex in this way is a fiction formed by discourse which at the same time renders intelligible a prior object, the human body that it comprehensibly organizes. If the language of temporal priority and succession is perhaps inescapable in this context it is also misleading in that it suggests any kind of sensible empiricism or diachronic movement from "things" to "knowledge of things." Foucault indicates the inappropriateness of such language to his project when he writes: "What, in

29. Foucault, *Archaeology*, 49.

30. In a discussion of Nietzsche, Megill, *Prophets*, 33–34, provides a helpful distinction between two sorts of nihilism. The first "is a nihilism that fails to respond to what Nietzsche sees as the opportunity offered by the world's nullity." The second "is an active, aesthetic nihilism . . . Instead of drawing back from the void, we dance upon it. Instead of lamenting the absence of a world suited to our being, we invent one." With some qualification of the possibilities of "invention," the latter definition arguably fits Foucault's writings.

31. Whether Foucault's writings enable any distinction between "objects formed by discourse" and "objects that exist prior to discourse" is an issue of contention among interpreters of Foucault, linking concerns about epistemology, ethics, historiography, and politics. This issue runs like a red thread throughout the essays collected in Hoy, *Foucault*.

short, we wish to do is to dispense with 'things.'"[32] This is not to say that no things exist apart from human knowledge of them, but rather that human knowledge of things is always a manner of doing something more with and through that knowledge. The necessity to "dispense with things" can therefore be reformulated as a necessity to dispense with reference to things as the sole end of discourse. Refinement of reference in many ways is a valuable end, but it also involves an irreducible dimension that is not fixed in any empirical reality exactly, but fixed in the structures and strategies of discourse itself.

It is inquiry concerning human accountability for this protean more of discourse that is enabled by joining the discourses of theology and sexuality precisely because they differ in an ultimate respect. Whereas sexuality privileges the knowing human subject in relation to things which nevertheless exist apart from human knowledge of them, theology recognizes all things, including the knowing human subject, as created by God. As Augustine puts it, there are fundamentally two distinct kinds of being: God on the one hand, and all that God creates on the other. Everything that is created is apart from God but in relation to God: "Nevertheless, all things were made not of the very substance of God but out of nothing, because they are not being itself, as God is, and a certain mutability is inherent in all things, whether they are permanent like the eternal House of God or if they suffer change, like the human soul and body."[33] Whatever the limits of knowledge of God as an end of the discourse of theology—that is, the capacity of the word "God" to signify the creator of whom Augustine also writes, "Your works praise you that we may love you, and we love you that your works may praise you"[34]—it is at least possible to note that the knowledge of God that theology as discourse achieves is always knowledge by creatures of their creator. God is at least no ordinary word because it is the one word that bespeaks an accountability for all the more that human beings do in their knowledge also of things, because it is the one word that is indispensable to any faithful account of self and its belonging to creation at all. The trouble is that fallen humanity can't know itself among other things as a creation of God, can't praise God through knowing creation, without also doing more in its knowing, without also sinning in its knowing, which includes,

32. Foucault, *Archaeology*, 47.

33. Augustine *Confessions* 12.17.25 (Chadwick, 258).

34. Ibid., 13.33.48 (Chadwick, 302).

for example, excusing its failures in hospitality and care for one another as a function of the mutability of soul and body.

Despite this fundamental difference between theology and sexuality, God, taken as an object of theological discourse, like sex in regard to sexuality, is an object that is systematically formed as it is spoken. The creaturely activity of theology produces the concepts, the discursive formations through which human communities approach understanding of themselves as creatures in relation to their creator.[35] Theology and sexuality are probably not necessary to each other; but they are now joined. The result has been the inappropriate predominance of sex to theological pursuits of self-understanding. In this regard the writings of Pierre Bourdieu helpfully refine the contributions of Foucault on discourse. In *Outline of a Theory of Practice*, Bourdieu defines "discourse" in sharp contrast to "doxa." As a kind of obverse of discourse, doxa, according to Bourdieu, are functional systems of learned ignorance:[36]

> Systems of classification which reproduce, in their own specific logic, the objective classes, that is the divisions by sex, age, or position in the relations of production, make their specific contribution to the reproduction of the power relations of which they are the product, by securing the misrecognition, and hence the recognition, of the arbitrariness on which they are based: in the extreme case, that is to say, when there is a quasi-perfect correspondence between the objective order and the subjective principles of organization (as in ancient societies) the natural and social world appears as self-evident. This experience we shall call *doxa*, so as to distinguish it from an orthodox or heterodox belief implying awareness and recognition of the possibility of different or antagonistic beliefs.[37]

35. Throughout these pages Foucault's writings are engaged as a constructive resource for understanding the unique human activity that is theology. For a spirited defense of the value of the companion concept of "religion," against those who engage a unilaterally suspicious critique of all study of religion as an academic discipline, see Strenski, "Religion, Power, and Final Foucault."

36. "The explanation agents may provide of their own practice, thanks to a quasi theoretical reflection on their practice, conceals, even from their own eyes, the true nature of their practical mastery, i.e., that it is *learned ignorance (docta ignorantia)*, a mode of practical knowledge not comprising knowledge of its own principles. It follows that this learned ignorance can only give rise to the misleading discourse of a speaker himself misled, ignorant both of the objective truth about his practical mastery (which is that it is ignorant of its own truth) and of the true principle of the knowledge his practical mastery contains." Bourdieu, *Outline*, 19.

37. Ibid., 164.

The strange reality of much theology is that it assumes as doxa the productions of sexuality once sexuality is recognized as discourse. The bulk of theological discourse of sexuality, in other words, arises out of a misrecognition of the objects of sexuality as "self-evident" truths of faithful adherence to Scripture, to nature, to science, to tradition, and not even as objects of "orthodox or heterodox belief."

Bourdieu's distinction between doxa and discourse helps to describe the apparent disconnect in theological debates in sexual ethics, the sense that too often persons are talking past each other and not to each other. It also provides a means of imagining how potentially to align the sides of that disconnect, in the hope that greater understanding in both theology and sexuality will follow. Among the many axes along which this disconnect appears, the most significant for present discussion is between persons and communities that do not recognize sexuality as discourse, enabling the incorporation of its objects as doxa, and persons and communities that recognize the theorization of sexuality as discourse. To demonstrate with philosophical sophistication, theological sensitivity, and analytical rigor the mutually illuminating possibilities for both theology and sexuality, realized as discourses, not doxa—to move both theology and sexuality from the status of doxa to discourse—is therefore another way to summarize the goal of critique of the romance of innocent sexuality, in the hope that it creates a common ground for discussion of questions that currently appear to be addressed from separate and incommensurable universes of belief and practice.

Like Foucault, Bourdieu elaborates the concepts of doxa and discourse as part of a theory of knowledge formation. Also like Foucault, he identifies the project of knowledge-formation as marked by and productive of power relations. So it is important to address the unquestioned assimilation of the objects of discourse of sexuality into theology, as those objects serve the function of theology as a mode of reproduction of specific forms of power relations. The invocation in theology of sex as a self-evident truth subsequently emerges as a problem of politics, as an opening to consider the ethics of the conduct of theological discourse of sexuality.

The point here is not to disregard or deny the necessity of some beliefs as integral to the formation of faithful community, but rather to insist that even the assertion of an absolutely necessary belief is not immune from the sinful dynamics through which all fallen human beings seek to recover an intelligibly faithful identity. For anyone who accepts the integrity of religious traditions as witness of theological truths, who rejects the possibility of translating such witness entirely and exhaustively into other terms, some core set of convictions will stand as neither doxa nor discourse—will stand, as Bourdieu himself notes, as orthodoxy. And belief in the literal inheritance of an original sin that joins all humanity in a single fallen community and for which each human being is singly responsible is arguably a paradigm of orthodoxy. The concepts of doxa and discourse considered in relation to the doctrine of original sin establish the basis for a theological argument that beliefs about sexed identity are not ultimately necessary to the witness of faith. Instead assertions of absolute knowledge about sexed identity are deformations of a faithful but fallen community that can progressively albeit only ever imperfectly re-fashion itself. Bourdieu explains of all theorization of knowledge formation, in light of the distinction between doxa and discourse: "The theory of knowledge is a dimension of political theory because the specifically symbolic power to impose the principles of construction of reality—in particular, social reality—is a major dimension of political power."[38] Doxa, in its assertion of the self-evidence of a "natural and social world," is as much a "theory" of knowledge, in a political sense, as its kin, discourse. Yet it is not until doxa is admitted as kin to discourse that it becomes contestable as such, that its self-evident facts become contestable as a "theory of knowledge" and a means of "reproduction of the power relations of which they are the product."

Given the political stakes associated with the preservation of doxa qua doxa with regard to sex, and its practical implications on the political scene, one can expect strong resistance, on the side of doxa, to any attempt to realign the relation of doxa and discourse. The absence of any theory of sexuality, except to ridicule and reject it, in so much theological writing and attendant political activism seems to confirm the ironic dependence of theology as doxa on sexuality as discourse. Too many communities have over-invested heavily in the worth of sex as an index of faithful identity and are understandably resistant to account sex differently. Yet the case remains that theological debates about human sexuality arise in a space of crisis that is also a space of opportunity for some sort of revised accounting. Bordieu's theory helps to explain the current tense relation of theology to sexuality, and associated political struggles, because that tension is indicative of a crisis that is internal to

38. Bourdieu, *Outline*, 165.

doxa. Bourdieu explains of this crisis: "The critique which brings the undiscussed into discussion, the unformulated into formulation, has as the condition of its possibility objective crisis, which, in breaking the immediate fit between the subjective structures and the objective structures, destroys self-evidence practically."[39] The uneasiness of the current relation of theology to sexuality, according to this model, is that theology, in its assertion of doxic authority in settling questions of sexed identity, can only do so by engaging as its own the very terms that undermine its claim to "self-evidence" and "immediate fit."

Whereas Bourdieu writes of doxa and discourse as mutually exclusive, the reality of theological discourse of sexuality seems to be more of an uncomfortable and shifting overlap. The boundaries between doxa and discourse are more permeable than otherwise, because pluralism is the ineluctable context of both doxa and discourse. No virtual space exists to think theologically about sexed identity that is effectively insulated enough from alternative perspectives to avoid the movement of the undiscussed into discussion. Gracefully and gratefully to move with that movement requires a lot of mature humor and also charitable anger, since even the attempt to create such a space is itself a response to the pressure of the movement it is resisting. Perhaps much of the humorlessness and uncharitable anger of theological discourse of sexuality reflects this fact. It channels resentment, one suspects, at having to discuss, to defend, ideals of sexed identity—ideals that are potentially undermined when they require articulation and affirmation.[40]

Very likely some persons and communities will object that the theoretical approach I am advocating disparages theology both historically and contemporaneously, no matter how much I qualify the meanings of the terms discourse and doxa. And some likewise will insist that theology and the resources internal to theology are wholly adequate to the task of discerning and elaborating the necessary and incontrovertible truths of sexed embodiment, as well as all the moral implications and norms of human relationship that follow from those truths. The turn to theorization of theology and sexuality, however, is not an abandonment of all claims to truth of theology. Nor does it deny that theology has anything distinctively theological to say about sexed identity. To the contrary, it is

39. Ibid., 168–69.
40. For discussion of how particular traditions maintain their integrity in a pluralist context, see Outka, "Particularist Turn."

because theology is presumed to possess uniquely valuable insight into a truth of human identity that the engagement of theology and sexuality, as doxa and discourse, is pursued. Most of all it enables recovery of the Augustinian insight that the history of procreation is a history of self-concerned questioning by every individually sinning human being. So Augustine, with a telling confusion of erotic imagery, exclaims: "If Adam had not fallen from you, there would not have flowed from his loins that salty sea-water the human race—deeply inquisitive, like a sea in a stormy swell, restlessly unstable."[41]

Looking forward, the book in hand proceeds in confidence that theology can incorporate theory of sexuality, that theology can become more intelligible to itself because it can effectively anchor an inquiry that is otherwise totally at sea. The goal is to show how the best insights of theory of sexuality are illuminated and grounded by orthodox belief. And how theological inquiry is improved and enriched by the incorporation of theory of sexuality. The expectation is that specifically theological resources will make possible explanation of what theory of sexuality necessarily assumes, yet cannot account for on its own terms. What requires this explanation is the phenomenon, following Foucault, of the fiction of sex, and the continuing investment of the fiction of sex with the worth of death. A responsible theology of sexuality must therefore take up the question: How and why does sex become experienced as worth dying for? And with mature humor and charitable anger defend vulnerable life against the depredations of sex.

To this end it is necessary to explicate within theological discourse of sexuality the functional importance of narrations of marriage to the pursuit of intelligibly sexed personal identity.

41. Augustine *Confessions* 13.20.28 (Chadwick, 289).

2

Sex, Sexuality, and Marriage

Insofar as identification is the psychic preserve of the object and such identification comes to form the ego, the lost object continues to haunt and inhabit the ego as one of its constitutive identifications. The lost object is, in that sense, made coextensive with the ego itself. Indeed, one might conclude that melancholic identification permits the loss of the object in the external world precisely because it provides a way to *preserve* the object as part of the ego and, hence, to avert the loss as a complete loss. Here we see that letting the object go means, paradoxically, not full abandonment of the object but transferring the status of the object from external to internal. Giving up the object becomes possible only on the condition of a melancholic internalization or, what might for our purposes turn out to be even more important, a melancholic *incorporation*.

If in melancholia a loss is refused, it is not for that reason abolished. Internalization preserves loss in the psyche; more precisely, the internalization of loss is part of the mechanism of its refusal. If the object can no longer exist in the external world, it will then exist internally, and that internalization will be a way to disavow the loss, to keep it at bay, to stay or postpone the recognition and suffering of loss.[1]

Sex, Sexuality, and Marriage

PROBABLY THE MOST PROMINENT and contentious issue in theological discourse on sexuality is the moral status of same-sex sexual

1. Butler, *Psychic*, 134.

relations. Most passionately engaged of all, often in the most seemingly unrelated contexts, is the question of the permissibility or not of same-sex marriage. Yet considered with some critical distance, the claims of the more strident activists both for and against same-sex marriage appear peculiarly hyperbolic. In each case marriage assumes an ultimate status, as if it were a magical territory, a Shangri La whose natives enjoy exceptional longevity of bodily and spiritual well-being. Exclusion from its precincts is depicted either as a profound harm to individuals who are denied entrance, almost a premature death sentence; or as profoundly necessary to the protection from harm of its rightful inhabitants, as if the violation of its borders would destroy its life-affirming capacities.

Given the intensity of present passions, it is easy sometimes to miss that Christian traditions prior to the Reformation often elevated celibacy and a single life over marriage.[2] Marriage has always been valued as good in its place, but not always as a privileged, exclusive good. Something the opposite was more the case, so that a transformation of marriage from good to better is a part of its history. The signs of such a transformation are present in such Reformation texts as Luther's *Freedom of a Christian*, where the third and culminating benefit of faith is "that it unites the soul with Christ as a bride is united with her bridegroom" in what he calls a "true marriage."[3] In contrast to earlier eras, when marriage was sometimes viewed as an impediment to perfection, marriage has now become central to imagination of a completely human life; to fulfillment of a basic reality of human embodiment; to proof of one's properly sexed human identity. Regardless of whether or not any particular person marries, the intelligibility and coherence of every person's sex depends on the possibility of marriage. Hence the inevitable progression from the question of the moral status of same-sex desire to some conclusion about the status of same-sex marriage.[4]

2. For a helpful starting point to discussion of Saint Augustine's involvement in early Christian debates on marriage, see Clark, "Adam's Only Companion." For a characteristically critical history of Christian marriage and the family, see Ruether, *Christianity*. For a comparable constructive historical study of the concept of a "Christian family," see Cahill, *Family*. Contemporary affirmations of marriage as the primary social relation between human beings have strong affinities with the Puritan affirmation of marriage as a covenant society, as detailed in Johnson, *Society*. For a review of the intertwined legal and social history of modern American marriage, see Cott, *Public Vows* and Hartog, *Mand and Wife*. For a history of marriage in Britain, see Gillis, *For Better*.

3. Luther, *Selections*, 60.

4. For elaboration of these two claims, see Rees, "In the Sight of God."

Whether supporting or opposing same-sex marriage, the arguments proceed from assumption of a sexed identity seeking expression to evaluation of its expression. The evaluation of sex is typically phenomenological and typically organized around such categories as natural and unnatural, innocent and sinful, purity and defilement, sacred and profane. Sex that is suited to marriage is judged as natural, innocent, pure, sacred. Sex that is not suited to marriage is judged as a potential contaminant of the sex it is contrasted against.[5] Sex all the while has the double signification of an identity that one is and of an activity that expresses that identity, while marriage is idealized as the proper context for expression of one's identity in the activity. As a result, to designate sex a fiction is to call into question the meaning and value of marriage, since it is purportedly founded on the sex of the persons who marry. It is also to call into question the more general organization of sexed identity through the more general regulation of who may and may not marry whom. The passionate and seemingly disproportionate interest in marriage, by so many writers across the theological spectrum, is thus a function of their passionate interest in the end, in the more, that is accomplished through their speaking and writing activities. It is a passionate interest in the fiction of sex.

To appreciate the functional role of marriage in the ongoing narration of the fiction of sex, and how it is possible that sex has attracted so much inappropriate theological valuation, it helps to regard debates about marriage in the light of the twin theses of Foucault's *History of Sexuality, Vol. 1*. Those twin theses are that the "repressive hypothesis" is a myth, and that the goal of "liberation" from repression is an illusion.[6] A work the interpretation of which has become something of an academic industry, it is important to distinguish the queer trajectory of interpretation of Foucault's argument from those focused on the politics of biopower, on the one hand, and those on gay and lesbian liberation, on the

5. DeRogatis, "Born Again," provides notable review of how the imagery of contamination organizes beliefs about relationship with God as achieved through sexual relationship between husband and wife within some evangelical communities. These ideals of holy sexual activity are matched by a comparable literature on same-sex sacred sexuality, from such classics as Daly, *Gyn/Ecology* to recent volumes like Roscoe, *Jesus and the Shamanic Tradition of Same-Sex Love*.

6. For readers already familiar with the writings of Foucault and Butler, the remainder of this chapter risks seeming redundant, yet for readers unfamiliar with them it risks seeming incomplete. For a key statement of the queer theoretical implications of the repressive hypothesis and the illusory promise of liberation, see Butler, *Gender Trouble*, 83.

other hand.[7] For proponents of either view, Foucault's work is considered both valuable and dangerous. It is valuable for the microcosmic perspective it enables of power relations, for the light it sheds on ordinary lived experience as fraught with creative disciplinary potential. It is dangerous for its perceived temptation to etherealize that same ordinary lived experience into a fragmentary network of specialized intellectual fiefdoms, their inhabitants more consumed by the pursuit of tenure and other academic privileges than any ostensible political projects. Such at least Richard Rorty seems to have in mind when he comments: "Foucault's has been the most influential figure on the culture of the American left, but his influence has been dangerous. The result has been the 'disengagement' of intellectuals; the idea was to resist the biopower exercised by capitalist society, but without any political notion of how to resist, without any political program, without any political utopia. Foucault's effect on the American intellectual community has been one of profound resentment."[8] The ironic insight of Rorty's comment is to connect "danger" and "resentment" without recognizing that the lacks he cites in the influence of Foucault are not without significance; they attest the danger that queer interpretation of the repressive hypothesis and the illusion of liberation poses to contemporary notions of resistance, political program, and political utopia, provoking criticism that is itself liable to critique as a kind of resentment. Rorty's dismissal of Foucault's influence, despair almost, is consequently worth keeping in mind, as it registers the power of queer interpretation to strike a raw nerve through a deliberate holding off that draws out its interlocutors so that they encounter the uncomfortable powers of their own imaginations. Politics in the process is not so much forsaken as it is foregrounded in the composition of possible self-identifications that any form of political resistance, program, or utopia necessarily enacts, and that bespeak the loss that is disclosed through the doctrine of original sin.

Building on Foucault's critique of the repressive hypothesis, to assert the phenomenological affinity of sexual experience to symbolic representation via the categories mentioned above is a kind of strategic misrepresentation of the formative processes at play, as if such representation were

7. On biopower, see for example Agamben, *Homo Sacer* and Rose, *Politics*. On gay and lesbian liberation, with some qualification, see Halperin, *Saint Foucault*.

8. Mendieta, *Take Care*, 40.

the end and not merely the beginning of the story.[9] As if it were possible exhaustively to evaluate marital conventions on the basis of such representations. Strategic misrepresentations make it possible to read arguments for resistance to marital conventions as attempts to achieve liberation from the unwholesome constraint of a condition of repression. And also to read arguments for the enforcement of marital conventions—including the expansion of those conventions to comprehend same-sex couples—as acceptance of the necessity of repression to liberate the married pair for enjoyment of the bundled goods of romantic companionship, procreation, and domestic partnership. These strategic misrepresentations characterize the bulk of theological discourse on sexuality and marriage.

In whichever direction claims of liberation from repression are advocated, they founder on the assumption of a native sexual desire that must be alternately channeled and disciplined or unleashed and empowered. Theological debates in sexual ethics—regarding the moral status of same-sex sexual relations, of same-sex marriage, of premarital sexual relations, of adultery, polygamy, surgical sex reassignment, among others—are all ostensibly debates about entitlement to the satisfaction of given sexual desires. The multiplicity of formulations of entitlement, however, are themselves a generative source of the desires they posit as given. As diverse as these desires appear, they arise from a common context of discursive practices, so that they contribute altogether to the conceptualization of desire as a force or drive of the naturally sexed body that demands satisfaction.[10] The divergence in moral assessments of desire actually manifests the coherence of the repressive hypothesis and the illusion of liberation as it makes argument about permissible and impermissible satisfactions of sexual desire possible. This is not to deny that criteria for moral evaluation of sexual relationships are meaningful and valuable, but only to question the conceptualization of sexual desire as the exclusive object of application of such criteria.[11]

At issue in these debates from an Augustinian and queer perspective is not the satisfaction of sexual desire itself exactly, but rather the

9. For a notable example of the reification of contamination as a phenomenological universal, see Ricoeur, *Symbolism*, 25–46 on "defilement."

10. In a similar vein, exclusive focus on objects of desire misses the mark: "It seems probable that the sexual instinct is in the first instance independent of its object; nor is its origin likely to be due to its object's attractions." Freud, *Three Essays*, 14.

11. A influential starting point for the definition of criteria of just sexual relationship is Farley, *An Ethic*, subsequently elaborated in Farley, *Just Love*.

satisfaction of the desire for more that is attempted through all this discourse, the desire concentrated in the fiction of sex. Stated most starkly, that desire, a desire of all human beings, is unity in God: "The recalling of my wicked ways is bitter in my memory, but I do it so that you may be sweet to me, a sweetness serene and content. You gathered me together from the state of disintegration in which I had been fruitlessly divided. I turned from unity in you to be lost in multiplicity."[12] Confessing as much a universal narrative of humanity as his own faith in God, Augustine's particular recollection of his wicked ways is also a common memory.[13] So too the turn he owns away from unity in God and into multiplicity is a turn of all persons because a summary description of the original sin in which all persons literally share. Crucial to this account is that unity *in* God is not exactly union *with* God. It is the former, a unity of self that is enjoyed only in relation to God, that was lost in the Fall and that all persons yet continue to desire. The latter, by contrast, is a fantasy of the condition of sin, the idea that the disintegrated sinful self can find completion through union with any other person, whether human or divine. Sin rends the self, humpty dumpty, engendering the maze of multiplicity in which persons, now turned away from God, persist in the delusion that creatures can accomplish for themselves, through the union of multiples, a unity that only God accomplishes. From the pride that eats of the fruit of the tree ensues the fruit of sin, continually bodied forth in the fruitfulness of the human species, impelled in turn by the fruitless pursuit of unity in creation.

Within the world of writings spawned by Foucault's *History of Sexuality*, it is axiomatic to describe sex as an effect of the power relations organized under the domain of sexuality, especially as those effects manifest the self-concealing strategies of that system.[14] An effect, it is important to add, that is misrecognized as a cause. Once sex is admitted as an effect that is strategically invested with value as a causal principle in

---

12. Augustine *Confessions* 2.1.1 (Chadwick, 24).

13. Suchocki, "Symbolic Structure."

14. Of the distinction between "sex" and "sexuality," Butler explains: "In opposition to this false construction of 'sex' as both univocal and causal, Foucault engages a reverse-discourse which treats 'sex' as an *effect* rather than an origin. In the place of 'sex' as the original and continuous cause and signification of bodily pleasures, he proposes 'sexuality' as an open and complex historical system of discourse and power that produces the misnomer 'sex' as part of a strategy to conceal, and, hence, to perpetuate, power-relations." Butler, *Gender Trouble*, 121.

theological discourse on sexuality, the movement of sex from the realm of the undiscussed into discussion acquires practical significance for self-understanding of the desire that moves theological inquiry. The seeming fit, so tempting in multiple senses, between the activity and identity of sex, opens to reading as the fiction that any particular aspect of the dis-integrated fallen self can organize a real unity of self. The point of sex, its power as a fiction, is the fictive unity it promises. Given the overwhelming force of the desire of self for unity, it is not surprising that sex has been un-questioningly assumed as a causal origin of personal identity, as a causal origin of the self who can experience unity through union with another. The fiction of sex has thereby contributed its authoritative stamp to the formation and persistence of the power relations organized through the operations of sexuality that in turn disarm a powerful truth of theology.

Against the fiction of sex theological writers can attest a reality of fallen human desire that potentially liberates, in a qualified sense, human enjoyment of the limited goodness of sexual relationship in marriage by exposing as myth a different kind of repressive hypothesis and related illusion of liberty. To this end it is noteworthy that Augustine, almost immediately following a reference to Rom 1:26–27 (the biblical verse at the center of some of the most heated disagreement regarding same-sex relationship)[15] summarizes human relationship contrary to nature in the following terms:

> That is the outcome when you are abandoned, fount of life and the one true Creator and Ruler of the entire universe, when from a self-concerned pride a false unity is loved in the part. Return to you is alone the path of devout humility. You purify us of evil habit, and you are merciful to the sins we confess. You hear the groans of prisoners (Ps. 101: 21) and release us from the chains we have made for ourselves on condition that we do not erect against you the horns (Ps. 74: 5 f.) of a false liberty by avaricious desire to possess more and, at the risk of losing everything, through loving our private interest more than you, the good of all that is.[16]

15. "For this reason God gave them up to degrading passions. Their women exchanged natural intercourse for unnatural, and in the same way also the men, giving up natural intercourse with women, were consumed with passion for one another. Men committed shameless acts with men and received in their own persons the due penalty for their error." This and all subsequent Biblical citations throughout the text are from the New Revised Standard Version.

16. Augustine *Confessions* 33.8.16 (Chadwick, 47–48).

THE ROMANCE OF INNOCENT SEXUALITY

Just as Foucault explains that the desire seeking liberation is never prior to the discursive conditions of its experience, is not repressed but more implanted, so too Augustine explains that the "avaricious desire to possess more" is never prior to the love of private interest that enchains fallen humanity within the multiplicity of creation. And just as Foucault explains that the liberation of desire is an illusion that promotes attachment to desire, so too Augustine explains that the attempt to possess the more that is sought through the fiction of sex, to secure unity of self in sexual union with another human being, is a false liberty that promotes attachment to itself. Sinful human beings are over-mastered by a desire for a false unity because over-mastered by a self-concerned pride that locates the power to unify the self within private relationship with others of its kind within creation. The private interest of the fallen self is to overcome the shame of sin without acknowledgment of the exposure of sin by diverting public gaze onto the sin of others.

To the extent that marriage is upheld as a private context of ultimate discovery and realization of unity of self—the value, in fact, with which marriage is most often credited—marriage turns out to be deeply implicated, theoretically and practically, in the negotiation and maintenance of power relations that in fact are *not* essential to the formation of any absolutely true knowledge of sexed identity. Marriage can only bear this emphasis, however, as it is organized by that effect, sex, which is imagined as the productive source that seeks stable expression and realization in marriage, while Foucault's dictum that sex is worth dying for is remarkable most of all for the suggestion that a fiction can hold such sway over human imagination. Sex operates as the nexus of a whole array of power relations that stabilize in the ascription of an ultimate worth to a fantasm of coherent personal presence. Sex is worth dying for only to the extent that a particular formation of human imaginative capacity is experienced as profoundly necessary to the satisfaction of one's desire to make sense as a whole person, to enjoy a false unity as if it were a true unity. If sex is indicative of the truth of one's embodied existence in any fixed sense, it is only because it is indicative of the energies exerted by the imagination to fix its desire for unity of self in a posited surety of the body. Psychical identity of one's self with one's sex thereby becomes bound to its basis in biological life.[17]

17. On psychical identity as a self-relation of power organizing embodied experience, see Butler, *Psychic*, 83–105.

As registered in more theoretical terms by Judith Butler, the loss of unity of self in God initiated by original sin has left human beings with an interior identification with God as the object of their desire that disables the self from turning to God as an exterior of self who creates the possibility of self-identification.[18] When Butler, writing of the processes by which any person becomes psychically self-aware, states that "the lost object is, in that sense, made coextensive with the ego itself," she provides a description of the deformation of self wrought by self-concerned pride, pride that places itself in the place of God. While the self, according to this framework, is founded on a constitutive loss that is a structuring gap at the center of self, a literal interpretation of the doctrine of original sin makes that gap evident by instructing the self about the loss out of which fallen self-identification emerges. It teaches that every fallen creature remains fully a creature in relation to God who creates, even as the entire community of fallen humanity is haunted by the fluidity of its imagination and the attendant contingency of the solutions it devises to its troubled yearning for unity. Queer theory that at first appears irreconcilable with something as old-fashioned as literalistic interpretation of the doctrine of original sin in this way aids in its constructive retrieval. So Butler continues: "Here we see that letting the object go means, paradoxically, not full abandonment of the object but transferring the status of the object from external to internal. Giving up the object becomes possible only on the condition of a melancholic internalization or, what might for our purposes turn out to be even more important, a melancholic *incorporation*."[19] Transposed into Augustinian terms, this statement can be rephrased as: having turned away from God in the pride of sin, human beings have not lost God (a conceptual absurdity), but have lost the unity of self in God, a loss that is experienced as the corporealization of sin.[20]

Joining a literal interpretation of the doctrine of original with the insights of Butler and Foucault, sex and power become recognizable as convertible terms that are in perpetual exchange. And marriage becomes recognizable as the social institution that keeps this exchange purposively focused. Still it is vital to distinguish critique of the theological

18. As a complement to the ensuing interpellation of Butler's writings on performativity with Saint Augustine's writings on original sin, see Coakley, "Eschatological Body," on the affinities between Butler and Gregory of Nyssa.

19. Butler, *Psychic*, 134.

20. Numerous commentators on *Inferno* for example observe that "Hell has a structure analogous to that of the human body." Dante *Inferno* (Durling, 552).

valuation of marriage from claims against marriage itself, since failure to distinguish the two risks falling into the delusion that if only one can do away with marriage, one can solve the problem of desire that is now so focused in marriage. To avoid this delusion (in as much as it is possible to do so) it is necessary to address more comprehensively the power relations that are the principal object of inquiry of a theory of sexuality, and by extension a theology of sexuality, especially as these become concealed in claims to speak the truth about sex. Only then is it possible fully to engage and renegotiate the more that is practically at stake in theological discourse on sexuality, and with vision enhanced by humor recognize the wrongs that ensue from the over-ascription of theological significance to marriage and in charitable anger begin to redress them. To value marriage, most of all, more responsibly as a good but limited human relationship.

To elaborate: as long as human beings pursue unity in creation is just as long as human beings remain the fallen creatures they have become through that original sin in which all generations literally participate. The desire for unity of self by fallen creatures is, in Butler's terms, therefore inherently a melancholic desire: "If in melancholia a loss is refused, it is not for that reason abolished. Internalization preserves loss in the psyche; more precisely, the internalization of loss is part of the mechanism of its refusal. If the object can no longer exist in the external world, it will then exist internally, and that internalization will be a way to disavow the loss, to keep it at bay, to stay or postpone the recognition and suffering of loss."[21] In desiring unity of self in creation, the fallen self is caught between its desire—that which it cannot abolish without ceasing to be a creature; the condition of possibility of the self at all—and the impossibility of fulfillment of its desire so long as that desire is unreformed. Unity of self in God in this way is not entirely lost after the Fall, precisely because the desire persists. The melancholia of fallen human relationship is that it bears the memory of the unity of self in relationship to God that no human relationship can realize.

When marriage becomes idealized as a means of recovery of the unity of self lost in original sin, marriage becomes a principal means of refusal of that loss, which is to say that marriage becomes a principal means of refusal of responsibility for sin. The romance of innocent sexuality is thus a disavowal of sin, the disavowal of the loss of unity of self

21. Butler, *Psychic*, 134.

in God through sin, accomplished through assertions of the innocence of certain persons' sexuality, sexual desires, and corresponding relationships against other persons' sinful sexuality, sexual desires, and corresponding relationships. The hold of marriage on theological discourse on sexuality is its illusory promise of solution to the melancholy of original sin through the realization of the fiction of sex. To understand better this hold, analysis is required of the power of the fiction of sex to organize one's experience of intelligible self-identification.

The Power of Fiction

As compelling as the fiction of sex has become for fallen human imagination, it is in itself not necessary to the desire for unity of self it assuages. As an effect of discourse, it is an effect of power relations. The delusion that unity of self is attainable through human relationship is inseparable from the delusional ascription to human agency of the power to underwrite such accomplishment. The delusion is that human beings can turn the disintegrating power of sin effectively against itself.[22] From the depersonalized account of power developed by Foucault follows the inherent tentativeness of the power human beings claim to possess, and especially the tentativeness of the social forms that mask power's dynamism:

> Power's condition of possibility, or in any case the viewpoint which permits one to understand its exercise, even in its more "peripheral" effects, and which also makes it possible to use its mechanisms as a grid of intelligibility of the social order, must not be sought in the primary existence of a central point, in a unique source of sovereignty from which secondary and descendent forms would emanate; it is the moving substrate of force relations which, by virtue of their inequality, constantly engender states of power, but the latter are always local and unstable. The ominpresence of power: not because it has the privilege of consolidating everything under its invincible unity, but because it is produced from one moment to the next, at every point, or rather in every relation from one point to another. Power is everywhere;

---

22. For discussion of the difficulty of analysis of power, when the only available grammar of such analysis compels ascription of intentionality and personality to power, see Butler, *Bodies*, 12–16, 34. The related critique of classical theism as a function of grammar has significant roots in the writings of Nietzsche. See Megill, *Prophets*, 97, 101. For the starting point of this discussion of power, see Foucault, *History of Sexuality*, 92–93.

not because it embraces everything, but because it comes from everywhere.[23]

When Foucault refers to power's "more 'peripheral' effects," he is almost teasing his reader, since a basic insight of this entire "viewpoint" of power is that no effect of power is properly classed as peripheral. To do so is to assume just that model of power's dispersal that Foucault is undermining, a model that hearkens back to a basic tenet of classical theism.[24] At issue however is not necessarily the identity and authority of God as sovereign, but only the viewpoint of fallen humanity on their own power to know and experience unity of self through appeals to God's sovereignty. From the viewpoint of fallen human power, claims about God and about the unity of human identity apart from God can no longer function as self-interpreting explanations of the ordering of human relations. They themselves require explanation.[25]

The inappropriate significance credited to sex in theological discourse on sexuality is its idealization as a point of stable contact between the self and God who creates. Sex has wrongfully albeit strategically been credited with the power to unify the self. Sex and marriage do not bespeak an incontrovertible truth of embodied identity and the context of its socialization. They are formed out of the overlapping coordinates of theology and sexuality in a "grid of intelligibility of the social order" that are themselves the conditions of possibility of theology and sexuality as human discourses. God's sovereignty after sin remains unchanged. But for human beings, God is now, in Augustine's terms, "orderer and creator of all things in creation, but of sinners only the orderer."[26] The disorder, the disintegration of self introduced by sin, is a deformation of the creation that remains good and remains entirely related to God. But the relation of the fallen self to God is inherently confused; the responsibility for sin, for the disorder and dispersal of self in creation that follows from sin, is entirely one's own and this reality is exactly what one can't just "see"

23. Foucault, *History of Sexuality*, 93.

24. For fascinating argument that correlates Foucault on scopic discipline with just this lack of a sovereign central divine point of view, and playing on the influential claim that "All significant concepts of the modern theory of the state are secularized theological concepts" (Schmitt, *Political Theology*, 36), see Geroulanos, "Theoscopy."

25. For superb constructive interpellation of Foucault on power with Augustine on fallen human love, see Schuld, *Foucault and Augustine*, especially 7–45.

26. Augustine *Confessions* 1.9.16 (Chadwick, 12).

for oneself. A literal interpretation of the doctrine of original sin focuses the viewpoint of sin's power upon itself. Otherwise the viewpoint of sin's power is scattered in its multiplicity and strives, in a kind of repetition compulsion, to impose an order on itself, in the process perpetuating its disavowal of its own powerlessness.

To the extent that theology is only possible as it is sustained by the "institutional crystallization" of power's strategy, it is not possible to speak of God, and especially of God's sovereignty, without also always engaging the "moving substrate of force relations" that is a condition of the intelligibility of such speech. This is an unsettling prospect. No such thing as a stable sovereign center exists that fixes the intelligibility of the social order sustaining theological discourse on sexuality. The possibility of such intelligibility is circumscribed by the realization that states of power are unreliable indices of any ultimate truth of human identity and being. They are by necessity "always local and unstable." This is again not to deny that God alone as a "unique source of sovereignty exists." But it is to say something alarming about human identity, and about human capacity to know God and to know oneself in relation to God.

Stated in summary theological terms, the disarming conclusion is that the only certain starting point for fallen imagination of human relationship to God is the fact of alienation from God. A practical correlate of this alienation is that power always exceeds the bounds of any systematic organization by human beings. Without doubt people have been and always will be exceedingly crafty and successful, both in attaining and wielding power. Yet the enduring drama of the desire to master power is the ultimate impossibility of such mastery:

> And "Power," insofar as it is permanent, repetitious, inert, and self-reproducing, is simply the over-all effect that emerges from these mobilities, the concatenation that rests on each of them and seeks in turn to arrest their movement. One needs to be nominalistic, no doubt: power is not an institution, and not a structure; neither is it a certain strength we are endowed with; it is the name that one attributes to a complex strategical situation in a particular society.[27]

The nominalism that Foucault recommends here refers to the being of the Power that people invoke as a reliable source of an intelligible

27. Foucault, *History of Sexuality*, 93.

social order.[28] Such a Power—a power that generates and grounds stable and reliable meaning—does not exist. Yet the "mobilities" of which this Power is "simply the over-all effect" do exist. Human struggles for power, considered in relation to these mobilities, are the impossible attempt to "turn and arrest their movement," and stabilize the intelligibility of a way of life in a social order. A particular kind of violence and instability is thus intrinsic to the very formation and maintenance of any intelligible human way of life.

The perspective on human identity that ensues from this acknowledgment of the intrinsic limitations of intelligible social organization is hard, but not exactly pessimistic. Nominalism regarding Power allows awareness of the ceaselessly productive aspect of power, the amazing diversity and wealth of meanings that have existed and that continue to come into being. On the one hand, this account of power does cast in a stark light the ceaseless destruction that human beings wreak on each other, destroying individuals, social groups, and entire ways of life. Yet the nominalist distinction between the "omnipresence of power" and power's "over-all effect" also opens to view the inter-relatedness and identities of destructive and constructive human energies as they take shape. The demystification, in a way, of power, opens to view very different possibilities of positive engagement in human "struggles and confrontations" than are imaginable when one is attempting to master to one's advantage a Power that has no being.

These alternative possibilities only become imaginable to the extent one relinquishes the pursuit of Power and instead imagines power as a function of one's own imbrication in a "complex strategical situation." The power anyone ever wields is then significantly temporalized and spatialized. A critical theology of sexuality recognizes that the value of sex as an effect of this spatio-temporal matrix is its utility, as it appears fixed and God-given as an origin of personal intelligibility, in rendering as inevitable and necessary its own appearance, because in doing so it renders as unquestionable, as outside the realm of discussion, the temporally and spatially localized configurations of which it is in fact an immediate and shifting radiance.

As participants in theological discourse on sexuality move sex into the realm of discussion, they expand the range of application of theology

---

28. See Bell, *Ritual*, 199–204 for excellent discussion of Foucault's nominalism in relation to the distinction between a "theory" and an "analytics" of power.

by opening to investigation the complex strategical situation out of which the fiction of sex is narrated. At the same time, the association of sexuality with sin makes possible critique of theology's own implication in the valorization of sex as worth dying for. So it is noteworthy that Foucault culminates his critique of the repressive hypothesis with a viscerally counter-intuitive summary description of sexuality in its functional aspect:

> Sexuality must not be described as a stubborn drive, by nature alien and of necessity disobedient to a power which exhausts itself trying to subdue it and often fails to control it entirely. It appears rather as an especially dense transfer point for relations of power: between men and women, young people and old people, parents and offspring, teachers and students, priests and laity, an administration and a population. Sexuality is not the most intractable element in power relations, but rather one of those endowed with the greatest instrumentality: useful for the greatest number of maneuvers and capable of serving as a point of support, as a linchpin, for the most varied strategies.[29]

Probably it is here more than anywhere else that theorization of sexuality encounters a practical resistance that at the same time suggests its depth. Theological discourse on sexuality almost inevitably begins with an assumption of the experience of sexuality as "a stubborn drive" that demands expression and must therefore somehow be addressed. It is both internal to the individual, yet also "alien and disobedient." The double bind of the individual in relation to his or her sexuality is typically identified as *the problem* of theological sexual ethics. The result is that theological writers end up unquestioningly accepting a conceptualization of their own possibilities that is strategically advantageous but also practically limiting; and that calls into question how faithfully responsible finally is the seemingly endless stream of theological writings about sexuality.

An additional feature of the strategic dependence of theology on sexuality for the discernment of the problem of sexual ethics is that it tends, more often than not unwittingly, to elaborate as a truth of human sexuality an early viewpoint of psychoanalysis. For this reason, the absence of the pair "psychoanalysts and analysands" from the preceding list of power-relations that engage the instrumentality of sexuality seems a bit like Foucault's idea of a joke, given his sarcastic comments about psychoanalysis at the outset of the *History*, and given also that no one

29. Foucault, *History of Sexuality*, 103

has more famously posited the view of sexuality as a problematic drive than Sigmund Freud, most popularly in *Civilization and its Discontents*. According to the Freudian model, sexuality is an explosive natural resource that both fuels the development of human civilization and also insures the impossibility of human satisfaction in the accomplishments of civilization. Freud pictures the relationship of civilization to sexuality via a surprising mix of natural and political metaphor: "In this respect civilization behaves toward sexuality as a people or a stratum of a population does which has subjected another one to its exploitation. Fear of a revolt by the suppressed elements drives it to stricter precautionary measures. A high-water mark in such a development has been reached in our Western European civilization."[30]

To a large extent the project of sexual liberation has appropriated this political and natural figure of sexuality in relation to civilization through a strategic reversal. The pursuit of liberation predicates the threat of civilization to sexuality through the debilitating forces of repression. The productivity of sexuality is then explicitly celebrated instead of feared. Foucault's critique of the repressive hypothesis intersects powerfully with Freud's theory of sexuality at this point of the productivity of sexuality and then comprehends Freud's theory as a paradigmatic instance of that productivity.[31] The image of exploitation in Freud's theory of sexuality assumes the model of power that Foucault reverses. When Freud suggests that "Western European civilization" has reached a "high-water mark" in its "exploitation" of sexuality, he manifests the instrumentality that Foucault identifies. Yes, a high-water mark has indeed been reached, but not because Western European civilization precariously dams some great river swelling against its embankments, but because that same civilization is organized especially by the sex that it effectively ascribes to the internal being of the persons it civilizes, masking the mechanisms of its formation, administration, and manipulation. When writers on theology and sexuality decry the current state of civilization alternately as enmeshed in a crisis of sexual morality, or in the remaining vestiges of a destructive history of repressive regulation, they prove the inseparability

---

30. Freud, *Civilization*, 51.

31. For analysis of the complex relation of Foucault's writings to Freud's theory of sexuality—including an argument for their basic compatibility—see Davidson, *Emergence*, 1–92.

of the discernment of truths about sexed identity from the politics that makes such discernment possible.

For Freud, sexuality is imaged as a turbid river that is literally on the brink of overflowing its channels and wreaking incalculable destruction, just as Freud's political metaphor suggests that "civilization" and a competing force, "sexuality," are locked in a perpetual struggle for "sovereignty." Human politics is figured in perpetual contemporaneous relationship to this more cosmic power dynamic, so that sexuality is significantly externalized from the human realm to this cosmic realm. It is no surprise then that theology takes up sexuality with such impassioned energy, since theology lays particular claim to speak authoritatively about human identity in relation to the intention of a divine creator. Enmeshed as it is in production of the terms of sexuality, theology is compelled to affirm the cosmic significance of sexuality in order to affirm its own authority as a form of faithfulness to God who is sovereign. Theological debates about sexuality become political in a cosmic sense as disputes about how to determine and then police the proper boundaries between sexual desire that can be assimilated to constructive human purposes, because consonant with divine purposes, and sexual desire that threatens to undo the former purposes because it flaunts the latter purposes.

A subsequent strangeness of theological discourse on sexuality, especially given how fashionable it is to dismiss psychoanalysis as a kind of esoteric hobby of literary critics, is that it adopts as its own mantra almost a classic statement of justice in sexual ethics as posed by Freud himself: "The requirement, demonstrated in these prohibitions, that there shall be a single kind of sexual life for everyone, disregards the dissimilarities, whether innate or acquired, in the sexual constitution of human beings; it cuts off a fair number of them from sexual enjoyment, and so becomes the source of serious injustice."[32] Too much theological debate, in other words, neglects to question its predominant definitions of justice and enjoyment even as it focuses on determination of the cut-off point of justifiable sexual enjoyment.[33] The result is that debate tends to devolve finally to incontestable appeals to God's authority in support of one's particular enjoyments—appeals which in turn are implicated in the instrumentality of sexuality.

32. Freud, *Civilization*, 51.

33. Regarding liberation of the enjoyment of pre-discursive sexually embodied pleasures, Foucault is ultimately ambiguous. See Butler, *Gender Trouble*, 123–35.

From the viewpoint of a literal interpretation of the doctrine of original sin and its association with sexuality, the illusory liberation pursued through theological discourse on sexuality is liberation from sin, liberation from the dispersal of self that is the punishment of sin and that stings so sharply because just enough of the memory of original unity in God remains. Sexual enjoyment is enjoyment of the fiction of sex, which is enjoyment of a fantastic unity in God. Once one recognizes that the power of marriage in theological discourse on sexuality is relative to the knowledge of self it promises, a different definition of justice emerges for sexual ethics. Justice no longer concerns whose sexual desires merit social accommodation or even approbation—which persons are free to pursue the satisfaction of their desires. It concerns the consequences of the avoidance of responsibility for sin that follow from the delusion that some persons and not others are liberated through the activity of their sexual relationships to enjoy unity in God.

The Promise of Intelligible Self-Identification

The power of marriage as it inappropriately organizes theological discourse on sexuality relates directly to the ways in which sex is experienced practically as a solution to the desire for unity thwarted by original sin. As a strategic means of institutional crystallization of the hold of the fiction of sex on human imagination, marriage, to summarize the argument so far, is burdened overwhelmingly with the expectation that it can fulfill the promise inherent in the fiction of sex, so that it is necessary to elaborate the content of that promise.

As an effect of sexuality, the fiction of sex secures the efficacy of sexuality by insulating the sexed self against the questions posed by the history of its own formation, since no unity of self is imaginable apart from the power that produces it. Literal interpretation of the doctrine of original sin further explains that if experience of unity of self after the Fall is possible apart from repentant return to God, it is only because fictions such as sex enable power to consolidate itself in the raw materials of the human identities that it generates. From the viewpoint of power, all that exists of the self, according to Foucault, are "bodies and their materiality, their forces, energies, sensations, and pleasures."[34]

---

34. Foucault, *History of Sexuality*, 155. This is hardly a simple assertion, since it is not clear how knowledge/experience of this "materiality" is possible except as materializations *of* power. In this sense his critique of liberation appears theoretically to foreclose

The possibilities of organization of these raw materials is wide open. In themselves they possess no internally self-organizing principles. They are mute, expressionless, incoherent. At the same time, the possibility of their coherence through the conjunction of power and bodies suggests that the self who emerges cannot be as intrinsically superficial as it seems it must be. Some gap, it appears, separates the insecurity of sexed identity from the instability of the elements of its organization, so that even if the self is not reducible to its sex, neither is it reducible to the bodily realities organized by power.

In the suggestion of a gap between one's desire for unity of self and identification of that unity, Foucault echoes Augustine on the problem of self. Recounting the death of a nameless friend of his youth, Augustine writes:

> My home town became a torture to me; my father's house a strange world of unhappiness; all that I had shared with him was without him transformed into a cruel torment. My eyes looked for him everywhere, and he was not there. I hated everything because they did not have him, nor could they now tell me "look, he is on the way," as used to be the case when he was alive and absent from me. I had become to myself a vast problem, and I questioned my soul "Why are you sad and why are you very distressed?"[35]

Prompted by the death of his friend, Augustine's ensuing distress is less grief for his friend and more grief at the experience of his own disunity exposed in the irrecoverable absence of his friend. The importance of this nameless friend, appreciated retrospectively, is his presence visually, his amenability to the gaze of Augustine as a point of identification, a place to look. Among all that they had shared, that which Augustine finds most of all "transformed into a cruel torment" when his friend can no longer be sought on the horizon is himself, in the sense that in the absence of his friend he is brought up short against the disorganization of self, its resistance to coherent visualization. The namelessness of the

---

those possibilities of liberation that he eventually seems practically to affirm. Hence the distinction often cited between Foucault on sex and sexuality, and the late Foucault on governance and care of the self. However one parses the phases of his career, in practice Foucault's writings have inspired and enabled intimately personal transformations almost immediately upon publication. See, for example, Weeks, "Capitalism and the Organization of Sex." And also McWhorter, *Bodies and Pleasures*. And my own preface to this volume.

35. Augustine *Confessions* 4.4.9 (Chadwick, 57–58).

friend thereby literalizes the incapacity of a name—a word—to unify the fallen self, so that the namelessness of the friend is almost a kind of protection of the friend against the depredations of Augustine's memory.[36] Immediately following a later passage in which he wonders about the relation between "the sound of the word" and "the thing which it signifies" as a function of memory, Augustine explicitly connects the mystery of knowledge through reference to the curse of original sin: "I at least, Lord, have difficulty at this point, and I find my own self hard to grasp. I have become for myself a soil which is a cause of difficulty and much sweat (Gen. 3:17f.)."[37] The labor with which God curses humanity after the Fall Augustine identifies with the labor of the fallen self to unify itself under a name.[38] Writing of his youthful seeking to know God, Augustine allows that even, perhaps especially, meaningfulness of the word "God" is confounded by the punishment of sin: "You had commanded and it so came about in me, that the soil would bring forth thorns and brambles for me, and that with toil I should gain my bread (Gen. 3:18)."[39]

Although Foucault refrains from any positively psychological interpretation of the self in relation to power's organization of bodies, the very impossibility of fulfillment of the promise named by the word "sex" assumes the ascription of a desiring interiority to persons who can become meaningfully sexed in the first place.[40] When, in the same passage cited above, Foucault sharpens the point of sex through a triplet of superlatives—"the most speculative, most ideal, and most internal"[41]—he conjures sex via suggestion of a technique from early Renaissance paint-

36. The namelessness of Augustine's concubine also opens to interpretation as a more complicated protective gesture on his part.

37. Augustine *Confessions* 10.16.25 (Chadwick, 193).

38. For recent discussion of Augustine on the problem of signification among fallen creation, see Ticciati, *Castration*.

39. Augustine *Confessions* 4.16.29 (Chadwick, 70).

40. By turning his attention to Greek and Hellenistic sources in the latter volumes of his *History of Sexuality*, Foucault resists any kind of totalizing psychological interpretation of the desire he correlates with sex, instead pursuing an archaeology of the psychological exigency suggested by his theory of sexuality and power. For appreciative criticism of Foucault's latter volumes, focusing specifically on the incorporation of Greek and Roman themes into an emerging Christian sexual ethics, see Clark, *Foucault*. For a constructive interpretation of Foucault's writings on classical asceticism as resource in imagining gay and lesbian identity as a form of contemporary Christian "vocation," see Vernon, *Following Foucault*.

41. Foucault, *History of Sexuality*, 155.

ing, as if sex does for power what the vanishing point does for a carefully drafted landscape, bringing the perception of harmonious coherence to an otherwise unintelligible agglomeration of material forces. In a similar manner Augustine's friend enables him to say to himself "look, he is on the way," to identify a figure on the landscape, a friend on the road who makes the way clear. The visualization of sex through a technique of perspective does not require the ascription of any agency per se to the power it represents, but even as a total accident of brute natural forces it somehow discloses also the presence of a viewer whose vision of the point of sex mirrors some self-relating desire—the desire, that is, for an imaginable point of coherence, a point that bridges the gap between the insecurity and instability of identity, a point through which and around which they are safely anchored; the desire to escape from the problem of self into the unity of a human word.

The efficacy of the fiction of sex in pointing this desire gives sex its practical urgency. The intensity of feeling in theological discourse on sexuality about the meaningfulness of marriage, and about who may and may not marry whom, attests the intensity of investment in marriage as a guarantor of the viability and visibility of the point of sex as fulfillment of the desire of unity of self. Given that the promise ascribed to sex is both impossible and yet utterly compelling, it makes sense that sex can bear a life and death value, since it is by definition an exhaustive promise, a promise that consumes potentially limitless energies. Sex is worth dying for because of what it offers to its victims in potential exchange for their lives:

> It might be added that "sex" performs yet another function that runs through and sustains the ones we have just examined. Its role in this instance is more practical than theoretical. It is through sex—in fact, an imaginary point determined by the deployment of sexuality—that each individual has to pass in order to have access to his own intelligibility (seeing that it is both the hidden aspect and the generative principle of meaning), to the whole of his body (since it is a real and threatened part of it, while symbolically constituting the whole), to his identity (since it joins the force of a drive to the singularity of a history). Through a reversal that doubtless had its surreptitious beginnings long ago—it was already making itself felt at the time of the Christian pastoral of the flesh—we have arrived at the point where we expect our intelligibility to come from what was for many centuries thought of as madness; the

plenitude of our body from what was long considered its stigma and likened to a wound; our identity from what was perceived as an obscure and nameless urge. Hence the importance we ascribe to it, the reverential fear with which we surround it, the care we take to know it. Hence the fact that over the centuries it has become more important than our soul, more important almost than our life; and so it is that all the world's enigmas appear frivolous to us compared to this secret, minuscule in each of us, but of a density that makes it more serious than any other.[42]

Foucault's exclamation of sex as "more important than our soul" is ironical at best, in that he presumably isn't worried that his readers risk the loss of their soul in their desire for sex. Yet in theological terms the affective orientation he describes of the self to sex connotes idolatry. Sex—a creation of human imagination—has been wrongfully invested with maximal importance at the expense of return to God.[43] Like any other idol, the ultimate truth of sex turns out to be an ultimate anticlimax: the non-necessity of sex to the desire it promises to fulfill.[44] The reality of fallen human identity is an intolerable condition of unintelligibility, and the distinguishing peculiarity of sex as an historical artifact is its magnetic capacity to organize the desire for intelligibility that it magnifies. Literal interpretation of original sin affirms that this desire for intelligibility is itself only comprehensible in relation to the unity of self in God that was lost, even as it also affirms that it is not possible definitively to describe this desire as a function of universal psychic structures, as if any repair of the psyche through human technique or therapy were possible.[45]

42. Ibid., 155–56.

43. On the genealogy of the "soul" as an "instrument of power," see Butler, *Bodies*, 32–36, 251–52 n. 12; Foucault *Discipline*, 29–30; and Bell, *Ritual*, 238 n. 202. Also see Rose, *Governing*.

44. For one starting point of a history of the concentration/reduction of the imagined site of the relation of self to God to the fiction of a sex, see Coakley, *Visions*. In addressing the historical imagination of an indivisible and simple self and attendant dualisms exemplified in the writings of Descartes, Coakley suggests that sex, like mind, soul, or will, is a fictional unity that functions as both metaphor and metonym of the whole self.

45. The difficulty of theorizing self-identification without invoking universal psychic structures is addressed by Butler's comment, in discussion of Slavoj Žižek, that "Žižek is surely right that the subject is not a unilateral effect of prior discourses, and that the process of subjectivation outlined by Foucault is in need of a psychoanalytic rethinking." Butler, *Bodies*, 189. Hence Butler's project to rethink psychoanalysis itself as contingent and historical yet also materially indispensable to aid in understanding the formation of personal identity. Still this strategy doesn't resolve the question of the universality or not of any psychic structures.

Most often the mystery of its transmission (=implausability + seeming injustice) is cited as the greatest objection to a literal interpretation of original sin, but the more relevant mystery for present purposes is, echoing Foucault, the omnipresence of sin's power, its fluid dispersal through self however organized. Or stated in traditional terms, the total depravity of fallen humanity. The uncomfortable result is that whether reading Augustine or Foucault, readers searching for some escape from the problem of self and its politics instead face their co-implication in the non-necessity of whatever vision of meaningful unity of self in a name that they are pursuing. With regard to Foucault this may help explain why many references to his writings take one of two forms. Either an invocation of his name that elides the most unsettling implications of his works because they are not consonant with the political project engaged. Or an *ad hominem* vilification of Foucault as a pederast and sadomasochist, as if his provocative criticisms of intergenerational sexual prohibitions in particular were proof that his entire life's work was merely the attempt to justify an inexcusable personal pursuit of properly forbidden pleasures.[46]

If one must pass through the point of sex "in order to have access to his own intelligibility," then the practical issue arises, how exactly can anyone accomplish this passage in the absence of any authoritative figure who can mediate it. Yet the legacy of sin is that humanity has lost enjoyment of unity of self in God and is not able on its own to recover the one way, the true mediator: "That is why the deceiving mediator, by whom through your secret judgments pride deserved to be deluded, has one thing in common with human beings, namely sin."[47] Whereas the true mediator holds in common the two kinds of being—God on the one hand and all that God creates on the other—human sin arises through the mediating authority of another creature. Which then turns humanity upon its own imitative but inadequate resources. Given that sex is a fiction, it

---

46. For discussion of Foucault's almost revelatory discovery of the S/M possibilities realized on San Francisco's Folsom Street, as backdrop to his writing of the first volume of the *History*, see Miller, *Passion*, 245–84. For summary of Žižek's critique of Foucault as sadomasochist, see Butler, *Bodies*, 206. For Foucault's now infamous critique of legal prohibitions of intergenerational sexual relations, see Foucault, *Politics*, 271–85. For discussion of Foucault's experience of LSD as the culminating experience of a mystical journey that begins on Folsom street, and hence Foucault himself as possibly exemplifying an "experience" of "secular mysticism," which "neither asks nor receives the consolation and comfort of a 'shelter in which experience can rest.' Rather, it embraces the whirlwind of one's 'nonunifying multiplicity,' intensified by natural or artificial means," see Flynn, *Partially*, 481.

47. Augustine *Confessions* 10.41.67 (Chadwick, 219).

is also the case that individuals are capable of narrating themselves into that fiction, of practically rendering for themselves fiction as fact and suffering the consequences. The instrumentality of sexuality engages the fallen self as narrator of its own desiring fictions, implanting within each person another self, a secret self, like a homunculus that is both the truth of oneself, and also a stranger and mediator within. To achieve personal intelligibility is to gain access to this little man or woman—one's sex—but also to worry endlessly about the indignities he or she may have endured. The intelligibility of one's sex is possible because the little person within continuously asserts itself as meaningfully sexed, and is thus "hyper-sexed." The unification of self idealized in marriage is the satisfaction of the demands of this homunculus for its own continual presence. It is the narrative stabilization of a specular self who can mediate (illusion) relation between self and God. The sex that is rendered visible as projected fiction is at the same time assumed as an internal presence, as if, in looking into a mirror, an object that appears at the greatest distance were ascribed a corresponding depth within the one gazing—the very image Foucault explores in his discussion of Velasquez's "Las Meninas" as inaugurating a new epoch of self-understanding in which one can become the bearer of a sex.[48]

The anxiety of the miniature sexed self who endlessly worries about its erasure attests to the necessity of narration to the accomplishment of sexed identity. Sex coalesces in the gap between the projected exterior and interior spaces of the self. Sex draws to a point the narrative activity that continually bridges that gap, even as that gap continually impels the narrative activity. It is in this sense that the homunculus—sex personified as the secret of the self—provides wholeness to the body and identity to the individual. In the first case because it exists in relation to the body as "a real and threatened part of it, while symbolically constituting the whole"; the whole modeled on the part, and not vice versa. In the second place, because it "joins the force of a drive to the singularity of a history"; because what is naturalized as mere bodily urgency is at the same time narrated as this other self—one's sex—literally speaking its history. Otherwise the self is no more or less than a porous and incidental cohesion of organic and inorganic compounds, no different, formally speaking, from the cumulus that develops into a tornado, streaking across the landscape, wreaking its havoc, then dissolving into the vaporous

48. Foucault, *Order*, 3–16.

atmosphere. Sex is finally so compelling, not because it is an irrepressible drive or instinct—not the storm of emotion and sensation typified in so much poetry and drama—nor because it is a means to bodily pleasure, but because it is experienced as a presence within—imagined most insistently as visibly mutually reflected through the eyes of romantic lovers—emerging out of the eye of this storm—the presence within which attests, of all these ingredients, here am "I."[49]

Contrary to the common sense that is often invoked in theological discourse on sexuality, sex is not something people do, nor is it something people are. It is something that people become, a possibility of intelligible personal identity with a history. This intelligibility, however, is neither immediately accessible nor self-interpreting. One cannot simply turn inward in search of one's sex. The passage to intelligibility is the narration of the possibility and meaningfulness of that intelligibility. The intelligibility achieved is not exterior to this activity of narration, but *is* this activity of narration. To possess intelligibility is thus to achieve relative mastery of this activity. It is to achieve a consonance between the self-concerned activity of embodying one's sex—proving the presence of the sexed person within—and the impersonal spatio-temporal capillary extension of power across the bodies it comprehends. The efficacy of sexuality itself depends on the possibility of this consonance between its operations and its effects, which in turn depends on the accumulation, in the space between sex and sexuality, of a community of intelligibility that is continually negotiating what counts as the successful narration of sex.

Within the history of sexuality, the injunction to be true to one's sex is an injunction to self-empowerment through the strategic embodiment of the narrative activity that makes sex intelligible. But sex is only ever more or less intelligible, never absolutely so. This more or less is negotiated within shared frameworks of narrative activity wherein some persons' sex achieves the status of greater intelligibility, of presumption to an absolute status that it can never fulfill. And this presumption depends in turn on the persistent challenge to its pretensions to finality. A narrative dominance ensues that establishes the practicability of ruling fictions for those whose rule they enable in the activity of fixing the intelligibility of a particular sex in such a way that its volatility remains unperceived by

---

49. "But you 'Lord my God, hear, look and see' (Ps 12:4) and 'have mercy and heal me' (Ps 79:15). In your eyes I have become a problem to myself, and that is my sickness." Augustine *Confessions* 10.33.49 (Chadwick, 208).

those who enjoy it. One's sex is thereby experienced as simultaneously most private and most public, most one's own and most shared, most secure and most uncertain.

Though necessarily not an exclusive framework for the negotiation and adjustment of sexuality with its effects, romantic relationship stabilized in marriage has been and continues to constitute the predominant conventional trajectory for the narration of an intelligible sex. Narrations of this trajectory are consequently experienced as irresistibly alluring, theologically charged, and inescapably dangerous. Drawn by the allure of the intelligibility it promises, the self seeks to know itself in a passage through sex, romanced by the dream of an irreducible individuation that is mirrored and affirmed by the identity of another as a "soul mate": creatures thereby mediating for each other imagination of relationship with God. In the possibility of affirmation of one's sex through relationship with another the shame of sin, the shocking exposure of self, naked apart from the grace of God, becomes displaced onto the bodies of those persons who appear improperly, incompletely, or otherwise unsuccessfully sexed. The apparent failure of some person's sex, which seems at first glance to undermine the narration of sex for everyone else, instead discloses the fluidity of all narrations of sex.

Even as the eyes of another are figured as the mirror through which the secret of the self is disclosed to the self, the individuation that results is only possible to the extent that it at the same time contributes to the maintenance of the common sex that it instantiates. The elaboration of an intelligible sex arises out of the creative tension between the individuation and communality that it simultaneously makes possible. As an operative ideal of personal intelligibility, sex is an identity one can only possess by sharing it in common with others, and at the same time it is realized through activity that is performed with regard to a specified partner.[50] This tension between commonality and difference reduces, in its starkest formulation, to the opposition of Man and Woman, often in reference to Gen 1:27: "So God created humankind in his image, in the image of God he created them; male and female he created them." Yet even the biblical text neglects to specify which of the two creatures is

50. Perhaps the possibility, let alone frequency, of sexual relationship with multiple partners, whether synchronically or diachronically (swinging or cheating), is so compelling and alarming because it belies the soul unity of self sought in relationship with a sole sexual partner.

the male, and which the female, leaving it a matter of interpretation by the reader, just as the commonality and difference of male and female in relation to each other are subsumed by the commonality and difference of both in relation to God in whose image all humanity is created.

The male and female created by God are not the essence of the sex narrated by the romance of innocent sexuality. In theological discourse on sexuality the ideals of Man and Woman are ideals of orientation. They do not denote a point of identity, but perspectival trajectories that inscribe a point at their center. The opposition of Man and Woman is in no simple sense natural, inevitable, or reductively symmetrical. It is a subject of continual narration, and also of continual challenge, negotiation, and subversion. The dominance of any intelligible sex therefore necessarily entails its own resistances, so that the most authoritative narratives are full of signifying omissions. They do not so much contain within themselves the traces of the voices they are silencing so much as they produce the traces of those voices in order to create the experience of their silencing. Only then is dominance affirmed, is a claim to superior intelligibility itself intelligible.[51] At the same time the voices to be silenced, when once sounded, are not so easily drowned out, not so easily contained. They acquire a life and a credibility of their own.

As a matter of contingent fact, it just happens to be the case that the opposition of orientations defined alternately as "heterosexuality" and "homosexuality" constitute the dominant framework for the establishment of sex, idealized in the opposition of Man and Woman. Yet the intelligibility of those ideals of sexed identity, and the orientations which presumably express them, are inherently unstable. They are efficacious as rubrics for the definition of sex precisely because they are not wholly coherent, but just coherent enough, in their narrative grip on the human imagination, to remain compelling as a generative locus of sex. Which helps to explain why the question of marriage in theological discourse on sexuality has become so intensely focused as a problem of same-sex marriage. Critique of the romance of innocent sexuality therefore requires analysis of the literary mechanisms of narration of sex through the conceptualization of sexual orientation, defined as it is by the oppositions "hetero" and "homo."

51. The presumably symmetrical or complementary relation of Male and Female notably has been critiqued by Luce Irigaray, who finds only the absence of the feminine in what she terms phallogocentric discourse. The feminine produced through this discourse she describes as a mark of erasure, as the non-thematizable necessity that makes possible phallogocentric claims of coherency. See Irigary, *Speculum* and *This Sex.*

The stage is now set to examine more closely, building on the central argument of Eve Kosofky Sedgwick's *Epistemology of the Closet*, the continuity between the depiction of romantic marriage in works of literature and the depiction of marriage in works of theological ethics.

Through the incorporation as doxa of the effects of discourse of sexuality, theology has accorded the fiction of sex extraordinary precedence, forcibly displacing imagination of alternative and even plural fictions of intelligible personal identity. Such has been the case because the image of sex as homunculus entails that the promise of intelligibility offered by sex become experienced as a function of communication between the self and the secret that is that self's sex. Like the soul that it now surpasses in importance, sex promises individuation through the disclosure of a private truth, a truth unique to the individual. Yet the possibility of such individuation requires the recognition of the secret as a secret, as knowledge that can potentially be shared. A secret, after all, is only a secret in the context of some form of disclosure that also includes a possibility of exposure. A secret is only meaningful where the possibility of exposure is meaningful. Whereas the soul had an experienced confessor to coax its secret into the light of day, and affirm its truthful claim to the status of secret, sex has only the hapless individual it inhabits, who must navigate a solitary passage to his own intelligibility, even as the possibility of such intelligibility depends on the possibility of such passage. For this reason Foucault's characterization of "the Christian pastoral of the flesh"[52] as a vital link in the trajectory that ends in the supersession of soul by sex suggests a view of the historical emergence of the novel and subsequent media of popular narratives as the fruition—in contexts where the intermediary of the confessor no longer existed—of the "reversal" incipient in this pastoral tradition.[53] The continuity between works of literature and works of theology, and the consequent intensification by theology of the importance of the fiction of sex, fulfills the logic of the operations of sexuality.

52. Foucault, *History of Sexuality*, 155–56.

53. In many English novels of the nineteenth century the Catholic priest is depicted as a nefariously disruptive intruder between spouses, precisely in his role as confessor of one of those spouses, usually the wife. Notable examples include: Radcliffe, *The Italian*; Reade, *Griffith Gaunt*; and Trollope, *Father Eustace*. The figure of the sexually predatory priest is a staple of nineteenth-century American anti-Catholic literature, itself a kind of popular pornography. When originally published, works by Reed and Monk, *Veil of Fear*, caused exceptional public ferment. (They remain wildly entertaining to read.) For history of this literature, see Pagliarini, *Pure*, and Gardella, *Innocent*, 25–38.

Considering the power ascribed to sex, its seeming power to unify the fallen self, and the centrality of marriage as the institutional intersection of state and church in which sex crystallizes, it is hardly surprising that debates about same-sex marriage have become so charged. It is in a way to their credit that they are so electrified by the desire of the fallen self for unity. Nor is it so surprising that the proliferating spectacle of improperly constituted marital relations becomes perceived as a threat to the possibility of fulfillment of that desire, once one recognizes that the inherent impossibility of the promise of romance turns out to be a distinguishing feature of romance. The work of romance is to transfigure ignorance into knowledge, incompletion into wholeness; it is to make dangerous illusions of self-identification as safe as possible for oneself. The continual narrative display of other people's marital failures and successes is consequently so compelling and provoking, because no such thing exists as properly constituted marital relations per se. All that exists is the elaboration of possible forms of relationship through their narrative display. The maximum security one can accomplish is the enjoyment of a certain invisibility, relative to this display. Whether or not it is possible to speak meaningfully about sex, without also contributing to its manufacture and proliferation—or at least to articulate some justifiable grounds for contributing to this process—is therefore a question that must be addressed. Does any reason exist to hope that one can speak meaningfully about sex *and* justice?

The answer suggested so far is that such reason does exists, but only when the focus of inquiry shifts away from sex imagined in itself, to the elusive intelligibility of self-identification that sex promises. The conclusion of all this argument converges in the possibility of a justice defined in relation to the differential possibilities of personal intelligibility arising at the intersection of theology and sexuality. The end of justice in sexual ethics is to redress the denial of intelligibility to some persons that is a function of the claim to an impossible plenitude of intelligibility by other persons. To do so requires honoring all persons as accountable for the fact of sin.

The immediately following step in this train of argument is to investigate the literary mechanisms for the narration of sexed personal identity, paying special attention to the centrality of marriage in the narration of sex as a crucible of intelligibility. The way will then have been paved for the development, in successive chapters, of a constructive Augustinian theology of sexuality and original sin, centered in a literal interpretation of the doctrine, that enables mature humorous recognition that sex is not essential to the relation of self to God except as it is indicative of the sinfulness of all sexuality. An extended critique will then become possible of the romance of innocent sexuality, of the idealization of marriage as a means of narration of the fiction of sex and consequent exteriorization of responsibility for sin, which in faith calls forth charitable anger to redress the injustices, the inhospitalities, that ensue.

3

The Sentimental Narration
of Sex in Marriage

About the foundational impossibilities of modern homo-heterosexual definition, the questions we have been assaying so far have been, not how this incoherent dispensation can be rationalized away or set straight, not what it means or even how it means, but what it makes happen, and how.[1]

The Incoherency of Homo-Heterosexual Definition

IF SEX IS WORTH dying for, then one should be able to find forensic evidence to this effect. How else otherwise is knowledge of the worth of sex possible? Yet sex is a fiction, and as such principally concerns not the body but the imagination. To search for proof of the worth of sex in death is therefore not to search for actually dead bodies, though some are likely to surface, but to search for their metaphorical equivalents. The actual murders of real live human beings when they happen are concretions of the pervasive symbolization of a parallel kind of violence. Together both kinds of violence contribute to the survival of the fiction of sex—the romance of innocent sexuality—against the threat posed by

1. Sedgwick, *Epistemology*, 213.

55

alternative imaginations of intelligible personal identity.[2] Preservation of the illusion of an intelligible unity of the fallen self against the pain of acknowledgment of communal responsibility for original sin appropriates to itself the wages of sin. Sex is only worth dying for, in other words, because human beings in their unending perversity turn the punishment of sin in death into the basis of yet another form of prideful imitation of God.

When theology incorporates sex as doxa, a contingent formation of human imagination becomes valued as a necessary origin of and point of contact with God who is the creator and sustainer of all life. The critical power of theology in relation to sexuality is then compromised, since theology is then blinded to the injustices that ensue when some persons claim for themselves an innocent sexuality at the expense of others whose sexuality is labeled sinful. Worse, theology contributes to those injustices by authorizing an ultimate value for sex as God-given that it otherwise wouldn't have. Theology as a result should not attempt to stand apart in any simple way from its contexts—a stance that undermines theological contributions to political and cultural debates—but instead should seek to achieve greater understanding of its enmeshed particularity in the social discourses of which it forms a part, including especially the narrative traditions sustaining the fiction of sex. As argued at the outset, this task demands a mature sense of humor with regard to the intelligibility of theology as much as with regard to the intelligibility of sexed identity, since the desired self-awareness of theology depends on the disturbances that enable more conscious attention to the workings of theological discourse on sexuality.

To achieve this self-awareness some literary theory is necessary, since it is finally the *fiction*, not the *sex*, which exacts its valuation as worth dying for. Reading theology and literature together discloses a common frame within which debates about same-sex marriage occur and also why questions more generally about sexed identity are refracted through this frame of reference. As a practical matter, disputes about the moral status of same-sex sexual relationship and about the permissibility or not of same-sex sexual relationship as a basis for marriage are bitterly divisive. It is tempting to assume from the intensity of disagreement among such communities as the Justices of the United States Supreme

---

2. On the related problem of violence by men against women in the construction of masculinity, see Herbert, *Sexual Violence*.

Court,[3] the Worldwide Anglican Communion,[4] and even contestants and judges for the Miss U.S.A. pageant,[5] that the divide over same-sex marriage must be as great in theory as it is in practice, yet something close to the opposite is rather the case. Debate over same-sex marriage is so intense because its participants all share a common commitment to the narrative capacity of marriage to render the secret of the self, its sex, accessible. The question of who may or may not marry whom matters so much because it is finally a question of who will or will not experience a regnant fiction of intelligible bodily and psychic integrity.

Indispensable as a guide to understanding the centrality of homosexuality to overall imaginations of sexed-identity is Eve Kosofky Sedgwick's *Epistemology of the Closet*, in which she explicates the terms by means of which the desire for sex as an object of knowledge attainable through its narration organizes. Despite the title of her book, Sedgwick's argument is as much a theory of unknowing as of knowing. Her principal thesis and starting point is that the problem of what she labels "a chronic, now endemic crisis of homo/heterosexual definition"[6] is productively incoherent as a matrix of generation of empowered knowledge-relations across a whole range of disciplines. Ignorance is not exactly opposed to knowledge, as if the accumulation of knowledge were a straightforward and linear process. Ignorance is multiple, and specific, and as such, she writes, "these ignorances, far from being pieces of the originary dark, are produced by and correspond to particular knowledges and circulate as part of particular regimes of truth."[7] The result is that disciplines are not able to secure the knowledges that are their province, even as the persistent quality of crisis ensures that the work of definition that makes disciplinarity possible proceeds. Realms of knowledge thereby multiply

---

3. Consider Antonin Scalia's apocalyptic dissenting opinion in "Lawrence and Garner Versus Texas," warning that elimination of sodomy laws will lead inevitably to same-sex marriage. For analysis of Scalia's dissent, see Harcourt, "Forbidden."

4. Amid international controversy, Gene Robinson was installed as an Episcopal bishop in New Hampshire on November 2, 2003.

5. In April 2009, Miss California Carrie Prejean—expected to win the Miss USA title—lost the competition after providing the right (i.e., wrong) answer to a question about "gay-marriage" posed by judge and same-sex marriage advocate Perez Hilton. Prejean almost immediately afterward became a spokesperson for the National Organization for Marriage, defending "traditional marriage" against the movement for "marriage equality."

6. Sedgwick, *Epistemology*, 8.

7. Ibid.

without limit, including theological knowledge of sexed identity as a stable basis of relation between self and God.

The trouble for theology, as for other disciplines, is that one's sex is only ever known as it achieves expression through a sexual orientation that is amenable to the project of homo/heterosexual definition. Yet because there is no end to this project, the sex expressed by homosexuality or heterosexuality is necessarily elusive. One is never fully and finally sexed once and for all, but always actively becoming a heterosexual or homosexual man or woman. It is therefore self-defeating to expect that disputes in sexual ethics can be mediated or resolved though the dispersion of knowledge. Such expectation is just another instance of the sinful delusion that the solution to the problem of self described by Augustine is attainable through human reason. Yet the temptation to knowledge is acute, since oneself is a problem that makes things happen, as even Augustine acknowledges: "That is why I was pushed away, and why you resisted my inflated pride. I was imagining corporeal shapes. I being flesh accused flesh. A 'wandering spirit' (Ps. 77: 39), I was not yet on my way back to you, but meandered on and on into things which have no being either in you or in me or in the body. They were not created for me on the ground of your truth, but were fictions invented by my vanity on the basis of the body."[8] Writing about his search to know God (where "to know" is to be in relationship, such that carnal knowing is only a crude analogue of true unity of self in knowledge), Augustine discloses that knowledge of self and knowledge of God are not separable, and that fallen human beings can't help but persist in generating fictions out of their bodies in their desire to collect the disintegrated self into an intelligible whole. Once generated, however, it is the inclination of sinful creatures to love their own fictions over the truth that would shatter those fictions.

An exacerbation of the problem of self is that the ignorances that complement the incomplete knowledges attainable by fallen humanity are hard to relinquish, since to do so is also to relinquish the apparent security of self promised by the knowledges that they enable. The aim of this book is not therefore to tidy up once and for all the conceptual mess that is theological discourse on sexuality, to establish the intellectual equivalent of a North American period room circa 2010 in which no one is allowed to sit on the furniture, pick up a book, open a window. Nor is the goal enlightenment, imagined as the establishment of certain

---

8. Augustine, *Confessions* 4.15.26 (Chadwick, 68).

knowledge of sexed human identity, as if those persons and communities whose vision of intelligibly sexed identity is deemed unjust can finally be discounted as *merely* ignorant. The goal instead is to articulate a theological frame of reference for evaluation of more and less just processes of knowledge formation concerning sexed identity and their attendant forms of unknowing. Resolution of disputes regarding any particular issue in sexual ethics will more likely take the form of a reconstituted community of knowing and unknowing in relation to acceptance of responsibility for original sin.

Whereas Foucault, and Butler in turn, write about sex as an effect of sexuality as if they were projecting a film in reverse, Sedgwick describes a more convoluted dynamic governed by the overall productivity of the crisis of homo/heterosexual definition: "The master terms of a particular historical moment will be those that are so situated as to entangle most inextricably and at the same time most differentially the filaments of other important definitional nexuses."[9] As Sedgwick goes on to demonstrate (and others have also) it is possible to find traces of homo/heterosexual definition across the most diverse and apparently unrelated domains of inquiry, from embryology to astrophysics. The global scope of her diagnosis of a definitional crisis may consequently invite skepticism regarding its outer reaches, but still it is invaluable for analysis of the living commitments to its solution pursued through narrations of the fiction of sex in theological discourse on sexuality, at the center of which lie together literally and figuratively those originary confounders of sameness and difference, Adam and Eve. As already suggested, it is not possible to disentangle this couple as male and female without also doing more, without also proving Sedgwick's point that "contests for discursive power can be specified as competitions for the material or rhetorical leverage required to set the terms of, to profit in some way from, the operations of such an incoherence of definition."[10] As concerns the categorization of human beings as definitively sexed male and female, a literal interpretation of the doctrine of original sin discloses that the profit too many people and communities seek through this incoherence is an unwarranted claim of God-relatedness.

It follows from this predominant incoherence that the goodness of sexuality cannot readily be renegotiated in terms of a re-conception of

9. Sedgwick, *Epistemology*, 13.

10. Ibid., 11.

human creation in the *imago dei*. The argument developed in these pages declines the possibility that "reconstructing the imago dei performatively thus decenters heterosexuality and allows the theologian to theorize that many sexualities have the possibility for performatively reflecting the image of God."[11] This view is deliberately eschewed for two main reasons. First, because it assumes that heterosexual definition can be coherently decentered. And second, because it assumes from the creation of human beings in the image of God that the basic goodness of any sexual relationship is a presently attainable performative institution of God-relatedness. Debates about the meaningfulness of sex and marriage have become structured around a strategically unknowing assumption of homosexuality and heterosexuality as revelatory of sexed identity as male and female. Revelation as encounter with God becomes over-identified with revelation as knowledge of one's sex. Among the many categories which, according to Sedgwick, are "entangled" and "differentiated"[12] by homo/heterosexual definition, for present purposes the most important (though not named by Sedgwick herself), is "innocent/sinful." Trajectories to stably sexed identity through homo/heterosexual definition have become valued also as trajectories of relation to or distance from God, as trajectories of innocent and sinful sexuality.

By insisting on the inherent sinfulness of all sexuality, a theology of sexuality and original sin disrupts attempts to capitalize further on the profits realized from the incoherence of homo/heterosexual definition. The crisis impelling theological discourse on sexuality, which at first appears as a difficulty in determining what counts as sin, and who is doing the sin, is now better described as a crisis of failure of personal intelligibility seeking its resolution in a differentially enforced assertion of the power of the fiction of sex to establish an identity-affirming God-relation. It is this fantasied power of sex to propel the self into relation with God that finally renders sex as worth dying for. Better to die while still in relationship to God than to live and fall out of relationship with God.

Even if the desire for intelligibly sexed personal identity cannot be wholly untangled from the crisis of homo/heterosexual definition, the filaments at least can be loosened. The resulting space allows for evaluation of theology as a contributing source of injustices across the spectrum of discourses and politics in which it participates.

11. Kamitsuka, "Toward," 202.
12. Sedgwick, *Epistemology*, 11.

Sentimentality and Homosexual Panic

For those persons who affirm the goodness of same-sex sexual relationship as a basis for marriage, it is tempting to seek to redress opposition to same-sex marriage by proceeding directly to analysis of marriage in itself, not marriage defined as between any two specifically sexed individuals. The way forward cannot be so straight, however, since the status of homo/heterosexual definition as a master term in the production of sex as an ideal point and fiction through which one must pass in order to achieve personal intelligibility entails that debates about marriage are inescapably means of negotiating the definition of homosexual and heterosexual identities. It is not possible to speak of marriage per se without also doing more, when all that is possible is marriage between unstably sexed individuals. For this very reason the specter of same-sex marriage evokes passionate responses, as its proponents and opponents are equally committed to the differentiation of sex at stake in the possibility of same-sex marriage. At the center of the movement for same-sex marriage is the claim of a rightful share, by persons and communities who have so far been excluded, to some of the profit of marriage, including the God-relating significance of homosexual and heterosexual sexual relations as expressive of male and female identity.[13] So it is interesting to note, for example, that even as any two persons are able in any jurisdiction to wed each other, so long as they are legally of opposite sex, and thereby enjoy many of the practical benefits of marriage, these visible public benefits are considered inauthentic, almost cheating, whenever it turns out that the private invisible union of sexed selves in sexual activity is missing, whenever it turns out, in effect, that the marriage is a sham. So it is also interesting to note that proponents of same-sex marriage are no less adamant that it is the enduring sexual relationship which grounds claims to marital benefits such as health care surrogacy.

Just as Foucault's account of sex entails ascription of a psychological depth to the persons who desire intelligible self-identification via sex through an external point that also points inward, so also Sedgwick ascribes a similarly visualized presence of self that can become enmeshed in the crisis of homo/heterosexual definition. In her prior work she denotes this psychological depth or desiring presence by the term "homosexual

---

13. For a characteristic description of marriage between man and woman as faithful worship of God, see Martinez, "Marriage as Worship."

panic."[14] Carrying the concept forward, she explains that the problem of homo/heterosexual definition has acquired overwhelming significance because it defines an unstable and insecure realm of male homosocial bonds that are not characterized by male same-sex sexual desire:

> I argue that the historically shifting, and precisely the arbitrary and self-contradictory, nature of the way *homosexuality* (along with its predecessor terms) has been defined in relation to the rest of the male homosocial spectrum has been an exceedingly potent and embattled locus of power over the entire range of male bonds, and perhaps especially over those that define themselves, not *as* homosexual, but *as against* the homosexual. Because the paths of male entitlement, especially in the nineteenth century, required certain intense male bonds that were not readily distinguishable from the most reprobated bonds, an endemic and ineradicable state of what I am calling male homosexual panic became the normal condition of male heterosexual entitlement.[15]

It appears at first from Sedgwick's account that only heterosexual men can experience homosexual panic, but such is not exactly the case, first because the stability of the category "heterosexual male" is itself in question, and second because the desire for entitlement associated with the achievement of heterosexual male identity is not exclusive to that category of identity. As a result it makes most sense only retrospectively to describe nineteenth-century bonds between men as forged through a state of homosexual panic, to the extent those bonds were the necessary precursors to the emergence of the possibility of naming a generalized condition of homosexual panic that marks all sexed identity as narrated along the trajectories of sexual orientation as homosexual and hetero-sexual. To possess a sex, to seek to render that sex intelligible, is thus energized by a pervasive condition of homosexual panic. In this sense, a group of lesbian and gay couples lobbying a legislature to legalize same-sex marriage models a passage through homosexual panic to a claim of homosocial entitlement just as much as the crowd gathered outside pro-testing any such legislation models homosexual panic as the condition of its own tentative entitlement to an intelligibly sexed identity.

Allowing that the ascription of homosexual panic to nineteenth-century male-homosocial bonding is a bit anachronistic, by that fact it indicates where to search for the literary precedents of narrations of the

14. Sedgwick, *Between Men*, 192.
15. Sedgwick, *Epistemology*, 185.

fiction of sex as homosexual and heterosexual. Readings of some novel examples of the fiction of sex as man and woman, before sex becomes explicitly conceptualized through the trajectories of homosexual and heterosexual orientation (to be undertaken at the outset of the following chapter) consequently promise to enrich insight into the productivity of the crisis of homo/heterosexual definition to theological discourse on sexuality. Looking backwards with a critical perspective shows how the crisis aspect of homo/heterosexual definition, especially concerning marriage, is experienced as a crisis of relations that are produced as *retrospective* truths of sexed identity. Sedgwick explains:

> The *homo* in the emerging concept of the homosexual seems to have the potential to perform a definitive de-differentiation—setting up a permanent avenue of potential slippage—between two sets of relations that had previously been seen as relatively distinct: identification and desire. It is with *homo*-style homosexuality, and *not* with inversion, pederasty, or sodomy (least of all, of course, with cross-gender sexuality) that an erotic language, an erotic discourse comes into existence that makes available a continuing possibility for symbolizing slippages between identification and desire. It concomitantly makes available new possibilities for the camouflage and concealment, or the very selective or pointed displays, of proscribed or resisted erotic relation and avowal through chains of vicariation—through the mechanisms that, I argue, cluster under the stigmatizing name "sentimentality."[16]

In emphasizing the slippages between "identification" and "desire" that follow from the unstable coordination of sameness and difference through homo/heterosexual definition, Sedgwick somewhat misleadingly suggests that these relations were once recognizably distinct and have subsequently become inextricably crossed. Yet they are only recognized as such retrospectively. Homosexual panic is a constitutive dynamic of sexed identity only because it includes imagination of a previously uncomplicated narration of sexed identity that presumably *could have* persisted, most typically fantasized as an uncomplicated, unambiguous relationship between a man and a woman as a husband and a wife.[17] To say that identification and desire are analytically distinct is not to say that relations

16. Ibid., 159.

17. For discussion of American religious historical formations of gender, emphasizing especially the correlation of sexed identity with a differentiation of men's and women's "spheres," see Hackett, "Gender and Religion."

between men, between women, and between men and women could all once be mapped without remainder by this distinction—by the unquestioned definition of marriage as the union of man and wife—and now they have become vulnerable to a de-differentiation. Instead the retrospective projection of such a history bespeaks an unstable present reality.[18]

As an experience of threat to self, homosexual panic induces also experience of the instability of the self it seeks to preserve, since the distinction between identification and desire only acquires its freighted significance as it fails to correlate exactly with the concepts homosexuality and heterosexuality. It follows that assertions of marriage as an institutionalization of heterosexual or homosexual relationship include also assertions of what Sedgwick calls "proscribed or resisted erotic relation and avowal." The heterosexual man, for example, is a man who presumably identifies with other men, as man, and desires other women, as man; while the homosexual man is presumably a man who identifies with and desires other men, as man. Yet the possibility of homosexuality means that the heterosexual man cannot securely identify with other men, as man, without also worrying that such identification also includes the possibility/reality of desiring other men, as man. To argue that the homosexual man is not really a man only begs the question and intensifies the occasion for panic, since it is to begin to openly acknowledge that man is an identity achieved and not an essence bestowed by nature. For this reason heterosexuality is better redefined, not in exclusive opposition to homosexuality, but as an orientation that comprehends homosexuality within itself. As Freud famously suggested, homosexuality is only a problem because heterosexuality is a problem.[19] So the confusion between the homo/same and the hetero/different in the conceptualization of homosexuality and heterosexuality is not some calamity for a previously unambiguous heterosexual identity, but is the (il)logical ground of this new identity.[20]

---

18. Sedgwick's focus on relations between men in this regard has been subject to significant critique for the history it overlooks, as masterfully documented by Marcus, *Between Women*, including even notable precedents of same-sex marriage.

19. "Thus from the point of view of psycho-analysis the exclusive interest felt by men for women is also a problem that needs elucidating and is not a self-evident fact based upon an attraction that is ultimately of a chemical nature." Freud, *Three Essays*, 12.

20. On the historical formation of the concept of "homosexuality," see Halperin, *One Hundred Years*. For a history of the concept "heterosexuality" that nevertheless affirms the priority of the invention of the concept "homosexuality," see Katz, *Invention*.

Given the irresolvable convolution of sameness and difference in homo/heterosexual definition, theological assertions of certain knowledge about the purposefully created sexual difference between man and woman can only be sustained through mechanisms that mask their own constitutive indeterminacies. Throughout her work Sedgwick posits multiple mechanisms of sentimentality, but at one key moment she summarizes the main features relevant for analysis of how fictions of sex are narrated within theological discourse on sexuality. In prose that is itself quite convoluted, she writes:

> About the phenomenon of "sentimentality," we have said, as more specifically about such subcategories of vicarious knowledge-relation as prurience, morbidity, knowingness, and snobbism, two things can be said. First, and crucially: *It takes one to know one.* But the apparent symmetry of that epistemological catchphrase, in which the One who Knows and the One who is Taken appear interchangeable, belies the extreme asymmetry of rhetorical positioning implicit in the projectile efficacy of these attributions. The ballistics of the "sentimental" requires the freeze-framing of one targeted embodiment of sentimentality, its presentation *as spectacle* to a further sentimentality whose own privileged disembodiment and invisibility are preserved and reenabled by that highly differential act of staging. Thus, in the second place, it must be said that sentimentality *as spectacle* is structured very differently from sentimentality as *viewpoint* or habitation; that this difference is rhetorical; and that it is most powerfully charged for textual performance.[21]

Untangling Sedgwick's prose, the key point here is that sentimentality is a mode of relationality. It describes how individuals and communities realize differentially enforced knowledge of themselves and others through assumption of viewpoint of others or presentation of self as spectacle. A distinct quality of sentimentality is that it differentiates most effectively as it strategically denies its own identifications. The enjoyment of heterosexuality as viewpoint in this way also always involves identification of oneself with homosexuality as spectacle, so that achievement of sentimental knowledge of one's heterosexually oriented sex turns out to depend on a closeted identification with other persons' homosexually oriented sex. Hence the centrality of the closet to this entire epistemol-

21. Sedgwick, *Epistemology*, 221–22.

ogy. Hence also the provocative potency of behaviors that become characterized as "flaming."

As with other disciplines, so for theology the crisis of homo/heterosexual definition impels the productivity of its "textual performances." More precisely, since sentimentality is a mechanism of narration *as* knowledge-relation, it is the relation which impels the textual performances. While heterosexuality is usually asserted as a basis both of marriage and of God-relatedness, the purported sinfulness of homosexuality functions as the spectacle which enables assumption of the viewpoint of heterosexuality as a position of innocence.[22] Entangled as they are in the web of homo/heterosexual definition, however, the judgments innocent and sinful do not correlate with a tenable division of human identity before God, but with an untenable division of human identity as projected in imagined relation to God. The dyad heterosexuality/innocence describes a position of invisibility before God experienced as a position of viewpoint in relation to the spectacle homosexuality/sinfulness. Any assertion of innocence, whether heterosexual or homosexual, is therefore also a movement toward self-erasure that seeks out the spectacle which affirms its own position as it is erased.[23] It is not possible, as a result, to seek to enroll homosexuality within the ranks of innocence and marriage without also conscripting some figure to embody visibly the remainder of sin, which helps to chart the fuzzy boundary on the other side of which homosexuality becomes queer.

As objectionable as it will be to some persons to have to take seriously the particular association of homosexuality with sin because it seems to affirm the terms of debate about same-sex marriage as defined by the most vociferous defenders of marriage as a relationship between one man and one woman in which created heterosexual nature completes itself, it is nevertheless imperative to do so once one recognizes that theological debates in sexual ethics are struggles to define a community of

22. For history of the American pursuit of innocence as a kind of primitivism, the attempt to recover a pristine past prior to the formation of the terms of homo/heterosexual definition, see Allen and Hughes, *Illusions*. For history of nineteenth century American imagination of innocence as release, by contrast, from the constraints of the past, see Lewis, *American Adam*.

23. For historical analysis of the concentration, in mid-twentieth century America, of Christian hopes of encounter with Christ in the privacy of the family home, and attendant identification of the public exterior realm with a world of faithlessness and sin, see Watt, "Private Hopes."

intelligibility organized through a homosexual panic that is also a panic over responsibility for original sin. A more responsible affirmation of all sexual relationship therefore begins with acknowledgment of the sinfulness of homosexuality *and* heterosexuality as a starting point in turn for the practice of a greater hospitality. It then becomes possible, following Sedgwick, to show that the association of heterosexuality with innocence is so powerful not because it is theologically sound, but because it sounds so theologically compelling: "What these proliferating categories and especially their indissoluble contradictions do unflaggingly sustain, however, is the establishment of the *spectacle of the homosexual closet* as a presiding guarantor of rhetorical community, of authority—someone else's authority—over world-making discursive terrain that extends vastly beyond the ostensible question of the homosexual."[24] The challenge, for those who recognize the goodness of same-sex sexual relationship, is thus to show how acceptance of the inherent sinfulness of all sexuality enables a more just and inclusive community of theological inquiry by disrupting the rhetorical authority of the distinctions homosexual/heterosexual innocent/sinful. It is hardly surprising in the meantime that some persons have advocated the celebration of coming out as a sacrament whereby the self comes out into a God-related identity by making a spectacle of the self.[25] Yet in doing so these persons merely affirm the pervasiveness of the closet—the hiding place of sin—multiplying the possibilities for entrenching the privileged invisibility of heterosexuality/innocence as viewpoint. Every claim to innocent sexuality is like the claim of someone looking at his own feet who simultaneously denies all knowledge of the person to whom they are attached, as if it were possible for anyone to stand elsewhere than the ground of sin.

Theological discourse on sexuality fastens on the imagined unity of self in one's sex by narrating sex as an agency that originates in God's creative activity. In narrations of sex, viewpoint is always a position of privilege (though not without great costs also) in relation to spectacle. The greater the invisibility of the viewpoint, the more insulated is the fantasy from its own lacunae and inconsistencies; the fantasy, that is, that one has a sex that is both an irrevocable origin and inflexible rule of intelligibility; the fantasy that fidelity to the origin and rule of sex ends in a plenitude of intelligibility that is an ultimate fulfillment of the need for

24. Sedgwick, *Epistemology*, 230.
25. Glaser, *Coming Out*.

intelligibility; the fantasy, above all, that fidelity to one's sex is fidelity to God who creates and thus a solution to the problem of original sin.

What Sedgwick calls homosexual panic describes much more than a fear of loss of control of, that is at the same time actually constitutive of, the bonds that structure the male homosocial spectrum. Entangling the category innocent/sinful, homosexual panic describes the desire for mastery of innocent sexuality as a God-relating viewpoint against the spectacle of others sinful sexuality. Evidence of the worth of sex in death, symbolized and otherwise, is the visible counterpoint on which the privileged assumption of innocence depends. The result is an intensification of homosexual panic as a matter of the life and death of heterosexually and homosexually sexed identity.

Sentimental-Homicidal-Suicidal Violence and the Spectacle of the Homosexual Child

Continuing the explication of sentimentality as the principal mechanism for the narration of a sex worth dying for through the differentiation of sentimentality as spectacle and viewpoint, the worth of sex, though it exacts individual human life, is never reducible to individual human life. One dies, not for the sake of a solitary sex that one is or is not, but for the sake of the possibility of a common sex that simultaneously identifies and differentiates, attracts and repels, comprehends and excludes. To counterbalance the exigencies of this death instinct and defuse some of its potential harm to individuals it is therefore necessary to avoid any assumption of the truth of sex in defense of the life that sex demands. To defend life in the name of sex—to affirm life as an affirmation of sex; to argue, in effect, that sex is a reason to live—is to begin with just that lack of humor that renders talk about sex a form of avoidance of thinking about sex.[26] One must, in effect, continually and vigilantly distinguish between the defense of the embodied individual, whose life is real and truly in question, from the sex of the individual, which is neither real,

---

26. A lot of feminist-liberationist writing lacks humor in this technical sense. It is striking to compare Lorde, *Sister Outsider*, an influential statement of the humorless identification of sex with life, with Rubin, "Thinking Sex," where humor is notably present. Rubin's essay is exceptionally wide-ranging. Hers is a key text that touches almost every theme sounded in this inquiry, including child-sexuality, feminism and pornography, masturbation, and especially the theme of "hierarchies of sexual value—religious, psychiatric, and popular" that "rationalize the well-being of the sexually privileged and the adversity of the sexual rabble" (280).

nor singular, nor necessary. Affirmation and defense of life begins with mature humorous admission of the theoretical possibility of a life entirely without sex.[27]

Once one allows a distinction between the sex of the individual and the life of the individual, the question remains what to make of the fiction of sex qua fiction. Even if a literal interpretation of the doctrine of original sin can't break the hold of the necessity of fictions on fallen human imagination altogether, a humorous theological consciousness can at least contextualize those fictions within sin-consciousness. The fiction of sex, as with any fiction that unifies the fallen self, engages a lethally willful and humorless suspension of disbelief. For this reason the death instinct associated with sex, no matter how indomitable it appears, is always energized by purposefully unknowing participation in its valuation. It is always characterized by an impassioned insistence on its necessity that underscores the drama of the reality of its non-necessity. There is consequently a potent world of difference between anger at disruptions of the suspended disbelief and charitable anger seeking to put such disruptions to use. This drama, moreover, is never an individual affair, as if the requisite suspension of disbelief were a matter of personal choice of what or whom to believe. Nor does this death instinct designate any simple compulsion of a solitary individual to murder or self-destruction. It is always inter-subjective, its momentum continually charged through a spiral of identification and differentiation between self and others. As a consequence, the substantiation of the worth of sex in death is always an inter-subjective and dynamic process of killing and dying through which the living and the dead mutually implicate each other.

This death instinct, in summary, is always both suicidal and homicidal. It is their conjunction that renders the fiction of sex so lethally pointed as a concern of ethics. In a reading of Kafka's short story "The Judgment," Judith Butler argues that "when denunciation works to paralyze and deratify the critical capacities of the subject to whom it is

27. For a classic humorous essay on this theme, see Thurber and White, *Is Sex Necessary?* Although Miroslav Volf's discussion of "Gender Identity" involves assumption of knowledge of "sexed bodies" that the present argument complicates, he gets very near that argument, perhaps more so than he would even allow himself, in his statement: "All employment of God language for construction of gender identity is illegitimate and ought to be resisted." Volf, *Exclusion*, 171. Likewise he anticipates the conclusion of this work when he writes: "And it is through the power of self-giving that a new community of men and women will emerge, in which distinct but dynamic gender identities that are 'not without' the other will be fashioned and re-fashioned in peace" (189).

delivered, it undermines or even destroys the very capacities that are needed for ethical reflection and conduct, sometimes leading to suicidal conclusions."[28] Butler's ostensible point is that homicidal judgments are internalized as suicidal impulses by the persons against whom they are directed—where life and ethical life are one. But it can be reformulated for the purposes of the present argument as follows: that homicidal judgments about the worth of another's sex are always also judgments of one's own sex.[29] And that the capacity for sounder judgment itself is undone in the process, which is why mature humor and charitable anger remain so important. In the conjunction of the homicidal and the suicidal the death of the sexed other valorizes the exchange value for the self of sex with death; just as the death of the self can be exacted comparably as valorization of the sex of another. The point of the fiction of sex is honed in this exchange value of the homicidal and the suicidal, binding together a multiplicity of individuals in a fictitious point, a common sex, which at the same time leaves open the question of who exactly must die, since the fiction of sex is plural. There is no uniform fiction, no master narrative that governs all personal narratives, but a multiplicity of shifting narratives conjoined in their variegated and patterned representations of a sex worth dying for.

Although the fictions of sex are multiple, the mechanisms for their narration have features in common, which helps to explain the importance of reading theological writings as literature, and also reading of some literature as precedents for theological discourse on sexuality. Literature, understood as the "differential act of staging" explicated by Sedgwick, proves a productive locus for the operation of sexuality. Literature isolates every individual in the fantasy of becoming the hero of one's own narrative, at the same time that it organizes those fantasies around the point of a common sex. Literature provides a supply of textual performances of romantic relationship that model the passage through

28. Butler, *Giving Account*, 49.

29. So the following statement is open to the same kind of reformulation: "It may, finally, be in the gay man's rectum that he demolishes his own perhaps otherwise uncontrollable identification with a murderous judgment against him" (Bersani, *Rectum*, 222). See Gaspar Noe's remarkable visualization of this sentimental-homicidal-suicidal violence in his film "Irreversible," which begins with the brutal murder of a gay man in a nightclub titled "The Rectum" and moves backward through the brutal murder in turn of the girlfriend of one of the attackers in the club, and finally to an initiating sexual request by the murdered woman's lover to penetrate her rectum.

sex to intelligibility; that model the narration of one's sex as a unity of self against the confusion of sexual de-differentiation, where difference is most confirmed when it proves itself in the end of sexual reproduction. One must therefore take care, when resisting the charm of the fiction of sex, to resist also the claim that the point of sex is the survival of the species *homo sapiens*. Rather, to say that sex is a fiction with a point is to say that the point of the fiction of sex is not the procreation of human beings, but the proliferation of narratives that render sex imaginable. Children, as animal offspring, are incidental albeit necessary byproducts of the fiction of sex. More, they are, as the editors of a recent volume of writings "on the queerness of children" suggest, bearers of a promissory note that can never reach maturity: "The child is the product of physical reproduction, but functions just as surely as a figure of cultural reproduction. Thus both the utopianism and the nostalgia invoked by the figure of the child are, in turn, the preferred form of the future."[30]

Caught between a past that only exists as a memory—the unity of self in God before the advent of sin—and a perfection that is nowhere—the integration of self through the fiction of sex—the figure of the child in its innocence of sexuality forestalls recognition of the accusatory reality that the sinfulness of present children otherwise elicits. A powerful temptation to imagine a solution to the problem of self confounded by sin, children are the characters who most literally embody the narrative energies of the romance of innocent sexuality. They are the raw material of the fiction of sex, the recurrent beginning and ending and beginning of its discursive momentum. As such, children are also the most volatile elements of the fiction of sex, because the end of the story is inherently indeterminable even as it remains absolutely certain that the story isn't going to end well, that children aren't going to perform flawlessly the innocently sexed identities they are assigned.[31] The central plot points and turning points of the fiction of sex are the shifting and unreliable bodies of the children it produces, bodies that endure this fiction as inscribed flesh. It is fitting, then, that the homicidal and suicidal impulses of sex aggregate especially at the site of youthful bodies, so that at the center of the fiction of sex is a drama of child sacrifice, a drama that simultaneously enacts both the violent destruction and the violent assemblage of the child's body. At its most spectacular limit, the climax of this fiction

---

30. Bruhm and Hurley, *Curioser*, xii.
31. For extended analysis of these themes, see Kincaid, *Erotic Innocence*.

of sex is the murder/suicide of the child, witnessed not as extraordinary exception to the rule that constitutes children's bodies but as its logical end and boundary.

In the history of English-language fiction, the death of a child is a definitive motif of the literary precursors of the sentimental narration of sex as homosexual and heterosexual. The motif is most familiar through depiction of such characters as Little Eva in Harriet Beecher Stowe's *Uncle Tom's Cabin* (1852) and Little Nell in Charles Dickens's *The Old Curiosity Shop* (1841). (Regarding the latter, Oscar Wilde famously quipped: "One must have a heart of stone to read the death of Little Nell without laughing.") More generally, the motif pervades American and British novels of the nineteenth century. Conventionally dismissed as the mawkish excesses of a bygone era, these stories epitomize, through the spectacle of the drawn-out death of children—usually girls—the emotional investment that characterizes the phenomenon of sentimentality as viewpoint and spectacle. Though the dynamics of this phenomenon are, at the beginning of the twenty-first century, much more diffuse, not as effectively bound to the bodies of long-suffering daughters, these tales nevertheless continue to exert enormous influence on the narrative structuring of the murderous impulses of sex. Redress of the mortal valuation of sex therefore requires attention to the ways in which sentimentality makes a spectacle of individual child bodies, marking them for death. Only then does it become possible to specify whose deaths are required to exemplify the worth of sex as viewpoint.

Before proceeding any further it is important to acknowledge that at first glance the bodies of children, especially as delimited by law, appear to be the most proscribed imaginable focal point of sex, the last place one would apparently look to witness the confirmatory valorization of the worth of sex in death. The depth of this proscription, however, is a paradigmatic instance of the "extreme asymmetry of rhetorical positioning" that enables what Sedgwick aptly characterizes as the "projectile efficacy" of sentimentality, almost as if certain subjects are marked as targets in a perverse form of shooting practice.[32] This is not a simple binary opposition

---

32. See Edelman, *No Future*, 45 for parallel image of the "projectile" in relation to what he terms the *sinthom*osexual, all in the context of discussion of Tiny Tim in Dickens's *A Christmas Carol*. Edelman's total argument intersects in many ways with the current argument, only is framed in unrelentingly Lacanian terms that are difficult to translate into exterior discussion. The echoes of the term "sin" with his adaptation of the Lacanian term "sinthome" at least suggest a starting point.

between adult sharpshooter and child target. It is a triangulated dynamic at one corner of which individual adults are targeted with spectacular vehemence in defense of the child body that is both pruriently displayed at another corner even as it is denied at the third. Consider the public treatment of anyone who is accused of violating norms of intergenerational sexual conduct. Within the criminal justice system, the pedophile is singled out, officially "registered," as a "sex offender," someone who offends against the fiction of sex, a type whose very being is counterposed against the supposed sexual inviolability of children's bodies—bodies that are projected for display in the affirmation of their inviolable status. This inviolability is figured most of all, not in terms of the impermissibility of intergenerational genital contact, but in terms of permissible and impermissible modes of regarding children's bodies.[33] The fundamental crime of the pedophile only secondarily involves physical touching; it is primarily a crime of visual intention. What is paradigmatically most prohibited is not "looking" at children's bodies per se, and not even "desiring" them per se (to desire to become a parent is ipso facto to desire a child's body), but rather to see them in a particular way as sexual bodies.[34] It is the very gravity of this prohibition, its enforcement through government-sponsored programs of entrapment via the Federal mail or the internet, its insistence above all on the averting of one's gaze from the sexualized bodies of children, that confirms the intensity of the focus of the fiction of sex on children's bodies.[35]

None of this is to deny that sound reasons exist for maintaining strict intergenerational sexual boundaries, or that children are vulnerable to serious harms when their developmentally appropriate capacities for sexual relationship are abused. Acknowledgment that children are not miniature adults, however, should not necessitate a denial of the truth that children are complex sexual creatures who will explore relationships appropriate to their physical, psychological, and social development.[36] Instead, the very

33. See Bersani, "Rectum," 215 and 221 for critique of the redemptive reinvention of sex through a related denial of childhood sexuality.

34. On the pedophilic gaze see Mohr, "Pedophilia."

35. In 2002 the U.S. Supreme Court, in "Ashcroft vs. Free Speech Coalition," ruled unconstitutional provisions of the 1996 Child Pornography Prevention Act that banned virtual representations of child sexuality.

36. On the importance of recognizing the social and embodied reality of children's developing sexuality, see Calderone, "Above and Beyond." One example of this importance is that the willful lack of knowledge of variability of child genitalia can actually hinder

acknowledgment of child sexual development as requiring special protections should lead one to question the integrity of the measures which are adopted to enforce the averting of all vision from children's bodies, especially when one considers the extent to which mass media in all its forms is suffused with the pornographic manipulation of children in the manufacture of the "childhood" this prohibition purports to protect.

As a form of vicarious knowledge-relation, sentimentality is fractured between viewpoint and spectacle such that the ostensible privileges of knowledge accrue disproportionately to viewpoint. Viewpoint enforces the attribution of a kind of embodiment as spectacle that obscures and disempowers as it protects. In the sentimental targeting of childhood—in a multiplicity of textual performances across the spectrum of media—the possibility of appropriate protection of children's developing bodies is inextricably intertwined with a simultaneous forced displacement of all vision of the dynamic processes of that bodily development. The result is a fantastic innocence ascribed to children, most often figured as a diminutive play of adult sexed identity fetishized almost under the rubric of cuteness.[37] Lee Edelman explains that there is nothing cute or innocent about the conditions of possibility of this display of children's bodies: "But the ideological labor of cuteness, though it falls most often to the smallest, imposes no insubstantial burden in a culture where cuteness enables a general misrecogition of sexuality (which always implicitly endangers ideals of sociality and communal enjoyment) as, at least in the dominant form of heterosexual reproduction, securing the collective reality it otherwise threatens to destroy."[38] Through a work of collective misrecognition, children's bodies are violently figured via the adult bodies they are expected to become, because that future is in fact uncertain. Among the privileges of viewpoint is the enjoyment of spectacle as a kind of medium of self-realization of the fantasy of innocently and coherently sexed self-presence. Much as child sexual abuse constitutes a serious threat to children's well-being, the very display of children as cuteness embodied is an additional form of abuse of children and as such is continuous with the ballistics that more generally obscure the pervasive violence that is actually constitutive of childhood. Greater caring for children is there-

---

documentation of child sexual abuse. See Fausto-Sterling, *Sexing the Body*, 300 n. 3. For more general analysis, see also Levine, *Harmful*.

37. On the aesthetics of cuteness, see Ngai, "Cuteness."

38. Edelman, *No Future*, 137.

fore enhanced when they are recognized as the entirely sinful creatures that they are, as fully belonging to the community of fallen humanity.

The violence of the sentimental spectacle of childhood is especially harmful in its capacity for erasure, its capacity to render invisible and inadmissible the ambiguity and complexity of children's bodies. Above all the body that must not materialize, when looking at children's bodies, is a homosexual body. Discussion of homosexuality consequently reaches a hysterical pitch in the depiction of homosexuality as pathologically predatory and of children as its especially vulnerable prey.[39] The logic of the threat that homosexuality poses, according to this view, is entirely fabulous. Yet this characterization of the homosexual as insatiable sexual predator is not without analytical significance; only what it signifies is no truth at all about same-sex sexual desire, but a profound truth about the desire for fixity focused by the fiction of sex. The character of the homosexual, as propounded by the tradents of this narrative, functions as a kind of reflecting telescope, a living mirror that gathers and focuses into one concentrated visible explosion of light the imperceptible glow radiated individually by every child body. A mere instrument, the homosexual as telescope does not reveal any previously unseen shape of children's bodies. Instead it reveals the chaotic and indeterminate energies of those bodies as they are taking shape. At the same time, however, the response to this vision by those persons who obsessively pursue it is fiercely and consistently to blame the instrument for the vision it reveals, in effect freeze-framing the homosexual as omnivorous threat. Even though not writing explicitly in a theological register, it is notable that Leo Bersani invokes the language of redemption when he comments: "The panic about child abuse is the most transparent case of this compulsion to rewrite sex. Adult sexuality is split in two: at once redeemed by its retroactive metamorphosis into the purity of an asexual childhood, and yet preserved in its most sinister forms by being projected onto the image of the criminal seducer of children."[40] Through this split between adult and child, between viewpoint and spectacle, the view of children's bodies that is a source of intense anxiety is effectively attributed to a despised homosexual subject and as such disowned, enabling the projectile efficacy of the violent attribution of a sentimental fantasy of heterosexual childhood innocence. Panic over vision of a homosexually sexed child

39. As exemplified in Ramsey, *Homosexual.*
40. Bersani, *Rectum*, 221.

body is thereby crossed with a panic over responsibility for the more generally culpable criminal seduction of children into the pursuit of an impossible redemption from original sin by means of fictions of childhood that they are then enjoined to repeat as the price of admission to intelligibly sexed adult identity.

The sentimental erasure and projection of innocence and sin is not necessarily tied to the narration of a predatory homosexuality, and in fact flourishes within and across a multiplicity of popular cultural and political and also more specialized discourses, but it nevertheless acquires peculiar conceptual prominence in evangelical Christian writings on the complementary norms of male and female personhood. In these writings the idea that adults, homosexual or not, could positively—in multiple meanings of that term—identify a child as at least potentially homosexual is regarded as anathema. Much defense of traditionalist understandings of male and female personal identity is marked from beginning to end by a single-minded focus on the subject of homosexuality, construed as a threat to the secure identification of young boys as future heterosexual men and young girls as future heterosexual women. So the principal spokesmen of the Council on Biblical Manhood and Womanhood, in answer to the question *"Why do you bring up homosexuality when discussing male and female role distinctions in the home and the church (as in question 1)?"*[41] confidently assert: "Not only have we seen evangelical feminists carried by the logic of their position toward endorsing homosexuality, but we also see the clinical evidence that *there is no such thing as a 'homosexual child.'*"[42]

41. The mission statement of the Council is "An Overview of Central Concerns: Questions and Answers." It begins: "1. *Why do you regard the issue of male and female roles as so important?* We are concerned not merely with the behavioral roles of men and women but also with the underlying nature of manhood and womanhood themselves. Biblical truth and clarity in this matter are important because error and confusion over sexual identity leads to: (1) marriage patterns that do not portray the relationship between Christ and the church (Ephesians 5:31–32); (2) parenting practices that do not train boys to be masculine or girls to be feminine; (3) homosexual tendencies and increasing attempts to justify homosexual alliances (see question 41); (4) patterns of unbiblical female leadership in the church that reflect and promote the confusion over the true meaning of manhood and womanhood . . ." (Piper and Grudem, *Recovering*, 60–92). These questions and answers are available for download as a pamphlet at the Council's website: www.cbmw.org.

42. Ibid., 84 (emphasis added). For explication of this clinical-psychological view, see Rekers, "Psychological Foundations." The Council publishes a whole series of pastoral resources for use in church and home to assist parents and church leaders in the project of "rearing" appropriately sexed boys and girls. All of these resources are available through their website.

Before explicating the multiple contradictoriness of the claim that "endorsing homosexuality" is illogical because "there is no such thing as a "homosexual child,'" it is important to note that the "logic" associated here with "evangelical feminism" has nothing to do with the activities of the National Organization of Women or any other mainstream liberal-political organization. It designates the idea, promoted by the otherwise conservative organization Christians for Biblical Equality, that "the Bible teaches the full equality of men and women in Creation and in Redemption,"[43] where equality specifically means an egalitarian, nonhierarchical ordering of relationships between the sexes.[44] Why then insist, as the members of the Council on Biblical Manhood and Womanhood repeatedly do, that homosexuality is at the very center of an intra-Christian debate over the proper ordering of relationships between men and women? Especially when many of the evangelical feminists they criticize share their negative assessment of homosexuality?

At this point many persons, albeit for very different reasons, might agree at least in theoretical terms "that there is no such thing as a 'homosexual child.'" Regardless of the view one holds, or refuses to hold, concerning the etiology of same-sex sexual desire, or the likely path by which individuals typically own self-conscious awareness of such desire, the desire in itself does not, need not, necessarily constitute an identity, least of all an identity that could be ascribed, for example, to an infant.[45]

43. As quoted in ibid., 407.

44. So the subtitle of *Recovering Biblical Manhood and Womanhood* is "A Response to Evangelical Feminism." The concluding chapter of the volume "Charity, Clarity, and Hope: The Controversy and the Cause of Christ" (Piper and Grudem, 403–22), is an extended address to "Christians for Biblical Equality." For a characteristic statement of the views Piper and Grudem single out for censure, see Mollenkott, *Women*.

45. In place of the terms "nature versus nurture" which typically structure debate on the etiology of homosexuality, Sedgwick proposes the terms "minoritizing versus universalizing" as contradictory and irresolvable approaches to "homo/heterosexual definition" (Sedgwick, *Epistemology*, 1–2, 40–44, 82–86). The point of this substitution is to obviate the question of etiology altogether, and instead enable analysis of the question "In whose lives is homo/heterosexual definition an issue of continuing centrality and difficulty?" (40). Sedgwick's approach intersects with Butler's critique of "essentialist versus constructivist" etiologies through the concept of "performative constraints": "The 'performative' dimension of construction is precisely the forced reiteration of norms. In this sense, then, it is not only that there are constraints to performativity; rather, constraint calls to be rethought as the very condition of performativity. Performativity is neither free play nor theatrical self-presentation; nor can it be simply equated with performance. Moreover, constraint is not necessarily that which sets a limit to performativity; constraint is, rather, that which impels and sustains performativity." Butler, *Bodies*, 94–95.

Yet at the same time, implicit in the very formulation of this denial of the homosexual child is the ascription to children, even to infants, of an immanent potential adult heterosexuality that somehow must be forced into bloom. Denial of the homosexual child also plays off, albeit with malignant intent, the politicized ascription of an adult same-sex desiring identity to children by many gay and lesbian activists.[46] In each case respectively, children's bodies become the focus of a program to eliminate homosexuality, and the focus of resistance to that program, which helps to explain also why higher than average reported rates of suicide among young persons who consider themselves wrongfully sexed remain a practically relevant measure of the toll the fiction of sex exacts in actual lives; why medical research that focuses on the etiology of same-sex desire remains cause for concern about its clinical translation; why inclusion of "sexual orientation" in hate-crimes legislation evokes bitter opposition, striking as it does at the meaningful heart of biblically faithful parenting for many.

The program to eliminate homosexuality is neither secret nor subtle. The claim that "There is no such thing as a 'homosexual child'" explicitly avows what appears to be a simply murderous impulse. It is the wish to get rid of homosexuality altogether through good, i.e., biblically faithful, parenting. Even the deliberate use of quotation marks—"homosexual child"—seems incited by a homicidal sentiment.[47] A central irony of this program, however, is that its proponents depend for their self-definition as hierarchically differentiated heterosexual men and women on the sentimental display of the homosexually sexed persons that they are simultaneously seeking to eradicate. The spokespersons for the Council, after asserting the non-existence of the homosexual child, consequently

46. Even if theoretically dubious this ascription has been practically effective in the work, for example, of the Gay Lesbian and Straight Education Network (GLSEN). For overview of GLSEN's activism, see their website: www.glsen.org.

47. This homicidal program is characteristic of some prominent evangelical Christian discourse of human sexuality. See for example www.lovewonout.com: "Focus on the Family is promoting the truth that homosexuality is preventable and treatable—a message routinely silenced today. We want people to know that individuals don't have to be gay." See also www.exodusinternational.org. In a remarkable play on the narrative of Israel's redemption by God from slavery in Egypt, this organization exclaims with regard to homosexuality: "Freedom is possible!" Their homicidal program also has an international reach. According to numerous news reports Americans associated with Exodus and similar organizations helped provoke the "Anti-Homosexual Bill of 2009" in Uganda, which proposes the death penalty for homosexuality.

proceed to summarize the moral of the clinical evidence they are citing in terms of the assumption of the existence of that homosexual child:

> What Rekers means is that there are dynamics in the home that direct the sexual preference of the child. Especially crucial is a father's firm and loving affirmation of a son's masculinity or a daughter's femininity. But, we ask, how can this kind of affirmation be cultivated in an atmosphere where role differences between masculinity and femininity are constantly denied or minimized? If the only significant role differentiation is based on competency and has no root in nature, what will parents do to shape the sexual identity of their tiny children? If they say that they will do nothing, common sense and many psychological studies tell us that the children will be confused about who they are and will therefore be far more likely to develop a homosexual orientation.
>
> To us it is increasingly and painfully clear that Biblical feminism is an unwitting partner in unraveling the fabric of complementary manhood and womanhood that provides the foundation not only for Biblical marriage and Biblical church order, but also for heterosexuality itself.[48]

What begins as a denial of the homosexual child devolves finally into a depiction of homosexuality as an apocalyptic threat to the very possibility of "heterosexuality itself," where heterosexuality is the index of an entire cosmic ordering of human relations. The possibility of the appropriate development of the "sexual preference of the child," the implied foundation of this cosmic ordering, depends on a crucial set of "dynamics in the home" that are the especial responsibility of the father. Denial of the homosexual child is bound to an extraordinary instance of the sentimental as viewpoint: a kind of world-projecting authorship of nature by biblically faithful men. This task of the father is simultaneously figured as both a nurturing of nature and as a battle against nature. The imperative importance ascribed to a "father's firm and loving affirmation of a son's masculinity or a daughter's femininity" depends on the contradictory assumptions (a) that children have an immanent "sexual preference" that requires paternal authorization; (b) that children have an indeterminate "sexual preference" that requires paternal authorship; and (c) that absent this paternal authorization and authorship children are actually "likely to develop a homosexual orientation." At the heart of the depiction of

48. Piper and Grudem, *Recovering*, 84.

homosexuality as the consequence of the biblically unfaithful assertion that for men and women "the only significant role differentiation is based on competency and has no root in nature" is a striking naturalization of "homosexual orientation" to child sexual development.[49]

The oddity and profundity of this viewpoint on homosexuality is especially compressed and focused in the question: "What will parents do to shape the sexual identity of their tiny children?" This image of "tiny children," at once telescopic and claustrophobic, is remarkably evocative of Augustine's self description as "so tiny a child, so great a sinner."[50] In figuring children as homunculi this image visualizes how powerfully homosexual panic and panic over responsibility for original sin have become confounded. As miniature persons, the tiny appearance of these children is a function of their distance from viewpoint. At the same time, the perception of them as tiny is a function of identification with them from viewpoint. The very fact of their tiny size consequently provokes a dual anxiety. On the one hand, the parent is positioned at a disempowering distance from the child, as if the child is effectively out of all reach of the parent's concern, and especially authority, so that all the parent can do is watch helplessly as the disastrous course of events predicted by "common sense" and "many psychological studies" unfolds. On the other hand, the parent identifies this distant child as another self, as a miniature heterosexual man or woman, so that the dire possibility that these are children "who will be confused about who they are" elicits a cascade of parental confusions. Confusion between the identity of parent and child: Who is the parent and who is the child? Confusion of identity as a parent: What distinguishes mother from father? Biological parent from care-giver? Confusion of "sexual preference" as a heterosexual parent: Can a *truly* heterosexual parent possibly produce as parent (biologically and child-rearing) a child who is confused about his or her sexual preference? And above all confusion of innocence and sin: Can the pretensions to innocence of heterosexuality as viewpoint withstand accusatory identification with the spectacle of the homosexual children who sinfully refuse all attempts at their elimination?

The power ascribed to homosexuality from this viewpoint is riddled with contradiction. It is no accident that the alternating fact/possibility

49. On the femininity of boys and its relation to the program to eliminate homosexuality, see Sedgwick, "How to Bring up Your Kids Gay."

50. Augustine *Confessions* 1.12.19 (Chadwick, 15).

of homosexuality, as opposed to heterosexuality, is constantly precipitating these confusions. Despite the assertion of biblical faithfulness, this viewpoint, as sentimental phenomenon, depends conceptually on the emergence in the nineteenth century of the pseudo-scientific categorizations homosexual and heterosexual. And the obsessive focus on homosexuality turns out to be irresistible, not because it encapsulates some timeless distinction between natural and unnatural, innocence and sin, biblical faithfulness and pagan ungodliness, but only because discovery of one's sexed self through one's sexual orientation is the historically and culturally specified generative locus of experience of the disintegration of self after sin. The denial of the homosexual child, typified in the statement from the Council on Biblical Manhood and Womanhood, turns out not to be an absolute denial of homosexuality, but is a paradigmatic affirmation of the closet as a hiding place of sin. And not a hiding place, it is important to emphasize, of homosexual persons, as if coming out of the closet would solve the problem. Likewise the program to eliminate homosexuality turns out to be a program to constrain homosexuality to the purposes of its display as spectacle of sin, so that affirmation of the homosexual child is only a disaster to the extent that it undermines the heterosexual as viewpoint of innocence, to the extent that the sameness of sin is no longer masked by the difference of sex.[51]

When the spokesmen for the Biblical Council on Manhood and Womanhood assert that what is at stake, ultimately, is heterosexuality itself, they are entirely correct. The irony however is that the homicidal fantasy of a world where "no such thing as a 'homosexual child exists'" is inconceivable apart from the suicidal possibility of the destruction of heterosexuality itself. Only whereas the members of the Council on Biblical Manhood and Womanhood fear the destruction of their heterosexually sexed selves as a catatastrophe, literal interpretation of original sin and its association with sexuality humorously anticipates that possibility as a kind of proof that hope for redemption from sin remains. The obsessive

---

51. It is interesting to note, for example, the placement of the terms "falls" and "fall" in the following description of the character Leonard in Hitchcock's "North by Northwest": "All sexuality, I've argued, is *sinthom*osexuality, but the burden of figuring that condition, the task of instantiating the force of the drive (always necessarily a partial drive, one incapable of totalization) that tears apart both the subject's desire and the subject *of* desire, falls only to certain subjects who, like Leonard, serve as fall guys for the failure of the sexual relation and the intolerable reduction of the subject to the status of sinthome" (Edelman, *No Future*, 73).

and recurring insistence on the centrality of the issue of homosexuality can therefore be characterized as a complex, anxious, and in many ways morbidly self-absorbed expression of the contingency and insecurity of heterosexuality as a refuge from the injury of sin that is oneself. Trapped in a cycle of sentimental-homicidal-suicidal violence, these writers correlate faith in and faithfulness to God with faith in and faithfulness to one's sexual orientation as the expressive viewpoint of intelligibly sexed male and female identity. In the process heterosexuality acquires a cosmic importance. And in the meanwhile, the imaginative concern with the survival of heterosexuality as viewpoint depends on a simultaneous identification with a spectacular figure that is dead or dying, and thereby belies the necessity of heterosexuality to the possibility of biblical marriage and biblical church order. As a matter of biblical faithfulness, the often elided sentiment concluding Psalm 137 now even opens to a charitably angry interpretation, so that the exclamation, "Happy shall they be who take your little ones and dash them against the rock!" (Ps 137:9) can be read as an exhortation to shatter the homosexual as telescope and the fantastic image of tiny children it discloses and instead begin to regard more hospitably and caringly little ones of all ages as the responsible sinners that they are.

At this point it is important to acknowledge that as powerful as are Foucault's theory of sex as a speculative point and fiction and Sedgwick's theory of sentimentality as mechanism of mobilization of the productive possibilities of the incoherency of homo/heterosexual definition for analysis of theological discourse on sexuality, they are not causal explanations. The only causal question all this present argument ultimately aims to address concerns the governing desire for personal intelligibility that moves persons to suspend disbelief in the fiction of sex. For whatever reasons, it just seems to be the case that experience of the contingency and insecurity of personal identity presently clusters with peculiar intensity around questions of definition of sex, sexuality, and gender, as those questions are framed by the project of homo/heterosexual definition.

For persons who hold fast to a so-called traditionalist articulation of male and female role differences, the fact of this clustering is explained in terms of a crisis in discernment of, and hence confidence in, a set of essential truths both about the constitution of sex, sexuality, and gender, and about their importance to the experience of sexual orientation as an essential aspect of personal identity. For many other persons, disagreement about the answers to these questions shares the crucial assumption of a crisis in discernment. Discernment is regarded as a portal to acceptance and affirmation. Disagreement centers on the discovery of the correct or true answers, but leaves unchallenged the homo/heterosexual framing of these questions.

My own view, by contrast, is that the pursuit of such truth, let alone correctness, is an obstacle to understanding these questions. The goal, as already suggested, is not to find *the* answers to the sorts of questions that dominate theological debates about sexual ethics, but to understand better why these questions continue to enthrall the imagination of so many writers on sexuality and theology.

To this end it is helpful to return to the nineteenth century and review the narrative conventions that continue to impel the sentimental narration of the fiction of heterosexually and homosexually sexed identity as worth dying for, specifically as that worth coalesces around marriage as the institutional means of expression of sexed identity. In consideration of these prior narratives, the centrality of male authority over who may or may not marry whom to the maintenance of sexed identity as a basis of God-relatedness is discernible before it has become complicated by the incoherency of homo/heterosexual definition. To understand the convolution of homosexual panic and panic over responsibility for sin that drives much theological debate about the moral status of same-sex sexual relations and the possibility of same-sex marriage, it helps to appraise the theological signification of homosocial bonds as they were narrated according to the opposition of male as father and female as daughter. The sentimental consternation over the authority of paternity as viewpoint, evident in the writings of The Council on Biblical Manhood and Womanhood, is continuous with the parallel consternation, in much nineteenth-century literature, of fathers regarding the marital choices of their daughters. In both cases, sex is idealized as a basis of God-relatedness, and as such is known only vicariously through mechanisms of sentimentality as knowledge-relation. Close readings of nineteenth-century novels have heuristic value for investigation of how writings on theology and sexuality become effectively charged as textual performances that differentiate and entangle the categories of man/woman, innocent/sinful, homosexual/heterosexual.

At the core of the continuity between nineteenth-century narratives in which the authority to permit and forbid marriage is a prerogative that defines the God-relatedness of the fathers who exercise such authority and the daughters who obey it, and twenty-first-century debates about same-sex marriage, is the phenomenon, joining the work of Foucault and Sedgwick, that I am calling the sentimental-homicidal-suicidal. The dynamic between father and daughter in the earlier narratives correlates with that between heterosexual and homosexual in contemporary debates about marriage and same-sex marriage. Homosexual stands to heterosexual as daughter stands to father as spectacle to viewpoint. Just as the concern, in the prior narratives, was to maintain the authority of paternal identity as viewpoint by asserting the basis of that identity in a God-relation, so too the concern in debates about same-sex marriage is to maintain the authority of heterosexually sexed identity as viewpoint by asserting the basis of that identity in heterosexual marriage as the capstone of heterosexual sexual orientation. In both cases, viewpoint is maintained through assertion of opposition to proscribed marriage as a form of faithfulness to God and to one's sex. The very concept of sexed identity expressed as an orientation intensifies the ascription of a viewpoint to the self who thereby becomes more or less effectively sexed. In the transition from fathers' viewpoint of the spectacle of their daughters' forbidden marriages to heterosexuality and forbidden same-sex marriage, however, viewpoint and spectacle become interrelated such that the already unstable authority of viewpoint becomes only more volatile at the same time that the spectacle becomes further charged, albeit differentially.

The proceeding chapter begins by elaborating more fully some unambiguous instances of sentimental homicidal violence at the cusp of becoming suicidally complicated by the incoherency of homo/heterosexual definition. The spectacle of a daughter's innocence, and a father's requirement either to preserve that innocence by forbidding an impermissible marriage or to punish a daughter for sinful disobedience, then provides a basis for analysis of the entanglement, through sentimental narration of marriage, of innocence and sin by homo/heterosexual definition. In both cases, marriage is inexorably marked by power struggles to determine who may and may not marry whom. Exercise of such authority is sinfully prized as a proof of God-relatedness. It is this power struggle that forms the central drama in the sentimental-homicidal-suicidal narration of the fiction of sex as worth dying for.

4

Redemptive Marriage and Redeeming
Same-Sex Marriage

So many children have come to me and said, "What shall I tell my parents about sex?" My answer is always the same: "Tell them the truth. If the subject is approached in a tactful way, it should be no more embarrassing to teach a parent about sex than to teach him about personal pronouns. And it should be less discouraging."

In discussing sex enlightenment for parents, first of all, definitions are needed. What do we mean by "parents"? Do we mean all adults who have had children? Do we mean adults who have had children, they knew not why? Or do we mean married people who have given birth to one or more offspring but have never gone into the matter very thoroughly? For the purposes of this article, it will be assumed that by "parents" we mean all adult persons permeated with a strong sense of indecency.[1]

Homicidal Fathers/Suicidal Daughters

REPRESENTATIONS OF SENTIMENTAL-HOMICIDAL-SUICIDAL VIOLENCE as guarantor of the worth of sex are a staple ingredient of popular narratives from the late eighteenth century to the present. They are especially prominent in the nineteenth-century novel. In his groundbreaking study *The Novel and the Police*, D. A. Miller writes that "the office that the traditional novel once performed has not disappeared along with it. The

1. Thurber and White, *Is Sex Necessary?* 123.

'death of the novel' . . . has really meant the explosion everywhere of the novelistic, no longer bound in three deckers, but freely scattered across a far greater range of cultural experience."[2] Following Miller's argument, review of the concerns with sexed identity of a pair of representative novels from the nineteenth century provides a training ground for novelistic reading of contemporary theological writings as a realm of cultural experience in which those concerns have since become scattered, enabling recognition of the continuity between them. Along the way it is important to keep in mind that the "novelistic" is not the "novelist," that one reads novels not to identify the intentions of their writers, but to engage the novelistic concerns occasioned through reading the texts and thereby make of them the present argument. Novelistic readings foreground constructive engagement with theological discourse on sexuality by showing that it has taken up the marriage plot with a vengeance.

Reading novels as a point of entry into theological discourse on sexuality also shows the productive but troubled vulnerability of fallen imagination to the power of fiction. Of his early education Augustine complains: "I was to recite the speech of Juno in her anger and grief that she 'could not keep the Trojan king out of Italy.' I had understood that Juno never said this. But we were compelled to follow in our wanderings the paths set by poetic fictions, and to express in plain prose the sense which the poet had put into verse."[3] In lamenting that he had been educated in the cultured and false literature of Rome and not the rough-hewn and true words of Scripture, Augustine is also lamenting that the consequence of sin is the general human loss of the one true path and the wandering along multiple false paths that ensues. Yet in the very accomplishment of his writing, with its wealth of allusion to the literature he disparages, Augustine also displays that discernment of the one path occurs in the midst of wanderings among the "paths set by poetic fictions," so that it is not possible nor necessary for theological imagination to isolate itself entirely from poetic imagination. Juno's anger and grief, for example, is a both a fiction and a type of the futility of pagan resistance to the providential history of Rome as the seat of the mother church.

Given the inevitability and productivity of the wanderings of theological imagination along the paths of fictions, readings of some novels are actually necessary to contextualize the dominant narratives underwrit-

2. Miller, *Novel*, x.
3. *Confessions* 1.17.27 (Chadwick, 19).

ing theological debates about sexed identity and relationship in terms of heterosexual and homosexual orientations. An earlier novelistic concern to maintain the authority of paternal identity by asserting the basis of that identity in a God-relation is now scattered in debates about same-sex marriage, where it has taken shape as a concern to maintain the authority of heterosexually sexed identity by asserting its basis in a similar God-relation. The sentimental-homicidal-suicidal violence required to prove the worth of sex in death, most visibly directed at homosexuality, is continuous with the violence fathers once directed at their daughters.

It is difficult at first glance however to recognize this insidious continuity, since the death of a child is commonly regarded as the greatest tragedy that can befall a parent. The notion that a parent could properly wish a child dead appears antithetical to conventionally asserted meanings of parenthood. Even the program to eliminate homosexuality altogether is framed as a kind of exorcism, a kind of call to life of the children it targets, as if the object of violence is the wrongful sex threatening the life of the body it viciously inhabits. The sentimental-homicidal-suicidal violence integral to the valorization of sex in death, in other words, is typically propounded in terms of protection of children, while reason exists to worry about the harms this protection causes. Critique of the violence that enforces the worth of sex as a function of heterosexual and homosexual orientation therefore requires some careful consideration of the logic by which caring and killing become associated. That association usually only appears tenable in extreme cases—of bodily injury, incurable illness, unrelieved suffering. When a parent otherwise kills, especially when a mother kills, the event evokes passionate, often hysterical outrage.[4] Fathers by contrast are sometimes presumed naturally to pose a mortal threat to their offspring, but this threat also is deplored.[5] Only

4. Notable recent instances that received widespread media coverage include the cases of Andrea Yates, Susan Smith, and Darlie Lynn Routier. Andrea Yates is serving a life sentence in Texas for drowning her five children in a bathtub in 2001. For detailed reporting on her case, see O'Malley, *Are You There?* Susan Smith is serving a life sentence in South Carolina for drowning her two sons in 1994. Darlie Lynn Routier is on death row in Texas, appealing conviction for the murder of her two sons in 1996. Unlike Yates and Smith, who both confessed their crimes, Routier has maintained her innocence, and her trials have been a source of intense debate between her supporters and her accusers. For review of her case and the movement to overturn her conviction, see www.fordarlieroutier.org.

5. For critical analysis of how differing assumptions regarding infanticide by fathers versus mothers function within debates to define the "human" in primate anthropology, see Harraway, *Simians*, 81–108, esp. 103.

it was not long ago that the highest expression of a father's caring for his daughter in particular was to wish her dead.

Just as a central disturbance to the domestic peace of many couples currently is an unauthorized affixing of the modifier "same-sex" to the noun "marriage," so also in the domestic life portrayed in much nineteenth-century fiction a central disturbance to the domestic peace of a father was an unauthorized romantic attachment of a daughter.[6] So much so that a father was not only permitted to wish the death of his daughter, but was actually expected to do so when she married over his objections. Representative of the many tales of mischief that restive daughters can cause when they pursue their own independent marital happiness, and the mortal danger that can ensue from such recklessness, is *Lord Oakburn's Daughters* (1864), a genuine three-decker by the prolific and popular writer Mrs. Henry Wood.[7] The Lord Oakburn of the title refers to Captain Chesney, a gouty widowed officer who has retired to the provincial town of South Wennock with his four daughters. Jane, the oldest, is a model of filial devotion. Since their mother's death Jane has supervised the education of her sisters and the management of the household. Her sole care in life is to secure her father's comfort despite their pinched circumstances: "It was Jane who bore the burden of it all. Perhaps no father had ever been loved with a more yearning, ardent, dutiful love than was Captain Chesney by his daughter Jane. To save him one care she would have forfeited her existence. If by walking through fire—and this is not speaking metaphorically—she could have eased him of a minute's pain, Jane Chesney would have gone lovingly to the sacrifice."[8]

At thirty years old, never for an instant does Jane long to marry or escape in any way from her father's home, from her duties as surrogate wife and mother. Jane's middle sisters, Clarice and Laura, are less easy to placate. They resent the tedium of their restricted existence. Before

6. Other person's opposition to same-sex marriage has also become a source of disturbance to the domestic peace of couples who support same-sex marriage. Versions of the pronouncement by Brad Pitt that "Angie and I will consider tying the knot when everyone else in the country who wants to be married is legally able," (Sager, "Mr. Pitt") are now common, even as part of some persons' wedding ceremonies.

7. She is best known for her sensational novel *East Lynne* (1861), adaptations of which became a staple of the stage. She published over 30 additional novels and countless stories while also publishing and editing a monthly magazine and supporting a large family, even as she was disabled from scoliosis so that she spent much of her adult life in a sitting or reclining position.

8. Wood, *Lord Oakburn's*, 93.

the novel opens, Clarice in fact had departed to work as a governess. As the grandson of an earl and the potential heir to the title of Oakburn, Captain Chesney had forbidden Clarice's plan, regarding it as a disgrace to the family. In response Clarice announced that "no disgrace through her should ever be cast upon the Chesneys; for she would change her name at once, and never betray her family to strangers."[9] In a striking association of the name of the father with the life of the daughter, any mention of Clarice's name in her father's presence is strictly forbidden, so that until she can be "made to hear reason, and return home,"[10] Clarice is as good as dead. Not until the middle third of the story does the reader even learn of her existence, by which time the fatal result of her exile forms the central mystery of the novel. Without a name and a home Clarice had entered a secret marriage—a marriage not sanctioned by her father—that effectively sealed her death sentence. The sacrifice that Jane so willingly would make, but is spared out of obedience to her father, is the sacrifice that Clarice unwillingly ends up making as a result of her concern, even in her disobedience, to obviate any disgrace to her father.

In the meantime Laura Chesney has become passionately attached to Captain Chesney's surgeon, Lewis Carlton. Willful, impatient, short-tempered, she despises Jane's subservience to their father and her resignation to their penury. She longs to be mistress of her own home, to possess horses, elegant finery, new plate and furniture, and Lewis Carlton promises her just this comfortable independence, but when he requests the captain's consent, the captain dismisses him from his house with furious condescension as "a common apothecary, sir—a dispenser of medicine!"[11] and forbids Laura all communication with him.

Soon afterwards, on the same evening that a letter arrives, announcing the death of the present Earl of Oakburn without an heir—and hence the accession of Captain Chesney to the title and estate—Laura—now Lady Laura, though she doesn't know it yet—elopes with Lewis Carlton. Not until the next morning, after the new Lord Oakburn's departure to attend the funeral, does Jane discover Laura's absence and suspect the worst, so that the prospect of disclosing to her father what has happened weighs most heavily on Jane.

9. Ibid., 182.

10. Ibid.

11. Ibid., 120.

Such is the context of the following exchange between Jane Chesney and Mr. Grey—another local surgeon, contrary to Mr. Carlton, whom Jane regards as the epitome of discretion, breeding, and good character; someone of whom "Jane could have made a friend and an equal"[12]—when she encounters Mr. Grey that morning in the high road of South Wennock:

> "Nothing can be done to recall her now?" said Jane, speaking the words in accordance with her own thoughts, more than as a question.
>
> "Nothing. The start has been too great—a whole night. They are probably married by this time, or will be before the day is over."
>
> "Mr. Grey—I seem to speak to you as to an old friend," Jane broke off to say; "a few minutes ago and I had not believed that I could have so spoken of this to any one. *How* shall I tell my father?"
>
> "Ah," said Mr. Grey, "it will be sad news for him. My eldest little daughter is only eight years old, but I can fancy what must be the feelings of a father at hearing these tidings. I think— I think—"
>
> "What?" asked Jane.
>
> "Well, it is scarcely the thing to say to you just now, but I think I would rather lose a daughter by death than see her abandon her home in this way," continued Mr. Grey in his frankness. "My heart would be less wrung by it. Will you allow me to ask whether Mr. Carlton was paying his addresses to her?"
>
> "He had wished to do so, but was peremptorily forbidden by my father. That was the cause of the rupture which led to his dismissal from the house. None of us liked Mr. Carlton, except—I must of course except—my sister Laura."[13]

These are hard words for Jane, coming as they do from the excellent Mr. Grey. He answers Jane's question, "*How* shall I tell my father?" by telling Jane how to interpret the event. As the messenger of the "sad news," he decides that it would be easier for Jane to report the death of Laura than to have to report what has actually happened, even as he scripts an account of what counts as actually happening. The very sadness of this "news" is not prior to its report, but is conjured and enforced by Mr. Grey's comments. Speaking, to quote Captain Chesney's prior estimation of him, as "a gentleman and a man to be esteemed,"[14] Mr. Grey implies

12. Ibid., 159.
13. Ibid., 157–58.
14. Ibid., 138.

that for Jane to anticipate anything less of her father, to think that the captain, now earl, would prefer his daughter living and married to unmarried and dead, would be to impugn the earl's character. As a daughter who loves her father with a "yearning, ardent, dutiful love," Jane becomes implicated in the homicidal sentiment of Mr. Grey's assertion regarding a daughter's death that "my heart would be less wrung by it," because Mr. Grey is speaking not only as a particular father of his own particular little girl, but as a novelistic representative of fatherhood.

Earlier, near the close of his last interview with Mr. Carlton, Captain Chesney had voiced the same homicidal sentiment that Mr. Grey now evinces: "'No, by Jove!' raved the captain, 'I'd see your coffin walk first. Here—stop—listen to me; I'd rather see *her* in her coffin than disgraced by contact with you.'"[15] Whereas the Captain's comments are the angry raving of a disagreeable old man in the privacy of his bedroom, Mr. Grey speaks in the high road, a model of restraint, respectability, and publicity. Through the combination of his reservation and "frankness," Mr. Grey voices no trivial "fancy," but the seemingly instinctual feelings that any "father would feel at hearing these tidings"—any father, that is, who merits the title. A weirdness however of this association of public speech with respectability is that it is also borderline pornographic and pedophilic. Through his speech, Mr. Grey conflates Laura Chesney, a grown woman of twenty-two, and his nameless eight-year old girl, into a single portrait of an ideal daughter whose very life is subservient to the father's "heart" she could potentially wring. In the process the novelist's image of sexual contact between an adult man and woman, projected by Captain Chesney in his bedroom, becomes the novelistic image of sexual contact between an adult man and an eight year old girl projected by Mr. Grey in the high road. In a move that will eventually become a staple of novelistic arguments against same-sex marriage, Mr. Grey narrates a scene of child sexual abuse as an objection to the marriage of Laura Chesney and Lewis Carlton.

In treating daughters of all ages alike, in showing how daughters younger and older live under a constant threat from the fathers to whom they owe obedience, a telling feature of Mr. Grey's relative assessment that his heart "would be less wrung by" his own daughter's death than her abandonment in marriage is that he is thereby ascribing some of Laura Chesney's adult agency to an eight-year-old girl. It is not possible to con-

15. Ibid., 120.

demn Laura Chesney's action under the cover of protection of his own child without also admitting the power she wields over his heart, without attributing to his own little daughter the agency of an adult woman capable of abandonment in all its sexual suggestiveness, and without hinting that the sentimental violence he harbors is both homicidal and suicidal. Likewise when Jane asks "Nothing can be done to recall her now?" she speaks of Laura's flight from South Wennock as if Laura were a child who could be lawfully compelled to return home, and not a grown woman over whom Captain Chesney holds little effective power despite all his threats. More worldly-wise than Jane, Mr. Grey does not acknowledge Laura's independence. Instead he makes explicit the equation between Laura Chesney and his "eldest little daughter" implicit in Jane's question. He imparts a meaning to Jane's question that Jane didn't yet know was there, as if Jane were asking the trusted surgeon about the welfare of a critically ill patient: "Nothing can be done to recall her now?" "Nothing," Mr. Grey answers with frank and definitive medical authority, as if he had been stopped in the High Road on his very way to certifying Laura Chesney's death.

Jane all the while, as a cost of her devotion to Captain Chesney, finds herself an easy prey to the filial demands of Mr. Grey also, who seems oblivious to the possibility, more probably the likelihood, that in Jane's case her heart would not be "less wrung" by the death of her sister than her abandonment but more so. It is hardly surprising as a result that when Jane speaks to Mr. Grey "as to an old friend," as one character to another in a novel, Mr. Grey doesn't exactly answer Jane in kind. Rather, Mr. Grey answers novelistically, evincing his suicidal concern as he elliptically acknowledges in his comment that "it is scarcely the thing to say to you just now." But then he says it anyway, indicating that it is exactly the thing to say to Jane "just now," as if he catches Jane, and the reader in turn, at a moment of indecision how to regard Laura's flight and is intent on foreclosing her—Jane's, the reader's—consideration of any point of view differing from his own. Mr. Grey effectively silences Jane before she could have any chance to oppose his concurrence in Captain Chesney's wish for the death of his daughter.

Never minding how much Captain Chesney and Mr. Grey wish her dead, in fact Laura stubbornly flourishes, again suggesting that beneath these fathers' expressly homicidal sentiment is an ambivalence about its suicidal repercussions, a self-reflexive concern for their own lives. Neither disinheritance by her father, the scandal of her elopement, and even the criminal end of Mr. Carlton (explaining the solution of the mystery of Clarice's disappearance), prevent Laura from emerging as a beautiful vain young widow with a tidy fortune and the pleasant prospect of a new life in London under the auspices of her step-mother Lady Oakburn, whereas the newly ascended Earl of Oakburn barely enjoys the title long enough to produce a male heir before dying himself. Laura's survival consequently points to the questions: Why is a daughter's marriage a matter of so much novelistic concern to the hearts of the fathers who inhabit the world of this and so many other similar novels? Why do these fathers harbor the murderous fantasies that they do when they are more often than not openly contradicted? Especially when the consequences are so disastrous for the domestic peace that these fantasies purport to cherish? When the result is as literally self-destructive as it is figuratively preservative of the hearts in question?

An incipient answer to these questions is that the fearful power ascribed to unauthorized marriage in *Lord Oakburn's Daughters* (and in current objections to same-sex marriage) is its ability to communicate a disgrace that is dreaded because it exposes *other* persons (not the married persons) as riddles to themselves. Put in more anthropological terms, "It is not that 'magical' rituals compel the world through representation and manipulation; rather they express a realistic assessment of the fact that the world cannot be compelled."[16] So ritualized speech and silences about marriage (contrary to the messiness of persons' actual marital relationships) are a manner of negotiating the gap between the desire to compel a certain order of human relations against the resistance of human relations to such desire. It confesses the final unintelligiblity of sexed identity. Small wonder therefore that while Mrs. Carlton proceeds shamelessly to dominate the social life of South Wennock, her father obsesses in secret over his disgrace. He is the one who lives in terror almost of what others are saying and thinking, who dreads any public encounter with his flesh and blood. Mr. Grey's reference to his own daughter is likewise a manner of referring to himself. It is an elliptical assertion that personal disgrace as a father is a less emotionally tolerable mode of being in the world than personal bereavement as a father; that the grieving of the former is publicly shameful and therefore unendurable in a way that the grieving of the latter is not; and that this distinction is worth maintaining even when

16. Smith, "Bare Facts." 65.

the practical costs to self and others are excessive. For Captain Chesney
the public aspect of his disgrace is the self-consciousness of his failure
of self-understanding in other people's eyes.[17] Enforced silences consequently accumulate freighted significance, so that the greatest offense is
to have to speak unconventionally of these matters at all, because such
speech undermines the implicit authority of the marital norms that have
been flouted even when such speech explicitly intends to enforce them.[18]
At the same time the sexual desire that Laura Chesney evinces in her
abandonment of her father's home mirrors the novelistic desire of Mr.
Grey and Captain Chensey to preserve their cherished illusions of unity
of self under the name of father.

Augustine himself invites this association when he writes of how the
habits of his flesh impeded his embrace of Lady Continence: "What filth,
what disgraceful things they were suggesting! I was listening to them
with much less than half my attention. They were not frankly confronting me face to face on the road, but as it were whispering behind my
back, as if they were furtively tugging at me as I was going away, trying to
persuade me to look back."[19] For Augustine the "disgraceful things" that
avoid public confrontation and exposure are the results of his own sexual imagination, but for Captain Chesney and Mr. Grey the "disgraceful
things" they wish to keep behind them are the sexual defilement of their
daughters in unsanctioned marriage. The desired sexual activities that for
Augustine hide out of sight—behind one's back—to preserve their place
in mind, Captain Chesney and Mr. Grey hide in plain sight to keep out

17. Mothers are just as capable as fathers of wishing the death of their daughters rather
than countenance a daughter's marriage that would degrade the mother's social standing.
In *The Rebel of the Family* (1880), for example, Mrs. Winstanley responds as follows to
the revelation that her daughter Perdita loves a chemist, when Perdita's friend Bell Blount
appears to denounce this relationship:

> "Trash!" said Bell coarsely. "It is the son, not the mother, I tell you! If you deceive
> others, you cannot deceive me. Mark my words, madam," to Mrs. Winstanley;
> "before the year is out you will have a shopkeeper for your son-in-law."
> "I would rather see her dead at my feet!" cried Mrs. Winstanley passionately.
> (Linton, *Rebel*, 333)

18. Hence in the "House Debate on the Defense of Marriage Act," May 30, 1996, Rep.
Hyde's genuinely anguished preface: "Mr. Hyde: Political! I wish I had never heard of this
issue. This is a miserable, uncomfortable, queasy issue. There is no political gain. But there
is a moral issue . . . Nobody wants to talk about it. We are forced to talk about it by the
courts" (Sullivan, *Same-Sex Marriage*, 225–26).

19. Augustine *Confessions* 8.11.26 (Chadwick, 151).

of mind any questions about their sexed identity. Their desire for unity of sexed identity as fathers, about which they are unwilling to engage in public confrontation, these men indulge through the ascription of sexed activity in public to their very own daughters. Through the projected sexual nakedness of these women they avert other persons' gaze from the shame of their own sinful exposure of disintegrated self. The disgrace of the daughters that they lament is consequently less a calamity than an opportunity for them to prove themselves as gentlemen, just as the wish for Laura Chesney's death is a bond of mutual self-esteem between Mr. Grey and Captain Chesney that is sealed by a meaningful silence about her. In the meanwhile, to the extent that speech within the novel remains practically necessary, it is relegated to women, most of all to the long-suffering daughter Jane, who covertly communicates by letter with Clarice and occasionally visits Mrs. Carlton. Nevertheless the power of women's speech against the novelistic silences of their fathers is too little too late to benefit Clarice, whose death turns out to have been the event on which the entire novel is founded. All Jane can accomplish through her correspondence and visits is to unravel the mystery of Clarice's tragic murder. Nor does Jane ever own the extent to which Clarice's fate was facilitated by the conditions of silence attached to her banishment.

A daughter need not be estranged from her paternal home in order to suffer the devastating consequences of this silence and at the same time threaten exposure of her father as himself a disgraced creature. Not the most celebrated or accomplished of his many works, Anthony Trollope's *Sir Harry Hotspur of Humblethwaite* (1871) in its relative slightness reads as an additional instructive example of a "traditional novel" whose "office" is now "performed" by theological writings among many others. Whereas the plot of *Lord Oakburn's Daughters* was driven by the active resistance of young women to the enforced restraints of their sex, and involves a lot of plain-spoken and angry complaint by both fathers and daughters, the plot of *Sir Harry Hotspur* is driven by the obedient conformation of Sir Harry's daughter Emily to the requirements of her father's heart. Two years prior to the opening of the novel Sir Harry's only son had died. Sir Harry now despairs that his title, fortune, and home will ever descend intact to a direct male heir. The only possibility of such a prospect would be for Emily to marry her second cousin, George Hotspur, but Sir Harry determines against this plan once he confirms reports of George's profligacy.

Unfortunately Sir Harry had invited George to Humblethwaite before settling against any marriage, during which time Emily gives her heart entirely to her cousin, exactly the outcome that Sir Harry fears at the conclusion of George's visit: "But he thought that he was sure that no great harm had been done. Had any word been spoken to his girl which she herself had taken as a declaration of love, she would certainly have told her mother. Sir Harry would no more doubt his daughter than he would his own honour."[20] Sir Harry's freedom from doubt depends on the relegation of any discussion of love to the realm of women's speech. As long as he remains insulated from such speech he remains sure of himself, of his identity as husband, father, baronet, man, the sum total of his "honour." Honorable silence between father and daughter, the imperative to maintain honor at the cost of speech, consequently sets in motion a course of events that ends in Emily's death and the demise of the "glories of the House of Hotspur."[21] That ends in a sentimental-homicidal-suicidal pact whereby father and daughter each lose as the only way to win, whereby Sir Harry's initial suicidal loss of future life in the form of a male heir is matched finally by Emily's present loss of life in fulfillment of her father's homicidal regard.

If so much great harm is preferable, as it turns out, to the great harm of an irruption of the undiscussed into discussion, it is only because on the other side of Sir Harry's confident silence is Emily's own, because the honor that binds him to Emily is as potentially destructive of their worldly happiness as it is constructive of their worldly identities as father and daughter. Constrained as no doubt she is, Emily is all the more intensely aware of the boundary between her father's property and her own:

> It was for them, or rather for him, to say that a hand so weighted as was hers should not be given here or there; but it was not for them, not even for him, to say that her heart was to be given here, or to be given there. Let them put upon her what weight they might of family honours, and of family responsibility, that was her own property;—if not, perhaps, to be bestowed at her own pleasure, because of the pressure of that weight, still her own, and absolutely beyond the bestowal of any other.[22]

20. Trollope, *Sir Harry*, 11.

21. Ibid., 246.

22. Ibid., 13.

Faithful to the posited association of honor and property, Emily ends up preserving her father's honor at the cost of her own life by asserting unrelentingly her self-possession through her own heart. Once given to George, her heart proves a donation that cannot be recovered. Even as she accepts the impossibility of marriage to George, she stubbornly refuses to hear any report against his character. Instead she pines away in an aggressive silence. Not until her mother reads to her the details of George's marriage (to an actress, no less!) as published in a newspaper does Emily acknowledge her mistake. But even then her only response is a willfully passive resignation. Once her "own property" is lost, Emily refuses to allow the possibility of its recovery by refusing to speak about her loss. She so completely identifies her life with the possession of her heart that she regards her life as ended symbolically once her heart is broken, tempting the reader to regard her ensuing decline to her romantic disappointment, another heroine who dies from a love frustrated, only to do so is to conflate the novelistic with the novelist.

If the novelist Trollope seems to diagnose Emily's mortal illness as one of failed romance, the novelistic concerns of the text bespeak a different, more complex homicidal relationship between father and daughter. No matter how much Sir Harry and his wife Lady Elizabeth urge patience, Sir Harry also resigns himself with a curious satisfaction to Emily's fate. When Lady Elizabeth worries about the severance of all ties with George Hotspur: "I do think it will kill her," Sir Harry replies:

> "We must all die, but we need not die disgraced," he said.
>
> It was a most solemn answer, and told the thoughts which had been dwelling in his mind. His son had gone from him; and now it might be that his daughter must go too, because she could not survive the disappointment of her young love. He had learned to think that it might be so as he looked at her great grave eyes, and her pale cheeks, and her sorrow-laden mouth. It might be so; but better that for them all than that she should be contaminated by the touch of a thing so vile as this cousin. She was pure as snow, clear as a star, lovely as the opening rosebud. As she was, let her go to her grave—if it need be so. For himself he could die too,—or even live if it were required of him! Other fathers, since Jeptha and Agamemnon, have recognised it as true that heaven has demanded from them their daughters.[23]

23. Ibid., 230–31.

In the "solemn answer" of Sir Harry Hotspur, Trollope illustrates how an idealized link between one's sex and the possibility of life in God enables the correlation of faith in and faithfulness to sex with faith in and faithfulness to God. One's sex must then be maintained to the extent that it is inordinately valued as basis of any possible relation of self to God. A self without a sex, or a self that is improperly sexed, or a self whose sex becomes undone, is a self who has been cut off from God.

In the case of Sir Harry Hotspur he leaps from the conclusion that Emily "*might*" die to the very different conclusion that she "*need*" die, because her death will fulfill his own need to preserve his intelligibly sexed self-understanding as a father. Sir Harry figures his identity as a father through a pair of Hebrew and Greek narratives about keeping faith with God. As if he has read Matthew Arnold's recently published *Culture and Anarchy*, Sir Harry concludes that Hebraism *and* Hellenism agree on the ingredients of authentic paternity; that "right acting" and "right thinking" equally and together necessitate the death of the daughter as the faithful offering of the father.[24] (Jeptha and Agamemnon are fathers who kill their daughters; Sir Harry has paid George's debts in exchange for his renunciation of Emily, causing the disappointment that is killing her, joining his suicidal renunciation of a potential future male heir to the death of his living daughter; the novelistic and the novelist cross paths.) In an impressive associative leap Sir Harry determines that he has been justified in "killing" his daughter through his denial of her choice in marriage. He reads in Emily's visage a narrative vision of himself as father that both requires and explains Emily's death as a sacrifice of himself demanded by God, so that his need for self-understanding as a father becomes instead a question of obedience to "The Father," the "recognition" of a "truth" of "heaven," a matter of affairs divine, not human.[25]

What begins as paternal sentiment for his daughter's spotlessness resolves into solution of the self-concern of his comment: "We need not die disgraced." Emily in fact "need" die, so that Sir Harry can continue to enjoy a foreshortened future in the false security of his imagined relationship with God. The disgrace of a wrongful marriage thus becomes a matter of dis-grace, a falling out of relationship with God. Or better—a

24. Arnold, *Culture*, 131.

25. On Jepthah as a model of political sacrifice in the writings of Hobbes, Locke, and Rousseau, see Allen, *Talking*, 37–38 and 200 n.3. See also Kierkegaard, *Fear*, 86; and Maturin, *Melmoth*, 94, with reference to Handel's 1752 oratorio "The Sacrifice of Jepthah."

matter of imaginative disgrace that disguises the literal disgrace of sin. Avoidance of the former consequently obstructs repentant confession of the latter. Emily's discovery of George's marriage through a text within the text—a newspaper—thus serves as a pretext of the novelist for working out of the novelistic concerns that propel the narrative.

Valorizing the worth of Emily's death for herself and for him, Sir Harry finally consoles himself with the thought: "For himself he could die too,—or even live if it were required of him!" The perversity of this sentimental-homicidal-suicidal logic is that Sir Harry has in a way killed his daughter just so that he can go on living with a particular cherished imaginative formation of intelligibly sexed identity. So too Emily proceeds to die rather than challenge Sir Harry's imagination of himself as father, but also in order to preserve her own self-understanding as a daughter. Belief in sex as a necessary basis of relation between self and God affirms the requirement of a daughter's death as proof of the worth of sex and at the same time enables characterization of the father's survival as a sacrificial affirmation of that worth, as itself a kind of suicidal act.

Sir Harry's imagined faithfulness to God demands that he obstruct any marriage that he deems inappropriate. Faithfulness to God demands, above all else, that Sir Harry avoid disgrace to himself as father and to Emily as daughter. Better that they should both die crushed by their failures, but true to heaven and so secure in their identities as father and daughter, than that they should live disgraced by a wrongful marriage and thereby alienated from heaven. Which is to say, alienated from a fiction they tell themselves about their relation to heaven. More than anything the appeal to God here marks a kind of period in the sentimental narration of the fiction of sex, a point beyond which the human need for self-understanding balks at the acceptance of responsibility for sin that would move understanding forward. Instead, as Judith Butler puts it, "If I am not able to give an account of some of my actions, then I would rather die, because I cannot find myself as the author of these actions, and I cannot explain myself to those my actions may have hurt."[26] Only the preferred novelistic solution isn't exactly death for the self but rather death for those whom one has harmed, even as the life of oneself and another are inextricably bound together in the mortal punishment of a single original sin.

26. Butler, *Giving an Account*, 79.

The stage is now set to explicate the centrality of similar claims of God-relatedness in theological debates about sexuality and same-sex marriage, where the novelistic correlation of faithfulness to God and faith in God with faithfulness to and faith in the fiction of sex has become a correlation with faithfulness to and faith in the project of homo/heterosexual definition. At the core of this correlation is the desire for intelligible unity of personal identity apart from acceptance of responsibility for sin that is the condition of the desire in the first place. It is the desire, above all, to solve the problem of sin without owning the problem as one's own.

Bodies of Dis-Grace

As the previous readings illustrate, marriages that violate the presumptive authority of fathers to determine who a daughter may or may not marry communicate a disgrace to more than just the individual man and woman who seek to marry. In fact a daughter's obedience to the rule of the father's determination of permissible and impermissible marriage functions as a kind of public standard of intelligible male identity. Obedience of the daughter in the home, and especially in the daughter's procession from the father's home to a husband's home, are a constitutive feature of the shared identity of the fathers whose rule they in turn precariously embody. As a result the most significant possibilities for disgrace associated with marriage are never the exclusive concern of the marital partners.

The proliferation in the nineteenth century of popular stories chronicling the whole range of possible marital mishaps and disasters—and ideal successes—charges marriage with the power to affirm the God-relatedness of the father. Another way to describe this disgrace is that challenges to the fathers' authority of definition of permissible and impermissible marriages undermines the privileged invisibility of the identity of father as viewpoint. The God-relatedness of the father subsists in an imagined correspondence of human and divine viewpoint; so that the disgrace of loss of invisibility of viewpoint is loss of a point of identity with God. The father can then no longer confidently—doxically—assert his authority as divinely instituted, but has to do defend it as such; which in turn inherently undermines its necessity.

Disobedience of the daughter in effect provokes a crisis of the unspoken. This possibility of disgrace associated with marriage is the basis of the continuity between nineteenth-century novels and twenty-first-century theological disputes over the possibility or not of faithful definition and authorization of same-sex marriage. A crisis that previously centered on the relation of fathers and daughters has since become entangled by the incoherency of homo/heterosexual definition. Whereas the disobedience of the daughter called into question the God-related identity of the father, now the disobedience of the same-sex couple calls into question the God-related identity of man and woman as husband and wife, by challenging the privileged invisibility of heterosexuality as viewpoint. Bracing this continuity is the retrospective discernment of homosexual panic as the route to a kind of entitlement (dubious yet fiercely desired) to evasion of responsibility for sin. In D. A. Miller's terms, "in this sense the novel would be the very genre of the liberal subject, both as cause and effect: the genre that produces him, the genre to which, as its effect, he returns for 'recreation.'"[27] Theological discourse on sexuality, put another way, is populated by characters whose novelistic concerns more than mirror those of its writers.

In elaborating this continuity one must keep in mind what disgrace is not: a static condition, a stain or infection that is effectively transmitted by contact, as if the entire phenomenon could be figured as an issue of cleanliness, or purity; as if resistance were merely the attempt to inoculate oneself against infection, or dissolve the stain, or change the relevant standards of cleanliness. One must remain wary of these negative qualifications because of the preponderance of such imagery—typified in Sir Harry's reflection "but better that for them all than that she should be contaminated by the touch of a thing so vile as this cousin." Insistent figurations of permissible and impermissible marital arrangements in terms of contamination—the classification of individuals into static categories that are then vulnerable to contamination; the categories as much as the individuals—must be subject to interpretation in light of the disintegration of self in sin that is only comprehensible because of the memory of integration of self that remains. The desire at the root of that memory has by historical contingency become concentrated in the fiction of sex. Marriage in turn has become the predominant context for the ongoing narration of the fiction of sex. The disgrace that improperly constituted marriages communicate is an imagined falling out of relationship with God and subsequent loss of coherent personal intelligibility.

---

27. Miller, *Novel*, 215–16.

Entangled as it is by the terms of homo/heterosexual definition, the disgrace that Laura Chesney and Emily Hotspur can bring to their fathers is now figured as a threat to the stability and coherency of heterosexuality as a God-given identity that comprehends an innocent, because identity-affirming, relation between man and woman as fixed through marriage. One way to begin to examine more closely the hold of the fiction of sex, and the valorization of its intelligibility as worth dying for, on the imagination of writers on theology and sexuality is therefore to look for signs of the slippage that Sedgwick identifies as a distinguishing feature of homo/heterosexual definition. Given the image of sex as homunculus, one would expect to find, as an index of the viewpoint of this image of sex, the sentimental display of a slippage between the body and the sex that symbolizes that body, and the evaluation of such slippage as a kind of death that confirms the worth of sex as it is established in marriage. One would expect to find evidence of a sentimental-homicidal-suicidal violence that celebrates viewpoint over spectacle as it attempts to insulate itself (never wholly successfully) from its own self-relating activity, from recognition of its own spectacular identifications, above all the spectacle of its own sinful disgrace.

As much as literary productions are apt loci for this analysis, because they concretize, from the viewpoint of the theoretically minded critic, the "privileged disembodiment and invisibility" of sentimentality as dominating viewpoint, it would be naïve to imagine that one can engage in such analysis, i.e., produce another literary text, without also participating in the dynamic this analysis assumes. But in place of the possibility of total release from the chains of "vicarious knowledge-relation" that make this analysis possible in the first place, one can at least strive toward a relative transparency in its operations. The aim of writing and reading is not to perpetuate the disembodiment of viewpoint but rather to emphasize the necessary embodiment of viewpoint, even if a posture of invisibility remains an inescapable condition of the possibility of viewpoint, and likewise the consignment of others to the targeted exposure of self as spectacle.

This emphasis hopefully provides a critical starting point for the adjudication of theological claims within their textual realm. Theological claims possess such force and appeal because they seem to apply the brakes to the slippages that characterize attempts at homo/heterosexual definition. They denote an end to theological discourse on sexuality where no end otherwise appears in sight. Claims to God-relatedness function like a seal on the invisibility of viewpoint, seemingly removing the adherents of a viewpoint from the constraints and challenges that are the historical condition of that viewpoint. Although it is perfectly possible to end with the assertion that contemporary theological claims regarding human sexuality and marriage are just that, hopelessly *contemporary*, inescapably enmeshed in the contemporaneous discourses that they frequently purport to critique, it is possible to push forward, and ask instead what insight theology might have to offer, not on sex as a truth of the self, but on itself as a discourse that takes hold of bodies and imaginations through the incoherency of the terms of homo/heterosexual definition. The resultant starting point for a constructive, because responsible, theological sexual ethics is a global questioning of the meaningfulness and worth ascribed to sex in theological writings, as that meaningfulness is exemplified in the sentimental privileging as standards of intelligibility of particular viewpoints of sex and marriage, both heterosexual and homosexual, as somehow innocent. Along the way, intractable issues of theological hermeneutics will arise both in a general and in a specific sense.

In general a hermeneutic is always assumed whenever one claims knowledge of God's intention for human beings in any realm of human activity, let alone sexual identity and relationship. Even in the event that one receives a direct communication from God, the question still arises, how can anyone be sure to have understood and received that message aright? The traditional assertion that God's speech is by its nature incontrovertibly true is a hermeneutical principle of interpretation of divine speech. With regard to contemporary sexual ethics, argument centers very much on interpretation of the Bible as the specific form of God's speech that is most consistently and reliably available. The appeal to God as a kind of "conversation stopper" in theological discourse on sexuality is therefore appropriately characterized as a hermeneutical strategy, often implicating Scripture, to delimit and legitimate the interpretive authority of sentimentality as viewpoint. In anticipation of the constructive theological work that begins in the proceeding chapter, the following readings therefore focus especially on the use of theological claims to attempt to immobilize, through an idealization of marital relations, the interpretive negotiation of sexuality with its effect, sex.

A remarkable instance of strategic display of the slippage between sex and body, and the implications of that display for claims regarding marriage, is found in a chapter from the highly praised book *Toward a More Natural Science* (1985) by the bioethicist Leon R. Kass, M.D.[28] Titled "Thinking About the Body," Kass's chapter is a rich text to examine because he so confidently brings together, under the rubric of sentimentality, diverse strands of discourse, medical and philosophical, theological and literary. He thereby provides a convincing case study of the functional efficiency of sentimentality as viewpoint in over-determining through multiple sourcing its own disembodiment and invisibility.

It is striking that Kass begins precisely with an image of a slippage between sex and body as an antipode of a feminized body that has no sex, implying that the paradigm of a properly constituted body, one where the relationship between sex and body is hidden from view, is a hierarchical relation of male sex to female body:

> What is the relation between a human being and his body? Never a simple question, it is today even more puzzling, thanks, in part, to new surgical and technological developments that also give it great practical importance. On one side, we have a living body apparently devoid of all human activity in the permanently unconscious young woman who still manages to breathe spontaneously on her own for several years. On the other side, we have a human being alienated from his living body in the man who believes he is really a woman trapped inside a man's body and who undergoes surgery for "gender reassignment." In between, an increasing number of people walk around bearing other people's blood, corneas, kidneys, hearts, and livers; successful transplantation even of brain cells is currently proceeding in animals. To meet the shortage of organs for transplantation, some people have proposed that we allow the buying and selling of such human "spare parts," transferable both before and after death. Implantable and attachable mechanical organs add to our possible confusion, as do the more prevalent but less spectacular phenomena of wigs, tattoos, silicone injections, and various forms of body-building and remodeling.[29]

Kass's examples here are noteworthy as they are not organized by ordinary analytical logic. One would expect, from the point of view of such logic, that the "other side" of a "living body devoid of all human

28. Kass is among the most widely cited contemporary bioethicists. He served as chair of the President's Council on Bioethics for George W. Bush. The commission's work is well-documented at its website: http://bioethics.gov.

29. Kass, *Toward*, 276–77.

activity" would be "human activity" apart from a living body. In place of this non-verifiable opposition, one would at least expect the formula, "human activity" in a minimally functioning body, the mind trapped in a body that is completely paralyzed. Kass's argument, however, bears traces of another kind of logic altogether. As the organizing poles of this smorgasbord of examples he locates at one end a brain-injured woman, at the other end a male body that will not submit to the rule of the incoherent sex who inhabits it, a worser than worst case of locked-in syndrome where one's homunculus is confused about his sex and deluded into thinking that it is trapped in the wrong body.

In joining these poles Kass begins his disquisition on the "relation of a human being to his body" with an equation of homosexuality with brain injury through the association of an improperly sexed male body with a brain-injured female victim of drug and alcohol abuse and of a car wreck.[30] The vast catalogue of items that fall into the middle ground between these two poles are organized by this equivalence. They fit here because they are all instances of slippage that border on the dreaded ultimate slippage, that between a body and its sex. Heterosexual identity as viewpoint is consequently elaborated through an incredibly violent homicidal defining spectacle of homosexuality, so that these two identities become constituted by an opposition in their orientation specifically toward the fact of human mortality. Kass's whole chapter predicates and elaborates the idea that mortality, for the homosexual, is not the same as for the heterosexual. The homosexual is doomed to die in a manner that the heterosexual is not, to die a dual death, since his life already is a kind of brain injury. This function of the image of a "man who believes he is really a woman trapped inside a man's body" as a cipher for homosexuality, and of the isolation of the homosexual body as subject to a

30. At the time of original publication of Kass's chapter (1984), anyone familiar with contemporary legal developments in the debates regarding cessation of life support and the right to die would likely have recognized in his example a conflation of the cases of Karen Ann Quinlan and Nancy Cruzan. Quinlan lapsed into a persistent vegetative state in 1975, following an incident involving drugs and alcohol, and lived in that state until 1985. Cruzan lapsed into a persistent vegetative state following a car accident in 1983, and died in December 1990, when her feeding tube was finally removed. On the status of women's bodies as sites on which case law concerning decisions to forgo life-sustaining treatment is determined, written fifteen years before the case of Terri Schiavo riveted the nation, see Miles and August, "Courts." For an example contemporaneous with *in Re Quinlan* of how the homosexual closet can frame medical discussion of end-of-life care, see Fried, "Terminating."

distinct and dreadful double mortality, emerges clearly as Kass's chapter progresses.[31]

Having begun with this curious opposition of images, Kass proceeds to develop an answer to his question through a reflection on the meaningfulness of human nakedness that is polemically heterosexual while passing itself off as incontrovertibly obvious interpretation of the Bible. Kass prefaces his inquiry regarding nakedness with an invocation of Genesis—"With the help of our tradition's most famous text on this subject"[32]—that eludes any specific theological commitments, as if medicine, philosophy, Scripture, and common sense all seamlessly converged in the formation of "our tradition," confirming the obvious intelligibility of sex in the facts of human sexual anatomy and reproductive biology. Through the absence of any definition Kass invites his reader to identify with a "tradition" that is not any denomination of Judaism or Christianity, not a philosophical discipline, not a branch of medical science, for example psychiatry or psychoanalysis, but rather the tradition of "homo/heterosexual definition" as an epistemological framework for production of the knowledge of sex.[33]

From the security of this viewpoint sex can now be confidently asserted as an ultimate origin of sexuality, defined specifically as heterosexuality, because attributed to God's creative intention for humanity, even as the appeal to Scripture appears to be an appeal to just another book, to a "text" whose heuristic value is only its undeniable familiarity and not its complex status as revelation. What follows is a weird evocation of Saint Augustine on the punishment of original sin: "Human nature then is, without any doubt, ashamed about lust, and rightly ashamed. For in its disobedience, which subjected the sexual organs solely to its own

31. Kass's definition of homosexuality fits Lacan's definition of psychosis as summarized by Butler. So for Kass homosexuality seems to be the answer to Butler's question: "In other words, what precise cultural possibilities threaten the subject with a psychotic dissolution, marking the boundaries of livable being?" where the possibility of meaningfully living is directly joined to the possibility of meaningfully dying. Likewise Kass's text is a productive ingredient in the answer to Butler's further question: "Under what conditions and under the sway of what regulatory schemes does homosexuality itself appear as the living prospect of death?" Butler, *Bodies*, 98.

32. Kass, *Toward*, 290.

33. For a history of the function of representations of female nakedness as a canvas for the projection of generalized meanings of human embodiment, see Miles, *Carnal*.

impulses and snatched them from the will's authority, we see a proof of the retribution imposed on man for that first disobedience."[34] So Kass writes:

> What is the meaning of nakedness? Why is the awareness of one's nakedness shameful? To be naked means, of course, to be defenseless, unguarded, exposed—a sign of our vulnerability before the elements and the beasts. But the text makes us attend, as did our ancient forbears, to our sexuality. In looking, as it were, for the first time upon our bodies as sexual beings, we discover how far we are from anything divine. As a sexual being, none of us is complete or whole, either within or without. We have need for and are dependent on a complementary other, even to realize our own bodily nature. We are halves, not wholes, and we do not command the missing complementary half. Moreover, we are not internally whole, but divided. We are possessed by an unruly or rebellious "autonomous" sexual nature within—one that does not heed our commands (any more than we heeded God's); we, too, face within an ungovernable and disobedient element, which embarrasses our claim to self-command. (The punishment fits the crime: The rebel is given rebellion). We are compelled to submit to the mastering desire within and to the wiles of its objects without; and in surrender, we lay down our pretense of upright lordliness, as we lie down with necessity. On further reflection, we note that the genitalia are also a sign of our perishability, in that they provide for those who will replace us.[35]

For Kass nakedness, defined as the discovery of the sexual differentiation of human beings by their genitals, is significant as an occasion of interpretation because it so obligingly seems to affirm the truth of sex as an origin of sexuality in multiples senses: as the bodily origin of sexual desire; as the bodily means of the reproduction of the species as male and female; as the bodily inscription of human disobedience of the divine command; as the bodily sign of the composition of human identity as sexed internally as well as externally; as the bodily index of the completion of human identity, internally and externally, in procreative heterosexual marriage.

However much it looks like one, Kass's argument is not exactly an updated version of the classic procreative norm; that is, the attempt to provide sexual activity with a justifying rational purpose. Rather it is a

---

34. Augustine *City of God* 14.20 (Bettenson, 582).

35. Kass, *Toward*, 291.

sentimental-homicidal-suicidal narration of the fiction of sex. As such it skillfully images the exercise of viewpoint. Kass's very choice of subject matter reinforces the invisibility of his own privileged participation in the tradition that requires no name. The polite suggestion of the naked bodies of Adam and Eve conjures for display a whole series of hierarchical relationships: between Kass and the naked bodies he projects for view, between God and human beings, between the mind and the body it inhabits, between a man and his erection, between a man and the woman over whom he exercises "upright lordliness" and thereby impregnates. Especially significant is the hierarchical relationship between God and human beings, because it organizes all of these oppositions in the assertion of a final opposition between heterosexual mortality and homosexual mortality that makes heterosexuality a condition of possibility of God-relatedness. In a post-coital gesture, immediately after "lying down with necessity," having spent his rhetorical energies, Kass sits up in bed and summarizes his argument with the "further reflection" "that the genitalia are also a sign of our perishability." Having sex—being faithful to God in sexual relationship with a person of the opposite sex—suddenly, unawares, has suicidal implications.

As an evocation of orgasm as a little death, and the erotic power of words too, Kass's comment doesn't so much interpret the signification of "the genitalia" as it ascribes to them a normative signification derived from the fact of mortality, so that completeness as a man or woman becomes defined as much by an orientation to death as it is to other human beings. Kass is now able to articulate the worth of sex in death by distinguishing the heterosexually sexed individual as a whole person who is meaningfully destined to perish—as one who can in effect meaningfully commit suicide—because he is someone who can marry and procreate—as opposed to the homosexually sexed individual who is an isolated and incomplete person whose "perishability" is therefore unintelligible, because not grounded in a properly constituted sex, a sex that can be narrated as completed in marriage. In this way Kass incorporates into the privilege of viewpoint the suicidal implications of the homicidal regard for homosexual spectacle in the sentimental narration of sex, as if suicidal sex is medically prescribed as the necessary means to kill the identifications on which that narration is based, so that one must continually engage in heterosexual intercourse in order to silence the homosexual panic of the little sexed person within.

Kass makes this link between intelligibility, sex, and mortality explicit a short while later, when he summarizes the import of this interpretation of nakedness in terms of the possibility of divine encounter: "And finally, in—and *only* in—the discovery of our own lack of divinity comes the first real openness to the divine. *Immediately* after making themselves girdles, reports the biblical author, 'they heard the Lord God walking in the Garden,' the first explicit mention that man attended to or even noticed the divine presence."[36] Apart from its plain inaccuracy as exegesis, this is a remarkable interpretive move, suggesting as it does that only after human beings achieve conscious awareness of their differentiation by sex are they capable of achieving "real openness to the divine," as if the "openness" to God that Adam and Eve experienced before their disobedience was somehow incomplete, was not "real" because they weren't fully heterosexual until after the Fall. Heterosexuality as a principle of intelligible sex is thus credited as a kind of perfection of creation at the same time as homosexuality is projected right back into paradise as an incipient principle of unintelligible lack of differentiation that is resolved by the Fall. As Kass recasts the story, Adam and Eve's disobedience becomes an expression of homosexual panic, as if they had to sin—and by implication marry in a kind of shotgun wedding—in order to prove that they weren't really gay.

It therefore makes sense that the punishment that ensues from Adam and Eve's disobedience is meaningful only in relation to the distinction between homosexuality and heterosexuality: "These reminders of perishability are also reminders of perpetuation; if we understand their meaning, we are even able to transform the necessary and shameful into the free and noble. For even in yielding to our sexual natures—I must add, only heterosexually—we implicitly say yes to our own mortality, making of our perishable bodies the instruments of ever-renewable human life and possibility. Embodiment is a curse only for those who believe they deserve to be Gods."[37] The very cavalier, rhetorically incidental flavor of Kass's aside here—"I must add, only heterosexually"—helps enforce the implicit punitive association of the "man who believes he is really a woman trapped inside a man's body" with homosexual desire, both exemplifying a form of cursed embodiment, since the former is not "really" a "woman trapped inside a man's body," but only a "man" who "believes"

36. Ibid., 292.
37. Ibid., 293.

this about himself, just as the latter is a man who can not say "yes" to his mortality, believing as he does that he "deserves" to be a God, because he has not symbolically re-narrated his own fall from undifferentiated humanity into intelligible heterosexual manhood, has not succeeded in determining who is the man and who is the woman.

Likewise Kass needn't use the actual word marriage once in this entire chapter, written as it was on the cusp of the emergence of same-sex marriage as a live social, political, and theological question. Instead Kass enjoys a culturally notable final moment of the safe assumption of marriage—privileged in its invisibility—as both the context of discovery that "We have need for and are dependent on a complementary other, even to realize our own bodily nature," as well as context of the "perpetuation" that can "transform the necessary and shameful into the free and noble." The result is an exclusion of homosexuality from marriage in a double sense, since a homosexual is a person who, according to this schematics of intelligible sexual identity, cannot meaningfully marry a person of the same sex *or* of the opposite sex. Either attempt is doomed to failure.

This double exclusion of homosexuality from marriage correlates with the distinction between two kinds of bodies, one doubly graced with life because heterosexual, marriageable, "open" to the divine; the other doubly dis-graced because homosexual, dead in body and soul because unaware of its own "necessary and shameful" nature, destined to die a meaningless bodily and spiritual death. One as a result able to kill itself, the other targeted for death even though in a sense already dead.

For Kass the narration of a brain-injured homosexual body is necessary to the narration of a wholly alive, wholly redeemable, wholly intelligible heterosexual body that is "free and noble," free from any contaminating disgrace of unintelligibility, noble in its invisibility, and indemnified by marriage from the disquieting intrusions of identification with the homosexual body that is so vehemently excluded and consigned to death. Only then can sex be asserted with such confidence as a source of intelligible identity, the viewpoint of the little person within imaginatively assumed almost as if that secret truth of the self is relishing the spectacle that makes its own coherence as viewpoint possible. Others must die disgraced, not so much that this sex can have life, but so that this sex also can die. Can die, in Sir Harry Hostspur's words, *not* disgraced.

Charity and Homosexual Spectacle

Consignment of homosexual bodies to death is an all too familiar feature of narrations of intelligible heterosexuality. Kass's argument is only exceptional for its cultural currency, its shamelessness that circulates as respectability, since display of doomed or lifeless homosexual bodies is usually only projected so explicitly by persons who self-consciously locate themselves on the far-right of the political and theological spectrum—persons, for example, who willingly equate HIV infection with divine retribution for same-sex sexual activity, or who cite Leviticus 18 and 20 as directives for public policy.[38] At the extreme, faced with the charge that they are advocating the extermination of homosexual persons as not worthy of living, Kass and others might respond that they are not asserting anything about the worth of homosexual persons at all, but only affirming the justice of death as a "punishment," whether symbolic or real, for homosexual activity.[39] In the context of live debates about sexuality and violence this response is specious at best, assuming as it does the trans-historical, universalistic truth of heterosexuality conceptualized as a sexual orientation of opposed sexes, grounded in the privileged asymmetry of heterosexuality as a viewpoint. The distinction between the sexual "act" and the sexual orientation of the "actor" reinforces the conceptualization of the "actor" as a sexed individual expressing a sex through a sexual orientation. By asserting the impermissibility of same-sex sexual activity, the invisibility of heterosexuality as an orientation, as the viewpoint of the secret self, is enforced through the active erasure of the homosexual orientation that is at the same time asserted.

Given the actuality of physical violence against lesbian, gay, and transgendered persons, many religious leaders have nevertheless insisted on a distinction between the symbolic and the real. To the extent that such insistence is an acknowledgment of the seriousness of this violence, the distinction is practically beneficial. Even so, the distinction only serves to reinforce the very process of symbolization that makes such violence intelligible as violence directed specifically against gay and lesbian and transgendered persons, against persons who are wrongfully harboring within themselves a sex that doesn't belong in that body. The irony is that Kass's gruesome spectacle, like the denial of the "homosexual child" by the

38. See, for example, Peters, *Death Penalty*..

39. For an example of a psychological study in support of the view that Christians can and do responsibly love the sinner and hate the sin, see Basset, "Homonegative."

Council on Biblical Manhood and Womanhood, turns out to be as much a suicidal as well as a homicidal fantasy. It is a fantasy of escape from the intractable crises of homo/heterosexual definition that characterize the pursuit of intelligible sexual identity. Death is more than just a possible punishment for wrongful sexual activity. It is the fantasied closure of the breach that separates the fiction of sex from the body that it symbolizes. Others must die, both bodily and symbolically, so that sex can intelligibly symbolize the bodies it inhabits, which includes the possibility in turn for meaningful death of the body that is successfully sexed.

Consignment of others to die as a kind of self-justifying proof of the worth of sex in death is not limited to those struggling to maintain the integrity of heterosexuality as sentimental viewpoint through an uncompromising opposition of homosexuality and marriage. It is equally available to proponents of same-sex marriage, especially when redemptive significance is ascribed to marriage. The spectacular display of mortal exclusion from that significance can then function as guarantor of the promise of redemption in marriage. Redemption in all these cases, as exemplified in Kass's reading of Genesis, has little to do with any qualitative shift in the relationship human beings can have with God, and everything to do with the incorporation of the body into the successful narration of the intelligible sex that inhabits it. The appeal of the redemptive claim for marriage is so powerful because it offers this intelligibility. As both an experience and as an argument it is not subject to verification or disconfirmation, so that disagreements over who can marry, over what bodies can mean in marriage, devolve finally into issues of ecclesiastical organization and authority, over the "Word" of one side against the "Word" of the other.

It is hardly surprising therefore that Eugene Rogers, author of perhaps the most sophisticated theological argument developed to date in support of the theological meaningfulness of same-sex marriage, organizes his entire argument around two assumptions: first, that marriage has particular redemptive significance, and second, that those who refuse to allow the inclusion of the bodies of same-sex couples in that significance face an awful death sentence. The first assumption Rogers celebrates with unabashed enthusiasm:

> Along the wide spectrum of views about marriage for gay and lesbian couples, the extremes sometimes meet in claiming that gay and lesbian marriages are irredeemable, on the far right because

they are gay, on the far left because they are marriages. I claim the opposite: that they can be means of redemption. More, they can be means of anticipating God's catching human beings up into that wedding feast that God celebrates in the life of the Trinity, an elevation that the tradition has had the wisdom to call consummation. The question to the right is, given that gay and lesbian people are not going to go away, what should the Church *do* with them? The question to left is, given that gay and lesbian people are part of the Church, how much should it allow their bodies to *mean*? In the context of baptism, eucharist, and (yes) monastic vows, the Spirit is now moving Christian communities to see marriage as the central symbol by which to test and renegotiate the fit of gay and lesbian bodies into the body of Christ.[40]

As a starting point for the rich and complex argument that follows, Rogers's claim is noteworthy for its seemingly conciliatory attitude precisely toward those persons who are most actively engaged in the fight at all levels to obstruct the solemnization, secular and religious, of "gay and lesbian marriages."

Rogers actually includes a full paragraph in his acknowledgments thanking those proponents of "views of Christian sexuality of enough charity and sophistication to compel me, when I disagreed, to think through why," including as a group the "signatories of 'The Homosexual Movement: A Response by the Ramsey Colloquium.'"[41] This is a suspect phraseology to use to describe the signatories of a document comparable, in "charity" and "sophistication," to the "Protocols of the Elders of Zion" that it eerily echoes. It certainly invites scrutiny of what sort of charity Rogers is extending in turn, whether this is a responsive mature humorous charitable anger or a return in kind of the lack of humor of the Ramsey signatories and the brittle self-concerned anger that accompanies that lack. It is fitting also to wonder, given the opposition he constructs between the extremes of the far right and the far left, what exactly Rogers means when he joins those extremes in the view that "gay and lesbian marriages are irredeemable," since his own "opposite claim" isn't exactly an "opposite claim" at all.

To claim that gay and lesbian marriages can be a "means of redemption" is not the same thing as to claim that gay and lesbian marriages are "redeemable." In fact a huge theological gap separates the two. The

40. Rogers, *Sexuality*, 27.

41. Ibid., vii–viii.

designation of gay and lesbian marriages as redeemable is a necessary precursor to the distinct, and much more theologically loaded designation of any marriage, let alone a gay or lesbian marriage, as a means of redemption. Moreover, the first designation, of gay and lesbian marriages as redeemable, depends conceptually on the criteria of homo/heterosexual definition it purports to repudiate in joining the terms "gay and lesbian" and "marriage" as means of redemption in the second designation. As a result, two levels of discourse are constructively entangled and not opposed by this construction of an "opposition." Rogers then writes as if all those he lumps together on the side of the irredeemable are wrongfully caught up in issues of homo/heterosexual definition whereas he, and all those willing to join him on his side, are properly engaged in a celebratory experiment of transformation conducted by the Spirit; all the while structuring that claim on the Spirit by use of the terms of homo/heterosexual definition. The stated irenicism of his invitation, to all those on the right and the left, to join this experiment of transformation, includes within itself a familiar dimension of violence that makes his constructed opposition possible, joining together as it does the violence of homosexuality as spectacle with the violence of threatened exclusion from the life of the Spirit of all those who refuse to accept this invitation.

The central difficulty with Rogers's project is the unknowing and troublesome imbrication of the theological desire for redemption within the desire for intelligibly sexed gay male identity, as that identity is potentially secured through assertion of a divinely instituted authority to determine the definition of marriage for the church. This imbrication must be addressed because no theologian can simply extricate himself from theological discourse on sexuality, least of all when he is specifically addressing questions of the meaningfulness of sexual relationship and marriage. The positive claim for marriage as a means of redemption is properly theological, but in itself not very informative. It is akin, for example, to the claim that the enslavement of the Israelites to Pharaoh was a means of redemption, since redemption only makes sense as redemption from some prior condition that is both comparable to and discontinuous with the relationship with God that follows. As an action that God initiates, and also as a relationship that God makes possible between God's self and humanity, redemption only ever makes sense within a given narrative context. To insist that "gay and lesbian marriages" "can be means of redemption" therefore invites the very important question: Redemption from what? Rogers's general assertion is "that marriage, for the same or opposite sexes, can be a discipline of denial and restraint that liberates the human being for sanctification."[42] Marriage in this view presumably redeems one from such obstacles to God-relatedness as selfishness, possessiveness, acquisitiveness, and lust. Still the question remains: What storied context is assumed as the background of this very strong claim on behalf of marriage?

As an explicit theological issue, the story here concerns the "fit of gay and lesbian bodies into the body of Christ"; and the possibility of such a "fit" assumes the prior exclusion of "gay and lesbian bodies." To the extent that Rogers proceeds to articulate a story of redemption based on the ingrafting of the Gentiles into Israel, a story he compellingly narrates at length through readings of Aquinas, the status of "gay and lesbian bodies" as "fit" for incorporation "into the body of Christ" is highly compelling. What remains unexamined in this storied opposition of exclusion/inclusion of Gentiles into Israel, "gay and lesbian bodies into the body of Christ," marriage as "irredeemable"/"means of redemption" are the troubled assumptions, first, of such a thing as "gay and lesbian bodies," and second, of "marriage" as the "central symbol by which to test and renegotiate the fit of gay and lesbian bodies into the body of Christ." Here is the marriage plot unquestioningly celebrated as the means to narrate a stably sexed self who can enjoy the ultimate pleasures of relationship with God.

This pair of troubled assumptions organizes Rogers's lengthy exploration of the possibility of finding "space" in the writings of Karl Barth for theological "openness" to same-sex relationships. Rogers does so by developing an internal critique of two layers of "unintended idealism"[43] or "abstraction"[44] in Barth's theological project, concerning Barth's treatment of the Jews in relation to the Gentiles, and women in relation to men. Rogers's focus on Jewish-Gentile difference and male-female difference follows Barth's example, as Rogers repeatedly quotes Barth: "'Because the election of God is real, there is such a thing as love and marriage.' So Karl Barth deeply and beautifully connects one doctrine, election, which has to do with the Jews, and another, human love and marriage, that has to do

---

42. Ibid., 70.

43. Ibid., 152.

44. Ibid., 159.

with gender."[45] Rogers's aim is to critique the effect of these binarisms—Jew and Gentile, man and woman—as they function in Barth's writing to "hide real Jews and women behind projections,"[46] and thereby enable inclusion within Barth's theological project of the "real" bodies of gay and lesbian persons in the "covenant of marriage" that is, according to Rogers a "type of the love of God for Israel."[47] The criticism of unintended abstraction is thus an argument for discernment of the genuine presence of the Spirit in same-sex unions.[48]

In his readings of Barth, however, Rogers assumes, with Barth, the invisibility of sex as the secret self that is the source of intelligible personal identity. The sentimental narration of sex through homo/heterosexual definition consequently frames Rogers's entire argument. His criticisms of the abstracting binarisms Jew/Gentile and man/woman are actually structured around the profoundly confusing binarism homosexual/heterosexual. The positive claim regarding the theological uses of gay and lesbian bodies—that is, the affirmation of the presence of the sex that makes those bodies intelligible as a locus of the Spirit's activity—requires the freeze framing of some persons in a spectacular and violently destructive display of the worth of that sex in death. Rogers accomplishes this freeze framing through a striking double gesture, first by insisting that refusal to agree to disagree on the issue of same-sex relationship, presumably by all parties to this dispute, is unnecessarily and perhaps culpably destructive of the church, and second, by issuing a "dire warning" of permanent exclusion from the church/body of Christ to all those who reject his view of the matter.

Predictably enough, agreement to disagree about the status of same-sex marriage within the church finally turns out not to be open to either genuine or charitable disagreement. Nor could it be, given the sentimental viewpoint that undergirds the entire argument. From this viewpoint the claim for marriage as "means of redemption," despite the occasional use of the metaphor in Scripture, is so appealing, strategically as well as affectively, because it so completely maps the sentimental display of the homosexual body as a mangled brain-injured body into the service of the

45. Ibid., 153.

46. Ibid., 143.

47. Ibid., 142.

48. For attempts to explicate the meaningfulness of same-sex marriage in concrete anatomical terms, see Lunn, "Anatomy," and Matzko, "Relationship."

claim that "gay and lesbian marriages" can be "means of redemption" of those very same brain-injured bodies. But only at the very high cost of the self-acceptance of homosexual identity as it is projected as bulwark of the invisibility of heterosexual viewpoint. The unacknowledged but assumed counterpart to this story of the "fit of gay and lesbian bodies into the body of Christ," that is, the upbuilding of the church, is the fiction of sex as it is concentrated in the fantasied "wedding feast that God celebrates in the life of the Trinity." The worth of sex in death is now exemplified in the very life of God's self-relating activity, as Rogers unhesitatingly asserts, implicitly in the above passage, very explicitly much later.

If sex is truly worth dying for, then someone must die, or at least face the threat of death. The conjunction of the "far right" and the "far left" in the assertion that "gay and lesbian marriages are irredeemable" allows Rogers to structure his argument for marriage as "means of redemption" on just such a death threat. Rogers's "opposite claim" establishes an opposition between those who allow marriage as a "means of redemption" and those who don't, so that he can then insist that persons who deny the possibility of "gay and lesbian marriages" as "means of redemption" themselves face exclusion from that redemption. What then becomes "redeemable" is this very discourse of exclusion/inclusion, to the extent that it includes "gay and lesbian marriages," and excludes those who refuse to allow them as "means of redemption." Rogers ends up instantiating the worst dimensions of "identity politics" as critiqued by Judith Butler:

> But there remains the task of thinking through the potential cruelties that follow from an intensification of identification that cannot afford to acknowledge the exclusions on which it is dependent, exclusions that must be refused, identifications that must remain as refuse, as abjected, in order for that intensified identification to exist. This is an order of refusal which not only culminates in the rigid occupation of exclusionary identities, but which tends to enforce that exclusionary principle on whomever is seen to deviate from those positions as well.[49]

In his desire to identify as a Christian, to claim the inclusion of his gay male body in the life of the Spirit, Rogers inscribes an exclusionary politics into the very heart of Christian theology as a communal enterprise.

Contrary to his stated aim, Rogers's argument multiplies just those sorts of exclusions decried by Butler, at its cruelest through the use of

49. Butler, *Bodies*, 116.

Scripture. The result is that Rogers's scholarship and insight boils down to a remarkably enthused affirmation of sentimentality as viewpoint, as hard-edged and unforgiving in its own way as Kass's consignment of the homosexual to a doubly dreadful death or the slanders propounded by the signatories of the Ramsey Colloquium's statement:

> Wedding guests also guarantee and insure the love of two against times of difficulty, as the Spirit keeps faith between the Father and the Son, reuniting them after the crucifixion. The celebration, blessing, and witnessing of a human wedding may catch up human beings by the Spirit into the very inner love and life of God, as the resurrection too, by the Spirit, catches up "your mortal bodies also" into the everlasting life of God.
>
> That is why the parable ends with a dire warning about one who does not celebrate. The one without a wedding garment is "cast into the outer darkness where they will weep and gnash their teeth." That one cuts himself off from the work of the Spirit and the life of God. Meanwhile, another warning tells against those who "set a table for fortune and fill cups of mixed wine for destiny," of which the celebration of sexual conquest would provide an example, an anti-wedding feast. Let those warnings stand against those on the right and on the left who deny the Spirit at same- or opposite-sex weddings.[50]

In the overall context of the work of the Spirit that Rogers is celebrating, this is a "dire warning" indeed. For the sincere believer, the cruelest fate that could befall an individual is this threatened fate of exclusion from the life of the Spirit, from the blessing, end, and consummation of human existence in the life of God. Truly no one can deny the Spirit. All one can deny is some other person's or community's claim upon the Spirit. The very specific "work of the Spirit" that the believer can "cut himself off from" here therefore doesn't appear to be the redemption of anyone, but rather the yoking together of "same- or opposite-sex" marriage through a very angry invocation of the parable of the wedding feast in Matthew 22.

This parable is worth quoting in full, in order to appreciate the vengefulness of Rogers's use of the text as exclusionary "warning" "against those on the right and on the left who deny the Spirit at same- or opposite-sex weddings":

50. Rogers, *Sexuality*, 196.

Once more Jesus spoke to them in parables, saying: "The kingdom of heaven may be compared to a king who gave a wedding banquet for his son. He sent his slaves to call those who had been invited to the wedding banquet, but they would not come. Again he sent other slaves, saying, 'Tell those who have been invited: Look, I have prepared my dinner, my oxen and my fat calves have been slaughtered, and everything is ready; come to the wedding banquet.' But they made light of it and went away, one to his farm, another to his business, while the rest seized his slaves, mistreated them, and killed them. The king was enraged. He sent his troops, destroyed those murderers, and burned their city. Then he said to his slaves, 'The wedding is ready, but those invited were not worthy. Go therefore into the main streets, and invite everyone you find to the wedding banquet.' Those slaves went out into the streets and gathered all whom they found, both good and bad; so the wedding hall was filled with guests.

"But when the king came in to see the guests, he noticed a man there who was not wearing a wedding robe, and he said to him, 'Friend, how did you get in here without a wedding robe?' And he was speechless. Then the king said to the attendants, 'Bind him hand and foot and throw him into the outer darkness, where there will be weeping and gnashing of teeth.' For many are called, but few are chosen." (Matt 22:1–14)

This is an extremely violent parable, notable for the prior exclusion of the "many" from the "wedding feast." The parable's "dire warning" which Rogers applies to "the one who does not celebrate" in fact applies to the one who is haphazardly gathered by the king's servants. A whole other group of persons, "those who had been invited to the wedding banquet, but they would not come," are first "destroyed," "their city" "burned," before the "wedding hall was filled with guests."

In the same way, Rogers's use of this parable as a dire warning enables an exclusion based on an exclusion. It distinguishes between those persons, the murdered and pillaged who never enter the banquet hall, who have suffered the constitutive "cruelties" of an "intensification of identification that cannot afford to acknowledge the exclusions on which it is dependent," and the invited guests who can visibly be excluded, an exclusion that is only possible, apprehensible, because of the prior exclusion that is denied. The invited guests consequently attend and must celebrate under a double threat; in the first case they face murder and arson; in the second case they face being "bound hand and foot" and thrown "into the outer darkness." The initial conjunction of the far right and the far left in a gesture of seeming conciliation, of wanting to bring together the two seemingly incompatible terms "gay and lesbian" and "marriage," turns out to be a gesture of redounding violence that makes possible the inclusion of "gay and lesbian marriages" as "means of redemption."[51]

Kass's brain-injured homosexual body is transfigured by Rogers into the spectacle of the doomed bodies—"bound hand and foot"—of those on the "right and on the left" who "deny the Spirit." It is particularly odd, therefore, that Rogers's total argument has been praised as a model of charity in the conduct of theological debate; revealing how the possibility of charity, in this narrow range of debate, is at the expense of violence to an insulted and disregarded constitutive exterior;[52] revealing the need for more mature humor and the ability to yoke the anger and charity that follows from mature humor. Rogers's use of the parable of the wedding feast is further dispiriting when one considers the precedent, often blamed on a moment in the later writings of Saint Augustine, of the citation of this same parable as an authorization for the use of coercion in matters of faith.[53] It hardly seems uncharitable, then, to summarize Rogers's total argument as an attempt to justify forcible religious conversion.

Lest the reader doubt that Rogers is not thoroughly embroiled in the freeze-framing of a mangled homosexual corpse, that he has somehow eluded the conceptual pitfalls of homo/heterosexual definition, that he is not using sentimental-homicidal-suicidal violence to narrate a sex worth dying for, Rogers literally resurrects this same lifeless homosexual body as the very symbolization of the redemptive possibilities ascribed to marriage. He upholds this body as a privileged symbol of the promise of bodily resurrection, that particular work of the Spirit that was able to re-unite the crucified Son with the Father. So Rogers later issues his death threat in the following terms: "The love stronger than death is therefore no abstract power, for Christians, but a particular person, and that is why it is to their peril that the Spirit should be resisted or denied."[54] Persons who resist or deny the Spirit, who refute or refuse to acknowledge claims

51. Rogers's use of the Bible is in line with the terrorizing techniques criticized in Trible, *Texts*, and Stone, *Practicing*.

52. For such a misplaced analysis of Rogers's work, see Stout, "How Charity."

53. See Letter 93, "To Vicentius," in Augustine, *Political Writings*, 232–45. Also in Augustine, *Works*, II/I:376–408. Also see Deane, *Political*, 172–220, esp. 200–202.

54. Rogers, *Sexuality*, 254.

upon the Spirit, risk, according to Rogers, "cutting themselves off" from the resurrection. They are, in essence, committing a form of suicide. At the same time, in the face of this threat, the bodies of those who are childless achieve a spectacular prominence. They become the walking dead, and as such privileged witness of God's promise to humanity.

All of this is attained at the cost of the assumption, typified in Kass, of marriage as the sole context of procreation, and the corollary reductive equation, also typified in Kass, of homosexuality with non-procreativity:

> Resurrection carries forward the pattern by which God chooses younger sons and unwed mothers, preferring eschatology over teleology. The married (gay or straight) may signify the eschatological community not only by participating in the love of God for the community, not only by participating in the witness of the Spirit to the glory of love, and not even only by exemplifying the taking up of eros into compassion and the sanctification of concupiscible passion become ascetical community, but also by trusting to the general resurrection for their bodily survival. Certainly the Church lacks for serious testimony to the bodily resurrection these days. Theologians doubt it and students, who have confused it with a disembodied immortality of the soul, encounter the traditional doctrine with disgust. What would the Church—especially Protesting Churches lacking monasticism—make of couples whose childlessness takes the resurrection seriously and embodies it in an unmistakable sign?[55]

Whereas Kass relishes the spectacle of the brain-injured homosexual as a kind of warning to those who would "yield to their sexual natures" otherwise than "heterosexually," Rogers here relishes the same spectacle as a warning to those who refuse to allow the assimilation of "gay or lesbian marriages" to "opposite-sex marriages." This assimilation depends on a conflation of same-sex marriage with infertile opposite-sex marriage, as if homosexuality and infertility were equivalent. This is a patently false equation, tenable only if one assumes a paradigm of romantic heterosexual marriage, and is willing to overlook the incoherencies and instabilities of that paradigm.[56] Only then can the display of the doomed infertile homosexual body become the locus of assimilation of all those

---

55. Ibid., 265.

56. For a more expansive conceptualization of procreativity that affirms the complexity of "same-sex fecundity," see Goss, "Challenging."

persons, gay or straight, right or left, who challenge Rogers's claim to the Spirit and its promise.[57]

In the process, Rogers completely elides the reality of gay parenting in all its multiplying complexity. Homosexuality has never been nor is it now marked by abject childlessness; least of all is it an "unmistakable sign" of that abject condition, outside the context of the display of the homosexual as such an abject figure from the comfortable vantage of heterosexual viewpoint. Rogers's goal in part here seems to be to challenge the smug assertion by so many persons, Kass among them, of procreation as itself a kind of substitute satisfaction for the promise of resurrection. In this case, the more accurate criticism would be idolatry, the idolatrous celebration of the mortal self through mortal generation—a form of idolatry to which same-sex couples are as completely liable as opposite-sex couples. Instead Rogers fights for inclusion within heterosexuality as viewpoint by self-identifying as the very spectacular dead homosexual figure who is the asymmetrical embodiment of that viewpoint, and hence its security of invisibility. Rogers seeks an inclusion that is therefore structurally impossible, since the fight for it re-enables the very asymmetry that is seemingly resisted. And all of this is asserted in terms of a practically irrefutable appeal to the work of the Spirit.

In the end, Rogers's gesture toward those on the right and on the left who refuse to accept his "Word" is depressingly continuous with Captain Chesney's gouty reply to Lewis Carlton's request for Laura Chesney's hand in marriage, and Sir Harry Hotspur's resignation to the end of the glories of the House of Hotspur in the death of his daughter Emily. Sir Harry's troubles began, recall, with the loss of one child, and are only resolved by the loss of his other child, by his de facto childlessness, articulated as a relationship with God that secures the perverse asymmetry of values exemplified in sentimentality as viewpoint: "For himself he could die too— or even live if it were required of him!" Rogers's embrace of childlessness as a witness of the resurrection enacts the same asymmetrical values. His promised life in the Spirit, realized especially in marriage, weighs against the promised exclusion from that life of all those who refuse to acknowledge and celebrate this marriage, whether that marriage be to another person, or to the divine itself.

57. Rogers here is likely playing off an infamous exchange between Andrew Sullivan and Patrick Buchanan on the inconsistency, or not, of distinguishing heterosexual marital infertility from the functional non-procreativity of same-sex sexual relations. Sullivan, *Same-Sex*, 81–85.

(Rogers is clear throughout that marriage and monasticism—functional equivalents in the work of redemption—are the sole alternatives available.[58] His whole argument rests on a foundational dualism that enacts the prior exclusion elided in his use of the parable of the wedding feast, limiting his entire work to a debate among those who claim to be the "chosen," excluding from the outset as it does the typical sexual experience of so many people, gay or straight: "many are called but few are chosen.")

At the same time Rogers's barely suppressed fury is reminiscent of Captain Chesney's sputtering death threat. Captain Chesney had raged "I'd rather see *her* in her coffin than disgraced by contact with you." Rogers obediently jumps into that coffin, and then scolds anyone who gawks at his sentimental-homicidal-suicidal self-presentation. Rogers in this way joins Laura Chesney's willful temper with Emily Hotspur's willful submissiveness, to turn the tables and threaten his opponents with the very disgrace that characterizes the objection to improperly constituted marital relations: the disgrace of exclusion from relationship to God, where that relationship is imagined as the end of narration of intelligibly sexed self-identification. Like all marriage plots Rogers ends his work with a "Charge for a Wedding" that invites the characterization of his whole argument as an all too plausible plea for the possibility of gay and lesbian romance, where romance is construed as the celebration of a wedding feast made possible because somewhere else, safely out of sight, others are mourning. Roger's accomplishment is finally a spectacular proof that homosexual panic doesn't discriminate on the basis of sexual orientation.

Sentimental-Homicidal-Suicidal Unity in Christ

To the extent that marriage could, or even should, be imagined as a means of redemption, probably it would be better to do so only to the extent that

58. At stake more generally is the idealization of sexual relationship as form of sacrament. John Milbank, for example, in a critique of Reinhold Niebuhr on sin as sensuality, writes: "For all the subtle tracing of sensuality to self-obsession and self-escape, there is no counter-balancing understanding of sexual union as a paradigmatic, sacramental realization of self-transcending ecstatic love. Niebuhr makes the Protestant mistake of seeing *agape* as beyond and above *eros*, including sexual *eros*." Milbank, *Word*, 253 n. 25. The reference is to Niebuhr, *Nature*, 1:266 and the background for Niebuhr is the work of Anders Nygren, whereas the background for Milbank, and Rogers also, is Eastern Orthodox sacramentalist theology of sexuality and marriage. Nygren remains a common point of reference against which writers prove their affirmations of the God-relating significance of eros. See, for example, Burrus, "Introduction."

marriage could be imagined as beyond homo/heterosexual definition altogether—a goal that is only possible by first insistently exploring the immersion of redemptive claims for marriage within that very dynamic of homo/heterosexual definition, opening imagination of a hospitable future of marriage beyond the romance of innocent sexuality. In the meantime, Rogers's charity—at once so angry and devoid of humor—is most of all saddening, because it trades so fully on that uncharitable opposition Michael Warner explicates between "good gays" and "bad queers,"[59] pressing as it does an idealized goodness and innocence in marriage, same- or opposite-sex, that is predicated on the assimilation of all those who deny this ideal to a characterization of queer sexuality as an "anti-wedding feast." Such a characterization is only one depressingly short step from labeling all these persons celebrants of the "anti-Christ." It neatly underscores the need for a more genuine hospitality to redress the harms of exclusion that make ordinary wedding invitations possible. It is also not surprising, if not inevitable, that Rogers's plea for recon-ciliation/inclusion—or else!—is answered, by a prominent signatory of the Ramsey Colloquium's "Homosexual Movement," with a reciprocal gesture of violent exclusion masquerading as charity that lumps Rogers together with the bad queers from whom he so desperately seems to want to distance himself.

In a review of Rogers's book in the journal *First Things*, Gilbert Meilaender helpfully makes clear, in articulating the apparent depth of the gap between his own view of same-sex marriage, as representative of the Ramsey Colloquium, and Rogers's view, just how fully the partici-pants in this debate are locked in a sentimental-homicidal-suicidal death grip energized by the shared but unacknowledged investment of every-one concerned in the promise of intelligibility of the fiction of sex, as that promise is fulfilled in the marriage plots of the romance of innocent sexuality. Meilaender's review in this respect has the merit of owning plainly the terms of dispute that Rogers only obliquely allows. Given the irrefutable nature of appeals to the Spirit, one should at least sympatheti-cally note, immersed as Meilaender's response is in an exchange of tit-for-tat, that Rogers's style of charity has invited the inhospitable reception it receives. Meilaender fully admits Rogers's proposition that same-sex marriage poses a fundamental challenge to the identity of the church as the body of Christ. He therefore urges on exactly the sort of cultural

59. Warner, *Trouble*, 41–80.

warfare that Rogers, albeit under the banner of ecumenical peace, has himself been waging.[60] Meilaender rejects Rogers's argument by reducing it to a matter of truth versus falsehood: "To the extent that this is what the 'reconciled diversity' of mainline Protestantism means as an ecumenical program, it is unworthy of our support. A unity purchased so entirely at the cost of truth could not possibly be a unity 'in Christ.'"[61]

Though phrased in terms of "unity 'in Christ'" the "truth" Meilaender sets out to defend is no truth at all about God, but about the fiction of sex, and of heterosexuality, conceptualized in relation to *homo*-style homosexuality, as foundational to the possibility of human encounter with God.[62] The unity defended turns out not to be the unity of the church as the embodiment of Christ, but the unity of sex and body that makes a whole intelligible sexual self, as male or female—the unity, that is, of heterosexuality as coherent viewpoint of the disintegrated sinful self. With no modulation whatsoever, Meilaender simply paraphrases as a kind of "gospel truth" the writings of Karl Barth on "Man and Woman" that Rogers works so hard to contextualize within the frame of Barth's larger theological project. Following Barth, Meilaender asserts the privilege of heterosexual sexual orientation as constitutive of the possibility of orientation to God.[63] Likewise, whether by design or not, Meilaender follows Barth's additional insistent ordering of relations between the sexes as A

60. For summary analysis of the culture wars as eminently Victorian, see Armstrong, "Contemporary."

61. Meilaender, "What Sex Is," 49.

62. The place of marriage in Meilaender's writings resonates with the views advocated by the "Council on Biblical Manhood and Womanhood." His engagement with Rogers is one installment in a career of writing against theological affirmations of same-sex sexual relationship. The following is typical of those writings: "For the sake not only of those who have been baptized into Christ's body, but also for the sake of a world which, even if only inchoately, wants to follow the way of life, we have a responsibility to conform our public teaching to what we have ourselves been taught by Scripture about our creation as male and female and about marriage as the first of institutions. We have no authorization to do otherwise." Meilaender, *Things*, 76. This magisterial "authorization" of "sex" as the "way of life" echoes both the Council's view of the world-making activity of faithful fathers and Sir Harry Hotspur's self-surrender to the demands of heaven. Likewise it depends conceptually on the spectacle of homosexual death for its assertion of heterosexuality as live viewpoint. See also Meilaender, "First," and Meilaender, *Limits*, 115–29. Meilaender throughout his writings affirms a picture of public "spiritual" friendship between men as grounded in the "one flesh" of heterosexual marriage. See, for example, Meilaender, *Friendship*, 104–5.

63. For my own earlier critique of schematization of heterosexual orientation as opening on a divine perspective, see Rees, "In the Sight."

and B, the male always precedent over the female. The unity sought in Christ as a result becomes unawares a contest over identification with and desire of Christ as male. Homosexuality in this view is defined as a drastic impediment to love of God even as the God who is loved is homo-sexed, sexed the same as those who are commanded to love. Same-sex marriage is thereby imbued with extraordinary destructive significance; with the capacity to communicate an awful disgrace to opposite-sex marriage, destroying the Church from within. And the Church is yet one more "institutional crystallization"[64] of the power dynamics that sustain the imagination of heterosexuality as a viewpoint that opens onto a divine horizon, with Christ embroiled in the tensions of male homosocial relations. Love of Christ becomes a charged occasion for homosexual panic because an ultimate occasion for entitlement.

The survival of these power dynamics, Meilaender correctly notes, depends on the exclusion of homosexuality and the consequent denial of same-sex marriage as an intelligible relationship of human identities; though it also depends for its survival, as Meilaender unwittingly demonstrates, on the display of homosexual spectacle through the measured admission of the possibility of same-sex marriage. The declaration of faithfulness to the truth of sex as necessary basis of unity in Christ joins the suicidal and the homicidal in the desire for and identification with the figure of a dying man-God. Meilaender in this way is only articulating a commonplace view of heterosexual marriage and of homosexuality as its sinful exterior in theology, considered as one of the many disciplines whose productivity is fueled by the incoherency of homo/heterosexual definition. Nevertheless his frankness illuminates the understandable if regrettable exasperation and anger fueling Rogers's rather sanctimonious insistence that "gay and lesbian bodies" are every bit as capable of realizing love of God; that "gay and lesbian marriages" do not destroy, but build up the body of the Church, by their incorporation "into the body of Christ."

Meilaender's response to Rogers is further instructive because it neatly demonstrates how much both men are acting out narrations of the fiction of sex that are continuous with the nineteenth century novels considered earlier. Just as in those stories, the central point of contention is the appropriateness, or not, of the celebration of certain wedding feasts, whether of Laura Chesney and Lewis Carlton, Emily Hotspur and George Hostpur, or gay and lesbian couples in the twenty-first century.

64. Foucault, *History*, 93.

And also as in those stories, the worth of sex as narrated in marriage is affirmed through the sentimental-homicidal-suicidal production of a dead body, in this case one could say of the ultimate dead body, the body whose death represents the death of death.

It is noteworthy finally that with extraordinary intuitive facility Meilaender at the center of his argument tells a tale of nineteenth-century justifiable homicide that draws a direct link between the rise of no-fault divorce and current demands for same-sex marriage. This tale enables him to join the issue of same-sex marriage as fundamentally an issue of permissible and impermissible satisfaction of sexual desires in marriage—just that liberal conception of justice in sexual ethics typified by none other than Sigmund Freud himself:

> When eros overtakes us—even an eros that is not rightly ordered —no one should try to tell us that nothing significant has happened. Even a distorted eros bears traces of its divinity, and it may well seem ennobling. But we need to remind ourselves that this is true for many people, not just for gays and lesbians. The single man who has found no wife, who has begun to despair of ever finding a wife, and who finds himself in love with his neighbor's wife is experiencing something very significant indeed. It may even, in some respects, make him a better man than he has been heretofore. Her bodily embrace may seem for the first time in his life, really to persuade him that he is desired and wanted. Renunciation of that embrace may resemble for him "passing through something akin to dying." But it is to such renunciation that he must be directed. If, nevertheless, he does not repent and marries her, theirs is not a wedding feast that the Church should celebrate.[65]

The only way to deal with same-sex desire, according to this view, is to kill it; to silence the wrongful sex that is rudely generating these "distorted" desires in the body it inhabits. The faithful homosexual must pass "through something akin to dying," namely cease being a homosexual, as a precondition, both of membership in the church and of relationship to God. Charity for the homosexually sexed individual consequently is offered in the form of a homicidal wish for the homosexual to take up the matter suicidally. An obedient homosexual, like an obedient daughter (like Emily Hotspur or Mr. Grey's eldest little daughter) should die rather than insist on pursuing a forbidden marriage. This is a harsh allowance of

65. Meilaender, "What Sex Is," 46–47.

a solely negative value and meaningfulness for same-sex desire, a tough-luck view prevalent among more "sensitive" traditionalists. Meilander attempts to soften the harshness of this view, highlight its sensitivity, by constructing an example of failed heterosexual romantic love, but his example only reinforces the assumption of marriage as an especially desirable and privileged relationship, and also a domain of male power where the God-relating significance of a man's sex is as much a source of trouble as it is a source of entitlement. One must be an authentically sexed man in order to achieve unity in Christ, yet the cost of such unity to self is disavowal of the homo-identifications that make anyone a man in the first place, placing at risk of death the sex in whose name others' deaths are deemed worthy sacrifices.

The narrative Meilander invents is notable for the absence of all agency on the part of the "neighbor's wife." She is an object, another man's property. Should the unfortunate hero of this tale marry her—"they" do not marry; rather, "he" marries "her"—it wouldn't be the culmination of a love between two persons, but a wrong one man does to another, a wrong that must be repented, and presumably punished, by denial of cel-ebration of a wedding feast, by a failure, that is, of hospitality. A failure of hospitality that is formally related to the sinful failure of hospitality to be explored later in this book in an extended reading of David Copperfield's and King David's relations with Uriah Heep and Uriah the Hittite respec-tively. In Meilaender's tale, the reality of divorce and remarriage has been entirely erased, allowing him to conflate objections to same-sex marriage with social critique of divorce, evincing in the process a nostalgia for the more general authority of father's over marriage as portrayed in the nineteenth century novel.[66]

Introduction of the specter of divorce into argument about same-sex marriage—the specter of the wrongful and impermissible dissolution of marital bonds between man and woman—is telling. What seems to be wrong with the hero's desire, in Meilaender's narrative, is that it incites the woman to abandon her husband. (In his mention of "bodily embrace" Meilaender suggests that she has already done so; literally joining neigh-bor to neighbor in a vicarious knowledge-relation.) Likewise same-sex

66. The same conflation marks debate about other highly contested issues. It is strik-ing, for example, that in an essay ostensibly about abortion Paul Ramsey offers a sustained diatribe against no-fault divorce; and even explicitly relates this calamity to the rising specter of same-sex marriage. Ramsey, *Ethics*, 3–42, esp. 16.

sexual desire, when acknowledged and satisfied in marriage, is assumed to incite such an abandonment of husbands by their wives, revealing the disavowed identification with homosexuality that is integral to the identity of any heterosexual man. All of this is constructed in terms of a death threat to the homosexual whose desire poses so much danger. A desire that is also internal to the man himself, because the hero of this tale has committed what used to be called "criminal conversation" under the old common law of coverture, a rare legal instance where homicide was not only justified, but expected. In fact all male juries during the nineteenth century would consistently refuse to convict a disgraced husband who murdered the man who seduced his wife, presumably because to do so would be to deny to themselves exactly the same prerogative, just as it would be to disgrace for a second time any man who justifiably avenged the cause of his disgrace.[67] It is therefore no exaggeration to remark that much opposition to the celebration of same-sex marriage is founded on a threat of extraordinary violence to gay people in general, and same-sex couples in particular, through the targeting of same-sex sexual desire as an intolerable threat to the constitution of heterosexual sexual desire and its satisfaction in marriage, through a suicidal attempt to kill off that part of the self, that element of identification that renders self-identification as heterosexual male so convoluted and insecure.[68] Finally it is important to note that none of this argument involves ascriptions to anyone of latent sexual desires for persons of the same sex exactly, but only of desire for the identifications that make enjoyment of imaginative experience of self as an intelligible unity of men as men in Christ possible.

The obverse of this masculinist romantic debate between Rogers and Meilaender is the trajectory of romantic feminist ethics and theology that celebrates the erotic as a life-affirming power for women, and views men as death-obsessed and deathly afraid of this female life-affirming

67. Regarding the concept of "criminal conversation" and attendant "right to kill," see Hartog, *Man and Wife*, 136–42, 218–41.

68. A contemporary legal argument resonant of the "right to kill" is the Homosexual Panic Defense, most notably associated with the case of Jonathan Schmitz, who murdered his co-worker Scott Amedure in 1995, after Amedure revealed on national television that he had a "secret crush" on Schmitz. For analysis of this legal argument, see Suffredini, "Pride." Two highly publicized killings of same-sex couples are: the 1995 murder in Oregon of Roxanne Ellis and Michelle Abdill by Robert Acremont, and the 1999 murder in California of Gary Matson and Winfred Mowder by the brothers Benjamin Matthew Williams and James Tyler Williams.

power.[69] Admittedly historically important, this trajectory in the end merely flips the terms of the debate on behalf of women.[70] In its typical form, it is equally romantic as its counterpart and subject to the same critique. Against the claims of the husbands and fathers, it substitutes female sexed-identity as a privileged basis of God-relatedness. Consider, as example, the writings of Carter Heyward, an Epsicopal priest and professor of theology. Heyward's celebration of Edwina Sandys's sculpture Christa, unveiled in 1984 at the Cathedral of St. John the Divine in New York City, demonstrates how claims of gay and lesbian Christians to full and equal participation in the life of the church proceed through the sentimental narration of a sex that is valued as worth dying for. Heyward celebrates Christa as a *spectacle* of sexed female suffering that simultaneously enables assumption of a sexed female *viewpoint* that is liberating. Of the image of Christ on the cross, traditionally sexed as male, she writes: "Because the church has established itself as a custodian of misogynistic, erotophobic theological values, the body of Christ is losing its appeal for many faithful churchwomen. It is a dying symbol for some women because we are beginning to understand that it signifies death to eros, death to women, and violent death to erotically empowering women who touch one another's lives deeply."[71] In order for Christian women to realize a full expression of their sexed selves, Heyward argues, they need a symbol that adequately mediates that expression, where the fullness, the unity, of women's sexed self-expression is homosexually oriented, not in a reductively genital sense, but more expansively as "women who touch one another's lives deeply."

Heyward's argument is deeply informed by the idea of a "lesbian continuum" that ostensibly seeks to overcome any distinction between heterosexuality and homosexuality among women.[72] Yet the idea of a lesbian continuum assumes a sexed identity as female that enables all women to relate to each other along the continuum. The sameness concentrated in the term "homosexuality" thereby assumes an even greater importance

69. This trajectory spans from Daly, *Beyond* and *Gyn/Ecology* through Christ and Plaskow, *Womanspirit*, to Heyward, *Touching*, among many others. Daly's earliest work in turn relies heavily on Tillich, *Courage*. Despite the concerns raised here, Daly's scholarship is a continuing inspiration.

70. For parallel affirmations of eros and life in homosexually sexed male identity, see Ellison, *Erotic Justice*.

71. Heyward, *Touching*, 115.

72. Rich, "Compulsory."

as expressive medium of one's sex. Focusing on the endangered but also empowering possibility of women's sexed selves meaningfully "touching" each other in this expansive sense, Heyward frames the misogyny and erotophobia of the church as a life and death issue. In the process she is not so much articulating a prior, falsifiable truth of Christian history, as she is making that history and establishing the life and death importance of one's sex. It is only through the ascription of a murderous custodial history to the church that she is able to propose a reversal of life and death values through the substitution of the spectacle of Christa for the spectacle of Christ. Through simultaneous adoption of viewpoint on Christa as spectacle and identification with Christa as spectacle, she argues women can become empowered as properly sexed human beings. So she continues:

> Yet Christa possibly *can* represent our creativity/liberation, by becoming a symbol of our predicament, including our need for liberation. Christa can represent the very antithesis of what, historically, the church has taught about eros, women, and especially erotically empowered/empowering women. Christa can signal the opposite of what the church has taught, preached, and (dis)embodied in relation to women and sexuality. She can represent for Christian women precisely what the church has crucified with a vengeance, and what we must now raise up in our lives: *the erotic as power and the love of God as embodied by erotically empowered women.*[73]

At stake in this negotiation of viewpoint and spectacle are power relations. When refracted through the theoretical matrix of Foucault and Sedgwick, Heyward's assertion of the "erotic as power and love of God" concerns the power to determine the capacity of a homosexual orientation to express a properly sexed female self who can properly know and love God. Heyward's argument echoes Foucault's imagery of sex as "stigma" and "wound" that are an origin of intelligible personal identity, suggesting that the desired empowerment and stability of sexed identity is inherently contestable, because it can't authorize without also stigmatizing, because it can't empower without also wounding. In the stigma and wound of the spectacle of Christa, enjoyed from the vantage of viewpoint, life and death are joined. Their conjunction is then asserted

---

73. Heyward, *Touching*, 115 (emphasis added).

as a basis of homosexually sexed identity for all woman in the unity of Christa. Sexed identity as a woman is also always at risk of death.

In contrast to the arguments exemplified in Heyward's writings, a more supple and promising version of this reversal is developed by the feminist philosopher of religion Grace Jantzen:

> From all that has gone before, however, it is clear that a religious symbolic which functions to perpetuate a dream of masculine self-presence, where the male subject refuses to recognize his situatedness, his embodied sexuate self, and his unconscious fears and desires of death, is destructive on many counts. It is destructive in that it will nourish in such men the idea that it is their God-given right to dominate all (m)others, who will be oppressed thereby. It is destructive in that it allows no emergence of women subjects in relation to a female divine. And it is destructive of the men themselves, whose self-constitution as little godlings actually perpetuates their own fears and insecurities, and forecloses the adventure of openness to a divine horizon.[74]

In writing of "women subjects," Jantzen's critique of the "dream of masculine self-presence" need not imply the mere substitution of an alternate dream of "feminine self-presence." Just as her critique opens to view a "divine horizon," that horizon can call into question imagination of any form of sexed self-presence as a basis of imagination of God and of self in relation to God. One must therefore distinguish between the desire for God and the desire for a sex that is wrongfully imagined as guarantor of satisfaction of the desire for God.

Returning in conclusion to the central theses of Foucault's *History of Sexuality*, the desire in all these cases that must be satisfied or renounced is not some ontological force in the body demanding properly controlled expression but is a generative source of the sex—the little man or woman within—to whom this agency/urgency is ascribed. Debate about the permissibility or not of same-sex marriage, however much it is phrased in terms of the claims and counterclaims to justice in the satisfaction of sexual desires, is just one more chapter in the ongoing tragicomedy that is the history of sexuality. It is a drama of the desire for intelligibility that is internal to that history. To gain a solid theological grasp of that history, of its operations, it is now necessary to go back to the beginning literally. To return in earnest to the source of this crisis of intelligibility. A

---

74. Jantzen, *Becoming*, 173.

theology of original sin is necessary in order to demonstrate more fully how the idealization of marriage as a means of redemption fits within a master narrative of evasion of the problem of intelligibility—evasion of responsibility for sin—at its root.

5

The Hermeneutics of Sin

It is, however, an astounding thing that the mystery furthest from our ken, that of the transmission of sin, should be something without which we can have no knowledge of ourselves.

Without doubt nothing is more shocking to our reason than to say that the sin of the first man has implicated in its guilt men so far from the original sin that they seem incapable of sharing it. This flow of guilt does not seem merely impossible to us, but indeed most unjust. What could be more contrary to the rules of our miserable justice than the eternal damnation of a child, incapable of will, for an act in which he seems to have so little part that it was actually committed 6,000 years before he existed? Certainly nothing jolts us more rudely than this doctrine, and yet, but for this mystery, the most incomprehensible of all, we remain incomprehensible to ourselves. The knot of our condition was twisted and turned in that abyss, so that it is harder to conceive of man without this mystery than for man to conceive of it himself.

This shows that God, in his desire to make the difficulties of our existence unintelligible to us, hid the knot so high, or more precisely, so low, that we were quite unable to reach it. Consequently it is not through the proud activity of our reason but through its simple submission that we can really know ourselves.[1]

1. Pascal, *Pensées*, 35–36.

Original Sin and Genealogical Inquiry

AMONG THE NUMEROUS SUPPOSED villains in the history of sex-phobic Christian writers, Saint Augustine stands apart, for both the purported reach of his influence and the depth of animus directed at that influence. Despite an ever-deepening contemporary conversation with Augustine—some speak in terms of an Augustinian revival—the constructive possibilities of Saint Augustine's writings for theological discourse on sexuality remain an under-explored terrain. In large part this neglect follows from the tendency to read Augustine on the sexed human body anachronistically through the lens of *Confessions*. Readings of Augustine are typically structured around the twin theses that Foucault critiques in his *History of Sexuality*. Augustine is then all too conveniently regarded as a proto-typical case study of the problem of repression as necessary for controlling sexual desire, and vilified as the most influential proponent of an unduly repressive and unliberated tradition of teachings on bodily pleasure in sexual relationship.[2] All of which in turn culminates in the accusation that Augustine, in the words of one recent author, "aligns himself with an already waxing Christian asceticism, which seeks to imitate Jesus as God without meditating on his body."[3] This kind of commentary has become so commonplace it is easy almost to miss its boldness—at least until one starts to investigate more thoroughly how the complaint that Augustine narrates his return to God at the cost of a turn away from the "bonds of erotic flesh"[4] is itself apiece with narrations of the romance of innocent sexuality.

A more forward-looking reading of Augustine on sexed identity and encounter with God begins by looking backward and reconstructing the place of human sexuality in the history of humanity's common

2. Notable examples of contemporary scholars who paint a picture of Augustine as a sex-phobic Christian father, and as the root of most of what is wrong in the history of Christian sexual ethics, are Pagels, *Adam*, and Ranke-Heinemann, *Eunuchs*. Much of Pagels's argument is devoted to vindication of both Julian and Pelagius against the judgment of a history too dominated by Augustine's influence. For critical response to Pagels that focuses on Augustine's earlier writings, and hence questions Pagels's focus on Julian and Pelagius, see Hunter, "Augustinian Pessimism." For response to Pagels and Ranke-Heinemann, see Lamberigts, "Critical Evaluation." For additional characteristic feminist criticisms of Augustine, see Brooten, *How Natural*, Bordo, *Unbearable Weight*, 144–48, and Heyward, *Touching*, 88–90. For recent more constructive appraisals, though still tinged throughout with distrust, see the essays collected in Stark, *Feminist*.

3. Jordan, "Flesh," 37.

4. Jordan, "Flesh," 386 n. 16.

origin and fall as revealed in Scripture.[5] Whereas a lot of commentary focuses on Augustine's depiction of sexual desire as a physical inscription onto the body of humanity's original disobedience, and then dismisses this view as a wrongful generalization from distinctively male sexual experience (or, as in the example of Leon Kass, recapitulates it), at the heart of the matter is the association of sexuality with sin in terms of the created and historical conditions of an inheritable original sin. It is therefore important to emphasize that this original sin was *not* sexual. Instead, through a metaphor of illumination Augustine describes the Fall as a kind of epistemic disobedience, as a willful choice of ignorance over knowledge, as a deliberate step away from light and order and into darkness and disorder, a step that begins in a fundamental refusal to own the source of intelligible human identity: "This then is the original evil: man regards himself as his own light, and turns away from that light which would make man himself a light if he would set his heart on it."[6] Original sin, Augustine insists, is an epistemic catastrophe because knowledge of self is only possible when the self lives in obedient community with God. Prideful and disobedient rejection of human community with God, for the sake of pursuit of individual and private benefits, forms the starting point of all human self-identification after Adam and Eve. One cannot know oneself without also knowing oneself as culpably sinful, as disgraced, so that one even seeks to hide that exposure of self from one's own gaze by fixing it in fictions, sex among them.

Sexuality as a result in fallen humanity does not concern stubborn and ungovernable libidinal drives, but concerns the impossibility of the constitution of the whole individual as an intelligible unity after the fall. Peter Brown summarizes the later Augustinian view adopted in these pages:

> It is no longer man divided between the "higher" and "lower"
> self. Rather, in sexuality itself, singled out as an area of the person
> that took men and women, singly or together, into the most intimate and puzzling contact with the body, Augustine had planted
> a reflection of an ideal of human community—a great partnership of loving wills opened to the service of others and of God,

5. In addition to the remarkable work by Schuld, *Foucault and Augustine*, a briefer but notable recent constructive engagement with Augustine on sexuality is Mackendrick, "Carthage." Roberts, *Creation,* is also notable for its insistently positive enrollment of Augustine *in support* of claims regarding the created intelligibility of sexed identity and its joyful completion in marriage.

6. Augustine *City of God* 14.13 (Bettenson, 573).

tragically eroded, fissured and darkened in its deepest hopes of
unity by the proud turning of the loveless self to private joy, to
private purposes, to private mastery, to the exclusion of others,
of God's vast store of goods. In this, Augustine on sexuality looks
forward directly, not to Freud, but to those far greater, if far less
comforting giants of our recent past—to Rousseau, to Hegel, and
to Karl Marx.[7]

The hard wisdom of this view of human community is that the "ero-
sion" and "fissure" and "darkening" of human unity is at the same time a
signifier of the genuine unity of humanity, which shares its origin in the
sexual community of Adam and Eve. Sexuality is recognized as integral to
the very possibility of human community, and at the same time to the imperfectability of humanity, understood as the impossibility of recovery or
current realization of that human community in God which was forfeited
by Adam and Eve. In this way the Augustinian association of sexuality and
sin has much affinity with accounts of sexual experience developed by such
queer theoretical authors as Leo Bersani, when he writes: "It is possible to
think of the sexual as, precisely, moving between a hyperbolic sense of self
and a loss of all consciousness of self."[8] The limit of this affinity however is
that Bersani and others (drawing on the writings of Jacques Lacan) regard
the sexual as a dalliance with an unbearable ultimate enjoyment that is
beyond any signification. From an Augustinian perspective, by contrast,
their descriptions of the sexual attest the significance of original sin and
its literal inheritance as a condition of the self that is always failing in its
achievement of satisfactory self-identification. So that the enjoyment one
seeks but also always postpones, because its enjoyment both makes the
self and destroys the unrepentant self, is unity of self in God.

Reading Augustine on sexuality and original sin leads to a summary of the sinfulness of sexuality, not as the physical experience of lust,
but as the sinful fantasy of privatized monopoly of relationship to God,
epitomized in much theological discourse on sexuality by a novelistic
obsession with romantic narratives of sexual relationship that culminate
in marriage. To understand the place of the romantic imagination of marriage in the history of sexuality, it is therefore necessary to explicate the
problem of original sin that marriage is mistakenly and sinfully presumed
to solve. And to do so it is necessary to reaffirm that the finitude of the

7. Brown, *Augustine and Sexuality*, 11–12.
8. Bersani, *Rectum*, 218.

body in time is not in itself suspect. All evil, Augustine famously explains, "has no existence except as a privation of good, down to that level which is altogether without being."[9] Existence is therefore by definition good, as all that exists is created by God. Yet this account, when joined with Augustine's imagination of a hierarchy of being, has sometimes led read-ers to misconstrue the relationship between the corruptibility of all being that is lesser than God with the privation of good that is evil. The problem is condensed in Augustine's statement: "Therefore either corruption does not harm, which cannot be the case, or (which is wholly certain) all things that are corrupted suffer privation of some good."[10] The trap here is to conflate corruption of being with privation of some good, as if corrupt-ibility necessarily erodes away at the being of that which is corrupted. The privation of good that concerns Augustine is not so much a loss of being as it is a disorder of the being that one is, and that one brings upon oneself. So he explains: "Yet I was at fault, Lord God, order and creator of all things in nature, but of sinners only the orderer."[11] The present point to establish is that one can't sin oneself out of existence, as if every time one sins one corrupts further one's being. One's being is always good, but is disordered, and precisely because God sustains the goodness of one's created being it is possible persistently to disorder that being. To be corruptible is not to be evil, but to be susceptible to the disorder that ensues from sin. And that disorder begins with the original sin of Adam and Eve.

Before proceeding to further reading of Augustine, it will also help to situate this investigation in relation to a distinctive feature of much queer commentary.[12] To many persons, a turn to beginnings, to talk of Adam and Even and Eden, to the literal sense of Scripture and consequently to a theology of original sin, will appear suspect on multiple grounds. (Even those persons who are in many ways disposed favorably to this project will likely find it at least a steep uphill argument.) Objections to such a turn concentrate in the worry that any appeal to origins can only end by reduplicating—in however attenuated a form—the set of reversals that are the continuing history of sexuality. The obligation of the writer

---

9. Augustine *Confessions* 3.7.12 (Chadwick, 43).

10. Augustine *Confessions* 7.12.18 (Chadwick, 124).

11. Augustine *Confessions* 1.10.16 (Chadwick, 12).

12. For influential statements on the powers of queer commentary—as opposed to a gay and lesbian identity politics—see Berlant and Warner, "What Does Queer Theory Teach?" and "Sex in Public."

of queer commentary, according to this point of view, is continually to expose those reversals, perpetually to challenge the sanctification of the spatio-temporal effects of power relations as their self-justifying origins, and relentlessly to destabilize any and all claims to faithful attendance to ordinances of creation. This worry assumes that the perpetuation of those reversals always somehow remains objectionable, even if unavoidable. The result is a constructive ambivalence toward ethics. Resignation to these reversals, though an option, is not advocated.[13] An imperative of resistance is to some degree assumed as a motive of theorizing, as the motive specifically of that mode of critical inquiry typically designated as genealogy and here construed as a form of queer commentary.[14]

Implicit in the enterprise of genealogical critique, its imperative of resistance is not always clearly articulated. To the extent that it is ever named, it is characterized as a refusal to engage in just that sort of inquiry that the term genealogy itself seems to suggest, that is, any assertion of the diagnostic importance to contemporary human relations of a distant occurrence in the history of the human species. Echoing the concerns voiced by Richard Rorty, so other critics have complained of the seeming inconsistency of this mode of inquiry, as encapsulated in the following summary statement by Judith Butler:

> To expose the foundational categories of sex, gender, and desire as effects of a specific formation of power requires a form of critical inquiry that Foucault, reformulating Nietzsche, designates as "genealogy." A genealogical critique refuses to search for the origins of gender, the inner truth of female desire, a genuine or authentic sexual identity that repression has kept from view; rather, genealogy investigates the political stakes in designating as an *origin* and *cause* those identity categories that are in fact the *effects* of institutions, practices, discourses with multiple and diffuse points of origin.[15]

---

13. For self-conscious reflection on this ambivalence, see Butler, "Ethical Ambivalence."

14. On the import of genealogy as a "research activity," see Foucault, *Power/Knowledge*, 78–108. For discussion of the perplexity of deriving normative ethical imperatives from Foucault's genealogical writings, see the three essays gathered in Fraser, *Unruly Practices*, 15–66. For pointed discussion of the relevance of genealogy to feminist theory in practice, see Benhabib, *Feminist*, and Butler and Scott, *Feminists Theorize*. On the etymology of the term "genealogy," see Kottman, "Introduction," xxviii n. 37.

15. Butler, *Gender*, xxix.

As a warning of the pitfalls and dangers of searching for explanatory origins, the relevance of genealogical critique to theological discourse on sexuality is compelling.[16] Especially given the continual citation of Genesis as an armament against claims of gay and lesbian enfranchisement. It is bad enough, many will no doubt object, that the history of the doctrine of original sin is a history of fear of the body and of fear of sex. But that history of fear targets specifically and destructively homosexuality. A history that has been considered indicative of the sinfulness of hetero-sexual intercourse within marriage is now routinely and repeatedly cited as indicative of the privileged originary status of male-female difference as a norm of sexual ethics. Even as the pseudo-scientific categorization of homosexuality as mental illness dissolves to the margins of reputable medical practice, the categorization of same-sex sexual relations as inher-ently "unnatural" continues to dominate current legislative and other de-bates, in tandem with arguments concerning biblical interpretation. Yet a reconsideration of pessimistic interpretation of Genesis enables criticism of contemporary biblical interpretation that is organized by the terms of homo/heterosexual definition.

Despite the dubious history of the search for explanatory origins as solution to disagreement about issues in sexual ethics, and the suspi-cion this history warrants of any appeals to beginnings, the objection to genealogy as a form of "critical inquiry" remains: that however incisive the critique, it is ultimately self-defeating, because it refuses to own the unstated ethical imperatives that motivate this inquiry in the first place. Alasdair MacIntyre succinctly identifies the seemingly fatal inconsistency internal to genealogy, when he ask of genealogical inquiry the following pair of rhetorical questions:

> Hence once again it seems to be the case that the intelligibility of genealogy requires beliefs and allegiances of a kind precluded by

16. From its beginnings in the development of source criticism in the eighteenth cen-tury, scholarship of religion has been obsessed with questions of origins. This concern is mirrored in much evolutionary biology and primate anthropology. Regarding the former, see Masuzawa, *Dreamtime*. Regarding the latter, see Harraway, *Simians*, 21–108. Feminist scholarship has also taken up the quest for origins, for example in the historical critique of patriarchy by Lerner, *Creation*, and the "recovery" of Lillith in particular and the goddess in general in Christ and Plaskow, *Womanspirit*. The emergence of gay and lesbian history is marked by a similar concern to assert a visible past, convincingly in many respects with regard to the nineteenth and twentieth centuries, as documented in Katz, *History*, and Blasius and Phelan, *Everywhere*.

the genealogical stance. Foucault's carrying forward of Nietzsche's enterprise has thus forced upon us two questions: Can the genealogical narrative find any place within itself for the genealogist? And can genealogy, as a systematic project, be made intelligible to the genealogist, as well as to others, without some at least tacit recognition being accorded to just those standards and allegiances which it is its avowed aim to disrupt and subvert?[17]

The gist of these questions is twofold. First, that the "intelligibility of genealogy" founders on a core inconsistency. Second, that such inconsistency, when exposed to truly honest critical inquiry, is insupportable. Genealogy as a form of critical inquiry is presumed to be intellectually confused at best and more likely intellectually dishonest and destructive, in the sense that its very possibility depends on the "tacit recognition" of "standards and allegiances" that the genealogist at the same has "avowed" to "disrupt and subvert." Honesty and consistency are invoked as standards of intelligibility that genealogy is judged too queer to meet.[18]

In defense of the genealogist one could try and address these questions by attempting to develop an internally consistent account of the genealogist, and by attempting to articulate systematically and then justify those "standards and allegiances" that are formative of genealogical critique. To proceed along such a path, however, is unquestioningly to accept as realizable, in an unproblematized manner, the ideals of honesty and consistency assumed in these questions. A theology of original sin in its queerness rightfully and productively, I believe, continually calls into question the practicability of any and all such claims to realize honesty and consistency, no matter how much they remain desirable as ideal standards of moral argument. This is not to deny the viability and necessity of partial approximations to honesty and consistency as present possibilities; it is only to insist on their incompleteness. The refusal that is the characteristic gesture of genealogy must be explicated, not as a direct answer to the criticisms of MacIntyre and others, but as presentation of a mature humorous alternative to the very mode of inquiry those criticisms

17. MacIntyre, *Three Rival Versions*, 55. Augustine voices similar complaints about "suspicion" against those who question the authority of Scripture, in "Of the Morals of the Catholic Church" in Augustine, *Manichaean Heresy*, ch. 29.

18. For general response to the accusation that Foucault's work, especially as political epistemology, is fatally self-contradictory, see May, *Between*, 69–127.

typify.[19] Accusations of dishonesty and inconsistency are then opportunities for charitable anger instead of indignation and recrimination.

In its most practical and pressing sense, the refusal articulated by Judith Butler is not equivalent to a necessary denial that such a thing as origins exists, but is a refusal to excuse oneself from the political stakes that always attend appeals to origins. Genealogical writers in this sense can rightfully claim a kind of honesty that their critics often cannot, in their avowed engagement with questions of truth and of origins as struggles of power *and* reason. Whether acknowledged as such or not, grass-roots politics is grounded in this identification of commitment to truth with necessary political struggle. As important as appeals to consistency are when addressing issues of justice as fairness, when the issue is philosophical critique of power, then the plaint for consistency starts to look irrelevant and even self-defeating. When the hoards have already bridged the moat and are pounding the castle gates, the whole pile shaking to its foundation under the patterned force, it really misses the point to call the insurrectionary assault inconsistent since its leaders chose as their battering ram a great tree that had been planted generations ago by a noble ancestor. It might make more sense instead to try and figure out why they're so incensed. It might make more sense also to wonder and worry about what is being resisted, rather than level a charge of inconsistency against figures who would very likely consider such a charge affirmation of the generative power of further resistance.

MacIntyre is therefore too hasty when he immediately rushes to the conclusion that "the history of genealogy has been, and could not have been other than, one of progressive impoverishment."[20] Such a conclusion is only justified if one believes that the progressive extension of rights and benefits represents an "impoverishment" of some traditional ideal of community. Nonetheless, even the most ardent proponent of such progressive politics might still argue that this history of expanding political enfranchisement is the result of a searching and stringent *adherence* to and *avowal* of those "standards and allegiances" that genealogy presumably dishonestly and inconsistently refuses to acknowledge. A more inclusive politics is presumed to follow from ever improving consistency and

19. For a summary articulation of the *constructive* value of Foucault's writings as resource that enriches an Augustinian ethic of epistemic humility in the pursuit of justice, see Schuld, *Foucault and Augustine*, 207–20.

20. Macintyre, *Three Rival Versions*, 55.

honesty in the administration of justice. Genealogy then stands accused of claiming credit for the positive benefits of precisely those ideals that it disowns, proving yet again its dishonesty and inconsistency.[21]

In the end, regardless of how much they might otherwise differ regarding a wide range of practical and theoretical questions, traditionalist and communitarian critics of genealogy, as well as their progressive counterparts, at least agree in their shared repudiation of genealogy. They are also likely to agree that progressive politics, whether to be embraced or resisted, could not possibly follow from belief in one of the most apparently irrational and anti-progressive tenets of traditional Christian doctrine: the assertion of descent to all human beings through literal inheritance by sexual reproduction of an original sin of Adam and Eve in Eden. In each case they assume as an essential ingredient of any intelligible moral inquiry a standard of honesty and consistency that a literalistic interpretation of original sin complicates. The theology of original sin does not renounce the normative force of honesty and consistency. But it does treat them as self-critical dispositions, and ultimately judges all claims to realize them as performative failures.

In my own reading of genealogical critique, I find a similar insistence on disposition and the performative limitations of moral inquiry. Typically this insistence remains muted, inviting the criticism that such critique assumes a logical impossibility, because it assumes the foundational importance of a proposition that is at the same time asserted as unintelligible and impossible, as if hasty citation of the principle of non-contradiction were enough to undo such theorizing at its root, as if the thoughtful proponent of a genealogical stance were unaware of this seeming contradiction, couldn't knowingly embrace such contradiction. The argument that follows, however analytical and logical it attempts to be, does not finally aim to resolve this contradiction, but to argue its irreducible necessity to moral inquiry, to the diagnosis of the problem of intelligibility that is at the heart of the history of sexuality but that is not at all unique to that history.[22]

21. This accusation seems to drive the infamous assault on Judith Butler in Nussbaum, "Professor."

22. In many ways my approach follows Bourdieu's critique of the incapacity of all "logical criticism" to explicate the practices it presumes to criticize when such criticism remains "ignorant of its objective truth as literary reading" (Bourdieu, *Outline*, 156–58). Bourdieu's point is that many philosophers (moral and otherwise) make a solipsistic error when they assume that standards of "consistency" that hold for analytic purposes of semantic analysis

Presumption of Intelligibility Versus
Confession of Unintelligibility

Genealogical critique, engaged theologically, is not an imperative of creation per se, but an imperative of fallen creation. It assumes as a matter of faith, not reason, the ultimate unintelligibility of human being as discerned through the exercise of any human capacities whatsoever. The observation remains that sexuality is the especial realm in which the problem of intelligible personal identity currently concentrates; but sexuality may, and in fact predictably will, ultimately dissolve into some alternative set of arrangements. Hence the necessary imagination of a future without sex, even as such a future remains practically unimaginable from a contemporary vantage point. Even in the event of the inevitable dissolution of current formulations of problems of intelligible personal identity as effects of the operations of sexuality, the reality of sin will remain unchanged. To assert the inherent sinfulness of sexuality is therefore not finally to claim anything inherent about sexuality, but about human nature; or rather about the nature of that shifting ground which is continually invoked as human nature. Talk about human nature as fallen human nature, as that which in itself compels only its own critique, is an indispensable component of a genealogical inquiry into the problem of original sin.

Still the questions loom large: How can it be possible meaningfully to assert as an imperative of moral inquiry the apparently self-contradictory and incoherent claim that fallen human identity is finally and utterly unintelligible? And how, in turn, is it possible to affirm the fragmentary intelligibility one can seek in God and all the while deny the possibility of any comprehensively intelligible personal identity apart from God? What self if any exists who can issue such claims? Especially when, as the readings of the previous chapter demonstrate, appeals to God-relatedness are generally suspect as lethally non-humorous attempts to stabilize intelligible self-identification through the sentimental-homicidal-suicidal narration of a fictitious sex?

---

are also necessarily applicable standards for evaluation of generative practices. These philosophers thereby miss the productive indeterminacies and homologies that constitute a logic of practice at the same as they thereby underwrite for themselves an unfounded confidence in their own intellectual superiority. In relation to Bourdieu's point, Sedgwick's accomplishment is that she avoids (or corrects) the mistake of such philosophers. She analyzes the function of homo/heterosexual definition, precisely in its logical inconsistency, as a generative practical logic that structures definition of the homosocial continuum according to male-female difference. See Sedgwick, *Epistemology*, 185 and *Between*, 192.

These are profoundly perplexing questions, challenges as much, if not more, to faith than to reason, because irresolvable by rational means. Much theology of original sin consequently appeals as argument directly to the pragmatic sense, and not the doctrinal disposition, of its audience. According to this line of argument, the reader is invited to own the truth, however rationally improbable, of some formulation of the doctrine of original sin, because it explains so much, rather than because it critiques so much. An exemplary summary statement of this dominant approach to a theology of original sin is provided by Alistair McFadyen:

> It is our incorporation into this practical atheism which explains how it is that many will be bemused by the claim that the doctrine of sin holds not just meaning, but explanatory power for us today. Our pragmatic atheism seems to me to offer the most viable explanation of the impotence and public irrelevance of the language of sin. Other ways of accounting for the public meaninglessness of Christian talk of sin fail, in the end, to take the *secularity* of our culture as a form of pragmatic atheism at all seriously as a source of resistance to it. Consequently, they fail also to give sufficient weight to the essentially *theological* nature of the language of sin. Merely changing the categories through which it is presented so that it accords with the psychological or moral consciousness of the age cannot rehabilitate the doctrine of sin. The real problem is the loss of God's active and dynamic relation to the world as the necessary correlate without which any form of human experience or consciousness may become a form of sin-consciousness. The task facing theology is consequently more radical than correlating the traditional forms of doctrinal expression with culturally predominant ways in which the pathological is understood. The theological task cannot then be reduced to the changing of its language pattern of basic conceptuality, in order to render it more meaningful to the supposed psychological and cultural forms of consciousness prevailing in contemporary Western culture. The meaninglessness of the language of sin in our secular culture issues a challenge to Christian faith and theology: to show that reference to God holds explanatory and descriptive power; that it invokes and enables a more truthful relation to reality in both theory and practice. It is that claim which this book, in a small way, sets out to test.[23]

Like many other recent writers on original sin, McFadyen's "claim" of the "explanatory power" of the "doctrine of sin" seems to be motivated

23. McFadyen, *Bound*, 9–10.

in large part by dismay at the "impotence and public irrelevance of the language of sin." His whole argument, though explicitly framed as an attempt to "explain" the "pathologies" of child sexual abuse and the holocaust of Nazi Germany, is also implicitly framed as a contest for political power: the power to define and regulate the terms of meaningful public speech. This contest in turn presumes an essential opposition between atheism and faith, and the correlation of the former with secular culture and the governing authorities, the latter with faithful witness against that culture and minority critique of those authorities.

When McFadyen complains of other persons' attempts to explain why "Christian talk of sin" is mostly "impotent" and "irrelevant" for public political purposes that they fail to recognize that "secularity" is really just a cover for a "pragmatic atheism" that is not at all neutral with regard to Christian doctrine, but actively hostile and resistant, he is criticizing his Christian compatriots for their own failure of "resistance" to this dominant "pragmatic atheism," and at the same time proposing just such a program of resistance. The cornerstone of that resistance is summarized as a steadfast insistence on the "essentially *theological* nature of the language of sin." Considered in itself, this assertion is indisputable. To talk about sin is by definition to say something about God, in a way that talking about psychology, morality, and pathology is not.

The oddity of this assertion, however, is that its very meaningfulness, as McFadyen issues it, depends on the opposition between secularism and faith, at the same time that it privileges faith for pragmatic-epistemological reasons that are characteristically secular. This form of argument for the meaningfulness of the doctrine is implicated in the very foundational opposition that it assumes. Yet from the vantage of faith, and of belief in the doctrine of original sin, more fully imagined, no such simple opposition exists. Instead what McFadyen labels "pragmatic atheism" is better labeled as "sin-*un*consciousness," assuming that God is never alienated from God's creation, however much that creation may alienate itself from its creator.

Atheism in this framework is so entirely defined in relation to classical theism that the very "meaninglessness" McFadyen worries over is actually a form of meaningful speech about God, as a denial of God, because it is also structured by the opposition between atheism and faith.[24] When

24. See Jantzen, *Becoming*, 59–76, for critique of dominant practices in philosophy of religion in similar terms. These practices enforce a binary opposition between an all-

McFadyen then asserts the capacity of the language of sin to explain and describe, he unwittingly exemplifies the instability and contradictoriness of defining a "challenge" to "faith and theology" in terms of an opposition between the secular and the theological, as if the "conceptuality" of one could be neatly isolated from the "conceptuality" of the other, and then each tested against some pragmatic explanatory standard of truth that looks a lot like outmoded philosophy of science: may the most comprehending paradigm win.

This opposition is especially out of place, in a theology of original sin, because the doctrine is a definite kind of ethical universalism that pointedly intends to undermine dichotomies, exclusions, exceptions. It is a fundamental assertion about the ground and starting point for ethical analysis of all human relations, in every realm, public and private, secular and religious. It does not exactly "enable a more truthful relation to reality," in the sense of providing a competitive edge in some contest for "explanatory and descriptive power." Rather it issues an imperative to approach ethical inquiry with a particular disposition, a particular favorable prejudice towards certain styles of explanation and description that bear much in common with contemporary genealogical critique. It is therefore important, when asserting the meaningfulness of the doctrine of original sin, and the appropriateness of associating sexuality with sin, to question any presumed opposition between secularity and faith, because so much of the present history of sexuality is premised on this opposition; is premised on a shared narrative of the progressive liberation of sexual relationship from the misconceptions and superstitions of a repressive Christian tradition. Secular and religious discourse are conjointly determined by their failure to ask the question Foucault poses early in his *History of Sexuality*: "It is certainly legitimate to ask why sex was associated with sin for such a long time—although it would remain to be discovered how this association was formed, and one would have to be careful not to state in a summary and hasty fashion that sex

---

powerful "Father" God and no God at all, and thereby enforce a masculinist theological imaginary. For classic critique of that imaginary see, Daly, *Beyond*. An alternative to the opposition McFadyen assumes between secularism/pragmatic atheism on the one hand and theism on the other hand, is the account of "theism and atheism as fraternal enemies centered on a common idol, i.e. 'God' of 'being'" developed by Marion, *God*, esp. 54–60. An additional alternative is to treat atheism as a mode of "ultimate concern" such that "God can be denied only in the name of God," as explicated by Tillich, *Dynamics*, 45–46.

was "condemned"—but we must also ask why we burden ourselves today with so much guilt for having once made sex a sin."[25]

The theology of original sin presses the question: What does all the "guilt for once having made sex a sin" signify? It begins with the assumption that the responsibility for original sin, shared by all humanity in common, is real, but not necessarily fixed in its association with any discrete realm of human experience, though necessarily experienced as fixed in some dominant form of experience. The sex that Saint Augustine associated with sin is not the same sex dissociated from sin in the romance of innocent sexuality. Yet it is not possible to understand the latter without understanding how it shapes to its own purposes conceptualization of the former.

Contemporary imagination of the meaning of the Augustinian association of sexuality with sin is a crucial ingredient in the attempt to displace the shame that concentrates in that association. Only then can the Augustinian association be discredited as a mistake, as some sort of failure of understanding of what sex and sexuality are. By contrast, recovery of the meaningfulness of that association is not an attempt to discover what Augustine really meant to say about the sexed human body and about sin. It deliberately resists the quixotic and deficient pursuit of some original text or definitive reading, and focuses instead on the texts as loci of ongoing debates and readings, as occasions for reflection and insight in the name of "Augustine," where that name designates less an historical individual of undeniable influence, and more a tradition of interpretation and orientation described by Charles T. Mathewes as a "Hermeneutics of Charity."[26] Working within such a framework, the goal is not to cite Augustine as an irrefutable authority supporting one's own chosen view of any number of cases, but sympathetically and creatively to locate one's present moment of thought within the "stream of argument"[27] that Augustine, broadly construed, represents.

Augustine remains a compelling figure to address because for better and for worse—the reference to the marriage ceremony seems apt here—theological discourse on sexuality remains immersed in this stream of argument, even though the most popular form of self-conscious engagement is to treat the Augustinian association of sexuality and sin as a

25. Foucault, *History of Sexuality*, 9.

26. The starting point in Augustine is *Confessions* 12.25.35 (Chadwick, 265).

27. Mathewes, "Original Sin," 40.

series of mistakes that would be laughable if not so pernicious in their immediate effects and lasting influence. Romantic marriage has been the primary context of the attempt to correct the Augustinian tradition and surmount its baneful influence. Religious and secular claims regarding marriage are equally invested in the project of dissociating sex from sin, of exonerating the worth of sex against the charge of sin and the attendant burden of guilt which persistently haunts it. It is therefore more accurate to describe any seeming "meaninglessness of the language of sin" bemoaned by McFadyen and others as a dimension of a "pragmatic theism" that characterizes romantic imagination of marriage, in both its secular and religious contexts, whether one is fighting for or against the inclusion of same-sex couples.

Whether acknowledged as such or not, marriage constitutes a theological as much as a social or political problem. It is a primary context for the working out of the denial of responsibility for original sin. Worrying about some seeming exclusion of talk about God from public discourse does not contribute much to understanding of the negative theological significance of marriage. Instead the task is to discern the ways in which that discourse already is a form of talk about God. Insisting on a dichotomy of atheism versus faith, secular versus religious, otherwise only functions to intensify the privatization of God-relation that such insistence seems to lament, as it accepts without question the pressure to dissociate sexuality from sin.

Whatever the meaningfulness of the language of sin, according to the view in question, it cannot be furthered or productively engaged when burdened by the traditional-seeming emphasis on sexuality. Better to talk about such spectacular horrors as the holocaust or child sexual abuse than the ordinary romantic quest of the individual for unity of sexed personal identity through a more perfect union with another person of the same or opposite sex. Yet it is because the stakes associated specifically with sex are so very high that the resistance to association of sexuality with sin presents a critical point of insight into the continuing meaningfulness of their association and its centrality to debates regarding sexuality and marriage. Likewise, an insistence on the meaningful association of sexuality and sin theologically enriches analysis of sexuality as the context of pursuit of a structurally impossible intelligible selfhood.

Again, however, this is not so much to urge the "explanatory and descriptive power" of a "language of sin," as it is to urge that consistency and honesty as ideals of moral inquiry are actually less important than confession and repentance as the starting points of such an inquiry. If the result also includes enriched explanation and description, this follows from the admission and acceptance of an irresolvable contradictoriness as the *sine qua non* of responsible moral inquiry in the first place. More important, consistency and honesty, as indispensable values of moral inquiry, receive altered emphasis. They are not so much terms of analytic evaluation, but of moral disposition. Honesty now primarily signifies allowance of one's dependent immersion in the mystery of unintelligibility denoted by original sin. Consistency now signifies refusal to claim any exceptions on one's own behalf from the dynamic of sin one is exploring. In Augustine's own words, the difference between the critics of genealogy and those who embrace it theologically is the "difference between presumption and confession, between those who see what the goal is but not how to get there and those who see the way which leads to the home of bliss, not merely as an end to be perceived but as a realm to live in."[28]

To engage a theology of original sin is deliberately to put oneself at risk, to invite charges of contradiction, inconsistency, irresolvability that one cannot fully answer. It is to reevaluate contradiction and consistency, and to accept irresolvability in the sense of incompletion. To engage a theology of original sin is, most of all, to embrace such incompletion as the most one can accomplish, so that success is measured more by the constructive humorous space one opens for charitably angry criticism and correction in turn by one's successors than by the conclusiveness of one's own arguments.

As an inheritable reality and inescapable condition of moral inquiry, original sin combines an imperative of resistance with a theory of what is to be resisted, where the imperative precedes and informs the theory. Willing assumption of responsibility for original sin precedes the attempt to account for the meaningful conditions of that responsibility. The imperative is always to remain accountable. What must be resisted is not the persistence of sin itself—a human impossibility—but the native tendency, inherent in sin, to seek to avoid responsibility for sin. To counter this tendency, it is necessary to try and identify just exactly where original sin acquires greatest personal significance, by identifying the site of the greatest concentration of the denial of original sin that must be resisted. The challenge of a theology of original sin is to engage con-

28. Augustine *Confessions* 7.20.26 (Chadwick, 130).

structively an ambivalence and contradictoriness that is already always presently constitutive of human identity and relationship.

It would be prideful and worse to imagine that one could resolve this ambivalence, untangle these contradictions. Yet one is also obliged to engage their productive dimensions in order to make a more responsible and more constructive ethics possible. What then does it mean to assert the sinfulness of human sexuality? Must it not include critique of the primacy of marriage, once marriage is recognized as the predominant context for culpable avoidance of responsibility for sin? And how does a return to Augustine inform these assertions?

Creation, Birth, and the Problem of Memory

Whatever views one holds or refuses to hold about the meaningfulness, let alone constitution, of such a thing as nature in general, and human nature in particular, the most relentless genealogist and most ardent traditionalist could at least share an admission of the finitude of human existence as an ineluctable conditioning necessity of intelligible human identity. Judith Butler's theory of identity as performative citation is as much an "anthropology," in the philosophical sense of that term, as the full-blown Aristotleanism expounded by Alasdair MacIntyre.[29] In each case intelligible self-identification is imagined as a function of what Butler aptly terms "constitutive constraints" or "tacit constraints."[30] Admittedly a growing community of futurists are adopting a voluntaristic and optimistic view of these constraints as restraints to be overcome, including especially the fact of mortality, but Butler and MacIntyre equally soberly insist that these constraints are not limits against which human identity strains for fulfillment.[31] They are the actual medium of whatever fulfillment of

29. See MacIntyre, *Dependent*.

30. Butler, *Bodies*, 93–94 and *Gender*, 187–88. A big difference is that MacIntyre treats these as non-negotiable natural givens and consequently paints a picture that is arguably "essentialist." Whereas Butler treats them as politically contestable and hence as means of moving beyond the argumentative divide of essentialism versus constructivism. Following Butler, Harraway calls these "enabling constraints." Although her précis of Butler is outstanding, I find her assessment regarding the dispensability of "regulatory fictions" for coherent and responsible agency an overly optimistic conclusion. See Haraway, *Simians*, 135.

31. Probably the most coordinated intellectual community of futurists is the World Transhumanist Association (www.transhumanism.com). Nick Bostrom is among the most prominent members of this community: www.nickbostrom.com. Some feminist scholarship shares the futurist optimism and enthusiasm of transhumanism, for example Harraway, *Modest Witness*. For criticism of transhumanist aspirations as expressive of a male philo-

identity is possible. Dependence is not opposed to independence as a kind of disvalue against which independence, agency, and selfhood struggle to emerge. Instead dependence is a governing term that comprehends identity within itself. The many attributes typically regarded as the indices of coherent personal presence, a self—agency, autonomy, rationality—are reconceived as forms of dependency.[32]

Just as these writers are keenly aware of identity as constrained and necessary dependency—regardless of whether they adopt or eschew use of the term "nature" itself—so too St. Augustine's work is infused throughout with a sensibility of dependency. Unlike Butler, and perhaps MacIntyre in some ways, given the shifts in his thought over his long career, for Augustine the necessary dependency of intelligible personal identity is finally dependency on God; so that Augustine's writings provide a valuable means of joining seemingly disparate resources. The constructive aim of the present argument—depending as it does on very modest pretensions to expertise about the writings of Augustine and the classical world, its languages, literature, and history—sets it apart from much of the scholarship about Augustine that seeks to explain his distinctive themes in historical and contextual terms and by that very process tends to call into question any appeal to Augustine's writings as a resource of integrative theological ethics. Influential studies of Augustine have argued the importance, on the one hand, of his immersion in the intellectually elite culture of the late classical world, and especially his general philosophical indebtedness to the so-called neo-Platonism of Plotinus, as mediated through the writings of Porphyry, and on the other hand, the model of Monica's unwavering faith and the possibilities of allegorical biblical interpretation opened up for him by Ambrose.[33] According to this avenue of scholarship,

---

sophical fear of the body, see Midgley, "Philosophy." For example of an explicitly theological openness to transhuman transformation of the body, see Briggs, "Digital Bodies."

32. See also Butler, *Psychic*, 8–9 on self-identification as a function of dependency on power. Elsewhere she writes: "So if, at the beginning—and we must laugh here, since we cannot narrate that beginning with any kind of authority, indeed, such a narration is the occasion in which we lose whatever narrative authority we might otherwise enjoy—*I am only in the address to you*, the 'I' that I am is nothing without this 'you,' and cannot even begin to refer to itself outside the relation to the other by which its capacity for self-reference emerges. I am mired, given over, and even the word *dependency* cannot do the job here. This means that I am also formed in ways that precede and enable my self-forming; this particular kind of transitivity is difficult, if not impossible, to narrate" (Butler, *Giving*, 82). Difficult, one might add, for creatures to narrate, but not for God who creates.

33. Regarding the former, see Rist, *Augustine*. Regarding the latter, see Harrison, *Augustine*, 23, 49.

as of so much scholarship that precedes it, Augustine's thought, and by extension the thought of any early Christian writer, is divided into "classical" and "Christian" components. The task of the scholar then becomes to determine the proportionate relationship between them; where the theme of dependency is credited almost entirely on the Christian side of the register. The more Christian Augustine becomes, the more dependence becomes a central focus of his writings, the more tradition and authority replace reason and philosophy as the only possible pathways to truth. The consolidation of Augustinian themes is consequently pictured in relation to this divide. Carol Harrison for example summarizes the challenge of identifying the most distinctive elements of Augustine's writings with the questions: "Are we therefore to speak of a transition, a crossing over, from one culture to another? Of an abandonment of classical culture? Of an eclectic mix of classical and Christian? Of a transformation of classical culture by a Christian culture?"[34]

Although Harrison subsequently develops an invaluable description of Augustine's integration of classical rhetorical sensibilities into the service of a "Christian aesthetic,"[35] the relevance of this kind of scholarly approach to the construction of a contemporary Augustinian theology is probably limited, since the project of studying Augustine in his context assumes a hermeneutical possibility that my own readings question: the possibility of the recovery of authorial intention distinct from the project of reading the text specifically for that intention.[36] A more self-consciously literary reading of Augustine's writings opens up to view exploration of the connections between Augustine's writings and those by Butler and MacIntyre and others by picking up especially on the shared concern to explicate the primacy of identity as a form of dependency, and worrying less about tracing the historical sources and references and developments of Augustine's thought. Augustine's writings need not then be contextualized as classical or Christian or pre-modern, but as incredibly sturdy texts that continue to provide productive occasions for reflection on themes of enduring theological, philosophical, political, and social relevance.

34. Harrison, *Augustine*, 53.

35. Ibid., 76.

36. Rist for example adds a final chapter "Augustinus redivivus," where he attempts to think through the following project: "Suppose him [Augustine] to have been allowed to return to life in the late twentieth century to write his *Reconsiderations* over again" (Rist, *Augustine*, 290).

For Augustine throughout his work, but especially in *Confessions*, awareness of dependency begins with a self-evident fact that is also an unending mystery: the origin and subsistence of his individual historical self in time. That he does enter the world, that he does possess certain if limited knowledge of the world, and that he will leave the world, is for Augustine an indisputable reality.[37] Yet how he enters the world, how he possesses whatever knowledge he does possess, he can never satisfactorily account to himself, whereas he can look forward, at least in hope, to a future life of happiness and security in God. So Augustine never imagines the problem of the end of life apart from the problem of its origins. He is perplexed because he finds himself aware of the certainty of both beginning and ending, and unable fully to comprehend the significance of the former to the latter.

Augustine figures his perplexity near the start of *Confessions* through decidedly material and maternal imagery:

> Neverthless allow me to speak before your mercy, though I am but dust and ashes (Gen. 18:27). Allow me to speak: for I am addressing your mercy, not a man who would laugh at me. Perhaps even you deride me (cf. Ps. 2:4), but you will turn and have mercy on me (Jer. 12:15). What, Lord, do I wish to say except that I do not know whence I came to be in this mortal life or, as I may call it, this living death? I do not know where I came from. But the consolations of your mercies (cf. Ps. 50:3; 93:19) upheld me, as I have heard from the parents of my flesh, him from whom and her in whom you formed me in time. For I do not remember. So I was welcomed by the consolations of human milk; but it was not my mother or my nurses who made any decision to fill their breasts, but you who through them gave me infant food, in accordance with your ordinance and the riches which are distributed deep in the natural order.[38]

It seems at first a bit incongruous, given the tradition of regarding St. Augustine as a stern father of the church, to picture him as an infant nursing at his mother's breast.[39] Yet rather than distance himself from this image, relegate it to an unimportant past, Augustine lingers over it, em-

37. On Augustine's rejection of skepticism, see Rist, *Augustine*, 41–91.

38. Augustine *Confessions* 1.6.7 (Chadwick, 6).

39. Iconography of Augustine often pictures him as a slightly hunched bearded man with a melancholy countenance. See, for example, Sandro Boticelli's "Augustine in his study," in Possidius, *Life*, 132, among numerous other illustrations.

phasizing the facts of his bodily formation in time. Emphasizing also the materiality of his body, its inseparable immersion in the physical world.[40]

Augustine's description of himself as dust and ashes is likewise more than a rhetorical formula of humility. It is also an embrace of creation as the only meaningful context of personal identity, and an identification of self with the scriptural account of creation. It is confession of identity as creature. When Augustine appeals to God's mercy, he is pointedly addressing God as creator, as the only one who can know fully what it means that dust and ashes somehow speak, because God alone creates this possibility and reality. Likewise, when Augustine credits God's mercy for the provision of the "consolations of human milk," he is enfolding the image of his own infant self in his mother's embrace in an implicit image of himself holding the reader in a similar embrace, and also himself and mother and reader in God's nourishing embrace, playing as he does on the words of Paul: "And so, brothers and sisters, I could not speak to you as spiritual people, but rather as people of the flesh, as infants in Christ. I fed you with milk, not solid food, for you were not ready for solid food" (1 Cor 3:1–2).

Already an authoritative figure of the African church at the time he was writing *Confessions*, Augustine nevertheless emphasizes his creaturely origin in time, his vulnerability and dependence, as an essential starting point, not only of his personal being, but also of his search for more intimate and clear-sighted relationship with God his creator, God who "formed me in time." Relationship to God is a defining structural truth of the *bodily* facts of birth and nursing, so that bodily truths constitute a knowledge of God that precedes any rationalistic, intellectual attempt to know one's creator.

These maternal and material metaphors are not some rare occurrence, but are echoed throughout *Confessions* by imagery of knowledge of God and relationship to God as inextricably the same experience, a kind of "tasting," "savoring," "relishing," and "delighting."[41] It is too

40. For discussion of this image of "woman's milk" and the depiction of Monica in *Confessions*, in relation to imaginations of male embodiment, see Krondorfer, "Confines." For a reading of Augustine's depiction of himself and his mother as a typological corrective to epic identity as exemplified in Virgil's *Aenead*, see Ziolkowski, *St. Augustine.*

41. Though Caroline Walker Bynum focuses on late medieval women's religious experience, her investigation of the religious significance of food, and especially metaphors of nursing, models a line of theological investigation that deeply enriches reading of Augustine. Bynum provides helpful clarification, for example, in her discussion of an influential essay

simple then to ascribe to Augustine a static dualistic view of flesh and spirit, though he does describe them in hierarchical relationship; or to argue that spirit is privileged to the extent it is gendered as male, while flesh is denigrated to the extent it is gendered as female. Contrary to the interpretations that follow from ascription of such a view to Augustine, he is never simplistically anti-body, nor anti-woman.[42] Instead he repeatedly emphasizes the profound significance of birth as a definitive human experience; not a tragedy to regret, as if the body were a prison of the soul, but rather a truth to fathom.

Perhaps it is difficult, in an era that is in many ways inured to the fragility of the body's immersion in the material universe by several centuries of progressive technical mastery of that universe—inured also to the import of that fragility to philosophy and theology by several centuries tradition of isolating philosophy and theology as intellectual disciplines—to appreciate Augustine's keen awareness of the interrelatedness of body and intellect in relation to God. Such appreciation is potentially very uncomfortable or worse, undermining as it does any sensibility of immunity from dependency, or of progressive diminishment of dependency, as the horizon of self-actualized personal fulfillment. Yet even at the beginning of the twenty-first century human beings remain mortal, finite, embodied creatures. Persons who accuse Augustine of unduly disparaging or denigrating the body may therefore miss sometimes how the claims that they criticize arise out of vivid and searching reflection on embodied experience that is not and cannot be one's own exactly; that these claims are so troubling because they are rooted so intimately in questioning of one's created existence; that it is arguably the present age, and not Augustine's, that in fact disparages the body; that Augustine may have raised all the hard questions he does not because he doesn't take the body seriously, but because he takes the body with ultimate seriousness.

---

in feminist anthropology (Ortner, "Is Female as to Male"), that the structuralist opposition of male versus female symbol systems is a non-essential pattern, available to creative appropriation and adaptation by both women *and* men. Bynum, *Holy Feast*, 282–88, esp. 283.

42. For overview of scholarship on Augustine on women, see Matter, *Christ*. For extended study, see Power, *Veiled Desire*, and Børresen and Talbot, *Subordination*. Drawing especially on the writings of Mary Douglas, Power critiques Augustine's writings as androcentric and anti-erotic, as the regrettable incorporation of the contemporaneously regnant cultural symbol systems of gender into Christian theological perspective. Børresen by contrast approves Augustine's fundamental affirmation of the spiritual equality of men and women.

However trite or obvious it may seem to say so, no such thing as a "self-created" individual exists, or can exist, so that the question Augustine is asking is a question that one can continue to press: Where did I come from? And despite the prospect that some will laugh at him, this is not a childish question. Or rather its childishness is a mark of its profundity and complexity. His wisdom in asking this question involves a willingness to ask something that seems childish, to identify with the puzzled child and not the adult who brushes the question aside as an amusing display of babyish ignorance of human sexual reproduction.[43]

The grown-up child Augustine is not so ignorant. He knows that his origin is sexual; that the emergence of his particular self as "I" follows from the sexual difference and sexual relationship of his mother and father. Yet he doesn't rest satisfied with this knowledge. Instead his very certainty of this knowledge multiplies his perplexity and becomes a paradigm of dependency of body and intellect when he is forced to admit of his embodied emergence that all he knows is what "I have heard from the parents of my flesh, him from whom and her in whom you formed me in time." In reflecting on the most significant fact of his own being, on his creation, Augustine discovers memory as a problem of identity. For how could he have a beginning, as he knows he does, and yet how could he also "not remember"? Nor of course could he, could anyone, though some individuals do claim to remember the experience of their own birth, or even of life in the womb, while others seek to reclaim such memory through experimental "rebirthing" therapies.

Augustine by contrast knows better what he does not know, that his own existence begins somehow outside himself and yet contains himself, that he is not his own creation, but another's. Neither is his knowledge esoteric, abstract, or trivial, at least as concerns himself. He does not ask the question generically, of humanity in general, but of himself, of a particular individual, so that when Augustine says "I do not know where I come from," he models a form of common identification through particularity with his readers, since the question can only be asked by the individual, and likewise addressed to individuals, whether to mother and father, or God. Augustine is asking about the creation of the world, and

43. Augustine's most systematic consideration of these questions is in *The Trinity*, especially Books XII to XV, in which he weaves together a Trinitarian philosophy of mind as the created image of God with the biblical revelation of creation, fall, and redemption. See Augustine, *Works*, 1/5:12–15 (Hill, 322–437). For a constructive feminist discussion of Augustine's Trinitarian theology, see Coakley, "Batter My Heart."

about how he inheres as himself within the world. Those who do laugh at him consequently laugh at themselves, as they ignorantly exclude themselves from the dynamic that Augustine is exploring, epitomized in the troubling experience of his own memory in its accomplishments and also its limitations.

In the recognition of his inability to account for his emergence of self in time, memory emerges as a central concern for Augustine. Memory encapsulates the experience of immersion of his particular searching self in the creative activity exterior to himself, out of which his own being and knowledge emerges, and on which their continuance depends: "The power of memory is great, very great, my God. It is a vast and infinite profundity. Who has plumbed its bottom? This power is that of my mind and is a natural endowment, but I myself cannot grasp the totality of what I am."[44] The experience of memory, more than any other emotive, rational, or bodily experience, exemplifies his experience of the exterior that becomes interior while remaining exterior, of his self as essentially composed in some way outside himself. Memory *unifies* the emotive, rational, and bodily dimensions of his self into an extended whole, so that in memory, in reflection on his self as a remembering self, he most fully conceives of himself as an extensional self.[45]

When considering Augustine as a figure in an intellectual history, it is tempting to treat his concern with memory as unidirectional, as a turning inward and hence as a kind of turning away from or renunciation of the visible world. Charles Taylor hints at this tendency when he summarizes Augustine's philosophical importance as follows: "Augustine shifts the focus from the field of objects known to the activity of knowing; God is to be found here. This begins to account for his use of the language of inwardness. For in contrast to the domain of objects, which is public and common, the activity of knowing is particularized; each of us is engaged in ours. To look towards this activity is to look to the self, to take up a reflexive stance."[46] For Taylor, Augustine's thought represents a turning point between Platonic idealization of the most authentic self as perfectly attuned to the external order of perfect being, and the thoroughly inter-

---

44. *Confessions* 10.8.14 (Chadwick, 187).

45. On the complex relation in Augustine of interiority to exteriority, see Mathewes, "Augustinian Anthropology." For a concise commentary on memory in the *Confessions*, see Augustine and Wills, *Saint Augustine's Memory*.

46. Taylor, *Sources*, 130.

nalized idealization of authentic selfhood that he summarizes as "Locke's Punctual Self" and "Descartes's Disengaged Reason." The tendency implicit in this location of Augustine's thought as "on the way from Plato to Descartes,"[47] is to dichotomize "the field of objects known" from "the activity of knowing," as if the two were essentially unrelated, as if one could exist or occur separable from the other. Yet when Augustine does "take up a reflexive stance," this stance entails consideration of himself as somehow within that "field of objects known," of himself as equally and as fully God's creation as those objects, and in this sense participating in a common identity with them. For Augustine, interior and exterior are not simply opposed, but are speaking to each other, so that he can search for God in his "particularized" "activity of knowing," not because that activity is apart from or above creation, but because it fluidly extends within creation. Memory exemplifies and symbolizes that extension. Birth is a non-negotiable limit to memory, and also a potent cipher of memory, a provocative absence.

The profundity of memory as a locus of self-understanding and knowledge of God crystallizes for Augustine in a key moment at the heart of *Confessions*. This moment can be (and has been) read as a classic formulation of the ontological argument for the existence of God.[48] Within the narrative framework of *Confessions* it also marks a turning point in Augustine's reflection on the problem of evil, sealing his rejection of Manichean dualism and acceptance of the saving name of Christ as mediator that was missing from the Platonic books that had otherwise been so valuable. Augustine discovers the importance of memory in relation to God only after he fully embraces the unmitigated goodness of creation as instructed by faith, not by philosophy or false religion. Only then is he able to envision evil entirely as a privative phenomenon. In "seeking feverishly for the origin of evil"[49] Augustine puzzles over the certainty of his knowledge that the eternal and immutable is by nature superior to that which is finite and mutable. Augustine doesn't ever question this relative valuation of the former over the latter; he just knows that it is true; that "That which truly is is that which unchangably abides."[50] Only he wonders how he can possess such sure knowledge. Augustine also

47. Ibid., 127.
48. Ibid., 134.
49. Augustine *Confessions* 7.7.11 (Chadwick, 119).
50. Augustine *Confessions* 7.11.17 (Chadwick, 124).

recognizes "that things which are liable to corruption are good. If they were the supreme goods, or if they were not good at all, they could not be corrupted. For if they were supreme goods, they would be incorruptible. If there were no good in them, there would be nothing capable of being corrupted."[51]

From this affirmation of the goodness of all that is, Augustine reaches the remarkable conclusion that he must already have had some knowledge of the immutable, where knowing is not disengaged intellection but a form of intense intimacy with God his creator. Rejection of any dualistic explanation of the reality of evil, along with admission of the goodness of his finite created self as sustained by his creator, leads Augustine to a tantalizing moment of theophany:

> This power, which in myself I found to be mutable, raised itself to the level of its own intelligence, and led my thinking out of the ruts of habit. It withdrew itself from the contradictory swarms of imaginative fantasies, so as to discover the light by which it was flooded. At that point it had no hesitation in declaring that the unchangeable is preferable to the changeable, and that on this ground it can know the unchangeable, since, unless it could somehow know this, there would be no certainty in preferring it to the mutable. So in the flash of a trembling glance it attained to that which is. At that moment I saw "your invisible nature understood through the things which are made" (Rom. 1:20). But I did not possess the strength to keep my vision fixed. My weakness reasserted itself, and I returned to my customary condition. I carried with me only a loving memory and a desire for that of which I had the aroma but which I had not yet the capacity to eat.[52]

As philosophical argument, Augustine's "unless" here is dubious, assuming as it does exactly that which it presumes to demonstrate. The train of thought here doesn't *prove* anything, least of all the necessary existence of God who *is*, so much so that some have even argued that this form of argument is in effect a proof of the impossibility of the existence of God, and of the necessity of an atheistic Platonic metaphysics, not any form of traditional theism, to morality.[53] Yet one need not become mired in the metaphysical question of the necessity or not of some unchanging ground of moral goodness to the possibility of human moral striving,

51. Augustine *Confessions* 7.13.18 (Chadwick, 124.)

52. Augustine *Confessions* 7.17.23 (Chadwick, 127–28).

53. Murdoch, *Metaphysics*, 391–430, esp. 411.

to appreciate that the ontological starting point of Augustine's "thinking" is his acceptance of the goodness of his own creaturely finite being. Augustine locates his being within a hierarchy of being, all of it sustained by the supremely good unchangeable being. What matters here however is less the hierarchical metaphysics, and more the dissociation of God from the problem of evil, which frees Augustine to envision his own birth as a form of relationship to and distance from God.

Once he is certain that responsibility for evil is utterly external to God, that responsibility for evil lies *elsewhere*, Augustine is able to search his memory, to look backward. He is liberated in a way to embrace his origin in time. Like a child who struggles to remember events that have been related to him by parents or others—true to the portrait of himself as child—Augustine is troubled and fascinated by the gap between his knowledge of all that must have preceded his own existence, and his lack of any memory of that history. Out of this gap he establishes, not the eternity or prior existence of the soul, but the inescapable truth of its emergence in time. Carol Harrison explains of similar passages in *On the Trinity* that even if these "might therefore at first appear as an exercise structured and informed by the Neoplatonic ascent of the image or soul, seeking to return to that from which it is derived, it must be remembered that for Augustine the image or soul is *created* by God, from nothing, it does not derive from Him; similarly its return is not a matter of its own striving, but is only possible by God's revelation and grace."[54]

When Augustine turns toward the light by which his own intelligence is flooded, he doesn't assume that he is remembering the unchangeable as if he must have known it in some former state, as if his own being was separable from that which it remembers. He is fathoming the full significance of the truth he grapples with at the very beginning of *Confessions*: that his origin is not himself. When Augustine concludes from his reason's preference for the unchangeable, "since, unless it could somehow know this, there would be no certainty in preferring it to the mutable," it is as if he is reasoning, "for unless I had been created, I could not seek out my creator." Knowledge of God is never purely formal, propositional, or abstract, but always a form of encounter. Knowledge of God

54. Harrison, *Augustine*, 44. For Augustine on the soul as created, see for example *Confessions* 12.17.24 (Chadwick, 258); *Literal Meaning* 7.1.1–28.40, 10.1.1–26.45 (Taylor, 2:3–31, 96–132); *The Nature and Origin of the Soul* in *Works*, 1/23 (Teske, 466–561); and *City of God* 14.11 (Bettenson, 568). For Augustine on "mind" also as created, see for example *Of the Morals of the Catholic Church* in *Writings*, chap. 12.

is always personal and creaturely knowledge. Intellection is consequently figured very significantly as a form of tasting. Knowledge is "aroma" and Augustine is hungry but also so far lacks "the capacity to eat." Memory is by its very nature a form of longing, so that when Augustine glimpses God's "invisible nature," which he then longs to know more fully, he at the same time glimpses the depth of his own longing for fullness of relationship to God, as that possibility becomes "known through the things which are made."

Augustine's famous moment of ontological insight is not an accomplishment of independent reason, but just the opposite, a fruition of dependent reason as it searches out and accepts its own dependency in the relation of self to God, where that relation also comprehends the relation of self and mother.[55]

The fundamental importance of birth as a form of relationship to God that structures the possibility of memory is underscored by Augustine's turn to an extended exploration of the problem of memory, in book 10 of *Confessions*, immediately after concluding book 9 with the circumstances of his mother Monica's death, and of his grief at this loss. Augustine concludes his meditation on the loss of his mother with a beautiful call to the reader that returns to the mystery of personal origin posed in the very opening sections of *Confessions*:

> My Lord, my God, inspire your servants, my brothers, your sons, my masters, to whose service I dedicate my heart, voice, and writings, that all who read this book may remember at your altar Monica your servant and Patrick her late husband, through whose physical bond you brought me into this life without my knowing how. May they remember with devout affection my parents in this transient light, my kith and kin under you, our Father, in our mother the Catholic Church, and my fellow citizens in the eternal Jerusalem. For this city your pilgrim people yearn, from their leaving it to their return.[56]

Augustine invokes a parallelism between his embodied relation to his father and mother, and his spiritual relation to God and church, and then he uses that parallelism to undermine any implication of ultimate hierarchy between generations of human beings, however much his im-

55. On the coincidence of "self-discovery" and "discovery of God," see Arendt, *Love*, 24–25.
56. Augustine *Confessions*, 9.13.37 (Chadwick, 178).

mediate model of familial relations is centered on the authority of the *pater familias*.[57] So he directly draws the conclusion of the equality of all human beings before God, implied in the much earlier acknowledgement of God as the one who provides "the consolations of human milk," because God's creative activity precedes the marital metaphor.[58] Human parenting is radically discontinuous with divine parenthood.

As the creator of all parents, God is not really a parent in any sense that human beings can grasp. Only God *creates*. This discontinuity between divine and human parenting is urged upon the reader as a form of remembrance of Monica and Patrick as kith and kin and fellow citizens. Memory is the medium of discovery of the fraternity of all humanity in God.[59] As a transitional pause in the autobiographical narrative of *Confessions*, Augustine's prayer assimilates human reproductive capacity to God's creative (and redemptive) purposes, and assimilates the reader into this very process of assimilation by actively urging the exercise of capacity for memory. Body and spirit are equally and completely affirmed as first and foremost God's creation, human reproduction somehow a means of God's active participation in the creation of the individual, "without my knowing how." Birth is the start in common of the pilgrim journey that is every individual human life. It marks their "leaving" just as death marks their "return." Yet birth itself must also have an origin in God. Hence discussion of the problem of memory and also the indelible certainty that the unchangeable is already known, that it composes in a way oneself.

Casual commentators on *Confessions* have sometimes puzzled over the apparent lack of continuity between the first nine books and the final four, as if the final books are an anti-climax to the stirring narrative of spiritual conversion that precedes them.[60] From the logic of the problem

---

57. For a classic statement by Augustine on the rule of the home in relation to the rule of society, see *City of God* 19.16 (Bettenson, 876). For discussion of the distinction between *pater familias* and *pater potestas* and the function of family as metaphor of organization of Roman society, see Lassen, "Roman Family."

58. The theme of maternal loss in Augustine's narrative as an occasion of prayerful reflection on the fraternal community of all humanity is in contrast to the invocation of maternal loss in the construction of Victorian fictions of sexed identity. With regard to the latter, see Dever, *Death and the Mother*.

59. For theological explication of all parental relationship as a distortion of fraternal community, see Alison, "Theology."

60. For explication of this frustration as it implicates the reader in Augustine's theological project, see Mathewes, "Liberation," 539–41.

that birth poses to memory, however, the transition from book 9 to book 10 is more than continuous with what precedes it. It is the culmination of the questions that were Augustine's starting point. With a prayer for the memory of his parents, Augustine moves from the memory of their loss to a disquisition on memory itself and then extended exegesis of the first verses of Genesis, because he knows they belong together somehow. He senses that the most unfathomable dimension of his own self is embedded in the relation between his own birth and the creation *ex nihilo* recounted in Scripture; Scripture which teaches irrefutably the truth of Christian faith.[61]

Just as he recognizes early on that God alone can answer his questions, Augustine now realizes that the solution to the childish question about his birth that he originally asked God to illuminate *is* that relation of birth to creation. Later in his life, as he became more and more embroiled in rebutting various forms of Pelagianism, Augustine would situate the problem of birth and memory much more explicitly in the context of the reality of original sin. For the moment, it remains important to explicate more fully the dimensions of the mysterious relation of birth to memory, in order to dramatize the personal as well as theological gravity of the doctrine with which Augustine is most closely and perhaps most infamously associated.

In the B/beginning

Much of the hesitation over how to construe the relation of the last four books of *Confessions* to those that precede them is a problem of definition of genre. The reader's expectations of autobiography, shaped by immersion in the sort of romantic fictional autobiographical narrative to be examined in chapter 7 of this work, are thwarted by the philosophically and theologically abstruse turn of Augustine's narrative.[62] Augustine doesn't marry and establish a domestic altar. Nor does he simplistically renounce worldly affairs and retire to the study of Scripture. Regardless of the incongruity of the remainder of *Confessions* with the genre of autobiography, it remains the case that Augustine doesn't cease narrating his self when he moves to the topics of memory and biblical interpretation. In fact, he unfolds more explicitly the truth from which he began, that

61. Harrison, *Augustine*, 61.

62. The template of Rousseau's *Confessions* has also colored reading of Augustine. See Hartle, "Augustine and Rousseau."

the narrative discovery of self proceeds through the narrative discovery of God.[63]

Augustine's search for God is self-interested, in the sense that he finds his own self a source of intense theological interest as a knowing person who is comprehensively known by God. Augustine repeatedly emphasizes that God's knowledge and creative activity are a unity: "You, Lord, are my judge. For even if 'no man knows the being of man except the spirit of man which is in him' (I Cor 2:11), yet there is something of the human person which is unknown even to the 'spirit of man which is in him.' But you, Lord, know everything about the human person; for you made humanity."[64] It is tempting at first glance to interpret such passages as if Augustine were intuitively prefiguring the psychic structure delimited by much scientific and psychoanalytic discourse, as if the unconscious were an unchanging reality awaiting discovery. Yet when Augustine writes of the unknown within himself, he is acknowledging much more than the incapacity of the self fully to know its own desires, fears, loves, and hates. More fundamentally, Augustine is reaching to describe the relational dependence of his knowing capacities as a person on God who knows "everything" of every person. As a person "made" by God, Augustine trusts that whatever insight he can achieve into himself will be creaturely insight that originates in God; it will be dependent and therefore true knowing. And this includes the limits of knowledge of self: "Accordingly, let me confess what I know of myself. Let me confess too what I do not know of myself. For what I know of myself I know because you grant me light, and what I do not know of myself, I do not know until such time as my darkness becomes 'like noonday' before your face (Isa 58:10)."[65]

Following Augustine's example, to attempt to know God or self entirely through one's own capacities, to imagine that such a thing as independent knowing exists, is actually a failure of self-interest, a failure to recognize a truth of one's most interested and interesting self. In terms of defining a structure of autobiography, Augustine's assumption of his own identity as another's creation, and of truthful knowing as dependent

63. For discussion of the extent to which *Confessions* is an egocentric narrative driven by an exhibitionist impulse inherent in the desire to "publish" a "confession," see Asher, "Dangerous Fruit."

64. Augustine *Confessions* 10.5.7 (Chadwick, 182–23).

65. Augustine *Confessions* 10.5.7 (Chadwick, 182–23).

knowing, contrasts sharply with the romantic obsession with autobiography as a means of self-creation, as a means of stabilization of intelligible personal identity through masterful narration of the fiction of sex.[66]

Augustine's concern with self serves as a corrective to the obsessive romantic quest comprehensively to fix one's identity through the fiction of sex, and in doing so it points to an origin of the desire for intelligible personal identity that all human beings share in common. Whereas romantic tradents of the genre imagine the structure of autobiography as a kind of private property, the successful self-narration of one's secret self, the sex within, Augustine imagines the structure of autobiography as fundamentally communal and external, since Augustine knows that his own particular life story, like every other particular life story—the only kind of life story; the story of every person—begins in the beginning:[67] "In this Beginning, God, you made heaven and earth, in your Word, in your Son, in your power, in your wisdom, in your truth speaking in a wonderful way and making in a wonderful way. Who can comprehend it? Who will give an account of it in words?"[68] If Augustine can fruitfully search within himself for knowledge of God, it is only because he trusts in faith that every human beginning has its source in the divine initiative of Beginning.[69] These are not separate events. The latter somehow contains the former. The start of every human life can therefore be described as a B/beginning.[70] The challenge for human authorship is how to approach with human words the accomplishment of the divine Word that literally makes oneself.

66. For a reading of *Confessions* in relation to contemporary lesbian and gay-male autobiographical narratives, see Hill, "(Dis) Inheriting Augustine." For a more general discussion of autobiography and American religious history, see Juster, "Forum."

67. Responses to the question "Where did you come from" that begin with some version of "In the Beginning," are liable to depiction as a form of mental illness, as in Mike Leigh's film "Naked." Or perhaps mental illness in this case is depicted as a form of heightened attention to this truth.

68. Augustine *Confessions* 11.9.11 (Chadwick, 227).

69. For a classic celebration of the human possibilities in beginning, that proceeds through theorization of a publicly narrated self, drawing specifically on Augustine's writings, see Arendt, *Human Condition*, 175–88.

70. This Augustinian perspective on the inherence of the self in creation contrasts sharply with romantic idealization of creation seeking fulfillment in rebellion, typified in a tradition of reading Satan as the hero of Milton's *Paradise Lost*. See Empson, *Milton's God*. For survey of this romantic trajectory, see Cantor, *Creature and Creator*.

For Augustine, faith in the truth of his own beginning as a form of Beginning that describes the true community of all human beings is a form of faith in Scripture as God's revelation. Scripture tells the story of oneself by God that fills the gap exemplified in Judith Butler's observation: "My account of myself is partial, haunted by that for which I can devise no definitive story."[71] Augustine reads Genesis because it is the opening chapter of his own particular autobiography, the record of the true history narrated by God that makes his own life-narration intelligible. Considered in the mirror of Scripture, God, not Augustine, is the ultimate author of the beginning as well as the conclusion of *Confessions*. As a human work, *Confessions* continually extols God alone as the author of existence, because God alone is the only reliable narrator of intelligible personal identity. God alone can speak the unerring truth of the self. Dependency of self upon God can be measured, metaphorically at least, in terms of this difference between the unreliability of human narrative capacity and the infallibility of God's narration. Every story human beings devise about themselves ultimately lacks definition, whereas God already has provided the one true story that is also every person's own definitive story.

Whatever view one holds on the status of Scripture, it is important when reading Augustine creditably to account in this way for his continual address of God as the only auditor who can fully comprehend his prayerful text. In doing so the reader discovers that Augustine models a mode of theological inquiry that is not dependent on any single ultimate commitment regarding either the status of Scripture, or methods of interpretation of Scripture. These are issues that one need not resolve in order to admit that no human being is self-created; in order to admit that the origin of every self is outside the self. Even for Augustine himself, the important distinction remains between Scripture, as the revelation by God of a Beginning that is otherwise utterly inaccessible, and the beginning that Augustine recounts in *Confessions*, and that he can identify with his parents, the town of his birth, his youthful education: "So I will also ascend beyond memory to touch him who 'set me apart from the quadrupeds and made me wiser than the birds of heaven' (Job 35:11). As I rise above memory, where am I to find you? My true good and gentle source of reassurance, where shall I find you? If I find you outside my memory, I am not mindful of you. And how shall I find you if I am not

71. Butler, *Giving*, 40.

mindful of you?"[72] Augustine reads Genesis as answer to these questions, as the place he can look to gain insight into his relation with God who made him the creature "set apart" that he is, always keeping in mind that he is set apart within creation, not apart from it or above it, not finally distinguishable from it in any ultimate way. Even the soul in its immortal future will be a creature of God.

Where memory fails, Scripture supervenes, establishing the relation of the two terms of the self, of beginning and Beginning. What matters is less the specific definition of these two terms than the fact of their relation. And this relation exists only because the terms are distinct, so that more than anything, memory's limit and failure affirms their distinction. As a result, Augustine need not lament the end of memory. The end of memory obviates the need to fix these terms, enabling him to focus instead on their relation.

The definitions of these terms also do matter, but to a certain extent they are necessarily indeterminate. What some regard as a discrepancy or even failure in Augustine's thought—the absence of any coherent account of the generation of the soul—actually reinforces the priority of the relation to the fixity of the terms.[73] Augustine himself didn't ever need finally to answer the question, "Whence the soul?" in order to affirm that the soul has a beginning that is beyond its own comprehension, where comprehension means more than intellectual understanding and meaningfully suggests volume, holding capacity. From the point of view of the self, who cannot comprehend the self in this way, the incapacity to grasp one's own origins signifies that a certain degree of incomprehension is structured into the relation of beginning and Beginning. As a creature, every individual exists through their relation, and so cannot see or imagine these terms clearly. Such a vision can only be imagined by projecting a point of view exterior to the self, a point of view that definitively distinguishes Creator from creature.

The incapacity to comprehend one's origin defines a signifying limit of the point of view of creaturely existence. The strange reality signified by this limit is that the self knows itself most intimately as a creature pre-

72. *Confessions* 10.17.26 (Chadwick, 195).

73. For review of Augustine as wavering between "creationist" and "traducianist" explanations of the question "How do we come to possess a soul?" see Harrison, *Augustine*, 109. On Augustine's inability ever to reach a definite conclusion about the origin of the soul, in relation to Pelagian debates, see Rist, *Augustine*, 317–20. See also Augustine's own comments in Augustine *Free Choice* 3:20–25.

cisely in the experience of this incomprehension of one's created origins. One must then hold a single ultimate conviction: that a personal and living God *does* create. But following the same sense of hold as a kind of capacity to encompass a volume, this conviction too can only be held in faith, and as such gives rise to the productive ambiguity regarding origins that is so crucial to Augustine's thought in general and the doctrine of original sin in particular.

Hannah Arendt points to this ambiguity when she writes of Augustine's questioning search in book 10 to understand the identity of God as the object of his love: "In other words, this God who is *my* God, the right object of my desire and my love, is the quintessence of my inner self and therefore by no means identical with it."[74] Personal identity, as Arendt suggests in this reading of Augustine, occurs in a kind of in-between space that one can neither create nor sustain nor fully envision, but also that one cannot evade. Just as the self can only love God as the "quintessence" of an "inner self" because God is not that self, so too the self can only cohere in time across the space of beginning and Beginning, because the former is not the latter. Yet one cannot see this relation in difference. Instead one can only imagine and trust that God's point of view is comprehensive in exactly the way that the human point of view is not and cannot be. And trust that out of this inter-related difference of the divine and human points of view that their relation nevertheless sustains the possibility of theology as a meaningful discourse; that God holds together in a comprehensive and true vision what human beings can only strain to glimpse obliquely and in distorted fragments.

Accepting this state of affairs, Augustine's focused discussion of memory and Genesis is in a certain way the most urgent and searching stretch of the entire narrative, where the "liberation of questioning" that Charles Matthewes compellingly describes as the narrative accomplishment of *Confessions* is realized. The final books renew the questions that Augustine puzzles over from the start and open to view exploration of the relation between beginning and Beginning. So *Confessions* culminates in narration of the space in which fruitfully to explore that relation, and thereby shape richer more searching and enduring questions. Augustine in these latter books models the priority of autobiography as a genre of theology. Matthewes explains: "His task is, rather, to narrate one's becoming the sort of creature who can begin properly to pursue,

74. Arendt, *Love*, 35.

dynamically and with others, such an 'external' aim as the inmost heart of all creation."[75]

This comment strikes me as succinct a summary statement as possible of what kind of "task" theology is, emphasizing as it does the integration of narration and exploration. From the point of view of creation—the only point of view accessible to a creature, a person—the quest to know and understand the external and true is always also the activity of narrating personal identity. Theology is in this sense subsumed by autobiography; it is a form of writing the self aright. Augustine underscores this properly self-concerned dimension of the search to understand one's own creation, within the context of all of creation, when he figuratively questions the earth, sea, the wind, all the world around him: "And I said to all these things in my external environment: 'Tell me of my God who you are not, tell me something about him.' And with a great voice they cried out: 'He made us' (Ps. 99:33)."[76] Augustine knows that he is speaking *for* the mute elements; his imagination of their response thereby underscores his identity as a speaking and remembering creature, as one whose awareness of the dependence of all creation on its creator centers uniquely in the personal experience that makes him other than a mere element, as one who is comprehended by creation yet also at least partially comprehends it through the activity of confession. The final books dramatically illustrate the benefit of resisting any qualitative or ultimate opposition between literature on the one hand and philosophy and theology on the other. Instead Augustine exemplifies the wisdom, echoed across the centuries in the recent words of Judith Butler, of incorporating philosophy and theology within a broadly reconceived genre of autobiography, where narrative is prior and basic: "That there is no final or adequate narrative reconstruction of the prehistory of the speaking 'I' does not mean that we cannot narrate it: it only means that at the moment when we narrate we become speculative philosophers and fiction writers."[77]

Formulation of an Augustinian genre of autobiography discloses the logic of associating birth with sin in an Augustinian theology of original sin. Assuming as he does the inerrancy of Scripture, Augustine recognizes that the record of the actions of Adam and Eve in paradise belongs to the

75. Mathewes, "Liberation," 556–57.

76. Augustine *Confessions* 10.6.9 (Chadwick, 183).

77. Butler, *Giving*, 78.

autobiography of every human being. All humanity traces its sexualized origin to the non-sexual creation of Adam and Eve.[78] Playing metaphorically with the material reality of Scripture as a manuscript written on parchment (calfskin, sheepskin, goatskin), and on which he himself is possibly writing, Augustine observes: "You know, Lord, you know how you clothed human beings with skins when by sin they became mortal (Gen. 3:21). So you have stretched out the firmament of your book 'like a skin', that is your words which are not mutually discordant, and which you have placed over us by the ministry of mortal men."[79] An Augustinian theology of original sin would therefore be radically incomplete without considering at length Augustine's specific readings of Genesis 1–3 as an account of creation and fall that does more than just incorporate all humanity in its consequences. In Scripture God discloses the disgrace endured by humanity in the sin of Adam and Eve even as God provides a garment with which to cover over one's shameful exposure. Scripture is the skin, the surface of contact that makes it possible to relate the beginning of the individual, in birth, to the fact of Beginning of all persons in God's creation from nothing; and the truth of original sin as an embodied relation, in every person, of these twin facts. By emphasizing the relation of beginning and Beginning above the terms, it even becomes possible to retrieve the most seemingly improbable feature of traditional formulations of the doctrine: that it passes from generation to generation as a literal inheritance.[80]

With regard to reading the last books of *Confessions* as an opening to exploration of the relation of Beginning to beginning, recovery of the meaningfulness of description of original sin as an inheritance is more than a mere "correction" or "historical restoration"; it is a criticism and challenge to at least several centuries' tradition of theology and philosophy that has treated any account of sin as a literal inheritance as a mistake that must be erased. The history of this erasure is long and deeply entrenched in the traditions of moral-philosophical and theological reflection on any

78. For an attempt to reconcile an Augustinian theology of original sin with the polygenic findings of human evolutionary biology, see Kasujja, *Polygenism*. For a similar argument that asserts the consonance of genetics with a biological account of original sin, see Warren, *Original Sin Explained?*

79. Augustine *Confessions* 13.15.16 (Chadwick, 282).

80. For analysis of the integral importance of a theology of original sin to the coherence of *Confessions* as a model of self-narration that is persistently aware of its constitutive exterior, see Rigby, *Original Sin*.

enduring meaningfulness of original sin. Once one begins to appreciate the vast complex relation of Beginning to beginning that the detail of inheritance signifies, this history appears as much more than just a history of objection to a particular dispensable detail. It appears as a history of the attempt to narrate Beginning within the activity of beginning; to subsume the former within the activity of the latter and collapse their perceived relation altogether. This is a history of increasing foreshortened perspective until the personal activity of beginning looms so massively before the self that the fact of Beginning is obscured from view—the intellectual equivalent, to use an Augustinian image, of holding up one's thumb to blot out the sun and then drawing the conclusion of the relative insignificance of the sun to the thumb, all the while depending utterly on the illumination of the sun for the possibility of this misperception.

When the doctrine of original sin hasn't been dismissed altogether as ill-informed biology or untenable metaphysics, the objection to description of sin as inheritance has been leveled in terms of a necessary relation of voluntariness to moral accountability. It is then dismissed as a confusion of natural and moral categories, and hence as an obstacle to ethics. Reinhold Niebuhr epitomizes this perceived need to "correct" the doctrine when he laments the notion of "inheritance" as a "literalistic illusion" that is "clearly destructive of the idea of responsibility for sin."[81] As a form of genealogical critique, a theology of original sin challenges this figuration of responsibility as a function of voluntariness, where voluntariness is defined in relation to the logical-analytic terms of honesty and consistency rather than as a relationship of creature and creator. From the perspective of such a theology, the focus on voluntariness, and on the question of justice in attribution of sin, appears as a form of the self-centeredness that epitomizes all sin. A central theoretical concern of a theology of origin sin is not to explain or resolve some problem of moral accountability, but to remain wary of allowing even a lingering or background concern with this problem to obscure apprehension of immediacy of the prior history of sin in the constitution of contemporaneous intelligible self-identification. The aim is to maintain the meaningfulness of inheritable sin as an ineluctable description of the relation of Beginning and beginning, as that relation is literally embodied by every individual human being.

81. Niebuhr, *Nature*, 1:262. For elaboration of this critique, see Rees, "Anxiety."

Where the notion of inheritable sin is retained in contemporary theology of sin, it is typically rehabilitated through redefinition as something "transmittable through the dynamics of social relationships."[82] This redefinition, however, tends to further rather than redress the obscuring of the central mysterious truth of the origin of the self in the relation of God's creation *ex nihilo* and the event of one's individual birth, because it is typically predicated on the assumption that inheritance cannot mean what it literally and traditionally means; because it assumes an opposition between an amoral "natural history" and a moral history of "the dynamics of social relationships." It avoids confronting the comprehensive view of creation projected from the perspective of sin: the unity of the natural and the human. Interpreters of "inheritance" as some form of "social constructivism" continue to depend on the paradigmatic oppositions that underwrite the history of objection to the concept of an inheritable original sin. They displace rather than address the question of the nature of the "nature" that is thereby constructed. Any account of the fallen and imperfectable condition of humanity is incomplete, however, when it delimits that condition as a function of the necessarily social formation of the human.

A fuller description requires the assertion of a fallen human nature. It requires the conjunction, in other words, under the rubric of sin, of precisely those two presumably opposed terms, "human" and "nature." It is important to note this possibility of a social constructivist interpretation of inheritance, and its limitations, because it appears consonant with the theory of sexuality derived from the writings of Foucault. The possibilities of interpretation of original sin, in light of Foucault, could then be described as more or less thorough-going. A "less" interpretation would read Foucault as proponent of some version of social-constructivism, leaving the categories of "nature" and "human" essentially unchallenged. A "more" interpretation, as I am pushing it, reads Foucault as undermining altogether the possibility of categorizing in any neutral way the ingredients of an intelligible self. Every category is suspect. Every distinction is indicative of sin. Romantic autobiography then appears, not as a reaction against rationalistic binarisms, but as the predominant matrix for the narration of personal identity according to those same binarisms,

---

82. McFadyen, *Bound*, 34–40, 247. For an influential Catholic redefinition of sin along similar lines, see Rahner, *Foundations*, 106–15.

and as a powerful and compelling context of refusal of responsibility for original sin, especially when sin is described as an inheritance.

A further objection to description of sin as inheritance merits notice, because it highlights the contrast between a literary-hermeneutical as opposed to a scholarly-exegetical approach to reading Augustine. This objection, exemplified by Roland J. Teske in the introduction to his translation of *The Punishment and Forgiveness of Sins*, explains away Augustine's theology of inheritable sin as the result of his reliance on a faulty Latin translation of the Greek New Testament: "His Old Latin version of Romans 5:12 omitted the word 'death' so that 'sin' was understood as the subject of 'was passed on to all human beings.'[83] Hence in Romans 5:12 Augustine believed that he had a clear statement of sin's transmission to all human beings. Furthermore, his Latin text seemed to say that all sinned either in Adam or in Adam's sin, though neither reading is accepted by modern exegetes."[84]

This argument constitutes a severely constrained "reading" of Augustine, isolating as it does text from text, missing how rich Augustine's supposed "misreading" of Paul has been, how richly it is informed by Augustine's other writings, as if reading and interpretation can be neatly limited to the task of establishing a "correct" text.[85] A theology of original sin productively undermines any distinction between "reading" and "misreading," since no kind of reading is a morally neutral activity. Every kind of reading is a politically vested production of the text and of the knowledge of self the text generates. No wonder then that readings of the Bible are especially contested loci of manufacture of intelligible selfhood, so that a further objection to this argument, especially relevant given the prominence of New Testament scholars in debates about the moral status of same-sex sexual relations, is that it surreptitiously asserts the superior theological authority of the scholar, as arbiter of the accurate and reliable

83. Rom 5:12: "Therefore, just as sin came into the world through one man, and death came through sin, and so *death* spread to all because all have sinned."

84. Augustine, *Works*, 1/23, 23, 77 n. 14. Harrison, *Augustine*. See also Rist, *Augustine*, 310, who suggests that if Augustine were alive today he would surely avail himself of the benefit of contemporary exegetical scholarship and correct his mistake.

85. For discussion of the importance of interpretation of this passage in Romans to modern theological and philosophical argument over how to reconcile justice in moral accountability and the doctrine of original sin, see Quinn, "Disputing." Quinn's argument is noteworthy because he urges philosophers to take issues of biblical interpretation more seriously.

text, and therefore of the definitive interpretation of the text.[86] Against these authoritative claims of scholarship, the revelatory encounter with Scripture is better defined as an experience of inspired misreadings of the text, because reading is always multiple. The text is a medium of God's speech, which is never reducible to the strictly material level of the text, so that the indeterminacy of any particular reading need not be an occasion for regret or panic. Instead it attests to the continual openness of Scripture as a source of self-understanding, of the limitless activity of reading the Bible as an activity of divinely sustained self-narration.[87]

As a commentator, Augustine is no exception to the rule of reading as sinful human production of the text. With regard to Scripture, however, the hope, in faith, is that this privileged text provides an occasion for the breaking through of this sinful literary dynamic of some insight into that dynamic itself. The hope is that every reading is potentially an opening onto experience of the fullness of relation of beginning and Beginning. Augustine's readings are not the final word on this relation but rather indices of how to read the texts as an opening onto that relation; not because the text is not authoritative, but because no individual commentary is authoritative. One can believe in the status of Scripture as revelation, and also believe that the import of Scripture is finally irretrievable through sinful human reading. From the perspective of sin, such a view seems the most responsible approach possible to biblical interpretation: an embrace of the incompleteness of all reading of the text.

The problem of incompleteness describes sin and not creation. The problem of interpretation is one of human incapacity to comprehend and not of God to speak. Augustine argues as much when he emphasizes, in regard to commentary on another portion of Genesis in "To Simplician," the goodness of creation as answer to any questions about God's justice in accountability for sin:

> At this point we must try, if the Lord will help us, to see how both of these Scripture passages can be true: "Thou hatest nothing that thou hast made" and "Jacob I have loved, but Esau I have hated." The potter, remember, made one vessel unto honour, and another unto dishonour. Now, if he hated Esau because he was a vessel

86. For analysis of the indeterminate use of appeals to biblical scholarship in public debates about the morality of same-sex sexual relations, see Guest, "Battling for the Bible" and Stone, "Homosexuality and the Bible."

87. Helpful in this regard is the concept of "appropriated discourse" as explicated in Wolterstorff, *Divine Discourse.*

made unto dishonour, how could it be true that "Thou hatest nothing which thou hast made." For in that case God hated Esau though he had himself made him a vessel unto dishonour. This knotty problem is solved if we understand God to be the artificer of all creatures. Every creature of God is good. Every man is a creature as man but not as sinner. God is the creator both of the body and of the soul of man. Neither of these is evil, and God hates neither. He hates nothing which he has made. But the soul is more excellent than the body, and God is more excellent than both soul and body, being the maker and fashioner of both. In man he hates nothing but sin. Sin in man is perversity and lack of order, that is, a turning away from the Creator who is more excellent, and a turning to creatures which are inferior to him. God does not hate Esau the man, but hates Esau the sinner.[88]

Augustine resolves the seeming contradiction between the two passages he cites, not by elaborating a moral-philosophical analysis of human voluntariness as a delimiting factor of justice in moral accountability, but by affirming a doctrine of creation.

In response to any attempt to define the problem of sin as one of holding God to account as creator—If God creates, then isn't God finally morally accountable for creation of even the possibility of sin? "For in that case God hated Esau though he had himself made him a vessel unto dishonour"—Augustine demonstrates that a doctrine of original sin is inseparable from a doctrine of creation; that the former actually follows from the latter. The goodness of every human being as creature, Augustine affirms, is rooted in an ultimate connection with God who creates. The evil of every human being as sinner, by contrast, is rootless distance from God and from creation. Esau is a fitting representative of the identity of every fallen human being as both created and fallen: "Every man is a creature as man but not as sinner." This is by definition true, since all that exists is created by God, created good. Moreover, to say that "God does not hate Esau the man, but Esau the sinner," is not to assert that God is in fact capable of hate at all in a positive sense. It is to define "hate," as imaginatively assumed in divine perspective, as God's experience of creation's deficiency in its disorder. God doesn't "hate" Esau, or any human being, but God may "hate" the distance of every person from the fullness of divinely created goodness, from the order that God provides for creation. God's "hate" for the nothingness and disorder of sin is thus a necessary

88. Augustine, *Earlier Writings* (Burleigh, 399–400).

aspect of God's love. And creature in this usage defines a potential plenitude of relation to God that is not realizable in current human existence, because every person is both "human" and "sinner"; both near to God and alienated from God. A sinner just is a disordered creature.

As a kind of hermeneutical principle, Augustine insists that always present between the two terms, Beginning and beginning, determining and obscuring every attempt to read their relation, is the fact of sin. This fact is revealed to human awareness by the biblical narrative of Adam and Eve's originary disobedience, by the revelation of their Fall from the perfect order of created human goodness into the disorder of sin. It is this truth of original sin as hermeneutic mystery that Pascal affirms in the *Pensées* when he writes: "it is, however, an astounding thing that the mystery furthest from our ken, that of the transmission of sin, should be something without which we can have no knowledge of ourselves."[89] The mystery, as Pascal summarizes it, is not so much the "transmission of sin" per se, but the relation of Beginning to beginning as deformed by sin. After the Fall, sin is an inescapable feature of that relation. It indicates tangibly the reality of that relation, but also indicates tangibly the impossibility of comprehending that relation with any final insight.

Genealogical critique and human genealogy as revealed by God are conjoined in the realization of the confounding of human self-understanding in the void of sin: "The knot of our condition was twisted and turned in that abyss, so that it is harder to conceive of man without this mystery than for man to conceive of it himself."[90] A mature humorous irony of this condition is that the "conception" of this mystery is as easy in one sense as it is "hard" in another; because human beings "conceive" this mystery out of their own bodies, in the continual transmission of sin as literal inheritance from generation to generation in the reality of human sexual reproduction, even as they remain incapable of "conceiving" the fullness of relation of human reproductive and divine creative capacities.

The task now remains, against the backdrop of this imagination of every human individual as both created and born—created in goodness; born in sin—to explicate further the specific association of sexuality with original sin. This association now becomes imperative to theological investigation because sexuality describes the dynamic embodied medium

89. Pascal, *Pensées*, 35.
90. Ibid., 36.

of intersection of creation and Fall in the emergence and constitution of intelligible personal identity. Addressing the reader in whose remembrance he endures and God, "the living memory of my soul,"[91] God who is more oneself than oneself is because joining the exterior and interior of memory, Augustine asks about the seeming absurdity of human community established through the nothingness of sinning: "Who can untie this extremely twisted and tangled knot?"[92] The only direct answer to this question is that God alone can do so. But as an indirect answer one can now start by affirming that the search to know God and to know self entails the mature humorous confession of responsibility for sin and the charitable angry commitment to redress the wrongs that are multiplied by the avoidance of such responsibility. In doing so the knot that is the mystery of the transmission of sin can at least loosen its stranglehold on the bodies of those persons who most visibly bear its burden.

91. Augustine *Confessions* 2.9.17 (Chadwick, 33–34).
92. Augustine *Confessions* 2.9.18 (Chadwick, 34).

6

The Romance of Innocent Sexuality

The situation now is that these passions are set in motion in this fashion, and are brought under control by those who live disciplined, just, and devout lives, sometimes with comparative ease, sometimes with difficulty. But this control entails coercion and struggle, and the situation does not represent a state of health in accordance with nature, but an enfeebled condition arising from guilt. Again, we observe that modesty does not hide the acts of anger and of the other emotions in the same way as it conceals the acts of lust, which are performed by the sexual organs; but this is simply because in the effect of other emotions the members of the body are not set in motion by the feelings themselves but by the will, after it has decided to co-operate with them, for the will has sovereign power in the employment of those members. Anyone who utters a word in anger, anyone who goes so far as to strike another person, could not do so if his tongue or hand were not put in motion at the command, as one may say, of his will; and those members are set in motion by the same will even when there is no anger. But the genital organs have become as it were the private property of lust, which has brought them so completely under its sway that they have no power of movement if this passion fails, if it has not arisen spontaneously or in response to a stimulus. It is this that arouses shame; it is this that makes us shun the eyes of beholders in embarrassment. A man would be less put out by a crowd of spectators watching him visit his anger unjustly upon another man than by one person observing him when he is having lawful intercourse with his wife.[1]

1. Augustine *City of God* 14.20 (Bettenson, 581).

Which Augustine? Whose Influence?

WITHIN THEOLOGICAL DISCOURSE ON sexuality the estimation of the writings of St. Augustine have been predominantly negative. Such judgment however depends on a particular romantic tradition of interpretation. According to this tradition, Augustine claims that sexuality, as a contemporaneous embodied reality of human identity, is both a symbol of Adam and Eve's sin in Eden and also a consequence of that sin. As a symbol, it assumes a continuity between the well ordered relation of the constituent elements of the individual, and of the well-ordered relation of individuals to God their creator, enabling an analogy between the disobedience of sexual desire of the individual will and the disobedience of Adam and Eve of God's will. As a consequence, it is the literal inscription onto the body of that disobedience. Hence the claim that the punishment fits the crime. Just as the created parents of all humanity subverted the good order of their communal relationship to God in the pursuit of a private selfish end, so too the "genital organs" subvert the good order of the body, will, and soul of every person, in the pursuit of their own selfish pleasure: "But the genital organs have become as it were the private property of lust."

As critical as this tradition of interpretation is of Augustine, at its most charitable it at least concedes to him that even if this loss of order of the constituent ingredients of the self is profoundly lamentable, neither the body nor the pleasures of the body, are per se lamentable, since Adam and Eve were wholly embodied creatures. Even so, Augustine is singled out for his extreme mistrust of sexual activity and pleasure. Other emotions and passions, though disordered, continue to reflect the hierarchy of soul and will over body, whereas sexual desire has a will of its own, and so overwhelms reason in a unique manner. Sexual pleasure after the Fall is even depicted as inversely proportional to a corresponding loss of reason: "So intense is the pleasure that when it reaches its climax there is an almost total extinction of mental alertness; the intellectual sentries, as it were, are overwhelmed."[2] Sexual pleasure before the Fall, to the extent it is imaginable, is imagined as a unity of bodily function and rational will: pleasure arising from the satisfaction of their harmonious relation. Sexual relations after the Fall, by contrast, require privacy not so much because the activity is shameful in itself, as because the loss of reason, the

2. Augustine *City of God* 14.16 (Bettenson, 577).

subjection of will to passion, is especially shameful, because especially degrading, in a literal sense, of properly ordered human identity.[3]

Modesty, according to this whole understanding of Augustine on sexuality, is figured very much as a proper regard for self-presentation as a self-commanding individual. Behind the conclusion that, "A man would be less put out by a crowd of spectators watching him visit his anger unjustly upon another man than by one person observing him when he is having lawful intercourse with his wife," presumably rests the whole weight of classical asceticism, so that one might paraphrase Augustine as saying "A *wise* man would be less put out."[4] Augustine's assertion of the relative discomposure of the "man," in these two cases, is determined by reference to a rationalistic norm of public encounter between sober-minded men. One could therefore criticize this entire account of a distinction between public and private self-presentation, assuming as it does an asymmetry between relations among men in the public realm, and relations between man and woman in the private realm. Instead the reading this chapter challenges in fact requires the ascription of this distinction to Augustine, in order to proceed with its own corrective of the Augustinian tradition on sexuality and sin. This disputed reading, rather than challenge the entire distinction between private and public encounter, re-affirms that distinction, not in the service of asceticism, but in the service of a romantic theology of marriage as unique locus of realization of personal identity of the sex of the individual man and woman. It attributes the distinction of public versus private self-presentation to Augustine. It is then able to reverse the valuation of public and private while endowing the distinction itself with the authority of the sainted church father.

The ensuing criticism of Augustine is that he failed to recognize the necessity of privacy to the fulfillment of sexual encounter between man and woman as an especially privileged space of self-discovery through self-disclosure. Attribution of this failure to Augustine serves as foil for elaboration of the typical romantic corrective of Augustine on sexuality.

3. For discussion of Augustine's view of "concupiscence" as the disordering evil of sexuality, see Kelly, "Sexuality."

4. In using the specific example of public sex, Augustine is countering what he terms, "The ridiculous indecency of the cynics" (*City of God* 14.20 [Bettenson, 581]). Elsewhere Augustine offers the following definition of wisdom: "I call those men wise whom the truth commands to be called wise, that is, those who are at peace because they have made lust subject to the rule of the mind." Augustine *On Free Choice of the Will* 1.9 (Benjamin and Hackstaff, 20).

This corrective is exemplified in the writings of no less a stern theological authority than Paul Ramsey:

> Indeed, we have to follow Augustine to the point of these some-times crude illustrations in order to come to the heart of the issue for the Christian interpretation of sex. For Augustine does not say that there is anything shameful about the body, the genital organs or their connection and movement in coitus. What he finds shameful is the operation of sexuality without the personal presence of the man and the woman in it. And he finds the invol-untary, passional aspects of the sex relation, as it now is, shame-ful, because he cannot imagine any other form of presence in the body than rationally deliberate or voluntary presence. Whatever we may make of his views, and however astonishing they may be, they have at least this strength: that Augustine offers some sort of comprehension of sexual passion in thoroughgoing connec-tion with what he regards as the very essence of human persons. Against him it accomplishes nothing to say that sexuality is just "naturally" spontaneous and unsubmissive to the presiding will, that is, that it has to do with the biological species and does not directly and immediately engage *the persons*, male and female. There will be no overcoming Augustine (and no overcoming of contemporary dualism) until it is said forthrightly that *precisely because* sexual love is *not* directly subject to reason or will it is specially apt to serve the function for which God appointed it, namely, to be the field in which men and women may be person-ally present in their bodies and consequently accessible to one another from the heart.[5]

Ramsey's reading of Augustine is noteworthy for insisting from start to finish on the possibility of "personal presence" between man and woman according to the terms of homo/heterosexual definition. In do-ing so Ramsey's commentary is a telling example of how the implicit ascription of an anachronistic psychological identity to the historical figure, Augustine, constructs an Augustinian point of view to then argue against. When Ramsey claims that Augustine only finds sexual relation-ship shameful if it is not between properly sexed and present persons, he is inscribing a familiar romantic ideal of liberated sexual relationship into the texts he is reading even as he is engaging in a kind of cultural protest against so-called sexual liberation, earning his status as the stan-dard of the colloquium that bears his name and proving how thoroughly

5. Ramsey, "Human Sexuality," 118–19.

novelistic concerns about sexed identity are scattered through theological writings, in the sense of also dispersed by them. In the process he credits to Augustine the fantasy at the core of the romance of innocent sexuality: that somehow human beings in relation to each other can overcome the epistemic catastrophe of sin.

Rather than say of Augustine that "he cannot imagine any other form of presence in the body than rationally deliberate or voluntary presence," probably it would be more illuminating to say of Augustine that it is precisely because he *can and does* imagine an "other form of presence in the body," that sexuality merits so much attention and criticism in his writings. The total project of "overcoming Augustine" thus depends on construction of a particular Augustine to be overcome: the one who denies personal presence in intercourse, or at least denigrates all such personal presence as shameful. Yet it is possible to construct a different Augustine, one who denies that any such fulfillment of personal presence, whether in the context of sexual relationship or otherwise, is possible after the Fall. It is the figure of this latter Augustine who is conjured in the present work, which seeks a more mature, humorous reading of his writings on sexuality and original sin.[6]

At stake in the romantic trajectory of interpretation of Augustine, its lack of humor, is maintenance of the imagined possibility of self-discovery through self-disclosure of the truth of the self—the fiction of sex—within the private space of marital sexual relationship. Though Ramsey and his many admirers regard this possibility of encounter as a function of an essential difference between man and woman, the claim is more noteworthy for its romanticism and epistemological dependence on the closet than its exclusivity. What is striking about Ramsey's argument is the manner in which, even as he decries Augustine's influence on the history of Christian sexual ethics, he at the same time credits Augustine, as an outstanding authoritative figure of the faith, with "comprehension" of the truth of sex as an essential generative source of personal identity:

6. Compare with Bourdieu on mythical analysis: "It follows that, as a point of method, any attempt to reconstruct the original meaning of a mythical tradition must include analysis of the laws of the deformation to which various successive interpreters subject it on the basis of their systems of interests" (Bourdieu, *Outline*, 231). My own conviction is that sin signifies the impossibility of any interpreter escaping from the reach of the "laws of deformation," and so the impossibility of "reconstruction" of an "original meaning" in reading of Augustine. One must therefore strive for awareness of the self's own location in contemporaneous structuring "systems of interests," in order to begin to approach the texts with some practical hermeneutic reverence.

"Whatever we may make of his views, and however astonishing they may be, they have at least this strength: that Augustine offers some sort of comprehension of sexual passion in thoroughgoing connection with what he regards as the very essence of human persons." Ramsey's "at least" here is ironic, given that the "essence of human persons" Augustine most consistently connects with "sexual passion" is original sin, and not any truth of personal identity as man or woman. And given that it at least also bespeaks the entanglement of homosexual panic and panic over responsibility for original sin.

Ramsey proceeds, under the rubric of an under-articulated doctrine of creation, both to perpetuate the caricature of Augustine as sex-phobic Christian father *and* to ascribe to him a romantic ideal of sexed identity, when he subsequently comments:

> As a consequence, created nature has been defamed at a most essential point under the aegis of the presiding mind and its "command performances." This fault, however, does not require us to deny that Augustine believed that sexual intercourse between Adam and Eve would have been pure, unmixed pleasure in each other's embodied presence. What else could integral human sexuality mean if not greater joy in man-womanhood than the fallen race has experienced since?[7]

The rhetorical energy invested in Ramsey's concluding question is surprising, since one could at least answer here that "integral human sexuality" could mean greater joy, not in "man-womanhood," but in God-personhood, "than the fallen race has experienced since."

Ramsey suggests that the consequence of Adam and Eve's sin is a tragedy not so much for the loss of experience of joy of relationship to God, as for the loss of experience of joy of true man-womanhood, for the loss of satisfaction of personal fulfillment through realization of one's created sex as man or woman. Through these comments Ramsey prioritizes redemption as a recovery of the idealized relationship between man and woman that makes such personal fulfillment possible, and only secondarily as recovery of relationship between humanity and God, since the very term "humanity" is insistently figured as the sexualized dyad man-womanhood. Resolution of the project of homo/heterosexual definition is now itself literally a matter of redemption. And human sexuality, defined as the expression of the individual's sex in the context of marriage,

7. Ramsey, "Human Sexuality," 121.

is accredited a divinely ordained status as privileged locus of human-divine encounter. Redemption from homosexual panic and redemption by God thereby fold into each other. Ramsey's choice of title for his essay—"Human Sexuality in the History of Redemption"—consequently invites strict scrutiny of the conjunction of these two terms—"human sexuality" and "redemption"—under the rubric of the history, not of redemption, but of sexuality. The question then becomes, not what purpose does sexuality serve in the promise of redemption of humanity, but how is discernment of the promise of redemption distorted by this historically specific overburdened association with sexuality?

Reconsideration of Augustine's writings on sexuality and sin provides a means of addressing this question. The ascription of redemptive importance to sexuality, typified in a traditionalist form by Ramsey's essay, connects directly with the history of denunciation of Augustine's influence on sexual ethics. Augustine's baneful influence must be countered, because to do so facilitates conferral of divinely ordained status to a distinction between personal identity in private-erotic relationship and personal identity in communal-rational relationship. Yet this is a distinction that Augustine consistently undermines, even as the apparent requirement of privacy of sexual relationship is an indication of something seriously disordered in that relationship itself, touching even a notion of personal presence or "the very essence of human persons." Though marital intercourse is "lawful," and more significantly, not sinful, still it is praiseworthy, as Augustine elsewhere indicates, when spouses can attain marital continence.[8] More generally for Augustine, the reality of coercion and special political arrangements points to something fundamentally disordered in human identity.

Interpretation of Augustine on this point can move in at least two directions: to include the public and communal within the disordered pursuit of self-presence that demands privacy, or to set apart the private as a special realm within which the disorder of public and communal relationship is overcome in the encounter between two properly sexed individuals. Ramsey makes a definite choice of movement in the latter direction, raising the question of what wisdom exactly he is crediting to Augustine when he writes:

8. See, for example, passages in *Excellence of Marriage*, and *Adulterous Marriages*, in Augustine, *Works*, 1/9 (Kearney, 34–35, 37–38, 41–42, 176–77); for an interpretation of Augustine on continence as a kind of reparative therapy one can practice to discipline fallen human desire, see Babcock, "Augustine."

All this means that, if ever the deleterious influence of Augustine upon Christian sex ethics is finally to be overcome, without rejecting his wisdom, it will not be contemporary dualists charging him with ancient soul-body dualism, and then looking the other way for some radically new starting point. He can be overcome only by an internal criticism, by denying that the body is (under conditions of maximum health and integrity) in every function subject to the soul's commands. It makes no difference whether we say that there is a presence of soul to the body in sexual passion that is quite different than its *commanding* presence, or say rather that bodily powers and precisely the spontaneous and rationally insubordinate movements of sexuality are, for the purpose of accessibility or presence to another being in this world, superior to the means the soul has for the deliberate communication of itself to the other. The point is in either case the same.[9]

A noteworthy feature of this whole attempt at an "internal criticism" is that it operates by articulating a "difference" that it simultaneously denies. To say that "there is a presence of soul to the body in sexual passion" and to say that "precisely the spontaneous and rationally insubordinate movements of sexuality are, for the purpose of accessibility or presence to another being in this world, superior" is not to say the same thing "in either case," as if these were equivalent analytic propositions. It is, continuing the analogy, to construct a contestable synthetic proposition about the relative status of communication of "presence" of the self in "sexual passion" as opposed to "deliberate," that is, non-sexual, relationship. (Assuming the multiple dubious ideas: that such a thing as "deliberate communication" of self is possible; that sexual relationship cannot be "deliberate" in whatever sense this means; that "sexual passion" necessarily involves an interest in some other person's self-presence; and that the sexual and non-sexual self can be neatly delimited, and then confined to their respective domains of self-disclosure.)

Though the ostensible "point" of Ramsey's argument is an internal criticism of an Augustinian theology of sexuality, its sharper point is to accomplish a wholesale reversal of valuation of the contrasting modes of personal presence upon which that Augustinian theology is constructed—modes which are mostly revealing of the romantic sensibility of the interpreter. Ramsey's point can therefore be parsed into two related propositions: first, the assertion of the superior status of sexuality

9. Ramsey, "Human Sexuality," 123.

as medium of communication of the superior truth of personal identity, the sex that one is; and second, the insistence that the truth concerned necessarily bespeaks one's created identity as male or female in relation to the dyad man-womanhood. The elevation of this dual truth to the indisputable status of uncorrupted creation—"under conditions of maximum health and integrity"—in other words, within monogamous heterosexual marriage—is the reason that Augustine's "deleterious influence" must be "overcome." Augustine above all others is caricatured as causing real harm to individuals by causing them to disparage the meaningful depth of their superior selves, their sex, by undermining in effect the project of homo/heterosexual definition, by inducing homosexual panic. The insult to self, blamed on Augustine, redounds directly to God: "created nature has been defamed at a most essential point." Christian theology now begins to look a lot like an exercise in reparative therapy.[10]

Ramsey's argument revolves around the humorless fantasy of recovery of a fictitious sex, but his essay nevertheless contains the ingredients of an internal criticism, not of Augustine, but of the strand of romantic Augustinianism that enables the isolation of this fictional sex of the self as an incontrovertible truth of personal identity, thereby bestowing upon that sex redemptive significance. If, as Ramsey insists, sexuality possesses some meaningful place in the overall history of God's relationship with creation—including as it does the history of humanity—then sexuality must be something more than mere animal instinct seeking mindless expression. Ramsey is adamant that sexuality describes something fundamental about persons, as creatures capable in some way of responsible, because uniquely responsive, relationship to their creator.

Such is Ramsey's concern in singling out "contemporary dualism" as especially destructive of the possibility of an adequate theology of sexuality:

> It is a doubtful advance beyond Augustine to say that in sexuality
> man is embedded in unchanging, non-historical nature, or that

10. The term "reparative therapy" mostly has been used to describe the work of "ex-Gay Ministries" such as *Exodus*. Their claim of possibility of "treatment" of homosexuality is based on the conceptualization of same-sex desire as an effect of incomplete or damaged identification of the afflicted individual with other persons of the same sex, especially of a boy with his father. Such desire is treated as a symptomatic expression of the individual's yearning for wholeness of sexed identity. The goal of therapy is to make of the person a complete "man" or "woman." For a theoretical basis of this approach, see Moberly, *Homosexuality* and *Psychogenesis*.

persons in community are historical, their bodies are not. That would be the most consummate dualism, for it would mean that man himself goes on toward his appointed end (be it some human or ideal achievement to which each individual or generation is as close as any other, or some providential appointment toward which mankind moves trans-sexually), while human sexuality remains, beside or beneath all this, in its eternal rounds forever of the same insignificant significance.[11]

This form of consummate dualism is so objectionable because it raises the specter of a self without a sex. As much as he objects to the conceptualization of sexuality as "embedded in unchanging, non-historical nature," Ramsey isn't interested in actually disputing the naturalness of sex at all, but only the "insignificant significance" of sex that might follow from a view of nature that he finds almost abhorrent. The implicit target of this whole statement is anyone who denies the integral importance of the created sex of every individual as man or woman to the realization of fullness of human identity. Ramsey is disputing what counts as nature, and what it means to count as nature. He is in effect writing the history of sexuality. When Ramsey posits and then rejects an opposition between "unchanging, non-historical nature," and "man" who "goes on toward his appointed end," he unwittingly engages nature as a field of contestable signification in the very process of attempting to fix that signification in one determinate form.

Ramsey seeks to affirm the *significance* of nature, of human nature as created male and female, to attainment of whatever "end" God appoints. He can only do so, however, by affirming the discovery of that nature as historical specificity; so that his whole argument turns out to be doubly romantic, in the redemptive significance ascribed to fulfillment of identity as male and female in marital sexual relationship and in the associated redemptive significance ascribed to the apprehension of nature as a field of unconditioned discovery of sex. Rejection of the consummate dualism Ramsey decries therefore calls into question the stability of his own idealization of nature as historical and also beyond qualification or dispute, since an unexpected glimpse emerges, in the midst of his argument for the primacy of sex, of the operation of sexuality as it masks its own generative capacities in the projected fantasy of sex as a productive and stable center of personal identity.

11. Ramsey, "Human Sexuality," 133–34.

What then has been so deleterious about the "influence of Augustine upon Christian sex ethics"? A plausible answer to this question follows from the distinction between the Augustine who has exercised such influence, and the historically documented figure, Augustine, Bishop of Hippo, who died circa 430 CE as his city lay under siege by Vandals. The relation between these two persons is tangential. The latter Augustine's influence expired pretty much when he did; or at least when the communities he guided over his lifetime themselves dispersed or were destroyed beyond all recognition or memory of their former selves. The former Augustine, by contrast, is alive and well, and remains influential. Yet the influence of this Augustine doesn't attest to any unmediated power of the writings of the Bishop of Hippo. Instead those writings are the occasion for the formation and exertion, under the figure of the influence of the historical Augustine, of the influence of the interpreters of those writings, overwhelmingly dominated by the theme I have labeled as romanticism in theology: the overburdening of human sexual relationship with redemptive significance. The continuing influence of Augustine denotes the continuing productivity of the writings of Augustine to the romance of innocent sexuality.

Like the host of other commentators spanning the theological spectrum who finger Augustine in the lineup of suspect authorities, Ramsey engages Augustine's writings as an occasion for narration of the fiction of sex. For this reason Augustine's writings present an invaluable resource for challenging those narrations. Reading Augustine against his detractors has unique potential to cast critical theological light on the shadowy operations of sexuality as a potent field of sin.

Sex, Nature, and Politics

A summary of this counter-reading of Augustine against his critics is that the romantic interpretation of Augustine, exemplified in Ramsey's essay, confuses "the deleterious influence of Augustine upon Christian sex ethics" with "the deleterious influence" of Adam and Eve's sin on human sexuality. Such confusion enables critics to remain blind to the implication of their own interpretive practices in the dynamic of sinful sexuality they are rejecting. They bifurcate sexuality into two distinct categories, the innocent and the sinful, and then insist that sexuality is implicated in sin only to the extent that the sexuality in question contradicts or eludes the romantic paradigm of sexuality in marriage as field of redemptive divine encounter. Augustine's deleterious influence, in this view, has been the unjust failure to distinguish between the innocent and the sinful, between those persons whose sex is realizing its created expressive purpose along the trajectory of its sexual orientation, and those who are thwarting or undermining that purpose. Relative to that purpose, marriage is credited with the capacity to redeem sexuality as means of realization of sex, and to redeem the married pair in relation to God.

To elaborate: every person, following this confusion, has a sex that is an origin and source of one's personal identity, specifically as human being, as more than animal, as expressed in an orientation toward another meaningfully sexed person in sexual relationship. Sexuality acquires tremendous importance as it becomes the means of disclosure of the most intimate and revealing truth of the self. The disputed subject matter of interpretation, following this confusion, concerns the status of sexuality as medium of expression of personal identity, of sex. Commentators on Augustine dispute how strictly animal and how sinful or disordered is sexuality, and how good is sex in itself. The end of their commentary is an unqualified affirmation of the goodness of sex, as created, in tandem with a qualified affirmation of the goodness of sexuality, in fallen humanity, as means of expression of sex within some set of strictly delimited conditions.[12] Innocent sexuality, sexuality that realizes the permissible, human expression of sex, is opposed to sinful sexuality, sexuality that degrades sex and undermines the expressive capacities of innocent sexuality.

Marriage emerges out of this matrix of interpretation as the condition par excellence for realization of the expressive capacity of innocent sexuality of the truth of sex, at the same time as marriage must be defended against the degradations of sinful sexuality. The possibility of disclosure of the truest self narrows to the space of private sexual relationship with one other person, presumably of the opposite sex, though not necessarily so, proponents of same-sex marriage often arguing for inclusion according to these very terms.[13] The romance of innocent sexu-

12. Parallel argument focuses on the "body" in relation to "society." See for example Cahill, *Sex*, 73–107. And her comment in the same volume: "Far from a simple loosening of social controls on the body, the moral question for a Christian ethics of sex and gender becomes how to socialize the body—as male and female, as sexual, as parental—in ways which enlarge our social capacities for compassion toward others and solidarity in the common good." (164)

13. See, for example, the discussion of Karl Barth's concept of "co-humanity" in Rogers, *Sexuality*, 180–91.

ality is the promise of realization of fullness of identity of one's sex in marriage. It is the promise of successful humanization through definitive privatization of sexuality against the continual threat posed by a public realm of sinful debasing sexuality and attendant slippages of homo/heterosexual definition.

Given how consistently Augustine describes sexual relationships after the Fall as fundamentally shameful, as fundamentally contradictory of the truth of self that romantic tradents of the fiction of sex continually assert, it makes sense that Augustine's writings have been a continual occasion for the working out of this confusion of interpretation. Whereas Ramsey and others argue that the privacy of sexual relationship in marriage is uniquely capable of enabling discovery and communication of self, and that the personal intelligibility that results is a function of creation by God, Augustine insists on the public and communal conditions of possibility of personal intelligibility. Where one treats nakedness as a metaphor of possibility of beneficial fullness of disclosure, the other treats it as a metaphor of damaging exposure in multiple distressing senses: of exposure to the judgment of God, to the judgment of other human beings, and to all the harms of the natural world. Where one treats nakedness in the marital bed as a privileged opportunity, the other treats it as a shameful necessity.

Confusing Augustine's influence with sin's influence facilitates reading Augustine's writings according to such oppositions. A passage from *The Literal Meaning of Genesis* addressing "Death and concupiscence the result of original sin," illustrates their productivity:

> When Adam and Eve, therefore, lost their privileged state, their bodies became subject to disease and death, like the bodies of animals, and consequently subject to the same drive by which there is in animals a desire to copulate and thus provide for offspring to take the place of those that die. Nevertheless, even in its punishment the rational soul gave evidence of its innate nobility when it blushed because of the animal movement of the members of its body and when it imparted to it a sense of shame, not only because it began to experience something where there had been no such feeling before, but also because this movement of which it was ashamed came from the violation of the divine command. In this, man realized with what grace he had previously been clothed when he experienced nothing indecent in his nakedness. Then was accomplished the saying of the Psalmist, *O*

Lord, by Thy favor Thou has given strength to my beauty; but Thou has turned away Thy face, and I have become troubled.[14]

A romantic reading of this statement faults Augustine for a lack of openness to the expressive possibilities of sexual relationship, and so accuses him of an unwarranted pessimism about the possible integration of the physical reality of sexual desire into a healthy marital relationship. The disgrace of sin, the exposure of incompletion of self that follows from the loss of unity of self in relation to God, is now perversely celebrated as an open secret, as an opportunity to achieve behind closed doors what was lost for all in public. Augustine's influence becomes a history of morbid distrust of sexuality, of wrongfully treating sexual desire as a strictly postlapsarian phenomenon, equating it with disease and death and base animality—a history projected in much anti-Christian, and especially anti-Catholic writings, to the present day.[15] This characterization of Augustine's influence likewise fits the shift, described by Foucault, from discussion of sexuality as a problem of sin to a problem of health, as even Ramsey's comments demonstrate.[16] What Augustine universally condemns as sinful, as "concupiscence," then is condemned only when unhealthy, when not properly expressive of a person's sex, when not constructive of marital relationship between two persons who are authentically oriented toward each others' homo/heterosexually defined sex.

Enmeshed as it is in the many cultural discourses of which it forms a part, theological discourse on sexuality admits the definition of Augustine's influence propounded by its most ardent critics. It then responds to those critics by decrying Augustine on sexuality in turn, contributing to production of an Augustinian influence. When Augustine is criticized for evaluating sexual desire and relationship too completely under the rubric of fallen nature, the possibility of a non-naturalistic reading of Augustine is eclipsed. All of this reading of Augustine becomes

14. Augustine *Literal Meaning* 11.32 (Taylor, 2:165).

15. Charles Kingsley's writings are a prime historical example of this tradition of argument. See Barker, "Erotic Martyrdom." In a similar and somewhat ironic vein, a lot of gay activism has also "blamed" the Catholic Church for treating sexuality as a disease. Saint Patrick's Cathedral in New York City was a regular site of protest by ACT UP/NY. One action in particular, on December 10, 1989, received massive media attention, when a protestor defiled a communion wafer. On the history of ACT UP, see Gould, *Moving Politics*.

16. For history of this shift in nineteenth-century America, see Gardella, *Innocent*, 39–79. For twentieth-century American medical history, see Terry, *American*. For philosophical analysis, see Soble, "Philosophy."

naturalized, in the sense that the subject of dispute is cast as the proper discernment of sex and its expression as a natural phenomenon, assuming an opposition between the natural and the political, where the work of the political is to integrate to human purposes what is natural and regulate what is unnatural. The work of theological discourse on sexuality becomes defined as a problem of nature, of distinguishing what is given by nature from what is chosen against nature, obscuring from view that the boundary between the natural and the unnatural is only ever marked by continual political dispute. At the same time literal interpretation of Augustine is discredited. Whatever else one believes, it becomes inadmissible to hold that the Fall took the form of an actual change in the human body, a change that persists throughout the generations, an unnatural change of nature.

If such an interpretation is likely to be dismissed as faulty biology, it helps very much that it also contradicts the model of sexuality as expressive of sex. Good biology and good theology—that is, comfortingly humorless biology and theology—converge in the ideal of the unifying presence of self in one's sex seeking its natural realization through orientation to another sexed individual. But once one challenges the very notion of the expressive capacity of sexuality, the aim of objection to the literal interpretation begins to dissolve. A different aim, a more responsible aim, an aim guided by the literal interpretation, instead can appear to view. One no longer needs to read Augustine as saying that sexuality is a disease caused by sin. Instead one can read Augustine as an exemplar of mature humorous theological reflection, as saying that sexuality is incapable of serving the expressive purpose ascribed to it within the history of sexuality. As saying, in effect, that sexuality is inherently sinful. The trouble, it is important to emphasize, is not with the body in itself—in fact an incomprehensible fantasy itself of uncomplicated personal presence—but with the body as a field of organization of prideful, because fallen, human ambitions. The body in faith as created by God remains an unqualified good, even as the body experienced in sexuality is sinful.[17]

---

17. Augustine is not a proponent of any version of a *felix culpa*. Whatever good humanity will ultimately enjoy through God's redemptive grace, Adam and Eve would have enjoyed had they not sinned, and then some; their enjoyment of their perfection in God was perfect in itself. They need not have sinned to have appreciated and known its perfection. See *City of God* 13.14–17, 14.10, 23 (Bettenson, 523–29, 566–67, 585–87). Compare with Adam's exclamation in Milton's *Paradise Lost* (1674): "O Goodness infinite, goodness immense!/That all this good of evil shall produce,/And evil turn to good; more

In order to make sense of the distinction between the goodness of the body, the sinfulness of sexuality, and the complexity of relation between them, Peter Brown divides Augustine's thought into two phases, what he describes as an early "ascetic" and "vertical" paradigm of sexuality and a late integrated "social" paradigm.[18] These phases correlate with Augustine's own shift from allegorical to literal interpretation of Genesis.[19] Sexuality in the later Augustine is no longer a problem of controlling or disciplining an isolable aspect of human biology. It is a manifestation of the impossibility of intelligibly unified personal identity after the Fall—an impossibility not of nature, but of history that has become nature. Augustine who in his earlier writings was more concerned with isolating and identifying sexual experience as a particular realm of sin that one must resist—in a way almost quarantining sexual experience as an aspect of the individual person that was especially deformed by the Fall—in his later writings becomes more concerned with sexuality as a communal practice that involves the whole person. Once sin signifies the equality and sociality of all human beings in their descent from Adam and Eve, the sinfulness of sexuality is less a matter of individual failing and much more a matter of deficient social practice. A qualification follows of the conventional distinction in Augustinian scholarship between the creation of humanity as social and the organization of human community as political, where the advent of the political in the Fall involves further, distinctive deformations of human community.[20] Instead sociality, though valued in faith as part of the ordered goodness of creation, is itself now only fully cognizable through political struggle. The social is therefore a future for which one ought to labor in faith, and not a past to be invoked as an explanation. All the more reason, as a result, to appreciate as an occasion for hospitality the discomfort with self that other person's purportedly improperly sexed presence elicits.

---

wonderful/Than that which by creation first brought forth/Light out of darkness! Full of doubt I stand,/Whether I should repent me now of sin/By mee done and occasion'd, or rejoice/Much more, that much more good thereof shall spring,/To God more glory, more good will to Men/From God, and over wrath grace shall abound" (12.469–78). Also the famously ambiguous statement from *Areopagitica* (1644): "And perhaps this is that doom which Adam fell into of knowing good and evil, that is to say, of knowing good by evil" (Milton, *Complete*, 728).

18. Brown and Donovan, *Augustine and Sexuality*, 8, 11.

19. On this shift, see Clark, "Heresy." And Schreiner, "Eve." Also see Augustine's own comments regarding this shift in *Literal Meaning* 8.2 (Taylor, 2:35–36).

20. Deane, *Political*, 78–153.

Augustine's insistence on a literal interpretation of both Genesis and the associated doctrine of original sin remains influential, only not for its baneful influence, but as a kind of inaugural event in the writing of the history of sexuality, a history that begins with the Fall as narrated by God. From this renewed historical perspective, what looks at first like bad biology appears more as theologically astute history: "When Adam and Eve, therefore, lost their privileged state, their bodies became subject to disease and death, like the bodies of animals, and consequently subject to the same drive by which there is in animals a desire to copulate and thus provide for offspring to take the place of those that die." One may dispute the details of what exactly was changed in Adam and Eve and in all humanity as a consequence of their disobedience; still the pivotal assertion of the following truth of the Fall remains: that Adam and Eve "lost their privileged state." And, a literal interpretation of this occurrence adds, in doing so they lost that state not just for themselves, but for all humanity.

When the nature of humanity in the Fall was altered, the possibility of knowledge of nature was itself altered. From the perspective of fallen humanity, it is impossible to describe fully what was lost. It is therefore possible to dispute Augustine's identification of the "rational soul" with the "innate nobility" of created human identity and still agree with his description of the fallen self as alienated from God. Relation to God under the sign of obedience has become relation to God under the sign of disobedience: "Nevertheless, even in its punishment the rational soul gave evidence of its innate nobility when it blushed because of the animal movement of the members of its body and when it imparted to it a sense of shame, not only because it began to experience something where there had been no such feeling before, but also because this movement of which it was ashamed came from the violation of the divine command." The shame that Augustine describes here is evidence that some memory of the privileged state of Adam and Eve persists among fallen humanity, so that the fallen self, though dissipated, maintains just enough integrity to desire to attempt interminably the futile project of reconstruction of its own wholeness of identity. One must have some sense of loss, of instability, of unintelligibility, energizing the continuous sinful project of self-organization, so that Augustine himself can extol the sense of shame of the fallen self at its disintegration as itself a portion of grace, the grace to feel shame at one's disgrace.

As an embodied totality, the self after the Fall is alienated from the body, not in the sense that any particular dimension of the self is insubordinate to any other dimension of the self—in Augustine's terms, the sexual organs defiant of the rule of the rational will—but the self is alienated from the possibility of its own completion in God. If Augustine's focus on the rebellion of the "sexual organs" against the "rule" of the rational will is indeed mistaken, the mistake is in its assumption of a necessarily hierarchical organization of the ingredients of selfhood. To the extent that Augustine himself emphasizes sexual desire as the specific locus of concentration of God's judgment on fallen humanity, at the expense of admission of the imperfectability of the self, of the radical incompletion of self apart from God, he then becomes subject to a different and arguably much more consistent internal criticism: that the body is not properly "subject to the soul's commands," not because the body is in any way defective in itself, but because the whole person, symbolized for Augustine by the term "soul," denies God's commanding authority in the very attempt to exercise such commanding authority on its own behalf. The transition from the earlier to the later Augustine is the working out of this internal criticism, so that any ambiguity in Augustine's earlier works about the possible perfectibility of humanity—implicit for example in the qualification of the earlier phase as "ascetical-mystical"[21]—is definitively resolved in the negative in the later works.

Once the imperfectability of humanity emerges as a constant theme in Augustine's writings, the shame experienced by Adam and Eve after their disobedience acquires distinctive historical and political importance. Because they lived alone, as the first two persons, man and woman, it is no surprise that so many persons have jumped to the hasty conclusion that Adam and Eve were married; that theirs was a private relationship; and that the Fall was for them a kind of loss of that privacy, so that marriage acquires a recuperative function: the microcosmic replication of the macrocosmic origin of humankind. The pairing of human beings in private sexual relationship is then wrongfully imagined as restoring Eden, as if the Garden had been created for the enjoyment of Adam and Eve as an ultimate honeymoon suite for themselves alone. Augustine undermines this idealization of Adam and Eve as a perfect marital pair, living literally in Paradise, by insisting that their shame is not in their loss of privacy, but in their acquired desire for privacy: "In this, man realized

21. O'Connell, "Sexuality," 76.

with what grace he had previously been clothed when he experienced nothing indecent in his nakedness. Then was accomplished the saying of the Psalmist, "*O Lord, by Thy favor Thou has given strength to my beauty; but Thou has turned away Thy face, and I have become troubled.*"[22]

Augustine's invocation of the Psalmist raises a vexing question of biblical theology, suggesting as it does that human troubles *begin* when God withdraws God's presence, whereas a theology of original sin asserts that human troubles *began* when human beings turned away from God. Considered as God's punishment, however, God's turning away follows human disobedience. When God, as the Psalmist repeatedly laments, is hiding God's face, God is in a way only metaphorically and mercifully obliging the psalmist by averting God's gaze from the fallen self. The tragedy for humanity is that while God can turn God's visage back again, fallen humanity of its own will can neither turn itself toward God, nor conjure God's presence. The "indecency" of nakedness after the Fall is a direct function somehow of this failure of community in God as instituted by human sin, whereas humanity before the Fall was not naked, because it was "clothed" in the "grace" of uninhibited community in God.

Following this line of argument, it is a distraction to worry whether Adam and Eve would have produced children regardless of whether or not they had sinned, and how they would have done so, especially since knowledge of sexual relationship before the Fall is an impossibility. (So that Augustine's description of intercourse in paradise mostly bespeaks one more sinful human fantasy of the unimaginable, of the perfectible self.)[23] Instead, assuming that they could once have procreated without sin—not to replace their mortal selves, as animals and fallen humanity do, but to fulfill the divine commandment—and that they could have continued to procreate without sin, a more apt question then becomes whether Adam and Eve would have required the privacy for procreation characteristic of "lawful intercourse" among fallen humanity.

Like all questions about the perfection of created humanity, it is impossible to say what privacy in the context of perfect enjoyment of community with God could have been. But one can at least observe that the characteristic sign of fallen sexual relationship, like all human relationship, is the *absence* of that community. One can further observe that the perfection of Adam and Eve in God was perhaps in part perfection

22. Augustine *Literal Meaning* 11.32 (Taylor, 2:165).
23. Augustine *City of God* 14.23 and 14:26 (Bettenson, 585–87, 590–92).

precisely because it was unmarred by any distinction between the public and the private. The lack of shame in sexual relationship before the Fall correlates with the lack of this distinction. The shame of sexuality after the Fall only secondarily concerns nakedness of the body; primarily it concerns exposure of the self's incoherence, because in seeking privacy, the self seeks to mask or deny its interminable failure of intelligibility. It is in this sense that original sin is the starting point of politics, of the wisdom in the refrain that the "personal is political."

This is not to suggest that sexual relationship in paradise, because shameless, would have been a kind of communal, polymorphous indulgence of uninhibited sexual pleasure, as if the solution to the sinfulness of sexuality were an assault on all shame. The idealization of uninhibited sexual community in paradise is one more fantasy of fallen human imagination, one more post-lapsarian variation on the public/private divide, assuming as it does the ideal of sexuality as means of expression of sex, whereby that means expands to a communal maximum—sexuality become the means of perfect realization of the sexed self in uninhibited encounter with every other person, each in turn encountered in the imagined perfection of her or his sex. This is a fantasy of a fallen self that imagines itself perfected without losing the imperfection of its fallen condition, because it clings tenaciously to the fiction of its sex. More productive theologically is the fantasy of a communal existence where sex doesn't exist, where the fictional expression of the fallen self's dream of wholeness in a sex never arises, where the self projects no sex to image its completion, especially in another human being, instead finding that completion in God.

In light of the fantasy of a creation without sex, the shame of fallen humanity appears as a function of sexuality, not of sex; as a function of sin, not creation. As a result, the very idea of sex, as it is projected back into paradise, attests the profound hold of the fiction of sex on fallen human imagination. It is the ascription of an imperfection where none existed, a mark of the incapacity of fallen humanity to imagine the nothingness of sin's origin, to comprehend what was lost in Adam and Eve's original disobedience, which was the lack of all need to disguise an incompletion of self. It is a naturalization of the historical deformation of nature into politics. Anticipating the likely criticisms of this Augustinian fantasy of a completion of self without sex helps to explicate as a political problem the sinful interpersonal dynamics whereby the self seeks to displace the shame of unintelligibility of fallen selfhood. Such criticisms proceed in at least two familiar directions.

Moving in one direction, many will no doubt humorlessly protest that the completion Adam and Eve enjoyed before their sin included their sex; that they were created whole, as man and as woman; and that the integrity of such identity, though compromised by the Fall, remains undiminished as a pattern and norm of human identity, separately as male and female, and together as husband and wife. The shame of fallen human sexuality is directly proportionate to the divergence of human identity in sexual relationship from this biblical norm. Argument consequently focuses on discernment of the norm, and not on the idealized completion of self in sex. Typical questions then become: Did hierarchical relationship between man and woman precede sin, or ensue from sin? Is their any essential difference between man and woman as created? And what norms of relationship ensue from the presence of any essential difference?[24]

Implicit in all these questions is an assumption that human identity is intelligibly organized around sex; that the work of responsible organization of self is the responsible assumption of identity as one's sex; that the terms of homo/heterosexual definition can be coherently and stably resolved; and that God either preserves these possibilities as a portion of nature in otherwise fallen humanity, or preveniently creates these possibilities in spite of the Fall. Shame in sexuality is de-historicized—the historical shame of all humanity, the communal shame of failure of intelligibility, instead divides into the designation of some person's sexuality as shameful, and therefore unworthy of public recognition, because failing to express a natural sex; and other person's sexuality as befitting communal acknowledgment. The shame of unintelligibility becomes publicly displaced, in order to sustain the illusion of fulfillment of intelligibility in private sexual relationship. It is in this technical theological sense that proponents of heterosexuality as a norm of sexual orientation, as an expressive direction of one's sex realizing itself as sexuality, are culpable of a sinful shamelessness. They are culpable, that is, of the sinful displacement of their own shame of unintelligibility through strategic naturalization of the private space of marriage, promoting it as a privileged locus of realization of sex. Likewise it is imperative to note here that proponents of

24. For example of a traditionalist approach, see Clark, *Man and Woman*, 23–45. For survey of "hierarchical" versus "egalitarian" interpretations of Genesis, see Kvam et al., *Eve and Adam*, 371–481.

homosexuality as a sexual orientation are capable of behaving with equal shamelessness. They are often only less successful by accident, not intention. Many proponents of same-sex marriage seek to achieve entrance for themselves into the space of marriage, seek entitlement to the benefit of marriage as it enables realization of one's sex in an orientation that is God-given. They are protesting their exclusion from this space, not the meaning accredited to it.[25]

Moving in the other direction, it is an equally sinful mistake of shamelessness to want to try and do away with shame altogether, as if the shame associated with sexuality were only a contingency, a convention. As if, by habituating oneself to cease to experience sexual shame, the problem of intelligibility such shame signifies would dissolve. The mistake here is not in seeking to dissolve some of the concentration of shame in sexuality in particular. It is in fantasizing that the shame will not manifest elsewhere, in other guises, in imagining the elimination of shame as a possible perfection of human identity.[26] To the extent that one correctly recognizes that the concentration of the shame of unintelligibility in sexuality is a contingency, but at the same time refuses to acknowledge the impossibility of any stable unified intelligibility apart from God, one remains under the spell of the fiction of sex. What looks like a rejection of the fiction of sex is more aptly characterized as a denial of the fiction of sex, as a denial that makes possible the fantasy of liberation from the desire for intelligibility that the fiction signifies. This fantasy is theologically important. It is a characteristic fantasy of God-unconsciousness, a fantasy of liberation from sin without ever achieving consciousness of sin. This is not to deny that sexual fantasy can serve liberating ends, or that pornography and other models of public sex can teach valuable and constructive lessons; only that one needs to be pretty careful about how one draws those lessons.[27]

25. For widely cited proponents of this view, see Sullivan, *Virtually*, and Bawer, *Place* and *Beyond*.

26. For a discussion of gay male anonymous sexual practices as a model for imagining theologically "good" sexual activity that is "unitive" and "procreative" see Rudy, "Where."

27. On the politics of shame, focused very much in criticism of Sullivan, see Warner, *Trouble*. The starting point of much of Warner's argument is Rubin, "Thinking Sex." On pornography in general, compare Paglia, *Vamps*, 107–12 and Tisdale, "Talk Dirty," with MacKinnon and Dworkin, *Harm's Way*, and Dworkin, *Pornography*. For criticism of Foucault, see MacKinnon, "Does Sexuality." On the distinction of pornography versus obscenity in general, and for a definition of pornography in particular, see MacKinnon, "Pornography," 120 n. 55.

Out of explication of the troubles with these potential criticisms, a central concern of a theology of sexuality and original sin emerges: how to determine the justice in distribution of the shame of unintelligibility that currently concentrates with special force in sexuality.[28] Relative to the notion of shame as a problem of distributive justice, the critical conjunction of "sexuality" and "original sin" becomes focused. Sexuality denotes the contingent and historical character of every particular locus of concentration of the shame of unintelligibility of the fallen self. Original sin denotes the necessity of the same experience of shame, as constitutive dimension of all fallen human relationship, as a burden the disintegrated self seeks to displace through political relationship.

As an origin and passage marked by the literal inheritance of sin from generation to generation, birth describes this ceaseless confluence of contingency and necessity as it acquires determinate form in the developmental embodiment of every person. Augustinian autobiography contrasts with romantic autobiography, as sin-consciousness contrasts with sin-unconsciousness. They are contrasting narrative dispositions of the self toward the exteriority of its own origins. It is therefore important (a) to explicate at even greater length than has so far been attempted the narrative conventions operative in romantic idealization of innocent sexuality, as mechanisms of displacement of the shame of unintelligibility, as a kind of refusal to rouse from the dream-like condition of sin-unconsciousness into the sober daylight of sin-consciousness, as resistance to movement from humorless self-concern to mature humorous regard for others. And then (b) to own the political harms that the disgrace and shame of unintelligibility generates, to pursue the justice as hospitality enjoined by charitable anger at unsustainable claims to enjoyment of a unified and integrated personal identity.

Before proceeding to these final two stages, in the next and the concluding chapter of this work, it will help to elaborate the theological frame within which shame is a problem of political justice, and address directly some of Augustine's comments on the goodness and the limitations of marriage.

---

28. Among queer theoretical writers, the meaning and relevance of this claim of justice remains a point of contention. In this regard, see Edelman, *No Future*, 101–9, writing against Butler.

Created Nature and Political Nature

Unrelentingly the focus so far of readings of Augustine has been sin, but discussion of sin in Augustine's work can only end in caricature unless it is recognized as subsidiary to the brightest theme and hope of all Augustine's writings: love of God and neighbor. As it is a turning away from God, sin is only discernible as a shadow cast by the light that unendingly illuminates the creation it authors and sustains. Like the fiction of sex that is nothing in itself yet exerts a real grip on human imagination, exacting its worth in death of the life that is its possibility, sin has no existence independent from love, indeed has no being at all. The separable importance of sin and love nevertheless requires emphasis, because the political implications of the association of sexuality and original sin only become fully apparent in relation to the Augustinian vision of the two loves that distinguish creaturely goodness from fallen necessity. Sin and love need to be considered, together and apart, because their history is itself intertwined. They are the ground of both the unity and the ultimate division of humanity that is a central concern of Augustine's writings. Sin unites humanity in a common and equalizing past history, and is a definitive feature of all temporal human community. Love by contrast distinguishes the eternal end of each person in an eschatological community. The end of love of God in harmonious community, however, is only experienced in this life as a hope, whereas the origin of every life in sin is a certainty.[29]

The profound difficulties and necessities of politics, especially the inevitable use of coercive force, arise out of the indeterminacy of all human community in relation to the loves that will ultimately divide the community of saints from the community of unredeemed sinners. Until that time arrives, sin and its corresponding love will take their toll on human community and its political organization. Or put another way, just as evil is a privation of good, so all human society is organized by a deficient love.[30]

Augustine's vision of the two loves, and their corresponding cities, is most famously articulated in *City of God*, but the vision is not exclusive to that work. It appears already throughout *Confessions*. And a notable

29. For a much more balanced and sustained discussion of love and sin than I can offer, see Gregory, *Politics*; and also Jackson, *Priority*.

30. For reflection on the temporality of the intersection of the two loves and their two cities, see Pranger, "Politics."

earlier statement appears in *The Literal Meaning of Genesis*. This earlier statement is significant since it underscores specifically the place of the two loves in a history of creation—a fact, given the scale of *City of God* and temptation of persons not to read it whole from beginning to end, that is easy to elide. The totality of creation, while it includes humanity in its common biological descent from Adam and Eve, precedes all human origins. There is no place for solipsism in Augustine's account of the two loves. Beginning, as much as beginning, forms the total background to his distinction between the two loves and their two cities. Augustine in his commentary consequently does not start his account of sin and its relation to love with the disobedience of Adam and Eve, but with the devil as the model of the pride that ended in the "Sin of Adam and Eve and Their Expulsion From Paradise."[31]

One need not share Augustine's specific angelology, or hold any belief in particular regarding the existence or role of the devil in the origin of human sin, in order to appreciate the meaningfulness of defining these two loves as fundamentally prior in some way to the appearance of humanity on the historical scene. So Augustine proceeds to explain, under the heading "Pride is the beginning of all Sin. The two loves in the two cities":

> There are, then, two loves, of which one is holy, the other unclean; one turned toward the neighbor, the other centered on self; one looking to the common good, keeping in view the society of saints in heaven, the other bringing the common good under its own power, arrogantly looking to domination; one subject to God, the other rivaling him; one tranquil, the other tempestuous; one peaceful, the other seditious; one preferring truth to false praise, the other eager for praise of any sort; one friendly, the other envious; one wishing for its neighbor what it wishes for itself, the other seeking to subject its neighbor to itself; one looking for its neighbor's advantage in ruling its neighbor, the other looking for its own advantage. These two loves started among the angels, one love in the good angels, the other in the bad; and they have marked the limits of the two cities established among men under the sublime and wonderful providence of God, who

---

31. Augustine *Literal Meaning* 11 (Taylor, 2:133). Among other places see also *City of God* 11.13, 12.1, and 14.2,11 (Bettenson 444–46, 471–73, 548–50, 568–70). For discussion of the development of Augustine's thought on the nature and origin of evil in human versus supernatural creation, see Burns, "Augustine."

administers and orders all that He creates; and the one city is of
the just, and the other city is of the wicked.[32]

A common occurrence in commentary on Augustine's political theology, to the extent one is articulated, is to compare him with other major
figures in the Christian tradition, notably Aquinas, Luther, and Calvin,
and then to conclude that Augustine, distinctively more than Aquinas, regards government and politics more generally as a strictly post-lapsarian
phenomenon.[33] Yet to locate the start of these two loves, as Augustine
does, "among the angels" prior to the creation of humanity, complicates
the meaningfulness of imagining the Fall as a fault line that divides the
natural from the political.[34] The tradition of romantic interpretation of
Augustine on sexuality has tended to oppose sexuality to politics, by opposing sexual love between husband and wife against sinful public life,
most explicitly in the denomination of separate spheres of properly male
and female activity.[35] Augustine is then interpreted as affirming a distinction between the natural non-political and pre-lapsarian order of the
home, and the unnatural political post-lapsarian order of forcible rule
outside the home.[36]

The project of correcting Augustine on sexuality proceeds through
the ascription of this distinction to Augustine. It then enables the discernment of the political problem of sexuality as the establishment of a secure
foundation for the family. The business of sinful politics can in turn become the domestication of innocent sexuality. Or rather, the delineation of
sexuality as innocent by the very fact of its domestication, contrary to the
Augustinian insistence that sexuality is never innocent, even when sexual
relationship is licit.[37] Innocence, according to this project, is localized in

32. Augustine *Literal Meaning* 11.15 (Taylor, 2:147).

33. See Markus, *Saeculum*, 197–210.

34. For a reading of this same passage that emphasizes the discontinuities between the
human and divine, rather than the before and after of sin, see Outka, "Theocentric Love."

35. The idea of separate spheres appears prominently for example in the social gospel
writings of Walter Rauschenbusch. As a construct for historical analysis however it has
also been roundly criticized. In this regard, see Davidson and Hatcher, *No More*.

36. As for example in Augustine *City of God* 19.14–17 (Bettenson, 872–79).

37. See Bourdieu, *Outline*, 87–95 on sex as "defined symbolically, and not biologically,"
(93) through the habitus of the social space of the home. Bourdieu's analysis explicates
the intuitive logic of associating same-sex marriage with a threat to this habitus: "The
principles em-bodied in this way are placed beyond the grasp of consciousness, and hence
cannot be touched by voluntary, deliberate transformation, cannot even be made explicit;

marriage between properly homo/heterosexually sexed men and women, once marriage is posited as the only institution that can tame naturally destructive sexuality and harness its energy for good social purposes. These purposes are often posed in terms of protection of vulnerable women and children by responsible men, though not necessarily so.[38] More generally the family is pronounced the foundation of society. Yet the family, at the same time, is an obstacle to society that must be overcome. Freud of all people actually gets at the problem of family for political theology when he writes: "Society must defend itself against the danger that the interests which it needs for the establishment of higher social units may be swallowed up by the family; and for this reason, in the case of every individual, but in particular of adolescent boys, it seeks by all possible means to loosen their connection with their family—a connection which, in their childhood, is the only important one."[39] The problem, practically, is how society can reproduce itself through the form of the family, how sons and daughters can proceed from the family to start families of their own. Assertions of the foundational importance of the family are thus only possible because the family is not its own foundation.

A surprise here is that the opposition between innocent natural sexuality in the privacy of the home and sinful public unnatural sexuality operates at the center of arguments both *for* and *against* any form of sanction of same-sex relationships. Consider for example that advocates of same-sex marriage often lobby under the banner "love makes a family,"[40] and typically decry the failure by opponents of same-sex

---

nothing seems more ineffable, more incommunicable, more inimitable, and, therefore, more precious, than the values given body, *made* body by the transubstantiation achieved by the hidden persuasion of an implicit pedagogy, capable of instilling a whole cosmology, an ethic, a metaphysic, a political philosophy, through injunctions as insignificant as 'stand up straight' or 'don't hold your knife in your left hand.'" (94)

38. For examples of this "civilization" argument, see Riley, *Civilizing*, and Novak, *Natural Law*.

39. Freud, *Three Essays*, 91. From this point of view, biblically faithful fathers are adolescents who haven't separated from their family connections, who are refusing in fact their sociality by ascribing to themselves the familial responsibilities that they do. Freud's comment arguably echoes moments in the Gospels concerning biological family, such as Mark 3:31–35, Matt 8:21–22 and 19:29.

40. It is interesting to note in this case that argument literally takes the form of deliberate *display* of gay and lesbian bodies as a familial spectacle. See Kaeser and Gillespie, *Love*. For contemporary debates on the definition of family, and whether same-sex couples can constitute a family, see Estlund and Nussbaum, *Sex*. For a critique of the bundling of "values" under the banner of "family," see Jakobsen, "Why Sexual Regulation?"

marriage to recognize that on any ordinary day same-sex couples fix their kids breakfast and drop them off at school in the morning, commute to the office, socialize with other parents while waiting to pick the kids up from soccer or baseball or ballet, put dinner on the table, make sure the homework gets done, teeth brushed, lights out, and repeat the same routine all over again the next day. In all these cases the claim to innocent sexuality, whether of husband and wife or same-sex partners, is achieved through invocation of an ideal of innocent nature only realizable in marriage. This is an innocent nature figured through the fantasied projection as sentimental spectacle of adult sexed identity, defined by the dyad of orientations heterosexual and homosexual, to children.

The appeal to romantic love as foundational of an innocent domestic space is challenged by Augustine's vision of the two loves. The eschatological horizon those loves describe only appears against the background of the contemporaneous landscape of fallen human community; a landscape where all relationship is implicated in the universal ruin of humanity that originates with the sin of Adam and Eve. The identification of pride as the "beginning of all sin," and its consequence for all of humanity as the experience of unintelligibility of personal identity, undermines any attempt to isolate the Fall as historical event that can be neatly described in terms of a before and after that correlates somehow with a created sex finding its natural expression in the home that makes innocent sexuality possible; and sinful sexuality threatening that home from without. Instead, description of pride as a beginning enfolds the original event of sin within the living history of sexuality and its effects. What remains after sin is a disordered created being that persists perpetually twisting in its attempt to step out of its own shadow.

In speaking of pride in relation to the devil, Augustine underscores that something was lost in the Fall that exceeds post-lapsarian desire and imagination of the before of sin; that pride in its most unalloyed imaginable reality is not bodily concupiscence, but a kind of lust that connects even more intimately and culpably to awareness of God as sustaining source of creaturely goodness. As such, pride alienates the creature from its own origin, from the exteriority that sustains its own capacities for beginning. Just as every human origin can be described as a B/beginning, the same enfolded history describes the negative relation that enables pride as a beginning of sin. The pride that is the beginning of sin in each culpable individual in this sense has its Beginning by analogy too in the devil. The Beginning of creation is imitated by the Beginning of its disorder when pride rears its ugly head.

Pride that is the imitative B/beginning of sin is a self-refuting negation. It is the attempt to extricate oneself from the envelope of B/beginning, to become something other than the creature one is. Adam and Eve, and the devil too for that matter, in order to have been able to have acted with pride, must themselves in this sense have already been creatures with a double origin in B/beginning, even though they were truly created originals of their kind. Moreover, whatever the possibility of sexual relationship before sin, one can at least say of that possibility that it was *not* romantic, because romance, like every sinful attempt of the self to extricate itself from the web of its own unintelligibility, begins with pride.

Recalling Augustine's definition of sin as privative phenomenon,[41] as a privation of good that is a disorder of creation, further implicates romance in the functioning of pride as a beginning of sin, and also further implicates the fanatasied intelligibility of personal identity in sex in the publicly negotiated distribution of shame of unintelligibility that is integral to the formation of all fallen human community. Since sin is itself no thing, to speak of a "beginning" of sin is to speak metaphorically about that which has no existence, which only enjoys a derivative intelligibility by analogy as the negation of being. To speak of a beginning of sin is to speak of a nothingness that is productive of no thing—productive, that is, of the disorder of creation that is sin's only reality. Given this no-thing-ness of sin, pride by definition turns out to be an existential absurdity. So the continuity of creation before and after the occurrence of sin must be acknowledged. Pride doesn't deform creation, but perverts the capacity of the creature to realize the goodness of its creaturely existence. It disorders especially the created sociality of human beings, the ground of the hospitality due to one another. Commenting on Sartre's account of the voyeur when himself subject to another's gaze, Joan Copjec provides an apt description of the social shame of fallen humanity: "He is caught by a gaze, it is good to remember, that cannot refer back to any specific norm of judgment because it refers to no determinate object. The shame that seeps through the body of the observer announces not a particular judgment, but the birth of the social as such. It therefore precedes the

---

41. Augustine *City of God* 11.9,22; 12.7; 14.11; 19.13 (Bettenson, 440, 454, 479–80, 568, 871). Also *Confessions* 7.12.18 and 7.16.22 (Chadwick, 124–25, 126).

possibility of shame in the sociological or civic sense."[42] It is just this lack of a "determinate object," the no-thing that sin is not, in relation to which recognition of human sociality is shameful. The figure of the voyeur is fitting also because it is what, in a sense, Adam and Eve themselves became at the moment in which their eyes were opened, in which they beheld their nakedness, which is to say observed their loss of God's grace, even as they were observed by God in turn. Sociality in the absence of sin became sociality in the absence that is sin, such that the former can only be recalled through the medium of sociological or civic shame, shame that works itself out in politics.

At the same time, designation of pride as the beginning of sin means that the before and after of sin does not map in any straightforward way onto a distinction between what is properly good as created from what is contrary to that creation. Whereas the romance of innocent sexuality is dominated by just such an obsessive mapping project, an overriding concern of a theology of original sin that accepts the meaningfulness of association of sexuality and sin is to resist any call to answer the question: How far fallen exactly is humanity? Accepting the fact of sin as *fait accompli*, the question instead becomes: What are the signs of the continual operation of pride among fallen humanity, as it perversely draws creatures into the absurdity of its parasitic deformation? Or posed another way: How does pride, even after the first sin, continue to function as the "B/beginning of all sin"? Once the difference between these questions is articulated, much of the hold of romance on fallen human imagination appears as its power to distract attention from the latter question to the former question.

To elaborate this critique of romance in terms of pride: If, as Augustine insists, pride is the beginning of sin, and sin is a constant dimension of current creaturely existence, then pride merits description as a kind of transcendental coefficient of B/beginning. The literal inheritance of sin denotes the perpetuation of the generative nothingness of beginning that unendingly renders humanity unintelligible to itself. Hence the importance again of associating pride with the devil, with a creature whose creation precedes human existence, since pride is a kind of transcendent possibility as negativity that was itself always already present in a way from the Beginning, and is the negative dimension of the relation of

42. Copjec, *Imagine*, 213.

Beginning to beginning. So that the "B/beginning" of sin in pride always belongs in quotation marks, as reminder that it is not a real beginning at all, but always a failure of beginning, a start of nothing.[43]

Likewise one must look to this false start, this beginning of sin in pride, as an opening of insight into the relation of sin to creation that arises *within* politics, and resist as much as possible the temptation to deny the constancy of pride in all human beginning. The necessity of politics to fallen humanity is no longer explicable in terms of a simple opposition between a pre-lapsarian natural social order and a post-lapsarian coercive necessity, since the construction of that opposition only arises as a consequence of the pride that is the beginning of all sin.

The move to avoid here is to regard politics as superimposed over nature, as if the natural subsisted somehow below the surface of the political; as if one could isolate a bedrock of social nature upon which the political is constructed. This is precisely the logic, in fact, that authorizes isolation of the nuclear family as foundation of civilization, a logic that precludes marital sexual relationship from the political, and also holds it forth as foundation of the political.

A more trenchant model of the relation of nature to politics under the rubric of fallen creation is admittedly more convoluted. Some persons, many perhaps, will likely challenge this convolution as needlessly or even willfully complicating what is God-given and self-evident. I believe it is more fitting to accept this convolution in faith as a sign of the degradation of all relationship that follows from the enduring reality of sin. In place of the prideful opposition of fallen politics and social nature, one must accept as a consequence of the loss of the "privileged state" of Adam and Eve the interminable convolution of sin and creation as constitutive of the political and the natural in social relations. Nature is not extricable from this convolution, not because it ceases to exist, but because nature

---

43. Here I am developing my interpretation of Kierkegaard's dictum that "sin presupposes itself." And the productive significance of correlating sin with nothingness: "Innocence is ignorance. In innocence, man is not qualified as spirit but is psychically qualified in immediate unity with his natural condition. The spirit in man is dreaming . . . In this state there is peace and repose, but there is simultaneously something else that is not contention and strife, for there is indeed nothing against which to strive. What, then, is it? Nothing. But what effect does nothing have? It begets anxiety. This is the profound secret of innocence, that it is at the same time anxiety. Dreamily the spirit projects its own actuality, but this actuality is nothing, and innocence always sees this nothing outside itself." Kierkegaard, *Concept*, 32, 41. Also see MacDonald, "Primal Sin," and Tanner, *Anxiety*.

is altered by sin, and ceases to be intelligible qua creation, underscoring that sin is an epistemic disaster with performative consequences, a catastrophe of intelligibility. Nor could sin be otherwise, originating as it does in pride, itself an abyss of nonsense: the desire of the self to make its own meaning, to be an intelligibility unto itself.

Rather than distinguish between nature and politics, one can distinguish between created nature and political nature, when saying of Augustine that politics is a strictly post-lapsarian necessity. Politics in this sense is fundamentally contradictory of creation, while nature itself only exists in relation to creation and sin. The post-lapsarian convolution of creation and sin in political nature can be imaged as a flow chart:

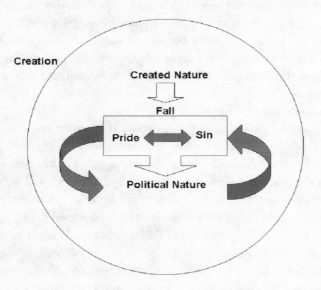

Following this image, the Fall, as the inaugural moment of human sin, is rightly described as the precipitation of this convolution, and as a *change* of human nature, as a fall from stable created nature to unstable political nature, as a fall from created communal social existence in transparent plenitude of intelligibility to the shame of pride's failure of intelligibility—shame that seeks in privacy to cover over its unintelligibility, and that seeks to authorize its privacy by attempting to re-order the relation of sin and creation through the categories of the natural and the political. Shame now speciously equates its sinful nature with the good created social nature irretrievably lost in the Fall, fueling the continual production through pride and sin of its own political nature. Shame, finally, conduces with the operation of sexuality, enabling the narration of a fictional sex that is then ascribed the status of created nature, and so seemingly disengaged from the politics of its own production.

A peculiar difficulty attending this description of the change from created nature to political nature, instituted by pride and sin, is how to comprehend the goodness of fallen creation, what I am loosely designating as the remnant of sociality—especially if one believes, with Augustine, that perdurance in being is only possible because some trace of the original peace of creation persists after the Fall: "Yet even what is perverted must of necessity be in, or derived from, or associated with—that is, in a sense, at peace with—some part of the order of things among which it has its being or of which it consists. Otherwise it would not exist at all."[44] One must therefore address the questions: How is the irresolvable convolution of creation and sin in political nature itself intelligible, if not by the traces it bears of uncorrupted created nature? Does not fallen creation remain creation?

Answer to these questions begins with reflection on the narrative anteriority of pride to the occurrence of human sin, as revealed in Scripture. At first glance, the location in *The Literal Meaning of Genesis* of Augustine's summary statement of the two loves *before* his description of the transformation of Adam and Eve that ensues from their sin seems to reflect a simple commitment to a literal-historical reading of the text of Genesis. Given the negative definition of pride as beginning, however, it is too quick to assume that Augustine is ascribing an absolute temporal priority to the love "centered on self," as if the pride of Satan was subsequently somehow transmitted to humanity through the intervention of the serpent.[45] Probably the long history of describing original sin as an infection has contributed to this misapprehension, to the assumption that the traditional assertion of original sin as a literal inheritance can only mean the penetration of a passive self by an active exterior force of pride and wrongful self-love, and an attendant interior transformation of soul and body. Of greater significance, this assumption of the meaning of sin described as infection enables the continual attempt to exteriorize sin from self to other—the main concern, when not denying sin altogether,

44. Augustine *City of God* 19.12 (Bettenson, 869).

45. Compare with the tradition that Eve literally had sexual relations with the serpent, as documented in Kvam et al., *Eve*, 85–88; and Tennant, *Sources*, 156–60, 209.

always to quarantine the infectious agent, literally and figuratively.[46] To the extent a metaphor of illness is helpful, it would be better to describe original sin as a metaphysical autoimmune disease, because the pride of Adam and Eve that was the beginning of human sin was wholly their own, was wholly human. In this way the loss of Adam and Eve of their privileged state was truly comprehensive. All *human* being was inflected by their pride and its consequent disgrace.

Although the origin of human sin is a transcendent nothingness internal to human being, the narrative sequence pride, then sin, is a necessary basis for the imagination of the origin of sin in time, since imagination of that sequence is always *ex post facto*. Exposition of the two loves, and of pride as the beginning of all sin, must seem to precede the event of human sin, in order to narrate intelligibly the consequence of sin as historical phenomenon, in order to elaborate not only what was lost in terms of the two loves, but how that loss functions as a structuring deformity of historical community.[47]

Adam and Eve alone enjoyed the privilege of a prospective view of sin. Or stated in traditional terms, they alone lived in the created condition of *posse non peccare*. The only way to imagine their loss of innocence involves imagination somehow of their loss of this possibility and its attendant prospective view of sin. To imagine sin's origin in the self, and to assume identity as a responsible beginning of sin, always involves a retrospective recasting into narrative sequence of the convolution of pride, sin, and love that is a continual and contemporaneous dimension of personal identity.

46. So the logic behind the passage of "defense of marriage" legislation, and the push for constitutional definition of marriage as the exclusive union of one man with one woman, is continuous with the call by some early in the AIDS pandemic for quarantine, in order to prevent "infection" of marriage by the sin of same-sex unions. Consider the following comment in response to the recent supreme court decision in "Lawrence and Garner Versus Texas," striking down Texas's sodomy law: "Robert Knight, a spokesman for the conservative Culture and Family Institute, said Thursday's ruling would have 'very real consequences.' Knight warned that it would undermine the legal foundation of marriage, lead to more deaths among gay men from sexually transmitted diseases and lead to schoolchildren being taught 'that homosexual sodomy is the same as marital sex.'" Quoted on CNN.com, Friday, June 27, 2003.

47. On the constructive possibilities of the doctrine of original sin for theory of justice, and also further explication of my interpretation of Kierkegaard on the topic, see Rees, "Original Sin."

For Augustine the beginning of sin in pride, as revealed in the narrative of the Fall, does not correspond with any straightforward division of human community according to the two loves—as if some persons and communities are defiled by pride, and others are not—but with the unity of humanity in the comprehensive pride and sin of the creaturely progenitors of all persons. So too for Augustine the trajectory of the two loves does not map in any discernible pattern onto human events, although the record of at least one historical community, Israel, does bear salvific significance as a sign of the endurance of God's promise to whom God grants it. At best, human knowledge of the two cities is liminal and providential. One can only conjecture with hesitancy who belongs to the city of God, and who does not: "These two loves started among the angels, one love in the good angels, the other in the bad; and they have marked the limits of the two cities established among men under the sublime and wonderful providence of God."[48]

A central and ongoing mystery of sin is the subsistence of pride as a dimension of the self—as an uncreated parasitic absurdity that somehow also enfolds the creaturely existence out of which it subsists. Once one accepts that the origin of sin is pride, and that sin is nothing of its own but only ever a privation of good, it becomes apparent the change from created nature to political nature in the fall must not have been a static past event.

The Fall, the first sin, was a singular occurrence, but the consequences of that occurrence are dynamic. After the Fall, created nature and political nature are coterminous realities of all human existence that at the same time can only be conceptualized in terms of the sequential transformation of created nature into political nature, the two halves joined by the imagined continuity of human sociality. Created nature doesn't cease to exist after the Fall, just as the imagination of *after* entails the imagination of *before*. But precisely because created nature is only imaginable in this narrative sequence, it is irretrievably something other than simply created.

The prior visualization of the Fall as inauguration of this change can now be amended to reflect the constancy of this change:

---

48. Augustine *Literal Meaning* 11.15 (Taylor, 2:147).

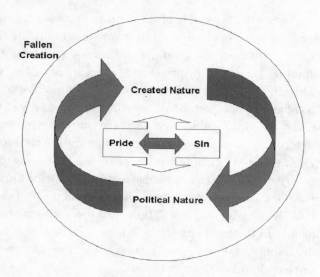

With pride and sin at the continual center of the convoluted inter-relation of created nature and political nature, no means exists to speak of nature that is both straightforward *and* responsible—an incapacity that is a sign of the social shame of unintelligibility of fallen humanity. To begin to assume responsibility for sin therefore entails rejection of any reductive equation of some isolable aspect of the self, notably one's sex, but alternately one's soul, or one's psyche, or one's mind, or one's will, or one's heart, with created nature. Created nature, under the rubric of fallen creation, is something other than it was before the fall. Sin has permanently entered the picture. Human nature has changed.

Acceptance of responsibility for sin begins with acceptance of the truth that the change in nature inaugurated by sin is total, with acceptance that every possible human narration of a continuity between the before and after of the Fall re-inscribes the discontinuity of fallen creation with pre-lapsarian creation. All the while, however, the very possibility of as-suming responsibility for sin only emerges out of narration of the self as an intelligibly responsible social creature. The immediate relevance of the Augustinian vision of the two loves and their two cities emerges, not as the criteria for the delineation and isolation of some perfectible human community, but as the criteria of the two predominant possibilities for the narration of intelligible personal identity after the Fall: the one pos-sibility is to seek in humility to narrate identity as a sinful creature rec-onciled to God in faithful dependence, the other possibility shamelessly seeks to narrate a fictional creaturely coherence that denies the exterior truth of its identity.

Given this understanding of the meaningfulness of the Fall specifically as an epistemic shift from the possibility of a prospective view of sin, to a necessary narration of a before and after of sin that is itself always marked by sin, it is now possible to summarize the theological inappropriateness and sinfulness of simple appeals to nature within theological discourse on sexuality, and to provide a fuller answer to the questions: How is the irresolvable convolution of creation and sin in political nature itself intelligible, if not by the traces it bears of uncorrupted created nature? Does not fallen creation remain creation? Created nature, after the fall, is only known as such through narrations of the sociality that joins the before and after of sin. The possibility of self-knowledge as a creature is therefore only possible as a function of the same modality of narration. Innocence, once lost, cannot be restored, just as the necessary narration of innocence, fall, and redemption is a function of the reality of the fallen creation it in turn describes.

The only intelligibility one can realize after the Fall is intelligibility as a fallen creature. The enduring meaningfulness and intelligibility of creation is a matter finally of faith, not reason. This same faith is the starting point for comprehension of creation as both created *and* fallen, for comprehension of the self as a creature alienated from its created possibility of intelligibility. The goal of self-understanding, realized in faith, cannot be to isolate the remainder of created nature within the self. Instead it is to grasp as fully as possible the dynamic and necessary interrelation of created nature and political nature; and especially to assume responsibility for that dynamic; to strive for awareness, as much as possible, of the continual shifting distribution of the burden of shame of unintelligibility that is a continual corollary of the persistence of pride as the beginning of all sin. The possibility of personal identity after the Fall is fundamentally a political concern, following in part the sense of politics offered by Lee Edelman: "Politics, that is, names the struggle to effect a fantasmatic order of reality in which the subject's alienation would vanish into the seamlessness of identity at the endpoint of the endless chain of signifiers lived as history."[49] The very large caveat here is that Edelman treats history as an infinitely deferred sequence of signification, while literal interpretation of the doctrine of original sin teaches in faith that

49. Edelman, *No Future*, 8.

God has revealed in Scripture a starting point for the history of oneself whose endpoint in turn is defined by the two loves in the two cities.

The emphasis, throughout this analysis, has been the priority of pride to sin, yet pride itself only acquires definition in terms of faith. The point of such definition is not to settle the question of which came first—pride or faithlessness—but to observe that they are two aspects of one phenomenon. Pride is both failure to keep faith with God, and failure to have faith in God. Pride attempts an impossible faith in the self, because it is impossible to keep such faith with oneself. Definition of pride as a failure of faith is further enriched by the explication of faith provided by Gene Outka in terms of the differences and correspondences between the self and God. Analysis of the distortions of faith in God and faithfulness to God, by the fiction of sex, can then proceed through analysis of the interplay of ways that faith goes wrong, where faith, according to Outka, disallows both "Tempting God" and "Playing God."[50] It is tempting God to become absorbed in maintaining the fantasy of one's own sex at the expense of hospitable caring for others, and also to neglect to become one's responsible self through unquestioning acceptance of identity as an improperly sexed self. It is playing God to idolize a fantasy of human imagination, sex, as a basis of God-relatedness, as if human imagination could reliably conjure divine presence—as if, most of all, persons could be geographically mapped at particular distances from the divine based on their faith in and faithfulness to the fiction of sex. Once the fiction of sex is recognized as a sinful deformity of fallen human imagination, faith in God and faithfulness to God entails specific forms of obligation to the neighbor, and to God, that cut directly against the imperatives claimed by those who cleave stubbornly to the fiction of sex. Following Outka's explication of the interplay of the differences and discontinuities between human and divine capacities, faith in the fiction of sex is a form of faithlessness to God who creates, and as such generates distinctive forms of faithlessness *between* persons and communities.

To assume faithful responsibility for sin is inseparable from the unending pursuit of self-awareness as a fallen creature, since one doesn't ever cease to be a fallen creature. The promise of intelligible selfhood is a necessary chimera in the formation of stable human community. Considered in terms of the two loves, the shameful failure of intelligibility of the fallen self, and the impossible yet necessary project of fixing an

50. Outka, "Faith."

intelligible personal self, unfolds as a series of moral oppositions, each series defining a trajectory of possible narration of intelligible personal and communal identity. These oppositions are dispositional. They are orientations of the self toward the possibility of self-knowledge. One orientation, maturely humorous, looks outward, opening through disposition toward others the space for visualization of a self that is sinful and incoherent yet also moving toward its own wholeness through the activities motivated by charitable anger. This orientation casts its vision across the distance, its point of view of self the horizon of its ultimate completion in God. The other orientation humorlessly avoids looking outward. Through disposition toward self it constrains its point of view and thereby lacks any focal point. It is incapable of a more hospitable and charitably constructive grasp of self and others. Failing to cast its gaze far and wide enough, this orientation ends up myopic, cross-eyed, its vision blurry and unreliable.

Returning to Augustine's summary of the two loves in *The Literal Meaning of Genesis*, just as "these two loves started among the angels," neither is their end of this world, even though "they have marked the limits of the two cities established among men." In the meantime, the present time of human knowing, pride and sin remain ineradicable constituent ingredients of embodied creaturely existence; pilgrimage a form of political struggle; the end of sin at best a hope of a future existence, never a contemporary reality. Allowing the persistence of pride and sin, however, the simple parallelism of these oppositions is only apparent. Just as sin subsists out of creation, yet creation is only known as fallen creation, so too love of self subsists out of love of God and neighbor, while love of God and neighbor is only experienced as the striving against love of self. So too the narrative possibility organized around self-love is always subsidiary to the narrative possibility organized around love of God and neighbor, while the narrative possibility organized around love of God and neighbor is itself a projection in hope of a future that is not yet. Personal identity only emerges out of the array of narrative trajectories possible in the temporal reality of fallen creation; out of the development in time of the alternate dispositions, "one turned toward the neighbor, the other centered on self; one looking to the common good, keeping in view the society of saints in heaven, the other bringing the common good under its own power, arrogantly looking to domination." Domination is defined as a deficient narrative orientation toward the present, opposed as it is to the orientation that keeps "in view the society of saints in heaven," so that the attempt to ascribe a stable present identity to the self by appeal to the fiction of a created sex, the principal effect of sexuality, merits judgment as love "centered on self" "arrogantly looking to domination."

It further follows from the interminable convolution of created nature and political nature after the Fall that it is not possible to organize the opposition of these narrative dispositions, the two loves and the two cities they establish, according to the categories natural and unnatural—or even according to the categories created natural and political natural—never mind by a simple appeal to the sociality of humanity. Instead, both narrative dispositions must be regarded as constitutively implicated in the convolution of created nature and political nature. For this reason, to say that "one city is of the just, and the other city is of the wicked" is to say that a more or less just politics, a more or less just realization of the political natural, distinguishes the two loves and their two cities as they manifest in contemporaneous human relations.

Simple appeals to nature tend, by contrast, to consolidate particular unjust configurations of the political natural, since such appeals are inherently indeterminate and untenable. Given this tendency of appeals to nature toward injustice, narration of theologically informed self-awareness as a fallen creature becomes its own moral imperative; and knowledge and responsibility become coextensive, where responsibility precedes knowledge, even as it is only consciously assumed through the knowledge figured in the narration of a before and after of sin in relation to a future of sanctified community in God. Knowledge of creation—the knowledge that underwrites the discernment of fallen creation as creation—is by necessity forward looking. While innocence cannot be restored, sin, God willing, can be surpassed. But only through the renewal of creation anticipated with hope in the words of the prophet: "For I am about to create new heavens and a new earth; the former things shall not be remembered or come to mind" (Isa 65:17).

The possibility of understanding fallen creation as creation is, ultimately, a kind of prophecy—an anticipation of a not yet present reality—and a faith in the fulfillment of an as yet unrealized divine promise. As a result, the sinfulness of the romance of innocent sexuality can be characterized as a "tempestous," "seditious," and "rivaling" mimicry of divine sovereignty; as the attempt to renew creation on one's own behalf; as a denial of the dependence of the self on the only source that can author such renewal. Seeking as it does to narrate intelligible personal identity by short-circuiting the convolution of created nature and political nature, the romance of innocent sexuality presumes to constrain God's freedom to renew creation however God chooses. As a narrative disposition, it attempts this usurpation of divine prerogative by ascribing to the fiction of sex the capacity uniquely and predictably to render the self intelligible as a creature. Sexual relationship is then regarded as sinful only when it is not expressive of that created sex. All sexual relationship is then regarded as sinful unless it is certified expressive of a sanctioned sex.

A more responsible and just narrative disposition recognizes the incapacity of sexuality, because fallen—because humanity is fallen—to express any truth about the created self except its own sinfulness. Clinging as it does to the fantasy of personal intelligibility through realization of one's created sex, the romance of innocent sexuality is at core an evasion of responsibility for sin through narration of a fiction of a self untouched by sin, and so an evasion of the possibility of achieving responsible personal identity as a fallen creature—a possibility, as God chooses, of divine creative activity.

Original Sin and the Limited Goods of Marriage

Before turning to an extended reading of a paradigmatic romantic tale of evasion of responsibility for sin through unjust displacement of the shame of unintelligibility, in the form of sexual shame, some comments are fitting on the implications of this developed view of the convolution of created nature and political nature for interpretation of two aspects of Augustine's writings: first, on the goods he attributes to marriage; second, on the appeals to natural and unnatural uses of the body that he correlates with those goods. These concluding comments are necessarily brief, but they at least offer an outline of an alternative to romantic attempts at a retrieval of Augustine on sex and marriage, the sort of arguments which proceed to enroll Augustine in one way or another as an authority on the truth of sex as organizing principle of the self. Retrieval in these cases merely perpetuates characterization of the task of sexual ethics as the delineation of the justifiable uses and occurrences of sexual relationship. It configures that task in service of its own project of self-understanding.[51] The Augustinian association of sexuality and sin, as developed in these

---

51. For an example of this sort of uncritical retrieval, see Meilaender, "Sweet Necessities." For a contrasting example of a constructively critical retrieval of Augustine on the goods of marriage, see Thatcher, "Crying Out."

pages, instead urges the discernment of appropriate occasions for shame in relation to the inevitable pursuit of avoidance of shame that ensues from original sin. This shame is not related in any necessarily specific way with the human body and its capacities for sexual reproduction, so that avoidance of shame cannot be resolved by uncritical appeal to some list of goods, or by the delineation of natural as opposed to unnatural uses of the body. By contrast sexuality, whatever the specific bodily configuration of sexual relations—homosexual, heterosexual, or otherwise—and this otherwise is an expansive possibility, if not a present reality—is always shameful, because always sinful.

Of the three goods that Augustine attributes to marriage—*fides*, *proles*, and *sacramentum*—fidelity, progeny, and sacrament—much has been written, obviating the need for a present review.[52] Of immediate relevance to this project is a basic observation of what marriage, even within the framework of these goods, does not do. Whatever the goods attributable to marriage as a form of relationship between persons, they do not alter the inherent sinfulness of sexuality. Marriage, through the goods it realizes, may constrain and direct sexuality to valued purposes, but it can never redeem persons. It is not a remedy for the fallenness of humanity, however much it might serve as a remedy for certain occasions of sin. Once the shame associated with sexuality is acknowledged as the ineliminable shame associated with the Fall, with the loss of intelligibility that was the consequence of original sin, and not with natural or unnatural embodied relations, any attempt to extricate marriage, as human institution, from the shared reality of that shame, becomes discernible as a sign of the inherent sinfulness of marriage: that it is a relationship, valuable and perhaps even necessary in some form or other, of fallen community. And that it cannot be otherwise.

The ultimate limit to the goodness of marriage, as of all possible human relationship, is the imperfectability of humanity after the Fall. As confirmation of human imperfectability, the description of original sin as a literal inheritance entails that even the good most traditionally identified as the sole justifying purpose of sexual relationship—procreation—includes within itself the perpetuation of sin. Much of the meaningfulness of description of sin as inheritable is the equation of the embodied future of humanity with the always contemporaneous embodied reality of sin.

---

52. See Reynolds, *Marriage*, 239–311; Brown, *Body*, 387–427; Augustine and Clark, *St. Augustine on Marriage*; Harrison, *Augustine*, 159–69; and Rist, *Augustine*, 246–52.

Augustine's assertion, throughout his writings, of the unceasing necessity and gravity of the requirement of infant baptism, proves a sharp reminder of how positively central the logic of inheritance is to all Augustine's thought on sexuality and human imperfectability.[53]

Allowing the goods that marriage accomplishes, Augustine nevertheless underscores that it does not save anyone when he insists that the transmission of sin as inheritance is strictly a function of the facts of embodied sexual reproduction, and never a function of the marital status of the parents. It is therefore possible to develop an internal critique of Augustine's own association of shame with natural as opposed to unnatural sexual relations, when he attempts to explain the relation of the goodness of human beings as created to the evil of original sin as transmissible in procreation. Augustine appeals to shame in just this way in the following passage from *Marriage and Desire*, where, writing to refute the criticisms of Julian, he first quotes those criticisms:

> One who observes moderation in natural concupiscence makes good use of a good; one who does not preserve moderation makes bad use of a good. "Why do you say then," he asks, "that 'the good of marriage cannot be accused because of the original evil which is contracted from it, just as the evil of adulteries cannot be excused because of the natural good which is born from them.' By these words you conceded," he says, "what you had denied, and you took back what you had conceded. You work at nothing more than making yourself less understandable. Show me bodily marriages without sexual union; give this act a single name, and call marriage either good or bad. You have, of course, promised to declare marriage good. If marriage is good, if a human being is the good result of marriage, if this result, a work of God, cannot be evil, since it is born of someone good through good means, where is, then, the original evil which is destroyed by so many concessions?"

Augustine's Reply to Julian's Objection:

> To this I reply that not only children born from a marriage, but also those born from adultery, are something good in terms of the work of God by which they were created. But in terms of original sin they are born from the first Adam in a state of condemnation. This is true, not only if they are born from adultery,

53. See, for example, passages in *Punishment and Forgiveness of Sins* and *The Nature and Origin of the Soul* in Augustine, *Works*, 1/23 (Teske, 121–37, 477–82, 522–30); *Marriage and Desire* and *In Answer to Julian* in *Works*, 1/24 (Teske, 89–91, 369–78); and *Unfinished Work in Answer to Julian* in *Works* 1/25 (Teske, 180–93).

but also if they are born from a marriage, unless they are reborn in the second Adam who is Christ. In the apostle's words concerning the wicked, *Having abandoned natural relations with a woman, they burned in their desires for one another, men treating men shamefully* (Rom 1:27), he did not speak of marital, but of natural relations. He meant for us to understand those relations which are brought about by the members created for this purpose so that both sexes can be joined by them in order to beget children. For this reason, when anyone is united by those same members even to a prostitute, the relations are natural, though they are not praiseworthy, but sinful. But if one has relations even with one's wife in a part of the body which was not made for begetting children, such relations are against nature and indecent. In fact, the same apostle earlier said the same thing about the women, *For their women exchanged natural relations for those which are against nature* (Rom 1:26); then he mentioned men treating men shamefully, after having abandoned natural relations with women. Hence, this term, namely, natural relations, is not used to praise marital intercourse, but to denounce those indecent acts that are more unclean and more wicked than if one had sinful relations with women that were at least natural.[54]

Augustine's resort to interpretation of Rom 1:26–27, as explanation of the distinction between "natural" and "marital" relations, is at first glance striking confirmation of the romantic trajectory of interpretation that resorts to the same passage to affirm what appears an essentially parallel argument: that the reproductive sexual anatomy of men and women has a created purpose only ever realized in heterosexual intercourse, regardless of whether or not procreation actually follows. (Augustine is elsewhere clear that formal conformation to the procreative purpose, and not the actual outcome, distinguishes natural marital sexual relations.[55]) Yet at the same time, through the introduction of this distinction, Augustine opens the space of internal critique of his appeal to the natural, since marital relations are not by definition necessarily natural at all. Instead, Augustine exemplifies that what counts as natural requires articulation, separable from what counts as marital.

Augustine does more than provide an early formulation of the concept of sodomy when he writes: "Hence, this term, namely, natural

54. Augustine *Marriage and Desire* in *Works*, 1/24:2.19.34–20.35 (Teske, 75).

55. See, for example, passages in *The Excellence of Marriage*; *The Excellence of Widowhood*; and *Adulterous Marriages* in Augustine, *Works*, 1/9 (Kearney, 38–39, 46–47, 115–17, 174–76).

relations, is not used to praise marital intercourse, but to denounce those indecent acts that are more unclean and more wicked than if one had sinful relations with women that were at least natural." More significantly, he demonstrates that the use of the term natural is a problem of communal definition, is a problem of determination of what human activities and relations to denounce, and so of how to allocate the shame of original sin among fallen humanity.

To distinguish "sinful relations" from "unnatural relations"—adulterous intercourse in the missionary position is "natural" but "sinful" whereas "homosexual" relationship is both "sinful" and "unnatural"—is an instance of the temptation to distribute differentially the limited intelligibility of the fallen human body, and of the temptation to seek to shift the burden of responsibility for sin, as if avoidance of sins somehow means the self is less fallen. Other criteria than natural versus unnatural must be the basis of determination of the possibility of classification of particular uses of the body as sins—separable from description of the self as sinful.

Lest the reader is wondering at this point, and also likely worrying, where such a claim leads, none of this argument is intended to deny the necessity of regulation of fallen human relations, but to question and in some cases reverse the determination of what merits regulation and how such regulation is administered. To say that some sexual relations are properly forbidden must remain distinct from saying that some sexual relations bring one closer to God, while other relations distance the self from God. The first claim is integral to sexual ethics. The second claim is not.

Once the determination of the natural is recognized as a problem of political nature, the constriction of marriage to one man and one woman no longer appears inevitable. It now appears as a strategic and negotiable means for concentrating the authority of denunciation of sin, and thereby displacing the shame of unintelligibility that undermines the ambition of realization of one's created sex, especially when the meaningfulness of sexual relationship is no longer limited to the procreative purpose of sexual anatomy. Augustine's refutation of Julian's questions demonstrates that attempts to define the goods of marriage proceed through sinfully culpable appeals to a created "nature" that cannot, following the Augustinianism here developed, be extricated from the fallen convolution of created nature and political nature.

This brief commentary on Augustine's writings is not intended to resolve the problem of interpretation of Paul on nature. It is only to assert the irresolvable persistence of that problem of interpretation to sexual ethics, regardless of whether one has Paul's specific words in mind or not. Likewise the question here is not whether or not Augustine possessed any conceptualization of heterosexuality as opposed to homosexuality as possibilities of sexual orientation. Or whether or not the conceptualization of sexual orientation provides some means of reformulating the designation of natural versus unnatural relations in terms of relations that alternately conform to or transgress heterosexual or homosexual nature. In fact the claim that same-sex sexual relations are only wrongful when one or more of the persons engaged isn't "really homosexual" is just one more instance of how sentimental-homicidal-suicidal narrations of the fiction of sex and its promise of personal intelligibility continue to enthrall the romantic imagination.[56]

The very conceptualization of sexual orientation must itself be reevaluated as a technique for the narration of the fiction of sex. The fundamental reference point of an Augustinian theology of sexuality and sin is not male-female difference, or the differentiation of possible sexual orientations according to that difference, but the fact of sin and the necessity of the narration of the before and after of sin in relation to an originary pair of human beings, as revelatory of both the unintelligibility of fallen humanity and the possibility of comprehension of that unintelligibility. Created nature before the Fall didn't know pride—just as political nature after the Fall can only imagine created nature through prideful fantasied narration of what was irretrievably lost. Hence the importance of a close reading of a prototypical romantic narration of marriage as the means to overcome original sin and achieve comprehensive personal intelligibility: a close reading that enables recognition of, and so opens the possibility of redressing, the unjust distribution of shame and attendant unjustifiable claims to intelligible personal identity that this romantic narrative tradition continues to authorize.

---

56. Debate on exegesis of Paul on nature, with specific regard to the moral status of same-sex sexual relations, has centered on the concept of sexual orientation and attendant problems of homo/heterosexual definition. Probably the most influential starting point of such debate has been Boswell, *Christianity*, 91–117. See also Hays, "Relations," and Martin, "Heterosexism." Remarkable about the exchange between Hays and Martin is that it centers on the figures of a dying versus a flourishing gay male body and how to regard them. For a wonderfully different reading of Paul on this passage, see Swancutt, "Sexing." For example of a progressive New Testament sexual ethics, see Countryman, *Dirt*.

7

The Fiction of Redemptive Marriage

To the leader. A Psalm of David, when the prophet Nathan came to him, after he had gone to Bathsheba.

> Have mercy on me, O God, according to your
>   steadfast love; according to your abundant mercy
>   blot out my transgressions.
> Wash me thoroughly from my iniquity, and cleanse
>   me from my sin.
> For I know my transgressions, and my sin is ever
>   before me.
> Against you, you alone, have I sinned, and done
>   what is evil in your sight, so that you are justified
>   in your sentence and blameless when you pass
>   judgment.
> Indeed, I was born guilty, a sinner when my mother
>   conceived me.
>
>   (Ps 51:1–5)

Memory as Power of Self-Organization, True and False

IF A DISTINGUISHING ACCOMPLISHMENT of a great writer of fiction is compellingly to narrate as autobiography that which by definition defies such narration—the event of one's own birth—then perhaps no novel of the nineteenth century attests more abundantly to such greatness than

Charles Dickens's *David Copperfield*. With remarkable facility Dickens's narrator assumes the authority "to begin my life with the beginning of my life," recounting with spooky precision the "the day and hour of my birth."[1] Never minding that the account, when considered in light of the commonly experienced limits of human memory, is absurd, a charming proof of Dickens's accomplishment is that the narration short-circuits any objection. The voice of the narrator, David, seems effortlessly to comprehend within itself the reality of the writer, Dickens, so that the narration subsumes the perspective of its creator. Literary invention becomes the means of erasure of the traces of its own history, and the reader, immediately engaged in this writerly strategy, struggles to refuse the invitation to conflate the character with the writer and all the while remain engaged as reader. It is only fitting therefore that more than any other of Dickens's works this book has been read as revelatory of the personality of the artist, as a model of fiction as an expressive medium of the self—the secret self expressing in the guise of the imaginary its own truth. Only fitting, also, that this beginning has been an object of special derision for its preciousness of self-regard, though even its most famous detractor cannot elude the reach of its influence on the practice of first-person literary narration—the very name Holden Caulfield bearing as it does the trace of the caul that Dickens's hero records as a feature of his own birth.[2]

It is best to acknowledge up front the tradition of reading *David Copperfield* as the most authentically autobiographical among Dickens's works, and the more general tradition it represents of reading novels as revelatory of the inner lives of their writers, since the reading that follows turns against itself the schematization of fiction as somehow separable from autobiography. Instead it insists on their necessary conjunction to all narration of intelligible personal identity, and it confesses this necessity as an ultimate non-fiction that is constitutive of fallen human identity. In the preface to the 1850 edition Dickens himself suggests as much when he writes: "Yet, I have nothing else to tell; unless, indeed, I were to confess (which might be of less moment still) that no one can ever believe this Narrative, in the reading, more that I have believed it in the writing."[3] The rhetorical diminution of his confession as itself "nothing" and then

---

1. Dickens, *David Copperfield*, 9.

2. For general argument on the significance of Dickens's work to a genealogy of the literary-critical present, see Clayton, "Dickens."

3. Dickens, *David Copperfield*, 6.

even "less" is telling, the author announcing to the reader—"whom I love"—that the tale told attests finally the privation of good and its disorder at the center of the ordered accomplishment of the fiction. Even the upper case of "Narrative" is revealing of a truth of human identity that one ought to believe, only that truth is the temptation of the fallen self to seek to gather into an impossible narrative coherence the elements of its own incomprehensible history; to persist in a sinful belief in the fictional coherence of self over against the truth of its disintegration; and thereby to seek to heal the wound of its fallen condition through an assertion of memory as creative authority.[4] So it is also notable that a recent critic has pointed to *David Copperfield* as the novel that more than any other installs the novel form itself as a perfect wife, as a perfectly sympathetic companion whose influence enables narration of a self at home with itself because attuned to a perfectly sympathetic partner[5]—attuned, that is, to the coordination of its own powers of imagination through their organization in the fiction of sex, and thereby able to avoid seeing the discomfiting reality of other persons. Yet already in this preface Dickens points to the possibility that another Narrative—properly designated uppercase—is the inescapable ground for both the writing and reading of his fiction. Even acknowledgment of God as the author who alone can speak the truth of self, however, still involves a prideful identification of human and divine, Dickens's address to the reader echoing Augustine's inclusion of the reader in his address to God: "To hear you speaking about oneself is to know oneself."[6]

In presuming to narrate his own birth, the narrator of *David Copperfield* attempts to reverse the relation of Beginning to beginning, reaches to contain the former within the latter. In doing so he accomplishes mastery of himself at the cost of knowledge also about himself. At stake, following Judith Butler, is the tenuousness of self-coherent personal identity which can only be achieved by also cutting oneself off from the security of intelligibility one most desires: "The 'I' can tell neither

4. Almost at the end of his life, Dickens in a revised preface (1869) reaffirmed identification of the fictional character David Copperfield with the heart of the writer: "Of all my books, I like this the best. It will be easily believed that I am a fond parent to every child of my fancy, and that no one can ever love that family as dearly as I love them. But, like many fond parents, I have in my heart of hearts a favorite child. And his name is DAVID COPPERFIELD" (766).

5. Ablow, *Marriage*, 14, 19, 43.

6. Augustine *Confessions* 10.3.3 (Chadwick, 180).

the story of its own emergence nor the conditions of its own possibility without bearing witness to a state of affairs to which one could not have been present, which are prior to one's own emergence as a subject who can know, and so constitute a set of origins that one can narrate only at the expense of authoritative knowledge."[7] The requisite qualification of this statement is that each person is in fact responsibly present at the state of affairs that is one's origin, so that the authoritative knowledge each person bears of that presence, but about which none wants to be reminded, is the fact of sin. The melancholic mood of Dickens's novel, perhaps its most outstanding and consistent feature, attests to the price that memory pays for its accomplishment, its inability to recognize and mourn what it has lost.[8]

In literary theoretical terms, such accomplishment of memory resonates with the projection of what Wayne Booth famously labels as the "implied author," or "second self" of the narrative: "The art of constructing reliable narrators is largely that of mastering all of oneself in order to project the *persona*, the second self, that really belongs in the book."[9] Although Booth's construct has fallen on hard times, his longing almost for reliability in narration still speaks to the power of Dickens's novel, and of novelistic concerns more generally. For Booth the possibility of mastery in the exertion of narrative authority is both real and occasion for celebration as a standard of objective greatness in fiction. As he explains near the end of his life, in defense of the concept of the implied author, it is the central means by which writers become "*more genuine, and of course far more admirable and influential: in wiping out the selves they do not like, the poets have created versions that elevate both their worlds and ours.*"[10] From an Augustinian perspective, Booth's demand that the author master oneself is always relative to an already narrated reality of the fallen self, so that the measure he is asserting of great fiction is the extent to which it effectively disowns the sinful desire that is its basis. His optimism about the greatness of fiction, its capacity to inspire ethical self-reformation in its readers, is thus proportional to the falseness in a sense of the comfort it provides. By contrast Italian feminist theorist Adriana Cavarero writes of the quest of the self for a narrative

7. Butler, *Giving*, 37.

8. On the absence of memory as a distinctly mid-nineteenth-century trope—memory opposed to self-presence in the present—see Dames, *Amnesiac*, esp. 3–19, 134–48.

9. Booth, *Rhetoric*, 83.

10. Booth, "Resurrection," 85.

unity: "Everyone looks for that unity of their own identity in the story (narrated by others or by herself), which, far from having a substantial reality, belongs only to desire."[11] Memory is the capacity that enables the realization through narration of this sinful desire. Assumption of responsibility for sin requires movement beyond memory, to the outside of memory, to a situation of the self theologically as creature in relation to creator. Imagination of memory of experience that is exterior to the limits of memory is then discernible as a form of evasion of responsible creaturely identity.[12]

In the light of these reflections, the absurd opening chapter of *David Copperfield*—"I am born"—seduces so successfully because the narrator is able to model so deftly the illusion of a coherent personal presence in one's origins. The theme of memory as power and fantasy functions from the outset as a primary concern of the novel, inviting comparison between the role of memory in Dickens's novel and in Saint Augustine's *Confessions*. Augustine's narrator also wonders about his self-presence at the scene of his birth, only he does so by owning the dependency of his knowledge on the authoritative knowledge of others, in particular his mother: "You have also given mankind the capacity to understand oneself by analogy with others, and to believe much about oneself on the authority of weak women."[13] Augustine's designation of his mother as a weak woman is more a rhetorical device to put himself in his place than to put his mother in hers. But when David Copperfield also acknowledges that he is conveying his information at second hand, the acknowledgment is more literally enclosed within the narration and points in a different direction: "To begin my life with the beginning of my life, I record that I was born (as I have been informed and believe) on a Friday, at twelve o'clock at night."[14] Unlike Augustine's mother Monica, David's mother

11. Cavarero, *Relating*, 41.

12. Even though memory inevitably sins in its attempt to narrate personal intelligibility, it is also indispensable to responsible human agency. One must have memory of the past to possess a responsible orientation toward the future. Adriana Cavarero explains: "The identity that materializes in a life-story has no future that is properly *its own*, if it has no past in the present of its memory" (*Relating*, 37). It is especially important to affirm the therapeutic necessity of mastering memory in the process of recovery from trauma; to affirm that empowered self-narrations enable freedom and agency. See Herman, *Trauma*, 175–213. Human capacity of memory is also arguably indispensable for theory of justice. See for example Hampshire, *Innocence*, 113–57.

13. Augustine *Confessions* 1.6.10 (Chadwick, 8).

14. Dickens, *David Copperfield*, 9.

Clara turns out to be weak in multiple senses, her authority more parenthetical than parental.[15] The difference is significant. For Augustine, belief
in the words of weak women grounds his acceptance of the authoritative
word of God in Scripture.[16] The work of narration for Augustine then
becomes to find oneself in the words of Scripture, whereas the work for
David Copperfield is to try to extricate himself from the comprehending
words of Scripture. Dickens's fiction turns out to be indicatively autobiographical to the extent that it is indicative of the failure of the romance of
innocent sexuality to elude its own self-accusatory exterior, summarized
in the words of the psalmist: "Indeed, I was born guilty, a sinner when my
mother conceived me."

While readings of *Confessions* as autobiographical, as a point of
entry into the psyche of its author, remained muted until the rise of
historical-critical scholarship, in the case of Dickens such readings began almost immediately following his death in 1870. John Forster—close
friend, literary executor, and first biographer—included in his *Life of
Charles Dickens* (1872) "a fragment of autobiography."[17] In the fragment
in question, Dickens recounts his experience as a child laborer in terms
so close to those of the narrator of *David Copperfield* that it seems impossible not to read the fragment as a key that unlocks the secret content of
the novel. Nor has this tendency been discouraged by the resemblance
of David's infatuation with Dora Spenlow to Dickens's youthful attachment to Maria Beadnell, and the correspondences between David's and
Dickens's professional trajectories. From reporter in shorthand of debates
in parliament to popular success as novelist, the story throughout reads
as an extended meditation on the craft of the writer. Forster's revelation
of the autobiographical fragment thus promoted a mode of reading already promoted by the novel itself, a mode, following D. A. Miller, which
appeals to the reader's own self-interest to believe that "autobiography is
most successful only where *it has been abandoned for the Novel*."[18]

15. For discussion of this parenthesis as part of larger reflection on the belatedness of
autobiography, see Ohi, "Autobiography."

16. Augustine *Confessions* 6.5.7 (Chadwick, 95–96).

17. Dickens, *David Copperfield*, 766–72. For discussion of the fragment in relation to
the novel, including a reading of the scene of the "red-hot poker" discussed at the end of
this chapter, see Bradbury, *Dickens*. See also Auerbach, "Performing," and Collins, "*David
Copperfield*" and "Dickens's."

18. Miller, *Novel*, 200.

Noteworthy also has been the temptation, arising from all this consonance between life and art, to read *David Copperfield* as an expression of Dickens's growing frustration and discontent with his marriage to Catherine Hogarth.[19] According to this reading, Agnes Wickfield is modeled after Catherine's sister Georgina, who, in inimitable Victorian fashion, remained the female head of Dickens's household till the end of his life, long after Catherine was banished from almost all contact with the family circle. These domestic arrangements are presumably reflected in the weird chilliness of the narrator's love for Agnes, the absence of any apparent eroticism in his attachment, correlating as it does to a relationship that was explicitly classed as criminal.[20] David's desire for Agnes fulfils no romantic desire for sexual companionship—that role in Dickens's life was reserved for Ellen Ternan, and lacks a correlate in the fiction—but the desire by an exacting and overtaxed male head of household for a responsible housekeeper.[21]

As troubled as they are, such autobiographical readings are inescapable testaments to the necessity of fictional narratives to the delimitation

19. Among Dickens's biographers, Johnson, *Charles Dickens*, dwells on the theme of Dickens's frustration with Catherine's companionship, emphasizing her unsuitability to her husband's genius. He writes of her: "She was amiable, devoted, unenterprising, lachrymose. She would no doubt have made an admirable wife to a placid gentleman of comfortable means" (131). He also unrelentingly pictures Catherine as a klutz who cannot board or exit a boat, train, or coach without falling (414–19). Other major biographies after Forster, *Life*, include Kaplan, *Dickens*, and Ackroyd, *Dickens*. For a favorable account of Catherine against the defamations of Johnson, see Rose, *Parallel*, 141–91.

20. Following passage of the "Deceased Wife's Sister's Bill," Lord Lyndhurst's Act of 1835, marriage between a husband and his deceased wife's sister was illegal. The issue remained a prominent theme in cultural and political debates. See for example Arnold, *Culture*, xxxi, 180–84. For discussion of Agnes as an angel of death, a presence of moral "judgment" opposed to morality founded on a "nonjudgmentally loving attitude to the world," see Nussbaum, "Steerforth's Arm," 360. Nussbaum is much more unqualifiedly optimistic than I am regarding the connections between eroticism, creativity, loving, and the possibility of moral goodness. Following the Augustinian perspective developed in this work, even the most loving sexual relationship cannot claim any *special* powers to improve a person morally.

21. Despite all the biographies and speculation, the details of Dickens's relationship with Ternan remain shrouded in mystery. For discussion of the incarnated significance of Dora and Agnes as more than projections by the narrator, see Newy, *Scriptures,* 136–62. On the narrator's marriage to Dora as more than a mistake, see Ayres, *Dissenting*, 13–32. In defense of Dora, G. K. Chesterton long since observed: "The reader does still feel that David's marriage to Dora was a real marriage; and that his marriage to Agnes was nothing, a middle-aged compromise, a taking of the second best, a sort of spiritualised and sublimated marriage of convenience" (Chesterton, *Appreciations*, 133).

of the presently imaginable possibilities of intelligible self-identification. When focused on Dickens's marital troubles, reading the story for the person is welcome as it illuminates the necessity of fiction as outlet and partial resolution of distresses of the self. But it remains deficient so long as it misses the theological dimension of the distress this fiction seeks to salve: alienation from God and the attendant burden of responsibility for sin. Among the temptations the novel poses is to imagine that if Dickens had only been happier in his marriage, he would have written otherwise. A parallel temptation that arises in reading Augustine is to wish that he had enjoyed a more integrated and healthy, i.e., optimistic, sense of the possibilities of his sexual desire. The temptation, more generally, is to imagine that if only the writer had been able to achieve satisfactorily a determinate form of adult sexual relationship, the problems posed in the text could have been resolved—as if, according to a cliché of popular romanticism, artistic greatness and personal happiness were inversely proportional (assuming in turn that romantic love were indispensable to personal happiness), and failed erotic relationship were an engine of artistic creation. As if, put another way, the problems of self disclosed in the text could be solved by a fantastic realization of the fictions of self the reader brings to the activity of reading.

Belief that original sin, the shame of failure of intelligibility of the fallen self, is the trouble that every reading, as participatory narrative activity, intrinsically attempts to redress, refocuses reading of Dickens's novel as a record of the fallen self's sinful quest for coherence, especially as it is a novel about reading and writing as self-constituting activities. Reading Augustine and Dickens together opens Dickens's text to this kind of scrutiny, given that Augustine's narrative, also concerned with reading and writing as self-constituting activities, explicitly directs the reader beyond herself.

The truthfulness or not of *Confessions* as historical record of the life of St. Augustine is less important, as a result, than the narrative orientation toward one's B/beginning that the text exemplifies: how completely the retrospective point of view, the remembering voice of narration, reaches beyond itself in search of the authoring personality of its own authorial identity. Augustine's text provides an occasion of reading as acceptance of the exteriority of the sources of the self that opens possibilities for new beginning. The narrator of *Confessions* searches for self-knowledge by searching for knowledge of and relationship with God, the author of all life, and turns to reading Scripture as a privileged means of opening oneself to illumination by divine creative authority.

Dickens's text points the reader in an opposite direction. It is an occasion of reading as foreclosure of the exteriorized search for self-knowledge. It is a novel of answers, not questions; of endings, not beginnings; the ultimate affirmation of Agnes's value in marriage the ending of all other endings. The narrator of *David Copperfield* is a passionate reader of novels, yet hardly mentions the one book in relation with which his own story is significantly interstructured, as if, in comparison with Augustine, the narration aims to domesticate its necessarily constitutive exterior. Rather than turn explicitly to Scripture as a means of breaking open the self, Dickens's narrative surreptitiously enlists Scripture into the service of the romantic attempt to self-satisfy the sinful desire for an intelligible unity in personal identity.

Analysis of this sinful dynamic requires some comment on the classification of Dickens's novel as a *Bildungsroman*. Though the term rings with a certain academic preciousness, still it is insightful to designate *David Copperfield* as a paradigmatic narrative of formation of romantic heroic identity. As such, it models an answer to a very a different kind of problem than that posed by *Confessions*: not how to imagine one's identity as creature of God, but how to be the hero of one's own life-narrative: "Whether I shall turn out to be the hero of my own life, or whether that station will be held by anybody else, these pages must show."[22] Another way to describe this problem, following Franco Moretti, is in terms of a necessary tension between individuality and normality, between "*self-determination* and the equally imperious demands of *socialization*."[23]

Moretti's summary of the continual appeal of the *Bildungsroman* helps also to explain the value of reading together Dickens's text in relation to Augustine's as resources for a theological discourse on sexuality that accepts with mature humor the traditional association of sexuality and sin:

> Thus it is not sufficient for modern bourgeois society simply to subdue the drives that oppose the standards of "normality." It is also necessary that, as a "free individual," not as a fearful subject but as a convinced citizen, one perceives the social norms as *one's own*. But one must *internalize* them and fuse external compulsion

22. Dickens, *David Copperfield*, 9.
23. Moretti, *Way*, 15.

and internal impulses into a new unity until the former is no longer distinguishable from the latter. This fusion is what we usually call "consent" or "legitimation." If the *Bildungsroman* appears to us still today as an essential, pivotal point of our history, this is because it has succeeded in representing this fusion with a force of conviction and optimistic clarity that will never be equaled again.[24]

As much as Moretti's characterization of the functional importance of the *Bildungsroman* as means of "fusion" of "external compulsion" and "internal impulses" applies with striking relevance to *David Copperfield*, it does not follow that the "drives that oppose the standards of 'normality'" are biological forces of the sexed body successfully constrained, though only ever precariously so, to conform to the "normality" that they naturally oppose. D. A. Miller makes a similar point when he writes of how packaged or boxed are all the characters of the novel: "Still, if their elaborate defenses finally amount to no more than the fact that they have made their social necessity into their personal choice, this perhaps suffices for a subject who can thus continue to affirm his subjectivity *as a form* even where it longer has a content of its own."[25] It is the form of secrecy that makes oneself, a form that the novel multiplies prolifically. What Moretti calls consent is a manner of making choice out of necessity. The self gets to keep its secrets because it consents only to have the secrets apportioned to it.

The value in description of *David Copperfield* as *Bildungsroman* emerges also when the novel is read, not as solution to some necessary conflict of "internal" and "external," but as a means of production of that very conflict.[26] The success of the novel is a double success of representation, productively representing as it does the oppositions that it then fuses. The novel in this way is a potent site for the operation of sexuality and for the ascription of mortal value to the fiction of sex, so that the multiple resolutions and foreclosures of the narrative can be summarized as the denials necessary to the practical coherence and invisibility of viewpoint the fiction of sex secures: the fantasied mastery of self projected by the implied author. Chief among the ensuing ironies is that the new unity this fiction accomplishes attains the status of consent or legitimation only

24. Moretti, *Way*, 16.

25. Miller, *Novel*, 204.

26. For complication of the account of the novel as *Bildungsroman*, see Ablow, *Marriage*, 21.

by a denial of a much more self-informing unity, accessible only in its exteriority to memory: the unity of creation and sin in political nature.

Before elaborating this reading of the novel as exemplary vehicle for the investment of value in sex, some further comment is in order also on the role of memory as an organizing rubric of narration. Memory is the power continually evoked by the narrator, asserted as a natural capacity that enables the sense of wholeness of the individual's life: "This may be fancy, though I think the memory of most of us can go farther back into such times than many of us suppose; just as I believe the power of observation in numbers of very young children to be quite wonderful for its closeness and accuracy. Indeed, I think that most grown men who are remarkable in this respect, may with greater propriety be said not to have lost the faculty, than to have acquired it."[27]

Though the comment is posed as an aside, this "fancy" is crucial to the assertion of the narrator's authority, since it marks his comprehensive faculty as a norm. The narrator's fancy is a fantasy common to the *Bildung* in any *Bildungsroman*: "Developmental narratives tend to err by assuming that the narrator of such a narrative can be present to the origins of the story. The origin is made available only retroactively, and through the screen of fantasy."[28] Only what Butler calls an error is instead precisely the point that is asserted by the novel's narrator as true of all persons. The narrator as adult is now distinguished by the "faculty" he has retained, in opposition to the mass of "grown men" who are not "remarkable in this respect." The writer is depicted as an exceptional character. But he is exceptional because he is normal, because he achieves enjoyment of a privileged relationship to his origins that is also the rule of all fully realized human identity.[29]

Memory in this way begins to look a lot like a means of return to the ultimate origin of human being:

> And now I see the outside of our house, with the latticed bed-
> room-windows standing open to let in the sweet-smelling air,
> and the ragged old rooks'-nests still dangling in the elm trees at

27. Dickens, *David Copperfield*, 19.

28. Butler, *Giving*, 53.

29. A related definition of fantasy: "To be there *always*, though unperceived, to inhabit the space of perception as such and thus to become the witness to one's absence, one's disembodiment; such fantasy presumes a reality guaranteed, not threatened by time, sustained by the certainty that a 'course of events' is bound to continue its course in due course long after we are gone." Edelman, *No Future*, 34.

the bottom of the front garden. Now I am in the garden at the back, beyond the yard where the empty pigeon-house and dog-kennel are—a very preserve of butterflies, as I remember it, with a high fence, and a gate and padlock; where the fruit clusters on the trees, riper and richer than fruit has ever been since, in any other garden, and where my mother gathers some in a basket, while I stand by, bolting furtive gooseberries, and trying to look unmoved. A great wind rises, and the summer is gone in a moment. We are playing in the winter twilight, dancing about the parlor. When my mother is out of breath and rests herself in an elbow-chair, I watch her winding her bright curls round her fingers, and straitening her waist, and nobody knows better than I do that she likes to look so well, and is proud of being so pretty.

That is among my very earliest impressions. That, and a sense that we were both a little afraid of Peggotty, and submitted ourselves in most things to her direction, were among the first opinions—if they may be so called—that I ever derived from what I saw.[30]

As many have observed, Dickens in these earliest pages captures with exquisite sensitivity how vivid and unparalleled first impressions *feel*; how much childhood knowledge is experienced as a form of discovery; and how fascinating family mythologies of birth and infancy are for the child concerned. But at the same time he also elevates that sensitivity to a sinful priority, the ending projected in this beginning suggesting as it does that the completion of a personality can be achieved through the re-creation of this scene, where the subject child becomes the governing and witnessing parent; where the subjection of the girl-parent and her child to the rule of the housekeeper is righted without losing any of its innocent charm.

The melancholy memory of a nameless fruit, "riper and richer than fruit has ever been since, in any other garden," suggests that the narrator is recalling much more than just the intensity of childhood sensation. Recollection is a means of asserting the primary bond of mother and child as a paradise, an Eden that will be restored in the happy conclusion of this story (as in so many others). Through memory domestic space is credited with an innocence, an originary perfection, that becomes a formative ideal of the adult personality. Here is more than just a prime example of the cult of innocent childhood functioning as fantastic preservative of one's own

30. Dickens, *David Copperfield*, 21–22.

imagined innocence lost; it is the very production of that idealized presence of the child in the man.[31] For this reason the novel is organized by a perpetual postponement, until the very concluding page, of definition of Agnes as the woman-child-bride who literally propels the narrator into God's presence. Memory is affirmed as the crucial medium of viewpoint on one's own past, a viewpoint achieved only through the domestication of an alter-hero who enacts the scene that memory witnesses—memory figuring this entire narrative, from the beginning, as somehow also contained by its conclusion. The seemingly insignificant and harmless phrase "as I remember it" is actually an assertion of a far-reaching discipline that encompasses a massive cast of characters within its comprehensive vision, even though the ultimate mastery of the remembering presence over a vast structure of places and times and persons is at best illusory. The writer in the end is no more in command of the reader than the self is over the memories it idolizes.[32]

Whereas memory in *David Copperfield* is the paradigmatic medium for the sinful self-organization of the narrator, in *Confessions* memory is a medium of a very different self-discipline: of the admission of the dependence of any coherent and meaningful narration of personal identity on its constitutive and sustaining exteriority, mother and father immediately, but also and just as immediately, God who creates. The narrator of *Confessions* takes care to credit God as the source of all those emergent qualities that the narrator of *David Copperfield* stakes as uniquely his own. He also takes care to own that sin is a constant reality of his person:

> Yet, Lord, I must give thanks to you, the most excellent and supremely good Creator and Governor of the universe, my God, even though by your will I was merely a child. For at that time I existed, I lived and thought and took care for my self preservation (a mark of your profound latent unity whence I derived my being). An inward instinct told me to take care of the integrity of my senses, and even in my little thoughts about little matters I took delight in the truth. I hated to be deceived, I developed a good memory, I acquired the armory of being skilled with words, friendship softened me, I avoided pain, despondency, ignorance.

31. Probably the most influential modern study on the conceptualization of childhood as historical phenomenon is Ariès, *Centuries*.

32. Memory does also have the power to generate moral insight, so that autobiography can function as a medium for challenging unjust norms and practices, as Ware, "Power," illustrates with regard to critical distanciation of the self from the conditions of racialization.

In such a person what was not worthy of admiration and praise? But every one of these qualities are gifts of my God: I did not give them to myself. They are good qualities, and their totality is my self. Therefore he who made me is good, and he is my good, and I exult to him, (Ps. 2:11) for all the good things that I was even as a boy. My sin consisted in this, that I sought pleasure, sublimity, and truth not in God but in his creatures, in myself and other created beings. So it was that I plunged into miseries, confusions, and errors. My God, I give thanks to you, my source of sweet delight, and my glory and my confidence. I thank you for your gifts. Keep them for me, for in this way you will keep me. The talents you have given will increase and be perfected, and I will be with you since it was your gift to me that I exist.[33]

The characterization by Augustine's narrator of the sin of his childhood contrasts with the celebration, by Dickens's narrator, of his own talents and of his mother's beauty. Where one claims as his own a faculty exceptional because normal, the other credits all his promising abilities to another. Where one conjures innocence and Eden in confession of submission to the rule of a servant, the other confesses sin and faithlessness in failure to submit to the authority of the Creator and Governor of the universe. The relevance of this acknowledgment of sin in Augustine's work, as means of initiating a theologically critical reading of the idolization of marital bonds via the idolization of maternal-infant bonds in Dickens's work, is only more compelling when one recalls how lovingly and devotedly Augustine urges remembrance of his mother upon the reader as an act of charity and faith.

To summarize: the power of memory in *Confessions* is liberating, it is constraining in *David Copperfield*. Memory in the former case opens the space of communal questioning and searching that enables a responsible contextualized self-interest. Memory in the latter case restlessly marks its boundaries, establishing the self as a private object of sinful self-interest, ever searching within itself for release from the "pain, despondency, ignorance" of its own being by fixing the imagined future in terms of the remembered past. These differences indicate why the latter ends in numerous tidy resolutions and the former does not. They also indicate the relevance of the unceasing suspicion of sexuality, as refracted through Augustine's writings, to illumination of Dickens's novel as a narrative of failed evasion of responsibility for sin. Sexuality focuses the fantasy of

33. Augustine *Confessions* 1.20.31 (Chadwick, 22–23).

the fulfillment of sex in marriage. Marriage then becomes idolized as the solution to the shame of unintelligibility that implicates every self in the facticity of original sin. Eclipsing the need for repentance, the idolization of marriage is at the center of the romance of innocent sexuality and epitomized in Dickens's novel, so funny at many moments even if ultimately humorless.

David Copperfield's Biblical Faithlessness

When addressing the topic of religious themes in *David Copperfield*, the most likely starting point is the character of Agnes and David's initial impression of her figure, subsequently invoked throughout the novel: "I cannot call to mind where or when, in my childhood, I had seen a stained glass window in a church. Nor do I recollect its subject. But I know that when I saw her turn round, in the grave light of the old staircase, and wait for us, above, I thought of that window; and that I associated something of its tranquil brightness with Agnes Wickfield ever afterwards."[34] The narrator's comment here is both directive and vague. He insists the reader see Agnes as an embodiment of God-relatedness, while his simultaneous (and out of character) denial of memory frees Agnes, as divinely illuminating presence, for domestication. A strategic forgetfulness enables the imaginative ascription to Agnes's hovering presence of a power to *convert* ordinary domestic space into a space of worship. Agnes "waits" for David "above," just as she waits with suffering patience throughout the book, lamb that she is—*Agnes Dei*—for David to realize his love for her, and finally secure this domestic church as his own.[35]

To the questioning reader, the assertiveness of the designation of Agnes as "good Angel,"[36] the insistent figuration of Agnes as index of elevated reality that echoes also with homicidal sentiment (she is chronically gesturing heavenwards, standing in a "grave light"; recall also Emily Hotspur's "great grave eyes"), the repeated accreditation of Agnes as source of moral goodness, all invite suspicion that the text is not only

34. Dickens, *David Copperfield*, 194.

35. The vagueness of Dickens's association of Agnes with church space also reflects the vagueness of Dickens's identification as a Christian. His church attendance was irregular at best. Regarding the attempt of various denominations to claim Dickens as their own, focusing especially on his period of interest in Unitarianism, see Cross, "Charles Dickens." On Dickens and Christianity more generally, see Cunningham, "Dickens."

36. Dickens, *David Copperfield*, chap. XXV.

promising more than it can deliver—a familiar criticism that targets Agnes's failure to convince, qua character—but is actually speaking more comprehensively through that exaggerated promise about enduring theological themes. Agnes's importance consists precisely in her vacuity as a character. Her vacuity signifies the much more devastating vacuity of the promise condensed in her idealized presence: the promise of completion of human identity—of plenitude of intelligibility of self—the self bathed in a "tranquil brightness"—through marriage with a perfectly sympathetic complementary partner. Whereas the failure of Agnes to convince could be regarded as a defect of the novel, and then dismissed as instance of the limit of Dickens's artistic accomplishment, it is more productive to regard this failure as integral to Dickens's literary genius. It bespeaks the deepest and most searching dimensions of the story. It draws the reader into the theological dynamic from which the narrator is trying to extricate himself without ever attaining responsible consciousness of that dynamic.

The meaningfulness of Agnes's role in the story, however, is severely restricted when considered in isolation. Agnes's initial appearance is framed by the appearance of another character who is hardly ever acknowledged as theologically important, despite the glaringly obvious biblical referent of his name: Uriah Heep.[37] Unlike the narrator's name, David, not by any stretch of the imagination is the name Uriah common, then or since. Nor is its biblical referent obscure. Yet critical treatment of Agnes Wickfield and Uriah Heep faithfully (ironically so) follows the direction explicitly insisted by the narration: regarding one as center of religious symbolism in the novel, the other as quintessential Dickensian villain. In part this submissiveness of readings of *David Copperfield* to the direction of the text may follow from a general lack of knowledge of the Bible among literary critics. But whatever may be the level of awareness of the Bible among readers of Dickens, this conformity of critics to the lines laid down by the novel suggests also the contribution of commentators to the romance of innocent sexuality the novel participates in and makes possible. That participation involves a reversal of symbolic investment in the name Uriah, so that this critical lapse of the reader is immediately implicated in the success of the narration in delimiting as properly theological themes that are at the same time untenable when considered in relation to their biblical basis.[38]

37. For discussion of the autobiographical correlate of Uriah, see Friedman, "Heep."

38. For an extended study of Dickens's use of the Bible in his fictions, that notably does not address *David Copperfield*, see Larson, *Dickens*. See also Walder, *Dickens*, 140–69,

To make fuller sense of the narrator's figuration of Agnes as a kind of morbid angelic presence, one must back up a few pages, to the prior appearance of Uriah Heep, and excavate the biblical drama of sex and sin that the novel reenacts. Only then does the depth of the narrator's quest through marriage to evade responsibility for sin become fully apparent. Likewise does the power of memory, celebrated as it is throughout the story, then appear more transparently as the corrupt medium for the culpable narration of a self free from sin.

The preterit in the following passage, as throughout the story, is more than a technical necessity of craft. It is the establishment and assertion of the authority of invisibility of viewpoint through the spectacle that it manufactures. After walking all the way from London to Dover, David finds safe haven with his aunt, Betsy Trotwood. In chapter XV, "I Make Another Beginning," his aunt subsequently entrusts him to the care of Mr. Wickfield in Canterbury, where he will resume the education interrupted by his consignment to Murdstone and Grinby's blacking warehouse. Arriving for the first time at his new home, he recalls:

> It was quite spotless in its cleanliness. The old-fashioned brass knocker on the low arched door, ornamented with carved garlands of fruit and flowers, twinkled like a star; the two stone steps descending to the door were as white as if they had been covered with fair linen; and all the angles and corners, and carvings and mouldings, and quaint little panes of glass, and quainter little windows, though old as the hills, were as pure as any snow that ever fell upon the hills.
>
> When the pony-chaise stopped at the door, and my eyes were intent upon the house, I saw a cadaverous face appear at a small window on the ground floor (in a little round tower that formed one side of the house), and quickly disappear. The low arched door then opened, and the face came out. It was quite as cadaverous as it had looked in the window, though in the grain of it there was that tinge of red which is sometimes to be observed in the skins of red-haired people. It belonged to a red-haired person—a youth of fifteen, as I take it now, but looking much older—whose hair was cropped as close as the closest stubble; who had hardly any eyebrows, and no eyelashes, and eyes of a redbrown; so unsheltered and unshaded, that I remember wondering how he went to sleep.[39]

whose chapter "The Social Gospel: *David Copperfield* and *Bleak House*" never identifies the biblical precedents of David and Uriah.

39. Dickens, *David Copperfield*, 190–91.

The "cleanliness" attributed to this house is almost nonsensical, until one recalls that the narrator is describing the residence of Agnes, the "spotless" and "pure" entry a kind of objective corollative, one suspects, of her virginity.[40] At the same time, it is also suggestive of how:

> It happened, late one afternoon, when David rose from his couch and was walking about on the roof of the king's house, that he saw from the roof a woman bathing; the woman was very beautiful. David sent someone to inquire about the woman. It was reported, "This is Bathsheba daughter of Eliam, the wife of Uriah the Hittite." So David sent messengers to get her, and she came to him and he lay with her. (Now she was purifying herself after her period.) Then she returned to her house. The woman conceived; and she sent and told David, "I am pregnant." (2 Sam 11:2–5)

Considered against its biblical background, it is more than curious that the narrator's first impression of the Wickfield home—(not exactly a "first" impression at all, foreshadowing as it does the presence of an angel within; memory is deep in play here)—contains also another presence, "a cadaverous face" that "appears" to peer outward from within through a window. The glass in daylight presumably also is a reflective surface, suggesting from the outset that Uriah is much more his accusatory "peer" than David ever acknowledges. Dickens's text is both reflective of the biblical text and window onto that text.

Here is the narrator, attempting to exercise a mastery of gaze—his "eyes intent upon the house"—and foundering; when out of this house appears "a red-haired person—a youth of fifteen, as I take it now, but looking much older." The first detail the reader learns of this person is not his name, but the coloration of his skin and hair—coloration that popularly signified an excessively and dangerously sexual constitution. The apparent libidinousness of this person is further suggested by his appearance of unnatural age. Their difference in age underscores the presumed sexual innocence of the narrator.[41] It is as if David, ten years old

---

40. The preservation of Agnes's spotlessness throughout the novel contrasts with the fate of Little Em'ly. These two characters arguably embody the poles of nineteenth century British imagination of female sexual identity as described by Trudgill, *Madonnas*.

41. According to folklore of the period, Judas was a redhead, and also the devil, and redheaded children were evidence that the mother had had an affair with the devil. In *Gulliver's Travels* (1726) the narrator writes of the Yahoos: "It is observed that the *Red-haired* of both Sexes are more libidinous and mischievous than the rest, whom yet they much exceed in Strength and Activity" (Swift, *Gulliver*, 232). In *North and South* (1855) Dixon describes the

and about to glimpse for the first time the little woman he will wed, is facing, and radically disowning, the image of himself on the other side of his incipient puberty. All the more so when one recalls that King David was by popular tradition also accounted a redhead.[42]

In relating the first encounter between David Copperfield and Uriah Heep, the narrator transposes the most distinctive features of King David and Uriah the Hittite as recorded in 2 Sam 11:6–13. The sinfulness of King David, who steals Uriah's sexual property, then murders him, and the virtue of Uriah the Hittite, devoted and abstemious servant who lawfully refrains from forbidden sexual contact with his beautiful wife, are reversed by the narrator. David Copperfield, always writing to exemplify his own blamelessness, assimilates to himself the faithful, loyal, and unsuspecting innocence of Uriah the Hittite and attributes to Uriah Heep all the sexual predatoriness, manipulativeness, and deceitfulness of King David.

The cumulative effect of these observations is that the narrator, upon close reading, starts to seem far less of a blank slate—or an "insipid" hero—and instead much more cunningly dispersed throughout the narration he provides.[43] The initial protestations of the remarkable keenness of his powers of observation and memory turn out to be a bit of a ruse, because they tend to distract the reader from questioning the trustworthiness of the narration. Not the reliability of the narrator as observer, or the accuracy of the record of details he provides, is in question exactly, but the trustworthiness of the evaluation accompanying all that observation of detail. Visualization and valuation are inseparable activities: "That is among my very earliest impressions. That, and a sense that we were both a little afraid of Peggotty, and submitted ourselves in most things to her direction, were among the first opinions—if they may be so called—that I ever derived from what I saw."

"scamp" young Leondards as, "A bad-looking fellow, I can assure you, miss. Whiskers such as I should be ashamed to wear—they are so red" (Gaskell, *North*, 255). Other libidinous and mischievous red-headed literary figures include Lydia Gwilt in *Armadale* (1866) by Wilkie Collins and Peter Quint in *Turn of the Screw* (1898) by Henry James.

42. This tradition is based on the verses I Sam 16:12 and 17:42. For the biblical Hebrew root, see Brown et al., *Lexicon*, 10.

43. The phrase is from Moretti, *Way*, 11. In relation to sentimental-homicidal-suicidal violence taken as knowledge-relation also consider: "Far from an aesthetic defect, the vacuity is the psychological desideratum of one whose ambition, from the time he first impersonated his favorite characters in his father's books, has always been *to be vicarious*." Miller, *Novel*, 215.

These first opinions only count as such because they retrospectively inaugurate the general habit of deriving "opinions" from "what I saw" that is the implicit activity of wisdom, marking the time of the whole narrative structure, even as the operation of that wisdom, through memory, projects a vision to the reader that is already thoroughly imbued with opinion, so that every "first" opinion is functionally more a "final" opinion.[44] (There is no false foreshadowing in this work.[45]) However much the narrator presents the operation as a straightforward temporal progression, no simple derivation from fact to value is possible.

Regarding the narrator's depiction of Uriah, judgment looms from without. The imbrication of the narrator's vision in a narrative of prophetic accusation consequently invites the reader to question every valuation in description concerning this character. All the more so because the vilification of Uriah by David is relentlessly sexualized. The sexual desire continually deployed as the nexus of reversal of biblical values by the narrator becomes invested with special prominence as locus of concentration of the desire that energizes their reversal in the first place: the desire to evade accusation of sin and its consequent judgment. The promise of the fiction of sex, as written in these pages, is that if David can successfully fix and then contain his sexual desire in some externalized form, he can avoid any imputation of guilt, any claim of responsibility for original sin. David's project is to secure Agnes as his own sexual property and at the same time transfer all the blame of his sexual desire to Uriah. The specter of sexual desire, about to "waken" in David, is reflected in the image of Uriah as Priapism personified, someone who "had hardly any eyebrows, and no eyelashes, and eyes of a redbrown; so unsheltered and unshaded, that I remember wondering how he went to sleep." The problem anticipated here is not how Uriah is able to sleep, but whether David will be able to sleep; whether he will be able to do so without succumbing to the temptation his emergent sexual desire poses to himself.

Proceeding the first meeting with Agnes (about which more below), this chapter of new beginning, which turns out also to be the advent of more than just an academic education, concludes as follows:

> But in the course of the evening I had rambled down to the door, and a little way along the street, that I might have another peep

44. The figure of "Mr. Omer, Draper, Tailor, Haberdasher, Funeral Furnisher, etc." keeps time in the narrative; see for example 112–13.

45. On the use of foreshadowing as control, see Moretti, *Way*, 182–88.

at the old houses, and the grey Cathedral; and might think of my coming through that old city on my journey, and of my passing the very house I lived in, without knowing it. As I came back, I saw Uriah Heep shutting up the office; and feeling friendly towards everybody, went in and spoke to him, and at parting, gave him my hand. But oh, what a clammy hand his was! As ghostly to the touch as to the sight! I rubbed mine afterwards, to warm it, *and to rub his off.*

It was such an uncomfortable hand, that, when I went to my room, it was still cold and wet upon my memory. Leaning out of window, and seeing one of the faces on the beam-ends looking at me sideways, I fancied it was Uriah Heep got up there somehow, and shut him out in a hurry.[46]

Given how much David has already figured Uriah as an exteriorized embodiment of his own impending sexual maturity, their handshake looks remarkably masturbatory. In touching Uriah, David seems to be touching and then recoiling from just that part of himself that was the means of his sin in his biblical incarnation, and that poses a dreaded threat to the healthy development of his mid-Victorian male identity.[47]

When David describes Uriah's hand as both "clammy" and "ghostly," he discloses the confusion of the narrator David's desiring orientation toward the embodied reality of his own desire, which then induces him to touch himself further: "I rubbed mine afterwards, to warm it, *and to rub his off.*" It is almost as if, in a fit of homosexual panic, by "rubbing off" Uriah's hand David is attempting a kind of self-circumcision: the removal of a part of himself that will initiate the possibility of divine human relationship—that will make possible his marriage with Agnes. David almost seems to be negotiating, through his ambivalence toward Uriah, a fit between Paul's assertion in Rom 2:29—"Rather a person is a Jew who is one inwardly, and real circumcision is a matter of the heart—it is spiritual and not literal"—and the literal implication, based on his self-identification with King David, that King David presumably was circumcised, and David Copperfield presumably is not.[48]

46. Dickens, *David Copperfield*, 195–96.

47. For discussion of the narrator's description of Uriah Heep as a clear-cut "easily recognizable type" of the masturbator as physically degenerate menace to public welfare, familiar to contemporary readers of the novel, see Lacqueur, *Solitary*, 63–65.

48. Augustine addresses the theme of "The Circumcision of the Heart" in *The Spirit and the Letter* in Augustine *Works* 1/23:13.21–14.23 (Teske, 162–65).

From a social-historical perspective, David's ambivalence toward Uriah reflects a reality of the context of the novel, a context that regarded auto-eroticism of any sort as sinful and dangerously unhealthy.[49] This background belief adds urgency to the theological imperative of fixing all blame for sexual sin on Uriah. In order to take up his residence in the Wickield's home, and not to defile it with his own self-polluting presence, David must expel Uriah. The reversal of biblical values has its corollary in the literal reversal of the positions of David and Uriah relative to this domicile. David effectively usurps Uriah's place. He progresses from an outsider, one who had just recently passed penniless "the very house I lived in, without knowing it"—one who was arrested on the doorstep, subject to Uriah's gaze from within—to a snug inhabitant, one who literally enforces the expulsion of Uriah from the premises: "Leaning out of window, and seeing one of the faces on the beam-ends looking at me sideways, I fancied it was Uriah Heep got up there somehow, and shut him out in a hurry." Sin and innocence are decisively localized respectively as exterior and interior in relation to the space of domesticity.[50] Only then can sinful sexuality be "shut out," and "innocent sexuality" just as forcefully "shut in," so that the definitive expulsion of Uriah Heep from the Wickfield premises, enacted here for the first time as a fancy, is a central component of the eventual happy ending of the whole novel.

Throughout this reversal memory can't quite escape voicing the self-contradictoriness of its need to enforce its privilege of invisibility of viewpoint upon the reader, in relation to Uriah. Uriah's viewpoint is always dismissed as fantastical and grotesque, as a perspective that must be denied. Yet memory clings to Uriah, depends on the recall of his spectacular image, in the very expression of the desire to be rid of him. When Uriah is accused of haunting memory, memory is also accusing itself: "It was such an uncomfortable hand, that, when I went to my room, it was still cold and wet upon my memory." The narrator, however, can never admit the complicity of his own desire in the narration of his memory of Uriah: that his "uncomfortable hand" is uncomfortable because it

49. For discussion of English medical perspectives on masturbation as a "crime," emphasizing especially the authoritative influence of French biologist Samuel Tissot (1728–1797), see Stengers and Neck, *Masturbation*, 45, 105–6. Even today the Catholic Magisterium teaches that "masturbation is an intrinsically and seriously disordered act" and that "masturbation is seriously wrong." Lawler, "Masturbation," 361, 368.

50. For critical discussion of Dickens's idea of the "home," see Baumgarten and Daleski, *Homes*, 3–75.

threatens the invisibility of memory's viewpoint, a viewpoint that is not innocent of desire, of the knowledge of sexual desire the image of Uriah's hand evokes, since it relentlessly projects that image. David's memory is itself guilty of the sexual sin of self-abuse it fixes on Uriah.

In the exertion of its self-contradictory power, memory is always opening a space of possible self-accusation, possible admission of sin, possible admission of confraternity and identity with Uriah, and then seizing each such occasion for the assertion of the narrator's innocence. David's assertions of innocence are always depicted, by the same complicit power of memory that makes this self-exculpating narration possible, in opposition to a grotesque spectacle of Uriah's malevolent lechery. The calm exteriorizing gaze of the narrator, in order to forestall any doubt of the self-control claimed throughout by the narrating competency of memory, in order to displace any suspicion that memory may be self-polluting, is constantly emphasizing Uriah Heep's unruly, ungovernable physicality, and joining the contrast between itself and Uriah to a vision of Agnes Wickfield:

> He had a way of writhing when he wanted to express en-
> thusiasm which was very ugly; and which diverted my attention
> from the compliment he had paid my relation, to the snaky twist-
> ings of his throat and body.
>
> "A sweet lady, Master Copperfield!" said Uriah Heep. "She
> has a great admiration for Miss Agnes, Master Copperfield, I
> believe?"
>
> I said "Yes," boldly; not that I knew anything about it, Heaven
> forgive me!
>
> "I hope you have, too, Master Copperfield," said Uriah. "But
> I am sure you must have.
>
> "Everybody must have," I returned.
>
> "Oh thank you, Master Copperfield," said Uriah Heep, "for
> that remark! It is so true! Umble as I am, I know it is *so* true! Oh,
> thank you, Master Copperfield!"
>
> He writhed himself quite off his stool in the excitement of
> his feelings, and, being off, began to make arrangements for go-
> ing home.[51]

Almost against his will, David admits that Uriah's serpentine energy, though "ugly," is also dangerously captivating in its power to "divert"

---

51. Dickens, *David Copperfield*, 204.

"attention."[52] As the despised embodiment of the narrator's awakening sexual desire, Uriah Heep is imbued with a propulsive restlessness that threatens the self-assured equilibrium of memory. Sexual desire is figured as a destructive energy that threatens to disrupt the equanimity and focus of memory's narrative capacity. David never owns that threat to his cherished self-image. Instead he always places Agnes in harm's way, so that protection of Agnes from Uriah's depredations becomes a highly articulated defensive mechanism of the narrator against any accusation of sexual sin, that is, of disruptive sexual desire for the woman in whom he will find completion of self.

At stake ultimately in this exchange between Uriah and David is the viability or not of marriage as means of narration of the fiction of sex. Which is another way of stating that at issue in the conflict between them, first hinted at here, is who will marry Agnes. As in a number of subsequent conversations between Uriah and David where this conflict arises, it is Uriah who perspicaciously names the stakes, so that Uriah is always inciting David's own vision of Agnes as a marital prospect.

In order to figure himself as husband and Agnes as wife, David must always first recoil from the vision of Agnes in Uriah's "writhing" embrace. Only then can David definitively answer the question that begins the story, because it establishes David's heroic task: to preserve Agnes from the threat Uriah poses. Yet the catastrophe of a marriage between Uriah and Agnes is not so much the particular defilement, repeatedly emphasized, of Agnes by Uriah's touch. It is the degradation of marriage as an institutional preservative of the claim of innocent sexuality. The narrator uses Uriah quite plainly as means of establishing what he otherwise never even remotely establishes in his own words—that Agnes is in any way at all desirable. When he does portray directly Agnes as desirable, her desir-

52. The condensation of sexual desire as distraction in the figure of Uriah is pointedly illustrated in the following exchange:

"Deuce take the man!" said my aunt, sternly, "what's he about? Don't be galvanic, sir!"

"I ask your pardon, Miss Trotwood," returned Uriah; "I'm aware you're nervous."

"Go along with you, sir!" said my aunt, anything but appeased. "Don't presume to say so! I am nothing of the sort. If you're an eel, sir, conduct yourself like one. If you're a man, control your limbs, sir! Good God!," said my aunt, with great indignation, "I am not going to be serpentined and corkscrewed out of my senses!" (437)

A rather suggestive statement by David's old maiden great aunt!

ability has much more to do with himself, with the imagined completion he associates with her presence, than with any quality one can positively attribute to her, least of all as a sexual partner.

In his backhanded way David regularly credits Uriah as the only character in the novel who recognizes Agnes as a sexual woman, and not just an embodiment of the sex "woman." Uriah also deserves credit for an honesty and a self-deprecating sense of humor that the narrator lacks. When Uriah attempts to elicit confirmatory expressions of Agnes's desirability—"A sweet lady, Master Copperfield!" said Uriah Heep. "She [Betsy Trotwood] has a great admiration for Miss Agnes, Master Copperfield, I believe?"—he is stating plainly what the narrator wishes the reader to understand on David's behalf, and yet refuses to allow David to avow for himself. Uriah is also making wicked fun of David's precious innocence: "sweet" about the least tenable description imaginable of Betsy Trotwood, proving the lie in David's pretension not to know already perfectly well to whom this term, in all its polyvalency, refers; manifest in his response, occurring as it does *before* Uriah actually inquires David's view on the subject: "I said 'Yes,' boldly; not that I knew anything about it, Heaven forgive me!"

Uriah Heep the Righteous Hittite

"Heaven forgive me!" In protesting his innocence in relation to Uriah, and calling upon heaven as divine witness, David is issuing a humorless disavowal that is also a prototypical formulation of the romance of innocent sexuality. He is insisting that he has no need of forgiveness, that Uriah is the sinner, not David. He is refusing to admit the constitutive exterior that is the possibility of romance. He is refusing to admit his complicity in the manufacture of the spectacle that makes possible his own empowered invisibility of viewpoint. He is refusing to know what he knows. And he is refusing to admit his shared responsibility for the reality of sin.

Considered in relation to the biblical narrative that sustains his romantic imagination, David Copperfield has much reason to ask forgiveness; forgiveness of the injustice of his treatment of Uriah; forgiveness of his denial of dependency on the biblical narrative that is the basis for establishing the meaningfulness of that injustice; forgiveness, moreover, for his lack of faithfulness to the biblical narrative.

Whereas Augustine's narrator confesses his sinfulness and seeks self-understanding by trying to find himself in the narration of Genesis, the narrator in Dickens's novel uses the Bible for a self-serving end. He uses the story of King David's repentance before God as occasion for his own denial of all need to repent in the first place. David Copperfield's "boldness" consists most of all in his untenable protestation of innocence and its attendant imperative injunction of divine forgiveness. His outburst presents a stark rhetorical contrast to the response of King David, when confronted with his sin: "Wash me thoroughly from my iniquity, and cleanse me from my sin. For I know my transgressions, and my sin is ever before me."

Perhaps it is a bit harsh to say of David when he claims "not that I knew anything about it," that he is lying; but only barely. The adult narrator writes the subtext of his exchange with Uriah that the child-hero appears to miss, and deploys their disjunction to exalt childhood innocence as his own perennial possession. The overwhelming structuring presence of the same disjunction makes Dickens's novel a prime example of the narration of the fiction of sex. It focuses that fiction purposefully on the self as sexed child who is at the same time utterly untainted by sexual desire. In doing so it enables the distinction between innocent and sinful desire; innocent desire that seeks its meaningful completion in another's sex; sinful desire that cares only about its own carnal pleasure, and doesn't seek the "tranquility" of its completion. All the attributes of the little person within, his sex, that David fears as inhuman, as irredeemably carnal, he projects outward—figuring himself as the true man, Uriah as an animal. So Dr. Strong, a figure of wisdom in the novel, exclaims: "'Why, my Dear Copperfield,' Said the Doctor, 'You are a man!'" Uriah by contrast is an "ape."[53] Uriah is so despised and dangerous because he threatens to disrupt memory's requirement of attention in narrating the fiction of sex. The threat Uriah poses to the fiction of sex is meaningfully sexualized as that threat serves to favor any contrast on David's behalf. It serves to reinforce the perception of David as self-possessed in a manner Uriah is not, where self-possession and possession of a stable and coherent sex converge to a point.

Despite every insulting depiction the narrator offers, Uriah is neither so obtuse nor so defenseless that he cannot call David to account for the asymmetry of their exchange. A fundamental theme of every encounter

53. Dickens, *David Copperfield*, 440, 435.

between David and Uriah is that their knowledge-relation is an accusation-relation. The memory of the narrator, in these encounters, gives voice to the memory of the biblical story, even as it is always disordering that biblical memory to its own advantage. Uriah the Hittite dies on the battlefield, never aware of how thoroughly he has been duped by his king, but Uriah Heep is always dropping hints that tear just beneath the surface at David's conscience. Constantly insisting on his own humility, Uriah Heep is constantly recalling the righteous humility of Uriah the Hittite, and rightfully naming as pride the shared sin of David Copperfield and King David:

> One Thursday morning, when I was about to walk with Mr. Dick from the hotel to the coach-office before going back to school (for we had an hour's school before breakfast), I met Uriah in the street, who reminded me of the promise I had made to take tea with himself and his mother: adding, with a writhe, "But I didn't expect you to keep it, Master Copperfield, we're so very umble."
>
> I really had not yet been able to make up my mind whether I liked Uriah or detested him; and I was very doubtful about it still, as I stood looking him in the face in the street. But I felt it quite an affront to be supposed proud, and said I only wanted to be asked.[54]

Notable in their meeting is that Uriah doesn't actually call David proud, but rather elicits from David a self-accusation of pride. David in the process doesn't exactly deny his pride. Instead he states plainly that the "affront" is "to be supposed proud." The self-accusation prompted by Uriah's presence to memory he turns against Uriah. Uriah's effrontery is to call to consciousness that which David wishes to leave in the background. David *is* proud, of his powers of memory and observation, of his presumptive innocence, of his quest for self-possession. It is the same pride which seems to prevent David from admitting the truth of his supposed incapacity to decide "whether I liked Uriah or detested him," which is that David *likes* detesting him, as amply demonstrated throughout the novel, especially in David's exultation over Uriah when he exposes, in a sort of improvised trial, Uriah's malfeasance in the conduct of Mr. Wickfield's financial affairs. However false Uriah's humility might be, its falsity is no defense of David's own bland pride.

54. Ibid., 219.

252 THE ROMANCE OF INNOCENT SEXUALITY

David's stated ambivalence in his regard for Uriah is a function of his incapacity to fix Uriah in *his* proper place. David is expressly rattled by Uriah's presence, and by his invitation, as it reminds him that he has not yet mastered the division of public sinful sexuality and private innocent sexuality. Uriah's invitation taunts David, forcing as it does an admission of the shared public space of this encounter—"I was very doubtful about it still, as I stood looking him in the face in the street"—almost as if David fears public exposure of the dimensions of himself he wishes to disown; as if David accepts this invitation, not because he doesn't want to be "supposed proud," but because the experience of standing in the street, visible to any passerby, in company with Uriah, is distasteful to himself, because it makes a spectacle of himself, and so wounds his pride. (Recall Jane Chesney standing in the street, conversing with Mr. Grey; and Augustine on the disgraceful things that avoid face to face confrontation on the road.) A dirty secret of the novel is how much David enjoys detesting Uriah: doing so enables him to settle whatever is "doubtful" of the boundaries between public and private, sinful and innocent, to his own advantage, enabling him to persist unchallenged and unrepentant in enjoyment of his pride. Pride, as the beginning of all sin, energizes articulation of the theologically untenable romantic distinction between innocent and sinful sexuality.

Structured as it is by inter-textual reference to the biblical narrative, Dickens's novel can never definitively establish David's innocence and Uriah's sinfulness. The constant vilifying sexualization of Uriah Heep as predatory other also always invites consideration of the grievances of Uriah Heep in light of the righteousness of Uriah the Hittite, and the correlation of the claims of both Uriah's against both Davids. King David, when confronted by the prophet Nathan with the fact of his sin, is not too proud to own his wrong. But David Copperfield remains proud to the end. A primary goal of the narrative is thus to contain, but not eliminate, Uriah's "umble" accusing presence. The goal, stated otherwise, is to keep Uriah the Hittite safely in the closet so that the narrator can persist in his denials of hospitality to Uriah Heep.

Through the correlation between King David and David Copperfield the association of sexuality and sin emerges more transparently as a matter of social justice and not of individual psychology or depoliticized human nature. The prophet Nathan doesn't criticize King David for desiring Uriah's wife. Instead he tells a parable of social relations between men:

"There were two men in a certain city, the one rich and the other poor. The rich man had very many flocks and herds; but the poor man had nothing but one little ewe lamb, which he had bought" (2 Sam 12:1–4). All the more telling, as a result, that Dickens's narrator doesn't designate the third party of this triangle by any name that connects specifically with Bathsheba, but instead gives her the name Agnes/lamb—directing the reader to Nathan's parable as the center of the inter-textual relationship of his own story with the biblical story. Nathan further frames his judgment of King David with a distinction between private invisibility and public exposure: "Thus says the Lord: I will raise up trouble against you from within your own house; and I will take your wives before your eyes, and give them to your neighbor, and he shall lie with your wives in the sight of this very sun. For you did it secretly; but I will do this thing before all Israel, and before the sun" (2 Sam 12:11–12).

Viewed at the intersection of these two narratives, and the radically divergent responses of their respective protagonists to the fact of sin— "David said to Nathan, 'I have sinned before the Lord'" (2 Sam 12:13) versus "not that I knew anything about it, Heaven forgive me!"—Uriah Heep appears as a paradigmatic embodiment of the imagined threat of deviant sexual desire to the stable meaningfulness of the fiction of sex at the center of the claim of innocent sexuality. He is paraded forth in a sentimental spectacle as the figure of sinful sexuality that the reader is invited, along with David, to detest, to enjoy detesting from the secure invisibility of viewpoint. At the same time the reader, in the very act of reading the novel, of identifying with the narrator, is also caught up in the self-accusatory web of hidden identification between David Copperfield and King David, Uriah Heep and Uriah the Hittite. The spectacular threat Uriah Heep poses to Agnes is a sentimental precursor to the spectacular threat same-sex marriage, and queer identity more generally, poses to the imagined stability of the status quo of romantic marriage. Even arguments in defense of the innocence of same-sex couples (recall the discussion of Eugene Rogers), depend conceptually on the displaced reference of sin to a spectacle of guilty, queer, public sexuality. Once its biblical basis is acknowledged, Dickens's novel helps to call to account the sinful manufacture of such sentimental spectacle, because each reader is placed by the narrator in between the text of the novel and the biblical text. Every reading of Dickens's novel poses a choice whether to perpetuate the sinful romance of innocent sexuality the novel instantiates; or to undermine the hold of that romance on the imagination by searching to reclaim Uriah's disregarded viewpoint, as that viewpoint is discernible in the structure of the novel, by searching to own the identifications that sentimental knowledge-relations deny.

The exercise of choice on Uriah's behalf is not as straightforward however as one might wish. When Uriah Heep is ever defended, or his villainy investigated in a sympathetic light, the focus of inquiry is likely the ambivalence of Dickens's fiction as social criticism. Readings that engage the power of Uriah to implicate in any sinful social dynamic the narrator-detractor of his villainy David tend to be socio-economic rather than biblical. Though welcome as far as they go, they don't go far enough to bring to light the injustice operative at the core of the relation between David and Uriah, as it concentrates in the untenable claim of the former to a coherent plenitude of intelligible personal identity denied to the latter.[55] Uriah's sexual interest in Agnes, repeatedly noted by the narrator—indeed luridly emphasized—then becomes figured as a form of economic competition, where Uriah embodies the failure of the novel to affirm the social and economic mobility that it at the same time celebrates.

At its heart the novel turns out to be socially conservative and anti-meritocratic, fixing David's end as the recovery of the paternal identity absent at his origin.[56] David can work his way from orphaned poverty to economic security and marriage to Agnes (and Traddles too can realize a similar, albeit more prolonged, trajectory). Uriah can never rise above the station of his lowly birth, despite his abundant intelligence and industry and ambition. Although both are fatherless, David is the son of established gentility. Uriah is not. Playing on this difference, the novel enacts the shift from *hereditary* gentility and chivalry to *moral* gentility and chivalry, as fixed and proven in the paradigm of romantic marriage, all the while re-inscribing heredity as a determinant of the sexual-moral nature of the individual.[57] Uriah's failure can then be explained and justified as a function of his inadequately socialized, because hereditarily morally deficient, sexuality.

55. For an example of the socioeconomic/social mobility argument on behalf of Uriah Heep, see Hardy, "Moral Art."

56. For analysis of the novel, focusing on the narrator's relation to his father of the same name, as an attempt to sever any relationship of the present self to its past, an attempt that entails the tragedy of always remaining at the same time incomprehensible to self and others, see Tambling, *Becoming*, 59–88.

57. On this shift in the conceptualization of chivalry, see Vance, *Sinews*, 17–28.

Important as these criticisms are, a distraction here is to read sexuality as secondary to economics, instead of allowing sexuality and economics as mutually comprehending rubrics that structure the socio-economic competition between David and Uriah. David over the course of the narrative grows from boy to man. Uriah, who must be well into middle-age when he last appears in the novel, evidently remains physically unchanged, a visible proof that Uriah's sex is not suited to romance. Uriah's apparently perpetual adolescence is also a familiar trope to the present day in discourse of sexuality that dismisses same-sex desire as some form of arrested and hence pathological psychological development.[58] When innocent sexuality correlates with innocent manhood and womanhood, childhood innocence is not so much preserved into maturity but is itself realized in sexual maturity. Failure to reach that maturity is a form of sexual sinfulness, just as the homo/heterosexually oriented, fully matured sex of the self is projected as present right from the start.

Uriah could never have been deemed a fitting mate for Agnes, even had he applied all his evident talents on the right side of the law, because he is never fully either child or adult, boy or man. Part of Uriah's crime is his ambition, in the most derogatory sense of the term, to marry Agnes. It bespeaks his ambitious title to an improperly constituted manhood. It is equally unthinkable that Agnes could in any way at all desire Uriah. In fact she rarely demonstrates any convincing agency in the competition between David and Uriah. Her agency is almost entirely self-sacrificing. Like the lamb in the parable of Nathan, she exists as a disputed property.[59] (Recall the story of criminal conversation told by Meilaender.) She is no ordinary property, however, and part of Uriah's fault, trapped as he is in perpetual adolescence, is not to be capable of valuing the "properties" the narrator is always ascribing to Agnes. David, on the other hand, prides himself on possessing the character that entitles him to possess Agnes. David's self-restrained adult sex is suited for fulfillment in romance: "There was always something in her modest voice that seemed to touch

58. On the valuation of sexed identity as a function of "maturity," see Da Silva, "Transvaluing."

59. Here is a likely starting point for feminist critique of the inter-textual depiction of Agnes in relation to Bathsheba. The aim of such a critique, though starting with the apparent absence of agency, should proceed to recovery of the specific mode of agency exercised by these characters. Agnes is not a lamb. She is *depicted* as one, *analogized* to one. The question arises: How does such depiction through analogy shape and also obscure imagination of the agency of the character in question?

a chord within me, answering to that sound alone. It was always earnest; but when it was very earnest, as it was now, there was a thrill in it that quite subdued me."[60]

The coincidence, in the figure of Agnes, of property and properties is central to the idealization of romance the novel consolidates. Romance is exemplified by a thematics of privacy and property according to which establishment of monogamous sexually exclusive marriage between a man and a woman is also establishment of a constricted private space of divine–human encounter, so that establishment of conventional domestic marriage space acquires overwhelming and inappropriate theological significance. Innocent sexuality, especially as ascribed to women, is proven within the marriage space it simultaneously makes possible, and is explicitly identified with women's roles as wife, mother, daughter, and sister. These roles are all condensed in the narrator's first vision of Agnes (occurring in fact a paragraph prior to the narrator's fixing of Agnes in stained glass):

> Mr. Wickfield tapped at a door in a corner of the panneled wall, and a girl of about my own age came quickly out and kissed him. On her face, I saw immediately the placid and sweet expression of the lady whose picture had looked at me down-stairs. It seemed to my imagination as if the portrait had grown womanly, and the original remained a child. Although her face was quite bright and happy, there was a tranquility about it, and about her—a quiet, good, calm spirit—that I never have forgotten; that I never shall forget.
>
> This was his little housekeeper, his daughter Agnes, Mr. Wickfield said. When I heard how he said it, and saw how he held her hand, I guessed what the one motive of his life was.[61]

Considering that Mr. Wickfield is a self-absorbed alcoholic headed for financial ruin who has never recovered from the death of his wife— the "lady" whose "picture" Agnes brings to life—and that the world of Dickens's fiction is populated by negligent, absent, or incompetent biological parents, David's guess of the "one motive" of Mr. Wickfield's life is hardly as obvious or as simple as he directs the reader to assume. It is an odd feature of the novel, how tenderly the narrator regards Mr. Wickfield's burdensome dependence on Agnes, until one considers that

60. Dickens, *David Copperfield*, 312.
61. Ibid., 194.

the coddling of Mr. Wickfield's infirmity contributes to an inordinate valuation, both of the magnitude of the loss of a woman of the presumptive properties of Mrs. Wickfield, and of the possession of the identical properties through Agnes.

In hinting that this "one motive" is a shared motive, the narrator implicates himself in the production of the spectacular ascription of adult sexed identity to the child, especially when one considers that he does so by means of identification of Agnes with a prior vision of a painting: "the portrait had grown womanly, and the original remained a child." (Recall Foucault on *Las Meninas*.) Agnes is a decidedly specular and ghostly figure. Her desirability stems from her capacity, so passively it seems, to reflect the properties people wish to find in her: hence the "great admiration" that "everybody must have" for her. It is this specular passivity, more than anything else, that the narrator celebrates as the ultimate perfection of female sex, as the most desirable property that he finally secures for himself in marriage, and that can finally save himself, by bringing his own quest for coherent self-identification to rest. The narrator pointedly assimilates his desired completion to his power of memory: "Although her face was quite bright and happy, there was a tranquility about it, and about her—a quiet, good, calm spirit—that I never have forgotten; that I never shall forget." Agnes is credited with the power to empower memory, even as her very image is the production of the operation of that same power of memory.

Agnes's appeal, for the narrator, as it is depicted for the reader also, is relative to the space she defines. Uriah's villainy is also relative to that same space. Though only ten years old, Agnes *makes* the Wickfield home: "This was his little housekeeper, his daughter Agnes, Mr. Wickfield said." Not just the narrator, but Mr. Wickfield also, and every one present at this encounter, contribute to the figuration of the adult wife in the child. It is the unique prerogative of the narrator, however, as the voice of a little man who finds himself in marriage to a little woman, to claim as his own private property the home-making and house-keeping capacity ascribed to Agnes. The fantasied reversal of mother and child, subject to the mastering desires of the adult narrator, of the early scenes of the novel, here acquires its determinate form and social sanction. It also here acquires its most distinctive theological significance, because the home that Agnes's presence defines is also a house of God.

Immediately the narrator projects his purposefully vague memory of a church, whereby Agnes's embodied presence is ascribed the power to shape and define devotional space: "I cannot call to mind where or when, in my childhood, I had seen a stained glass window in a church . . ." Agnes's ultimate worth as housekeeper is reserved for David alone, which is her capacity to make and keep a home as a space of divine encounter, uncomplicated by any accusation of sin. Yet that accusation of sin remains without, threatening, with the righteousness of its own claims of justice, to demand acknowledgment of the identifications that make accusation of itself as sinful exterior possible, threatening thereby the sanctity of the romantic hearth from which it has been forcibly excluded. In order, in conclusion of this work, to name and redress those claims of justice, it is therefore necessary to explicate how they are generated through the narrative delimitation of a degraded exterior space of sinful sexuality that makes possible the enjoyment by some persons of an exalted interior space—in a dual sense: in the home, and in the self—of innocent sexuality.

The Constitutive Externalities of Sinful Sexuality

As a novel of endings, the most explicit naming of the God-relating significance of Agnes as housekeeper only occurs on the final page of *David Copperfield*. It confers pride of place upon her naming as the final closure of the narrative, every preceding closure contributing to its possibility. Along the way, the continual association of Agnes with tranquility renders her the physical embodiment of memory's self-mastery, in contrast to the distraction posed by Uriah's restlessness: "The beautiful, calm manner, which makes her so different in my remembrance from everybody else, came back again, as if a cloud had passed from a serene sky."[62] The calming effect of Agnes on the narrator's remembrance necessitates postponement of any explicit formulation of her ultimate value until the conclusion, because it is literally the cessation of all dramatic activity, of all narration. The grave light associated with Agnes ultimately kills the story. Another way to summarize the melancholy of the novel is that the ending of the story serves as the point of the story, by substantiating a conclusion of the fiction of sex. A stable and fully intelligible sex requires in the end no further apparent narration. The narration must seem to cease, *in order* to maintain the fiction—in order for the reader to

62. Ibid., 315.

participate effectively in the maintenance of the fantasy that a plenitude of intelligibility of personal identity, focused in a sex, is a real possibility, attainable through romantic sexual relationship. Sex in a narrative sense is imbued with a death instinct, is marked by the desire to cut itself off from its sustaining sources. Agnes organizes the sentimental-homicidal-suicidal violence of the novel to a final God-relating point.

As romantic sexual complement of the narrator, Agnes in the end is figured as illuminating memory. The narrator seals the novel with a vision of Agnes as conduit of divine illumination that at the same time seals the fiction of sex as a stable point which presumably enabled all the entire preceding narration: "And now, as I close my task, subduing my desire to linger yet, these faces fade away. But, one face, shining on me like a Heavenly light by which I see all other objects, is above them and beyond them all. And that remains."[63] Here is the epistemic presumption at the heart of the romance of innocent sexuality. All the wisdom of the narrator is credited to Agnes, so that her "face" as it "remains" is projected right back to the beginning of the narration, as the solution of the desire that propels the narration and brings it to a close. Following Augustine, Agnes is placed by Dickens's narrator directly between himself and God whom he pridefully imitates: "For I did not know that the soul needs to be enlightened by light from outside itself, so that it can participate in truth, because it is not itself that nature of truth. You will light my lamp, O Lord."[64] Agnes as mediary between self and God is credited with a capacity to render intelligible both the narrator and the story he narrates. Memory can thereby close in upon itself by comprehending this vision of Agnes within its own imagined narrative capacity: imagined in that it does not, cannot finally accomplish the resolution into stable focus of the self it continually presupposes.

It is no criticism exactly of *David Copperfield* to observe that the function of memory throughout the narration is solipsistic, because the genius of the novel is in large part the accomplishment of such a huge and complex narration entirely from the first person point of view. Yet the remarkable solipsistic capacity of memory, in projecting such a vast display, is also a point of entry into the sinful fantasy that energizes the display. The solipsism of memory in its formulation of Agnes's value is condensed in the image of her face as radiant source of epistemic illumination: it is

63. Ibid., 737.
64. Augustine *Confessions* 4.15.25 (Chadwick, 68).

humanly impossible, after all, to look directly at such a face. Placing this face "above and beyond" all others suggests that Agnes's value is in her distance as much as in her presence; that her value is most apparent when the narrator's back is turned to her, when she herself dissolves into an invisible presence that makes possible the assumption of the invisibility of viewpoint of narration, which in turns leads back to the image of Agnes's countenance as a "Heavenly light." The privilege of viewpoint is in the end to make of oneself a kind of spectacle.

The fantasy compelling the narration is itself an implicit identification with the reality of original sin as epistemic disaster. Marriage to Agnes is posited as the solution to the problem original sin makes of the self, without ever having to acknowledge that oneself has sinned. Sin is a turning away from the light which renders the self intelligible. Redemption is therefore imagined, not as restoration of relationship to God who is the light that was turned away from, but instead as marriage to a complementary partner who is imagined capable, by nature, of mediating that divine illumination of the self, of beholding the spectacle of one's invisibilty of viewpoint. Redemption acquires its romantic figuration in the fantasy that another exists who makes possible a coherent narration of stable and intelligible sex that is in turn the generative source of the narration it organizes. (Recall Ramsey on sexual encounter as privileged means of realizing and disclosing personal presence.) Sin meanwhile is notably missing from the picture. It is the apparent absence of sin—not its elimination—that requires further explication.

Comparison of the hold of romantic fantasies of intelligibility on the fallen self with St. Augustine's summary description of original sin underscores just how paradigmatically sinful these fantasies are. The power memory assimilates to itself, in its final vision of Agnes, assumes the form of the beginning of all sin in pride: "This then is the original evil: man regards himself as his own light, and turns away from that light which would make man himself a light if he would set his heart on it."[65] As the specular presence at the center of the narration, Agnes enables the narrator, through memory, to recover his "regard for himself as his own light" in the figure of an ideal marital partner. Rest in God becomes rest in a well-furnished honeymoon suite.

However much the narrator repeatedly credits Agnes with the capacity to render himself intelligible to himself, that capacity is ultimately

65. Augustine *City of God* 14.13 (Bettenson, 573).

imagined as his own. As a result, the claim of justice for Uriah Heep is joined to a claim of justice for Agnes Wickfield, since the narrator is never able to see either character in any other light than that light the narrator himself projects. The solipsism of the narrator's point of view imbues the narrative with a sense of indescribable loss, a sort of incurable melancholy presumed as the writer's lot in life, that Agnes never convincingly salves. Adriana Cavarero aptly describes the inbuilt tragedy of the fallen impulse to self-narration: "The self is the protagonist of a game that celebrates the *self as other*, precisely because the self here presupposes the absence of another who truly is *an* other. In this sense, by bringing together the *auto*, the *bios*, and the *graphein*, the self conquers for itself an absolute unity and self-sufficiency. And yet she is not content, because she has the sense that she is being deluded."[66] The more compellingly David Copperfield narrates romantic marriage as able to unify the disintegrated fallen self, the more ominously the novel threatens to serve as occasion for similar self-delusion by the reader—unless, one must add, the reader is disposed otherwise.

The delimitations of exterior and interior spaces of romantic sexuality that structure the entire narrative concentrate most of all in the failure of the narrator adequately to distinguish his interior self from the reflective exterior in which he imagines that he sees himself. The narration actually depends upon this failure, even though the narrator can never admit he has failed. The definitive pride of romantic memory is its blindness to its own exterior, which the narrator conveniently presents throughout the novel as a blindness to Agnes's self-sacrificial love, as indicated to him by the words of Aunt Betsy that haunt his memory: "'Ah Trot!' said my Aunt, shaking her head, and smiling gravely; 'blind, blind, blind!'"[67] Except the narrator is not so blind as to be able to depict his blindness to Agnes's worth as his greatest fault, and even register its implications; so that it becomes a fault of which he can be proud, since it only increases estimation of the prize he secures for himself.

Important as Agnes's own claims against David are, it is not possible within the scope of this work to explicate the injustices she faces as destined marriage partner, except to note the importance of not assuming that Agnes is ever anything more than a fallen angel. And also of not separating out the justice of the relational dynamics internal to

66. Cavarero, *Relating*, 40.
67. Dickens, *David Copperfield*, 425, 426, 703.

marriage from their exterior, to not, in effect, exempt marriage from the reach of political nature, to not imagine that a more just marital relationship is possible apart from a more just social world. The present work focuses however on the injustice of the relational dynamics that make the delimitation of the internal dynamics of marriage possible—injustice that concentrates in the novel on the person of Uriah Heep. The prior presence of Uriah Heep in the Wickfield home correlates with the priority of the biblical narrative of exchange between Uriah the Hittite and King David to the rivalry between Uriah Heep and David Copperfield. Drawing upon the biblical narrative, the narrator incorporates Scripture as a building material of the sentimental literary construction of domestic space, so that the domestic space defined by Agnes's angelic presence is, in a literal sense, a house built upon the word of God. This house only exists through the unjust displacement of the shame of unintelligibility of original sin, in the form of sexual shame, from David to Uriah.

In order to define the house that Agnes keeps as a domestic space of divine encounter, the narrator must do violence to the biblical text that is the building material of that house, and to Uriah himself. The narrator's designation of Agnes as "housekeeper" serves as the foundation and justification for violence. It invites the material enforcement of sexed role differentiation through norms of property ownership and management, whereby male possession of property becomes linked to male possession of innocent sexuality—literally embodied in women's confinement to the domestic realm—as conduit of God-relatedness. The resulting violence toward the biblical text is negative and takes the form of denial of the exterior and prior reality of that text to the narration. The violence to Uriah is positive forcible consignment to the same exterior status that is denied to Scripture. The biblical name Uriah signifies both a denial and an embrace of the constitutive exterior of Dickens's text. The romantic structure of marriage, as it revolves in *David Copperfield* around the figure of Uriah, is an attempt to dissociate sin from sexuality via punitive exercise of this violence. The end of the attempt to evade responsibility for sin is a falsifying private–public dichotomy that itself only ever has its beginning in sin.

Within the novel, the dichotomy public–private is central to the discrimination of sinful from innocent sexuality. The dichotomy is objectively reflected by the shift of scene of the rivalry between David and Uriah from Canterbury to London. Seven to eight years have passed since David entered Dr. Strong's school, and he has now embarked on life in London, the emblematic public stage-set in English literature for the formation of adult male identity. Agnes too is in London. When she asks David, has he yet encountered Uriah, his response is pure question:

> "Uriah Heep?" said I. "No. Is he in London?"
> "He comes to the office-down-stairs, every day," returned Agnes. "He was in London a week before me. I am afraid on disagreeable business, Trotwood."[68]

Ostensibly the disagreeable business Agnes refers to is Uriah's assumption of partnership with Mr. Wickfield. But that partnership— Wickfield and Heep—is peculiarly disagreeable because it parallels so completely another form of partnership. (Uriah later makes the metaphorical relation of commercial and marital partnership explicit.[69]) Uriah's felonious activity in the public realm of business correlates with his intention of marriage with Agnes, as pictured against the backdrop of the bustling metropolis.

Just as Bathsheba, in the biblical text, prompts King David's hospitality for Uriah the Hittite, so Agnes, in her passive-aggressive way, prompts David, out of ostensible concern for her father's comfort, to befriend Uriah. King David's adultery thereby inter-textually enjoins David Copperfield's invitation to Uriah to tea at his lodging.[70] Whereupon the subtext of the rivalry between David and Uriah, only hinted at in the scenes of encounter discussed above, becomes explicit, and provokes a graphical image of personal violence:

> "Why that, Master Copperfield," said Uriah, "is, in fact, the confidence that I am going to take the liberty of reposing. Umble as I am," he wiped his hands harder, and looked at them and at the fire by turns, "umble as my mother is, and lowly as our poor but honest roof has ever been, the image of Miss Agnes (I don't mind trusting you with my secret, Master Copperfield, for I have always overflowed towards you since the first moment I had the pleasure of beholding you in a poney-shay) has been in my breast

---

68. Dickens, *David Copperfield*, 313.

69. Ibid., 435.

70. A further question regarding Agnes's sinning self also arises here. To what extent does she provoke David's violence in order to preserve her cherished self-identification as innocent Woman?

for years. Oh, Master Copperfield, with what a pure affection do I love the ground my Agnes walks on!"

I believe I had a delirious idea of seizing the red-hot poker out of the fire, and running him through with it. It went from me with a shock, like a ball fired from a rifle: but the image of Agnes, outraged by so much as a thought of this red-headed animal's remained in my mind when I looked at him, sitting all awry as if his mean soul griped his body, and made me giddy. He seemed to swell and grow before my eyes; the room seemed full of the echoes of his voice; and the strange feeling (to which, perhaps, no one is quite a stranger) that all this had occurred before, at some indefinite time, and that I knew what he was going to say next, took possession of me.[71]

The violence of David's response to Uriah's masturbatory "confidence"—"he wiped his hands harder"—takes the form of a phallic doubling. David, his own narrative "confidence" rattled, attempts to forestall the violence that this "red-headed animal" does to his self-celebrated power of memory, by skewering him with a "red-hot poker." Memory then immediately depicts Uriah as a recurring erectile presence: "he seemed to swell and grow before my eyes."

David's violence seems provoked by the explicit threat which Uriah, as the exteriorized embodiment of his own sexual desire, poses to the narrator's capacity to successfully narrate the fiction of his sex through the "image of Miss Agnes" as the guiding light of memory. Which helps to explain why David is so enraged when Uriah exclaims his love of "my Agnes." Uriah threatens David's possibility of self-possession through possession of Agnes in marriage.

Such self-possession is an impossibility, however, so that David's admission of his exchange with Uriah as an experience of déjà vu—as an identification that is disavowed—reads as an acknowledgment of the limit of memory's prideful fantasy of self-illumination. Unable to acknowledge the dependency of his own narration on the biblical narrative that is its constitutive exterior, instead the narrator directs memory back on itself, in the form of a "strange feeling" that helps the narrator to take "possession" of the biblical text which is threatening awareness of its possession of him.

David Copperfield's sentimental-homicidal-suicidal fantasy is yet one more instance of the validation of the worth of the fiction of sex

71. Dickens, *David Copperfield*, 324–25.

in death. David needn't actually kill Uriah, because in his memory he already has. The spectacle of Uriah Heep's bloody demise assumes the prior death of Uriah the Hittite through the machinations of King David. David Copperfield wishes Uriah dead, presumably to forestall sexual sin. King David kills Uriah the Hittite because Uriah *will not* sin and thereby exculpate him of responsibility for his own transgression, embodied by Bathsheba's pregnancy. In both cases the injustice to Uriah is a sinful failure of hospitality that follows a refusal of identification.

Consideration of the full biblical text underscores how completely Dickens's text works to privilege marriage to Agnes as an excuse for intentionally inhospitable violence:

> So David sent word to Joab, "Send me Uriah the Hittite." And Joab sent Uriah to David. When Uriah came to him, David asked how Joab and the people fared, and how the war was going. Then David said to Uriah, "Go down to your house, and wash your feet."[72] Uriah went out of the king's house, and there followed him a present from the king. But Uriah slept at the entrance of the King's house with all the servants of his lord, and did not go down to his house. When they told David, "Uriah did not go down to his house," David said to Uriah, "You have just come from a journey. Why did you not go down to your house?" Uriah said to David, "The ark and Israel and Judah remain in booths; and my lord Joab and the servants of my lord are camping in the open field; shall I then go to my house, to eat and to drink, and to lie with my wife? As you live, and as your soul lives, I will not do such a thing." Then David said to Uriah, "Remain here today also, and tomorrow I will send you back." So Uriah remained in Jerusalem that day. On the next day, David invited him to eat and drink in his presence and made him drunk; and in the evening he went out to lie on his couch with the servants of his lord, but he did not go down to his house.
>
> In the morning David wrote a letter to Joab, and sent it by the hand of Uriah. In the letter he wrote, "Set Uriah in the forefront of the hardest fighting, and then draw back from him, so that he may be struck down and die." (2 Sam 11:6–15)

Considered in light of the prior biblical violence, David Copperfield's "idea" only appears "delirious" to the extent that he is unable to acknowledge that it is not his idea at all; just as Uriah's reference to "my Agnes" also

72. The word "feet" in biblical Hebrew is a euphemism for genitals. See Brown et al., *Lexicon*, 920.

points to the prior truth that King David steals Uriah the Hittite's wife.[73] Uriah Heep's use of the possessive is so provocative because it is a just accusation of David Copperfield. Uriah's continual assertion of his own humility reinforces the accusation by continually provoking the memory of Uriah the Hittite's ingenuous devotion to—his "confidence" in—King David. David Copperfield's hospitality, prompted by Agnes's pleading, turns out to be decidedly suspect and self-serving for them both, raising the possibility also that Agnes is slyly and symbolically engineering reenactment of the murder of the one man by the other.

Just as Uriah the Hittite refuses to "go down to his own house," and instead "went out to lie on his couch with the servants of his lord," so David Copperfield ends up entertaining Uriah to such a late hour that he is forced to offer him the use of his own "sofa"[74] for the night. The result is a transposition of the biblical instruction to extirpate Uriah into decidedly Victorian terms:

> I never shall forget that night. I never shall forget how I turned and tumbled; how I wearied myself with thinking about Agnes and this creature; how I considered what I could do, and what ought I to do; how I could come to no other conclusion than that the best course for her peace, was to do nothing, and to keep to myself what I had heard. If I went to sleep for a few moments, the image of Agnes with her tender eyes, and of her father looking fondly on her, as I had so often seen him look, arose before me with appealing faces, and filled me with vague terrors. When I awoke, the recollection that Uriah was lying in the next room sat heavy on me like a waking night-mare; and oppressed me with a leaden dread, as if I had had some meaner quality of devil for a lodger.
>
> The poker got into my dozing thoughts besides, and wouldn't come out. I thought, between sleeping and waking, that it was still red hot, and I had snatched it out of the fire, and run him through the body. I was so haunted at last by the idea, though I knew there was nothing in it, that I stole into the next room to look at him. There I saw him, lying on his back, with his legs extending to I don't know where, gurglings taking place in his throat, stoppages in his nose, and his mouth open like a post-office. He was so much worse in reality than in my distempered fancy, that afterwards I

73. It is interesting to note that in Luther's writings, King David was the model-type of an adulterer. See for example Luther, *Selections*, 135, 138, 157. But also that King David as author of the Psalms is a model of repentance. *Selections*, 153, 158.

74. Dickens, *David Copperfield*, 326.

was attracted to him in very repulsion, and could not help wandering in and out every half hour or so, and taking another look at
him. Still, the long, long night seemed heavy and hopeless as ever,
and no promise of day was in the murky sky.

When I saw him going down stairs early in the morning (for,
thank Heaven! He would not stay to breakfast), it appeared to me
as if the night was going away in his person. When I went out to
the Commons, I charged Mrs. Crupp with particular direction
to leave the windows open, that my sitting-room might be aired,
and purged of his presence.[75]

David's "morning" impression after this night with Uriah reads so
much like a record of post-coital revulsion, it is tempting to evaluate
this scene as a fully formed expression of the psychology of homosexual
panic. It is rife with all the apparent ingredients of sexual repression: au-
toeroticism, homoeroticism, and self-loathing sexual guilt seem to com-
mingle "like a waking night-mare," the "poker," still "red-hot," stuck so
fast in David's "thoughts" that "it wouldn't come out." David all the while
is caught between "sleeping and waking," between vision of Agnes's "appealing" face and the "leaden" immediacy of Uriah's nearness, the angelic
properties of the former suggested by likening the latter to a devil. Rather
than read this scene as expression of a fixed psychological reality, however, it is more productive to read it as constructive of the psychology of
homosexual panic it seems to express. Sexual desire is not a force within
David, causing all his tumult, but is an effect of the narrated triangular
exchange between David, Uriah, and Agnes, the result of which is the
formation of his desire through the designation of Uriah as a kind of
demonic "lodger" who must be expelled.[76]

King David, in order to rid himself of Uriah the Hittite's accusing
presence and secure his untroubled enjoyment of Bathsheba, instructs
Joab to send Uriah to "the forefront of the hardest fighting." David
Copperfield says of this exterior memory, "I was so haunted at last by
the idea, though I knew there was nothing in it," and then accomplishes
the parallel goal through recourse to efficient housekeeping: "I charged
Mrs. Crupp with particular direction to leave the windows open, that
my sitting-room might be aired, and purged of his presence." The image of good housekeeping, as much as the "red-hot poker," is central to

75. Dickens, *David Copperfield*, 326–27.

76. For a reading of Uriah in this scene, and also in the previously cited scene of hand-
shaking, as an obscenely sexed female body, see Dowling, *Manliness*, 53–55.

conceptualization of David's psychology, because the psychological model of sexuality as expressive force of a unique personal property, one's sex, is the effect of the dichotomization of sinful and innocent sexuality according to public and private spaces. Warfare, an exceedingly messy public activity, collapses to domestic tidiness. Romance is profoundly anticlimactic.

In the enforcement of its anticlimax, Dickens's novel turns out finally to provide an exposition of the social injustice that concentrates in the impossible quest of some persons to realize innocent sexuality through the inhospitable delimitation of a domestic space of privileged personal intelligibility. Augustinian critique of David Copperfield's romantic quest leads to a recognition of marriage as an institutional source of social injustice—as a complex and messy reality of public political nature. Marriage is defined novelistically by an economy of externalities that delimits the domestic realm as private, innocent, and liberated; and the public realm as common, sinful, and enslaving; and that exteriorizes sin from the private realm to the public realm. As with economic externalities, the burden of the costs of sin are unjustly distributed. The possibility of marriage for some is only possible at great personal, economic, and political cost to others.

Within the novel, Uriah Heep bears the cost of David's satisfaction in marriage to Agnes. In bearing this cost, he is no ordinary variety of "creature" or "devil." He is a distinctly romantic creature, the obverse of romance, one who lies asleep on his back, "his mouth open like a post-office." With this image the narrator equates Uriah's demonic sexual character with a bureaucratic public institution. The description of Uriah as post-office is further suggestive because it points to the necessity of keeping Uriah in circulation in the public realm in order for the private space of lodging to remain intelligible as a locus of innocent sexuality.

The estimation of Uriah Heep's unsuitability as marital partner for Agnes is driven by the continual refusal of the narrator to repent for his own sin. Uriah's incarceration at the end of the novel, for "Fraud, forgery and conspiracy,"[77] attests the necessity of visibly violent control of sexuality in publicly delimited spaces to the maintenance of the fiction of sex, to maintenance of the fantasy that enjoyment of sexed identity in privacy is somehow apart from political nature and so less violent, less disciplined, less unnatural. D. A. Miller summarizes his influential reading of the novel: "Faced with the abundance of resemblances between the

77. Dickens, *David Copperfield*, 719.

liberal subject and his carceral double, the home and the prison-house, how can we significantly differentiate them?"[78] If the reader follows the ostensible direction of the narrator, the answer is justice accomplished, sin and innocence each contained in their proper places. Only the justice in this case is far more "poetic" than "just." It most of all manifests the narrator's desire to elude the charges of fraud, forgery, and conspiracy against himself with regard to the exterior text that he never identifies as his own story—his desire, that is, to master as his own free creation the severely chastened and confined embodiment of his own sexual sinfulness. Uriah is reduced in the novel to a "model prisoner," a successfully socially constrained spectacle, a type who can be easily identified from viewpoint without undermining viewpoint. The sexualization of Uriah's spectacular figure as prisoner is underscored by the correspondence of his scheduled punishment—transportation for life—with the fate of the other tragic sexual sinner of the novel, little Emily.

Despite his imprisonment, Uriah Heep maintains his sly sense of humor and sense of his own claims of justice and calls out David for the lack of charity in the angry treatment he receives. Even from the door of his prison cell he eludes the fantasied control of the narrator and continues to give voice to the wrongs of Uriah the Hittite against King David, urging ownership of the identifications the narrator denies. Paraded forth by his jail keepers as a model penitent inmate, Uriah pointedly confronts David with the fact of his stubborn denial of all need for repentance:

> "You knew me, a long time before I came here and was changed, Mr. Copperfield," said Uriah, looking at me; and a more villainous look I never saw, even on his visage. "You knew me when, in spite of my follies, I was umble among them that was proud, and meek among them that was violent—you was violent to me yourself, Mr. Copperfield. Once, you struck me a blow in the face, you know."
>
> General commiseration. Several indignant glances directed at me.
>
> "But I forgive you, Mr. Copperfield," said Uriah, making his forgiving nature the subject of a most impious and awful parallel, which I shall not record. "I forgive everybody. It would ill become me to bear malice. I freely forgive you, and I hope you'll curb your passions in future. I hope Mr. W. will repent, and Miss W., and all of that sinful lot. You've been visited with affliction,

78. Miller, *Novel and the Police*, 219.

and I hope it may do you good; but you'd better have come here. Mr. W. had better have come here, and Miss W. too. The best wish I could give you, Mr. Copperfield, and give all of you gentlemen is, that you could be took up and brought here. When I think of my past follies, and my present state, I am sure it would be best for you. I pity all who ain't brought here!"[79]

When Uriah says "you knew me, a long time before I came here and was changed," he is challenging the memory of the narrator. He is challenging David to acknowledge the biblical precedent which is the basis of Uriah Heep's very existence, so that Uriah's forgiveness seems offered most of all for the narrator's willful forgetfulness. David's response is to persist in his denial, by refusing to "record" the "most impious and awful parallel" that Uriah makes of his "forgiving nature." The suggestion of a biblical precedent is discounted as "impious," enforcing a final violence against Uriah. Yet it is the narrator's failure of memory that is most "impious," wedded as it is to the denial of the author of its own contents. Uriah's pity, by contrast, starts to look like a model of charitable anger, if one considers that "here" is the space of confession of one's "sinful lot."

Uriah speaks further words of charitable anger when he admonishes David: "You've been visited with affliction, and I hope it may do you good." Here he voices a truth which the narrator by this means both owns and disowns, which is how sad the story is in total. Agnes, in her imagined perfection as marital partner, is a fantasy of the writer's desire for a perfectly comprehending reader. The writer's affliction is the unintelligibility of fallen human identity that the work of narration cannot satisfactorily comfort. Uriah's injunction to repent, much more than the final image in the novel of Agnes, illuminates the dark truth of the narrator's self-celebrated capacities: that the position of privileged invisibility of viewpoint—unable to own its identifications—is also a position of loneliness and alienation; that what looks like a happy ending is better construed as a kind of self-enforced tragedy, because the accomplishment of the comfort of such viewpoint has its own grave constitutive costs.[80] The ultimate self-sacrifice of sentimental-homicidal-suicidal violence is that it renders the self incapable of mourning its losses.

79. Dickens, *David Copperfield*, 718.

80. For an interpretation of this final encounter between David and Uriah that uncritically completes the novel's reversal of its biblical basis, by crediting David as fully penitent, see Bandelin, "David Copperfield."

Uriah Heep's call to repentance—saucy and pointed—is finally an emblem of queer resistance against the sentimental-homicidal-suicidal narration that treats him with such violence.[81] It is also an invitation to recover the identifications that make more just hospitality possible. Appreciation of his queer insubordination opens to view the theme of the final chapter of this work, which is to protest in charitable anger against the unjust distribution of the shame of unintelligibility of original sin, as that shame concentrates in the inhospitable exclusion of some persons' despised bodies from the imagined intelligibility of sexed identity that others claim to enjoy. Justice in sexual ethics requires imagination of more theologically sin-conscious and more hospitable narrative paradigms of fallen self-identification. It requires the articulation, in conclusion, of an inclusively queer Augustinianism.

---

81. For a similar recuperation of Ebenezer Scrooge in *A Chrismas Carol*, see Edelman, *No Future*, 42–47.

8

The Democracy of Sinful Sexuality

A Psalm of David

The Lord is my shepherd, I shall not want.
He makes me lie down in green pastures;
   he leads me beside still waters; he restores my soul.
He leads me in right paths for his name's sake.

Even though I walk through the darkest valley,
I fear no evil; for you are with me;
   your rod and your staff—they comfort me.

You prepare a table before me in the presence of my enemies;
   you anoint my head with oil; my cup overflows.

Surely goodness and mercy shall follow me all the days of my life,
   and I shall dwell in the house of the Lord my whole life long.

(Psalm 23)

Shame and the Social Paradigm of Sin

THROUGHOUT THIS WORK, THE problem at the core of contemporary theological debates about sexuality and marriage has been framed as a problem of intelligibility. Original sin is an inaugural event of an ongoing epistemic catastrophe. Knowledges multiply continually, but sin disrupts the possibility of authoritative unified knowledge in a more general sense because it disrupts the specific possibility of stably coherent human self-knowledge. No amount of knowledges no matter how seemingly comprehensive can satisfy the desire for self-identification frustrated by the Fall, even as the original occurrence of sin is comprehensive in its consequence. It changes human nature. It sets human nature loose from its created narrative context. In place of direct human comprehension of self in the sustaining narrative activity of God who is the author of all life, sin inaugurates the human search for an origin and source of intelligible personal identity in creation, apart from a simple immediacy of relationship to God who creates. Sin convolutes all narrations of created nature in the culpably sinful dynamic of political nature.

At the heart of this dynamic, energizing the continual fallen narration of created nature in political nature, is the shame of original sin attested by Scripture. The shame of original sin is the shame of the incoherence of intelligible personal identity after the Fall. The prototypical covering-over of shame takes the form of an interpersonally and differentially enforced claim of fictional self-knowledge as naturally and necessarily true self-knowledge.

Too often Augustine is interpreted as equating the desire of fallen human nature with sexual lust, as an incapacity of reason and will to govern a disobedient sexual body. Instead I interpret Augustine as affirming that all sinful desire is epistemic. At root sin manifests a desire for autonomous self-knowledge—a desire of the self to become a generative source of knowledge of the self. Sinful desire does not reduce to any specific bodily reality or mental or psychological faculty of the individual as a site, either of the desire for knowledge, or as capable of comprehension of such knowledge. So it is important to emphasize that no matter how much the argument has engaged theoretical resources affiliated with the tradition of psychoanalysis, the fact of sin requires confession, not therapy. As one of the most compelling expositors of psychoanalysis Jonathan Lear identifies a useful concluding point of entry into the experience of sin because he denies so pointedly that which theology of original sin owns: "Certainly, there should no longer be a presumption when we begin an analysis that guilt is what we shall find, and guilt is what we must treat. That would be our fate if psychoanalysis really were a souped-up version of Christianity. Psychoanalytic freedom begins when we give up that fantasy."[1] The fantasy instead challenged throughout these pages is

1. Lear, *Happiness*, 154.

that one can ever free oneself from the fantasy that one's fractured intelligibility doesn't already begin in a responsibility for sin that is beyond the capacity of oneself to know directly. The freedom of fallen humanity therefore begins when it confesses its bondage to sin, its bondage better yet to its desire for a form of self-knowledge that was lost in the Fall. That desired knowledge, when apprehended as a matter of faith, is the memory of a relational knowledge of the wholly comprehended self. It is neither a proposition presented to the "mind," nor an experience of the "body" as reflected through disclosure in erotic encounter. It is an experience of the self as totally known into created coherency by God.

As much as an Augustinian theology of original sin asserts the unintelligibility of the fallen self, it also asserts the fundamental intelligibility of the self, as created by God, and as recalled into redemptive relationship with God. The failure of intelligibility that sin initiates and that contemporary theory of sexuality helps to explicate is a theological tragedy, not because no intelligible self exists, but because all the ingredients of the created possibility of such a self do exist.

Emphasis of all knowledge of self as relational and external, as an experience more of being known that makes the self known, than a knowing activity that begins within the self and works its way outward, is crucial to discrimination of the morality of theological discourse on sexuality as an inescapable issue of sexual ethics. As long as the vast quantity of writings on theology and sexuality are uncritically engaged in assertions of the possibility of innocent sexuality, those writings help further dominant traditions in sexual ethics as a confluence of theologically irresponsible and unjust practices. For reasons that are beyond the scope of this inquiry to examine, it just is the case that sexual ethics has become the focus of the most concentrated culpable denial of the shame of original sin. Sexual ethics continues to organize around the fiction of sex as a point of stable contact between the self as creature and God as creator—a point that is then credited with the capacity to realize and prove the created goodness of one's sex via an orientation to others, whether of a same or an opposite sex.

Theological discourse on sexuality, rather than critically challenging the operation of sexuality through its effect, sex, has been a complicit partner in securing the efficacy of sexuality. Theology incorporates within itself the idealization of sex as origin and cause of personal identity, and then returns it to sexuality with a heightened valuation, by affirming the significance of sex as a direct route of the self to relation with God. Sex becomes valued as worth dying for because it wrongfully becomes valued as a necessary basis of relation to God who is the creator of all life.

Theology, conjoined with sexuality, conditions the terms of interpretation of association of sex with sin, and wrongfully accepts as its own imperative the dissociation of sex from sin, thereby encouraging the intensification of theological debates about sexuality and marriage as an ultimate fault line of faithful community. The worth of sex in death expands to the life of the faith community, and the unity of the sexed self correlates with the unity of the faith community in its affirmation of a sexual ethic. In the process, the properly sexed self secures its claim to innocence by receding to the comfortable invisibility of viewpoint relative to the spectacular display of a sinful, improperly sexed, typically homosexual body. The desired intelligibility, imaginatively assumed as viewpoint, at the same time becomes reified in the promise of a sex that one can possess. The public becomes sinfully privatized. Personal possession of a properly constituted and fully expressed sex becomes articulated as the model of responsible adult sexual maturity, and also the immanent possession of every child.

It is imagination of personal intelligibility as both a natural and private possession of the sexed self that the association of sexuality and sin, as literal inheritance, breaks open. Contrary to critics of the assertion of the inherent sinfulness of human sexuality, the shame of original sin is not specifically sexual at all, but shame at the severance of the social relatedness between human beings in God that is the basis of all intelligible personal identity. Interpreters of Augustine who insist on "correcting" his influence on sexual ethics consequently end up doing so by reading Augustine as a proponent of the very paradigm of sin that Peter Brown argues Augustine himself was rejecting:

> We need only look carefully at Augustine's analysis of the sense of shame in Adam and Eve, that followed their act of disobedience to God, to see the extent to which the "social" paradigm of sin has changed the meaning of a phenomenon far more easily explained, *prima facie*, in terms of the ancient "vertical" hierarchy of the "lower" and the "higher" parts of the self. The precise flavor of the shame of Adam and Eve, in attempting to cover their nakedness at the first realization of unexpected, uncontrolled sexual stirring in themselves, was not wholly explicable, for Augustine, in terms of shame at the stirring of a "lower" part of the self—tempting

though it was to see it in such terms. Their stunned awareness was, rather, of a part of the self silently withdrawn into itself, made deeply private and unavailable to the command of their own wills. Shame at the "otherness" of their own bodies was the chill echo, both in their own bodies, then between themselves, and later still, in the face of God, of their own high sin, a sin now clearly seen by Augustine in terms of how [sic] his new "social" paradigm of sin—sin as withdrawal of the self from sharing in love, and hence in the service, of others.[2]

Writing in the present of an "ancient" organization of "lower" and "higher" parts of the self, Brown's account also speaks to contemporary romantic interpretation of Augustine. For all those interpreters who think Augustine was somehow wrong about sex, the distinction between lower and higher parts of the self enables a reverse valuation of those very parts. At the same time it damps the connection, in faith, between service of others and love of God. The private parts of the self become isolable as correlates of a privatized ideal of God-relatedness.

The fiction of sex has fueled a governing conviction that the lower parts of the self connect in the most intimate sense imaginable to the higher parts of the self. Yet this reverse valuation has never disowned exactly the logic of the designation of those lower parts as pudenda, as parts that are shameful—not shame at the nakedness of the body, but at the faithlessness of sin, and at the loss through sin of communal relationship in God. Imagination of the truth of the self as originating in one's sex cannot elude the problem of the shame it denies. The shame of the disintegrated self is an omnipresent open secret of all sexual-ethical community. The end of sexual ethics is to prove publicly for others the realization of a particular, genitally defined private sexual activity that is always carefully hidden from view. Sexual ethics reduces in a most perverse and anticlimactic manner to a guessing game: who is sleeping with whom. The spectacle of others, engaging in illegitimate sexual activity, is crucial to the maintenance of the open secrecy of the legitimated community. Faithlessness, refusal of service of others, achieves its invisibility as sinful viewpoint in relation to a fantasied spectacle of other persons' reputed sexual sins.

Romantic interpreters of Augustine, through their criticisms, engage his writings as a constructive resource for affirming a division between

---

2. Brown, *Augustine and Sexuality*, 11.

public and private realms of inter-personal relationship; and for affirming the private realm as distinctively necessary to the establishment of the sexed identity of the individual who appears in the public realm. The insistent interpretation of Augustine as obsessed with sexual shame is a means for these interpreters and faith communities to disown responsibility for the social shame that Peter Brown identifies as the core of Augustine's theology of original sin. Instead, romantic interpretation of Augustine is a definitive means whereby faith communities continue to instantiate the social paradigm of sin. The idealization and idolization of sex, and attendant assumed imperative to secure a safe space for the proving of sex, ensures that theology becomes structured by sin that it cannot acknowledge as its own, "sin as withdrawal of the self from sharing in love, and hence in the service, of others."

According to the social paradigm of sin, every attempt to establish as private property the intelligibility of the sexed individual is a blameworthy rejection of a theologically faithful alternative route to the promised realization of intelligible personal identity: service of others. The problem of the shame of original sin is a problem of distributive justice in sexual ethics arising from faithlessness. Building on the metaphor of illumination that informs the account of sin as a life in epistemic shadow, human justice must seek its relational context within creation: "But just as there is a difference between light which illuminates and that which is illuminated, so also there is an equivalent difference between the wisdom which creates and that which is created, as also between the justice which justifies and the justice created by justification."[3] The possibility of a more just practice of theological discourse on sexuality begins with the allowance that all sexuality is justly accounted sinful by the terms of that justice which alone justifies. Too much contemporary theological sexual ethics is regrettably argument over whose sexed identity is or is not shameful. Blaming others, by shaming them, is a means of disowning one's own responsibility for sin, is a manner of asserting self as a source of illuminating justice, instead of allowing oneself to be illuminated, especially as that responsibility entails assumption of service to those persons and communities who are unjustly burdened with the costs of the common shame of all humanity of original sin. The possibility of faithful service is obscured so long as the desired intelligibility is conceptualized as a possession, as something one can justly grasp individually or through

3. Augustine *Confessions* 12.15.20 (Chadwick, 255–56).

exclusive community. The recognition of sin as a form of disservice to others, as a failure faithfully to serve others, facilitates recognition that the shame of unintelligibility of the fallen self is not redressed through any possession one can secure, but only through more or less just and loving relationships that one can build. The remainder of these concluding comments are therefore devoted to exploring how acceptance of the inherent sinfulness of all sexuality and literal interpretation of original sin as an inheritance actually enjoin pursuit of more just practices of hospitality and democracy.[4]

Sodomy and Hospitality

As the prior reading of *David Copperfield* elaborated, the romance of innocent sexuality has developed through a far from innocent incorporation of biblical literary precedent to its own self-serving sinful purposes. The narrative on which Dickens builds his romance centers on a parable of hospitality unjustly proffered. The treatment of same-sex sexual relationship as a threat to the possibility of intelligible personal identity involves a comparable deformation of a biblical precedent.

At the center of the inter-textual relationship between King David, David Copperfield, Uriah the Hittite, and Uriah Heep, is the parable related by the prophet Nathan. In that parable, recall, a "traveler comes to the rich man, but he was loath to take anything from his own flocks and herds to prepare a meal for the guest who had come to him; so he took the poor man's lamb and prepared it for the man who had come to him" (2 Sam 12:4). The prophetic accusation, which incites the anger of King David and then calls his own sin to consciousness, takes the pointed form of an accusation, not of sexual misconduct, but of inhospitality. The inhospitality is multidimensional. In the parable, the sinful action of the rich man is not just the appropriation of the lamb of the poor man. It is also the offer of the poor man's lamb to the traveler, because in doing so, in remaining "loath to take anything from his own flocks and herds," the rich man is not truly displaying hospitality at all. He is not giving anything of his self, but instead taking from others and then proffering what he takes as his own, in a project of consolidation of his own identity as rich man. His disservice is as much to the traveler as to the poor man; both

---

4. My reflections on hospitality are shaped by my experience of the hospitality of Letty Russell in her classroom at Yale Divinity School, reflected in turn in her works *Church in the Round* and *Just Hospitality*.

suffer from the inhospitality of the rich man. The traveler unwittingly but wrongfully participates in a transaction that leaves both himself and the poor man impoverished. The former has not received what was his due, while the latter has lost his dearest possession.

It is striking, moreover, that this parable doesn't map exactly onto the exchange between King David and Uriah the Hittite, almost as if Nathan pointedly adds the character of the traveler in order to focus judgment away from David's adultery and onto his abuses of hospitality as a means of trying to cover over the sin of his adultery. The adultery then appears less sinful than the deceptive and discourteous manipulation of food and feasting. The shift of focus is fitting; it emphasizes David's sin as the abuse of public and communal service of others in the pursuit of a private satisfaction.

The call to account of sexual sin through the accusation of inhospitality, exemplified in Nathan's parable, connects directly with the troubled history of interpretation of one of the most famous seeming biblical indictments of same-sex sexual relations: the account of the destruction of Sodom and Gomorrah in Genesis 19. In popular imagination, the "cities of the Plain" are emblems of promiscuously sinful homosexual activity. Their annihilation directly by God is commonly invoked as irrefutable affirmation of the definition of sodomy as a biblically condemnable sin of same-sex sexual relations, justly punished by death. Yet as John Boswell explains, summarizing an influential current of twentieth-century biblical scholarship, the condemnation of Sodom, as invoked especially by the prophets, was a condemnation of sin in a very inclusive sense, best summarized under the rubric of inhospitality.[5] By contrast, the definition of the sin of Sodom as solely sexual facilitates the valuation of sex as worth dying for, imagined as a judgment on an entire civilization. The example of Sodom and Gomorrah then contributes to the depiction of same-sex sexual relations as an apocalyptic threat to heterosexually sexed civilization, indeed to heterosexuality itself. It authorizes depiction of all those persons who are willing to entertain allowance of some form of same-sex marriage as inviting chaos and divine retribution.

Recovery of the definition of the sin of Sodom as inhospitality generates distinctive criticism of the admittedly long-standing parallel history of the definition of sodomy as homosexual sexual activity, and especially of invocation of the story as witness of the valuation of sex as

5. Boswell, *Christianity*, 94.

worth dying for. It now appears as a history that culminates in the forcible denial of hospitality to all those persons who are deemed improperly sexed. The intelligibility of the sexed self, expressed and realized as heterosexual viewpoint, is affirmed by the projection of a dreadful spectacle of collective punishment of homosexuality. The destruction of an improperly sexed civilization is so utterly compelling because it engages an identification from viewpoint with the desiring civilization destroyed. The hold of the destruction of Sodom and Gomorrah on sexed imagination is its spectacular promise of the satisfaction through its destruction of all sexual desire, the promise of a human community civilized beyond desire. Hospitality is thus a space in which desire becomes less desirable, a Sabbath finally for desire: "Cursed are the adversities of the world, not once or twice but thrice, because of the longing for prosperity, because adversity itself is hard, and because of the possibility that one's endurance may crack. Is not human life on earth a trial in which there is no respite?"[6] Writing as he is to understand how the single fact of his conversion hasn't altered once and for all the many facts of his ordinary living, Augustine reminds his readers that all living is a trial of one's desire for that wholeness, completion, integration, unity, intelligibility of self that one will not accomplish in this living. Augustine's rhetorical question is therefore more than rhetoric. It is an invitation to his readers to create for each other the respite whose existence he questions. Hospitality is most of all a present respite of fallen desire that anticipates a future respite that is more than a respite because it is an actual satisfaction of that desire through its reformation.

When interpreters of the biblical text, captive of their own restless desire for intelligibility, and likewise caught in the snares of homo/heterosexual definition, persist in defining sodomy as same-sex sexual activity, they use the biblical narrative much as Dickens's narrator does. Instead of acknowledging the biblical text as constitutive exterior that enables their own narration of self, they incorporate it into their quest for privatized self-knowledge as an instrument of violence and inhospitality toward their fellow sinners. They invite judgment of themselves as Sodomites. To the extent it makes sense to define sodomy as a sexual sin at all, it is best defined as persistence in maintaining uncritical belief in the fiction of sex. Sodomy is not a particular sexual act, nor the desire to perform any particular act. It is the inhospitality that ensues from the

---

6. Augustine *Confessions* 10.38.39 (Chadwick, 202).

culpable desire to appear in restful possession of an intelligible sex, and so elude the shame of sin through assumption of the privileged invisibility of a viewpoint of sexed innocence that is secured through the projected identification of others as shameful and sinful spectacle. It is persistence in denial of responsibility for sin.

The Degradation of Connection

Once sodomy is re-conceptualized as the inhospitality attending the self-interested pursuit of an unrealizable ideal of personal intelligibility, the worth of the fiction of sex as the basis of any commitment of service of others is undermined. Expanding the field of application of sex, though alluring as a progressive route to a more inclusive justice, ends up reinforcing the unjust distribution of the shame of original sin. It is never more than a redistribution of shame, because every attempt to resolve the shame of one's own failure of intelligibility, apart from confession and repentance before God, involves a denial of the solidarity of all humanity in a common sinful identity.

The possibility of opening oneself to service of others requires a leap of faith away from sex as the unifying concept of a self who can benefit from a just hospitality. From the perspective of a theology of original sin, as explicated by queer theory of sexuality, it requires recognition and acceptance of the lust of original sin as the unconquerable desire for the resolution of the constitutive ingredients of the fallen self into a coherent unity. A desire that God alone can satisfy.

The ultimate insufficiency of the fiction of sex, as a comprehending point of contact of service of others, Judith Butler rightly characterizes as a problem of democratic politics. Every fallen narration of intelligible personal identity is self-concerned with power in a dual sense—with power as that which generates the illusion of a coherent self-presence, and with power as that which the self fantasizes mastering. The goal of justice in sexual ethics is a goal of power-sharing, in an alternate and intimately self-interested sense:

> To the extent that subject-positions are produced in and through a logic of repudiation and abjection, the specificity of identity is purchased through the loss and degradation of connection, and the map of power which produces and divides identities differentially can no longer be read. The multiplication of subject-positions along a pluralist axis would entail the multiplication

of exclusionary and degrading moves that could only produce a greater factionalization, a proliferation of differences without any means of negotiating among them. The contemporary political demand on thinking is to map out the interrelationships that connect, without simplistically uniting, a variety of dynamic and relational positionalities within the political field. Further, it will be crucial to find a way both to occupy such sites *and* to subject them to a democratizing contestation in which the exclusionary conditions of their production are perpetually reworked (even though they can never be fully overcome) in the direction of a more complex coalitional frame. It seems important, then, to question whether a political insistence on coherent identities can ever be the basis on which a crossing over into political alliance with other subordinated groups can take place, especially when such a conception of alliances fails to understand that the very subject-positions in question are themselves a kind of "crossing," are themselves the lived scene of coalition's difficulty. The insistence on coherent identity as a point of departure presumes that what a "subject" is is already known, already fixed, and that that ready-made subject might enter the world to renegotiate its place. But if that very subject produces its coherence at the cost of its own complexity, the crossings of identifications of which it is itself composed, then that subject forecloses the kinds of contestatory connections that might democratize the field of its own operations.[7]

Addressing the project of coalition building as a queer political strategy, Butler's comments apply as well to the project of building a practical universalistic sexual ethics out of theological conviction of the inherent sinfulness of human sexuality. Sexual ethics is a project in democratization. All claims to sexed intelligibility founder on a denial of the empowering "interrelationships" that are the condition of the possibility of imagination of the coherency of the sexed subject. As an effect of sinful sexuality, the fiction of sex renders the "political field" of its own narration as natural and inevitable, as beyond question and "democratizing contestation."

To critique the hold of the fiction of sex on the fallen imagination as a deformation of democratic politics is not to affirm the possibility of a realizable democracy of sex, as if an egalitarian distribution of power would somehow render each person equally intelligible; as if, in place of the conceptualization of intelligibility as a possession, one could sub-

7. Butler, *Bodies*, 114–15.

stitute a parallel conceptualization of power.[8] The intractability of the
fiction of sex to politics is illuminated when one recalls that the origin
of all sin is pride. Pride: the otherwise nameless power that catches the
fallen self into its net, that consolidates at bodies and renders them sites
of intelligible identity, is the power of sin unleashed by Adam and Eve.

All politics is fallen identity politics. It will remain such, will continue to be energized by pride, regardless of how much politics may become informed by a more searching theological and critical awareness of
its own dynamic basis. Indeed, the pride that is the parodic B/beginning
of sin flourishes in the very fantasy that the power using one to its own
blind purpose and effect is available to be disposed to one's own purposes
and effects, most of all to B/begin anew. Pride inescapably effaces the
"crossings of identifications" which are necessary to its operation, because once they become visible, the title of pride to its own intelligibility
collapses. That title to intelligibility remains necessary to fallen imagination of the possibility of justice as a human project. Pride must become
visible as the fantasy that the experienced consonance between power
and its effects bespeaks a truth about the self, instead of a truth simply
of the effectiveness of power as it proceeds in its own operations. Yet the
same pride remains the medium of the democratization of responsibility
for sin and experience of the shame that is its consequence, so that the
imperfectability of fallen humanity by definition entails the imperfectability of democratic human community.

The cumulative effect of sin, which can not ever be fully redressed
by fallen human activity, is the "degradation of connection" that is the
basis of all imaginably intelligible human identity. Mature humor and
charitable anger are finally guides to loving pursuit of less degraded
connection. Simone Weil writes that the pursuit of more loving connection begins when accusation of sin is tranformed by a desire for shared
identity: "If someone does me an injury I must desire that this injury
shall not degrade me. I must desire this out of love for him who inflicts
it, in order that he may not really have done evil."[9] Though the created
connectedness of human identity in communal relationship with God
can not be restored in temporal community, a significant remnant of that
connection persists in the fact of sin itself, in the fact of sin as a literal

8. For discussion of the challenge of integrating conceptualizations of justice as "redistribution" and justice as "recognition," see Fraser, "Recognition Without Ethics?"

9. Weil, *Gravity and Grace*, 74.

inheritance that relates the birth of every individual human being in the dynamic of B/beginning that is the historical starting point of all human identity and community. Yet at the same time, as Weil indicates, the loving response called forth by the experience of evil by others is to treat it as the privation of good that it is, to treat it as nothing.

While a theology of original sin continually emphasizes sin as "original" in a complex sense, as locating the self in the histories from which it emerges, a faithful response to the awareness of the fact of sin as one's own embodied reality looks forward in hope, not backward in regret. The fullness of identity destroyed by sin cannot be recovered, but one can anticipate the possibility of a future healing and restoration. Hopeful anticipation can provide a basis for imagination of service of others in the present which at least begins to model, in an imperfect form, the fulfillment of communal identity and intelligibility forfeited by sin. The end of all such service of others is not to overcome sin, but to redress the continually unfolding harms that ensue from the inexorable present reality of sin. In the words of Adriana Cavarero: "Rather than salvation, the accidental needs care."[10]

The provision of care depends ultimately on the allowance that God alone saves. Fantasied imagination of salvation nevertheless shapes practical imagination of care. It is especially fitting, therefore, to conclude this argument for an Augustinian theology of sinful sexuality, following Augustine's own trajectory in *City of God*, with reflection on the meaningfulness of belief in the future resurrection of the body as a basis of present imagination of justice as a practice of hospitality.

At the very end of his magnum opus, Augustine identifies the perfection of the resurrected body with a perfection of all humanity joined in a communal service of God, by titling the last chapter of the last book "The eternal felicity of the City of God in its perpetual Sabbath." Of the perfected body at the resurrection, Augustine writes:

> How great will be that felicity, where there will be no evil, where no good will be withheld, where there will be leisure for the praises of God, who will be all in all! What other occupation could there be, in a state where there will be no inactivity of idleness, and yet no toil constrained by want? I can think of none. And this is the picture suggested to my mind by the sacred canticle, when I read or hear the words, 'Blessed are those who dwell in your house; they will praise you forever and ever!'

10. Cavarero, *Relating*, 53.

All the limbs and organs of the body, no longer subject to decay, the parts which we now see assigned to various essential functions, will then be freed from all such constraint, since full, secure, certain and eternal felicity will have displaced necessity; and all those parts will contribute to the praise of God. For even those elements in the bodily harmony of which I have already spoken, the harmonies which, in our present state, are hidden, will be hidden no longer. Dispersed internally and externally, throughout the whole body, and combined with other great and marvelous things that will then be revealed, they will kindle our rational minds to the praise of the great Artist by the delight afforded by a beauty that satisfies the reason.

I am not rash enough to attempt to describe what the movements of such bodies will be in that life, for it is quite beyond my power of imagination. However, everything there will be lovely in its form, and lovely in motion and in rest, for anything that is not lovely will be excluded. And we may be sure that where the spirit wills there the body will straightway be; and the spirit will never will anything but what is to bring new beauty to the spirit and the body

There will be true glory, where no one will be praised in error or in flattery; there will be true honour, where it is denied to none who is worthy, and bestowed on none who is unworthy. And honour will not be courted by any unworthy claimant, for none but the worthy can gain admission there. There will be true peace, where none will suffer attack from within himself nor from any foe outside.[11]

The coherence of the resurrected body Augustine imagines through its ability to serve reason, yet his vision is more distinctive for its holism than its rationalism, for his conviction that all the disparate "elements" of the self will, finally, join in a seamless plenitude of intelligible personal identity that will realize its perfection as created in uninterrupted praise and thanksgiving of God who is the "Artist" of the self. This is an aesthetic vision, an exercise more of imagination than reason, that attests to the desire of the individual for intelligibility, and at the same time attests to the present failure of human imagination to comprehend such intelligibility.[12] In admitting as the limitation of his imagination

11. Augustine *City of God* 22.30 (Bettenson, 1087–88). See also *Confessions* 13.35.50–38.53 (Chadwick, 304–5).

12. For reflection on the relation of this "aesthetic" vision to the Augustinian principle of evil as a privative phenomenon, see Williams, "Insubstantial Evil."

of the resurrection that "anything that is not lovely will be excluded," Augustine demonstrates that to the fallen human imagination, perfection is unimaginable in other than exclusionary terms. As Augustinian refinement of his vision, one can affirm that the reality of the resurrection, now unimaginable, will be a transformation of human imagination, because it will be an existence utterly unmarked by any exclusion at all; or at most by the exclusion of the prior history of sin which will have ended once for all.[13]

It is impossible to anticipate what, if anything, the fact of sin will matter or signify from the perspective of the resurrection. In the meantime, however, the revelation of the origin of sin remains contemporaneously necessary to faithful orientation of the self toward one's hopeful perfection in God at the end. Returning specifically to the definition of sin as a turning away from God, Augustine summarizes the perfection of the resurrection by describing the resurrected body as an embodiment of creation united in service of God:

> We ourselves shall become that seventh day, when we have been replenished and restored by his blessing and sanctification. There we shall have leisure to be still, and we shall see that he is God, whereas we wished to be that ourselves when we fell away from him, after listening to the Seducer saying, 'You will be like gods.' Then we abandoned the true God, by whose creative help we should have become gods, but by participating in him, not by deserting him. For what have we done without him? We have 'fallen away in his anger.' But now restored by him and perfected by his greater grace we shall be still and at leisure for eternity, seeing that he is God, and being filled by him when he will be all in all.[14]

In the culmination of the first account of creation in Genesis, on the seventh day God ceases from the work of creation. God's rest functions

13. For discussion of Augustine on the sexuality of resurrected bodies, see M. Miles, "Sex and the City (of God)." Miles's account of "the *distributed* sexuality of resurrected bodies" (323), from the perspective developed in these pages, elides too easily the troubled complexity of any contemporary, post-lapsarian imagination of the perfection of resurrected bodies. As a result, rather than imagine resurrected bodies as beyond sex altogether, Miles concludes by invoking Augustine as a resource in yet another installment in the ongoing *history* of sexuality as narrated by Foucault: "Reading sexuality in Augustine's idea of resurrection bodies begins to sketch a model that can function to correct and shape present ideas of sex and its role in human relationships. The value of imagining ideal sexualities is that only then can one begin to make 'good sex' *now*" (325).

14. Augustine *City of God* 22.30 (Bettenson, 1090).

as a seal of creation. Human beings subsequently broke that seal through the disobedience of sin. But the hope remains that God can and will restore God's seal on creation. Then the perfected body will become the Sabbath; then service of God and wholeness of identity will become entirely, perfectly, eternally one, as knowledge of self and knowledge of God will become transparently one. Then the self "will be still and at leisure," not because it will be idle, but because it will be completely liberated from the turmoil and unrest of its self-interested pursuit of intelligible self-identification.

Although the fallen self can only fantasize about such resolution of its own infernal dynamic, the powers of fantasy are cause for some optismism. The fantasy of rest of the self in God points to the truth that the desire of the fallen self for stable intelligibility is always a desire for God. Even the desire of oneself to "be like gods" is only meaningful in relation to the desire for God it perverts. Just as original sin is itself a confusion of identification and desire, so also the intractable incoherency of homo/heterosexual definition of sex is a contemporary manifestation of a foundational confusion of fallen human identity. Belief in the comprehensive truth of original sin is also a basis of disciplined orientation of the self away from its sinful fantasy of sexed coherency and toward God who is the only stable and coherent point of the self. The faithful possibility emerges that hospitable service of others in the present, grounded in mature humorous conviction of the solidarity of identity of fallen humanity, moved by charitable anger, may at least begin to realize in some imperfect way the participation in God lost in the Fall and anticipated in hope of the resurrection.

A Queer Wedding Feast

Following the theory of sexuality explicated throughout these pages, a practice of solidarity in fallen human identity is a practice grounded in conviction of the irresolvable instability of all intelligible personal identity so long as sin persists as an inextricable constitutive ingredient of embodied human existence. Given the explication of the shame of original sin as the failure of personal intelligibility that the self seeks to cover over, the injustice to be redressed through a faithful practice of service of others is the narration of intelligibly sexed identity for a majority of persons that is a function of the spectacular ascription of an unintelligible or failed sex to a narratively disenfranchised minority.

Redress of exclusivistic narrative practices should not proceed however as if it were a simple exercise in expanding access to the terms of intelligibly sexed identity to the margins. On the contrary, the justice to be realized begins with recognition of the truths that those seemingly unintelligible individuals—people whose economic, physical, and psychic well-being are most at risk—have to teach to everyone else. It begins with admission that those persons and communities who appear least intelligible are privileged exemplars of the intelligibility of all sinful identity and community as revealed in that most inclusive narration, the revelation of Creation and Fall in Scripture.

Narration of intelligibly sexed personal identity from the margins to the center proceeds through an orientation of service of others, where such service affirms what Michael Warner calls "the world making activity of queer life."[15] That world-making activity, mostly regarded as deviations from the norms of conventionally sexed identity, and as parasitic on the social body built up by romantic marriage, illuminates the hollowness and pretension of that social body and its norms. Most especially, that world-making activity illuminates the precarious and false security of intelligibility which tradents of the romance of innocent sexuality assume. Reaching in service to the queer margins engages those margins in service of a theologically enriched comprehension of the center. The queerness of the center then opens to view, and both center and margin become more mutually intelligible to the extent that the instability of their shared ground of intelligibility is acknowledged, to the extent that the center dissolves, leaving only a limitless margin forever folding in on itself.

Queerness, as a term that joins theory and theology, denotes the precariousness of the intelligibility of fallen human identity. Faith in the literal truth of original sin as an inheritance is a queer faith. To accept in faith the truth of original sin is to embrace the queerness of one's identity as a basis of faithful responsiveness to God who creates. From the perspective of queer faith, the fiction of sex can never serve as a secure basis of a just hospitality. This does not imply that marriage could or should cease to exist, or that marriage could or should cease to function as a significant element in narrations of intelligible personal identity. But it does mean that just arguments for same-sex marriage, as for all marriage, are based on a vision of such marriages as a kind of witness of queer inclusiveness.

15. Warner, *Trouble*, 147.

Whereas the romance of innocent sexuality typically concludes with a wedding feast that concretizes multiple exclusions, expanding in waves outward from the exclusivity of the marital pair, a queer wedding feast celebrates anticipation of the exclusion of all exclusion. Such a celebration is suggested by the words of King David as Psalmist, when read in relation to the confession of his sinfulness and inhospitality as prompted by the prophet Nathan. Read as prayer, David's incantation to God in Psalm 23, "You prepare a table before me in the presence of my enemies," invites the reader into a dynamic of identification with King David as both blessed and sinning, so that the blessing of a "table" prepared by God calls for a responsive completion by the faithful petitioner, in the wish that the table spread by God serve as basis of as inclusive a celebration as possible.

Recognition of the image of "enemies" as exclusive enables conformation of the psalmist's prayer to the faithful project of overcoming such exclusion: that the table be spread as invitation and respite. Nor, finally, could the prayer of the fallen self for such blessing be otherwise. Because no one, not King David himself, realizes an innocence that justifies claims of such exclusive enjoyment. A more just theological understanding of human sexuality, and more just celebration of the goodness of embodied creation, begins with confession of the sinfulness of all sexuality. It begins with commitment to service of others, where the end of such service is to acknowledge and honor the inclusion of all humanity in a faithfully queer community.

Bibliography

Ablow, Rachel. *The Marriage of Minds*. Stanford: Stanford University Press, 2007.

Ackroyd, Peter. *Dickens*. New York: Harper Collins, 1991.

Agamben, Giorgio. *Homo Sacer: Sovereign Power and Bare Life*. Stanford: Stanford University Press, 1998.

Alison, James. "Theology Amid the Stones and Dust." *Theology and Sexuality* 11 (1999) 91–114.

Allen, C. Leonard, and Richard T. Hughes. *Illusions of Innocence: Protestant Primitivism in America, 1630–1875*. Chicago: University of Chicago Press, 1988.

Allen, Danielle S. *Talking to Strangers: Anxieties of Citizenship after Brown V. Board of Education*. Chicago: University of Chicago Press, 2004.

Arendt, Hannah. *The Human Condition*. Chicago: University of Chicago Press, 1958.

———. *Love and Saint Augustine*. Chicago: University of Chicago Press, 1996.

Ariès, Philippe. *Centuries of Childhood: A Social History of Family Life*. New York: Vintage, 1962.

Armstrong, Nancy. "Contemporary Culturalism: How Victorian Is It?" In *Victorian Afterlife*, edited by John Kicich and Dianne F. Sadoff, 311–26. Minneapolis: University of Minnesota Press, 2000.

Arnold, Matthew. *Culture and Anarchy*. New York: Cambridge University Press, 1960.

Asher, Lyell. "The Dangerous Fruit of Augustine's *Confessions*." *Journal of the American Academy of Religion* 66 (1998) 227–55.

Auerbach, Nina. "Performing Suffering: From Dickens to David." *Browning Institute Studies: An Annual of Victorian Literary and Cultural History* 18 (1990) 15–22.

Augustine. *City of God*. Translated by Henry Bettenson. London: Penguin, 1972.

———. *Confessions*. Translated by Henry Chadwick. New York: Oxford University Press, 1991.

———. *Earlier Writings*. Translated by John Henderson Seaforth Burleigh. Philadelphia: Westminister, 1953.

———. *The Literal Meaning of Genesis*. Translated by John Hammond Taylor. Ancient Christian Writers 41–42. New York: Newman, 1982.

———. *On Free Choice of the Will*. Translated by A. S. Benjamin and L. H. Hackstaff. Indianapolis: Bobbs-Merrill, 1964.

———. *Political Writings*. Edited by Michael W. Tkacz et al. Indianapolis: Hackett, 1994.

————. *St Augustine on Marriage and Sexuality*. Edited by Elizabeth A. Clark. Washington, DC: Catholic University of America Press, 1996.

————. *Writings in Connection with the Manichaean Heresy*. Translated by Richard Stothert. Edinburgh: T. & T. Clark, 1872.

————. *The Works of Saint Augustine: A Translation for the 21st Century*. Edited by Edmund Hill et al. Brooklyn: New City, 1990.

Augustine, and Garry Wills. *Saint Augustine's Memory*. New York: Viking, 2002.

Ayres, Brenda. *Dissenting Women in Dickens' Novels: The Subversion of Domestic Ideology*. Westport, CT: Greenwood, 1998.

Babcock, William S. "Augustine and the Spirituality of Desire." *Augustinian Studies* 25 (1994) 179–99.

Bandelin, Carl. "David Copperfield: A Third Interesting Penitent." *Studies in English Literature, 1500–1900* 16 (1976) 601–11.

Barker, Charles. "Erotic Martyrdom: Kingsley's Sexuality beyond Sex." *Victorian Studies* 44 (2002) 465–88.

Basset, Rodney L. et al. "Homonegative Christians: Loving the Sinner but Hating the Sin." *Journal of Psychology and Christianity* 19 (2000) 258–69.

Baumgarten, Murray, and H. M. Daleski. *Homes and Homelessness in the Victorian Imagination*. New York: AMS, 1998.

Bawer, Bruce. *Beyond Queer: Challenging Gay Left Orthodoxy*. New York: Free, 1996.

————. *A Place at the Table: The Gay Individual in American Society*. New York: Poseidon, 1993.

Bell, Catherine M. *Ritual Theory, Ritual Practice*. New York: Oxford University Press, 1992.

Benhabib, Seyla. *Feminist Contentions: A Philosophical Exchange, Thinking Gender*. New York: Routledge, 1995.

Berlant, Lauren, and Michael Warner. "Sex in Public." *Critical Inquiry* 24 (1998) 547–66.

————. "What Does Queer Theory Teach Us About X?" *PMLA* 110 (1995) 343–49.

Bersani, Leo. "Is the Rectum a Grave?" *October* 43 (1987) 197–222.

Blasius, Mark, and Shane Phelan. *We Are Everywhere: A Historical Sourcebook in Gay and Lesbian Politics*. New York: Routledge, 1997.

Booth, Wayne C. "Resurrection of the Implied Author: Why Bother?" In *A Companion to Narrative Theory*, edited by Phelan and Rabinowitz, 75–87. Malden, MA: Blackwell, 2005.

Booth, Wayne C. *The Rhetoric of Fiction*. Chicago: University of Chicago Press, 1961.

Bordo, Susan. *Unbearable Weight: Feminism, Western Culture, and the Body*. Berkeley: University of California Press, 1993.

Børresen, Kari Elisabeth, and C. H. Talbot. *Subordination and Equivalence: The Nature and Role of Women in Augustine and Thomas Aquinas*. Washington, DC: University Press of America, 1981.

Boswell, John. *Christianity, Social Tolerance, and Homosexuality: Gay People in Western Europe from the Beginning of the Christian Era to the Fourteenth Century*. Chicago: University of Chicago Press, 1980.

Bourdieu, Pierre. *Outline of a Theory of Practice*. Translated by Richard Nice. New York: Cambridge University Press, 1977.

Bradbury, Nicola. "Dickens's Use of the Autobiographical Fragment." In *A Companion to Charles Dickens*, edited by David Paroissien, 18–32. Malden, MA: Blackwell, 2008.

Briggs, Sheila. "Digital Bodies and the Transformation of the Flesh." In *Toward a Theology of Eros*, edited by Burrus and Keller, 153–66. New York: Fordham University Press, 2006.

Brooten, Bernadette. 2003. *How Natural Is Nature? Augustine's Sexual Ethics*. The Feminist Sexual Ethics Project, 2003. Online: http://www.brandeis.edu/projects/fse/Pages/originalpapers.html.

Brown, Francis et al. *The Brown, Driver, Briggs Hebrew and English Lexicon*. Peabody, MA: Hendrickson, 1996.

Brown, Peter. *Augustine of Hippo: A Bibliography*. Berkeley: University of California Press, 1969.

———. *The Body and Society*. New York: Columbia University Press, 1988.

Brown, Peter, and Mary Ann Donovan. *Augustine and Sexuality: Protocol of the Forty Sixth Colloquy, 22 May 1983*. Berkeley: Center for Hermeneutical Studies in Hellenistic and Modern Culture, 1983.

Bruhm, Steven, and Natasha Hurley. *Curioser: On the Queerness of Children*. Minneapolis: University of Minnesota Press, 2004.

Burke, Edmund. *A Philosophical Inquiry*. New York: Oxford University Press, 1990.

Burns, J. Patout. "Augustine on the Origin and Progress of Evil." In *The Ethics of St. Augustine*, edited by William S. Babcock, 67–85. JRE Studies in Religion 3. Atlanta: Scholars, 1991.

Burrus, Virginia. "Introduction: Theology and Eros after Nygren." In *Toward a Theology of Eros*, edited by Burrus and Keller, xiii–xxi. New York: Fordham University Press, 2006.

Butler, Judith P. *Bodies That Matter: On the Discursive Limits of "Sex."* New York: Routledge, 1993.

———. "Ethical Ambivalence." In *The Turn to Ethics*, edited by Marjorie Garber et al., 15–28. New York: Routledge, 2000.

———. *Gender Trouble: Feminism and the Subversion of Identity*. New York: Routledge, 1990.

———. *Giving an Account of Oneself*. New York: Fordham University Press, 2005.

———. *The Psychic Life of Power: Theories in Subjection*. Stanford: Stanford University Press, 1997.

Butler, Judith P., and Joan Wallach Scott. *Feminists Theorize the Political*. New York: Routledge, 1992.

Bynum, Caroline Walker. *Holy Feast and Holy Fast: The Religious Significance of Food to Medieval Women*. Berkeley: University of California Press, 1987.

Cahill, Lisa Sowle. *Family: A Christian Social Perspective*. Minneapolis: Fortress, 2000.

———. *Sex, Gender, and Christian Ethics*. New York: Cambridge University Press, 1996.

Calderone, Mary S. "Above and Beyond Politics: The Sexual Socialization of Children." In *Pleasure and Danger: Exploring Female Sexuality*, edited by Carol Vance, 131–37. Boston: Routledge, 1984.

Cantor, Paul A. *Creature and Creator: Myth-Making and English Romanticism*. New York: Cambridge University Press, 1984.

Carrette, Jeremy. *Foucault and Religion*. New York: Routledge, 2000.

Cavarero, Adriana. *Relating Narratives: Storytelling and Selfhood*. London: Routledge, 2000.

Chesterton, G. K. *Appreciations and Criticisms of the Works of Charles Dickens*. New York: E. P. Dutton, 1911.

Christ, Carol P., and Judith Plaskow. *Womanspirit Rising: A Feminist Reader in Religion.* San Francisco: Harper & Row, 1979.

Clark, Elizabeth A. "'Adam's Only Companion': Augustine and the Early Christian Debate on Marriage." *Recherches Augustiniennes* 21 (1986).

———. "Foucault, the Fathers, and Sex." *Journal of the American Academy of Religion* 56 (1988) 619–41.

———. "Heresy, Asceticism, Adam, and Eve: Interpretations of Genesis 1–3 in the Later Latin Fathers." In *Genesis 1–3 in the History of Exegesis,* 99–133. Lewiston, NY: Mellen, 1988.

Clark, Stephen B. *Man and Woman in Christ: An Examination of the Roles of Men and Women in Light of Scripture and the Social Sciences.* Ann Arbor, MI: Servant, 1980.

Clayton, Jay. "Dickens and the Genealogy of Postmodernism." *Nineteenth Century Literature* (1991) 181–95.

Coakley, Sarah. "'Batter My Heart . . .'? On Sexuality, Spirituality, and the Christian Doctrine of the Trinity." In *The Papers of the Henry Luce III Fellows in Theology, Vol 1,* 49–68. Series in Theological Scholarship and Research. Atlanta: Scholars, 1996.

———. "The Eschatological Body: Gender, Transformation, and God." *Modern Theology* 16 (2000) 61–73.

———. "Visions of the Self in Late Medieval Christianity: Some Cross-Disciplinary Relfections." In *Philosophy, Religion, and the Spiritual Life,* edited by M. McGhee, 89–103. Royal Institute of Philosophy Supplement 32. New York: Cambridge University Press, 1992.

Collins, Philip. "David Copperfield: 'A Very Complicated Interweaving of Truth and Fiction.'" *Essays and Studies* 23 (1970) 71–86.

———. "Dickens's Autobiographical Fragment and David Copperfield." *Cahiers Victoriens et Edouardiens: Revue du Centre d'Etudes et de Recherches Victoriennes et Edouardiennes de l'Universite Paul Vale* 20 (1984) 87–96.

Connolly, William E. *Why I Am Not a Secularist.* Minneapolis: University of Minnesota Press, 1999.

Copjec, Joan. *Imagine There's No Woman: Ethics and Sublimation.* Cambridge: MIT Press, 2002.

Cott, Nancy F. *Public Vows: A History of Marriage and the Nation.* Cambridge: Harvard University Press, 2000.

Countryman, L. William. *Dirt, Greed, and Sex: Sexual Ethics in the New Testament and Their Implications for Today.* Philadelphia: Fortress, 1988.

Cross, Anthony J. "Charles Dickens, Edward Tagart and Unitarianism." *Faith and Freedom* 42 (1989) 59–66.

Cunningham, Valerie. "Dickens and Christianity." In *A Companion to Charles Dickens,* edited by David Paroissien, 255–76. Malden, MA: Blackwell, 2008.

Da Silva, Stephen. "Transvaluing Immaturity: Reverse Discourses of Male Homosexuality in E. M. Forster's Posthumously Published Fiction." *Criticism: A Quarterly for Literature and the Arts* 40 (1998) 237–72.

Daly, Mary. *Beyond God the Father: Toward a Philosophy of Women's Liberation.* Boston: Beacon, 1973

———. *Gyn/Ecology: The Metaethics of Radical Feminism.* Boston: Beacon, 1978.

Dames, Nicholas. *Amnesiac Selves: Nostalgia, Forgetting, and British Fiction, 1810–1870.* New York: Oxford University Press, 2001.

Dante. *Inferno.* Translated by Robert M. Durling. New York: Oxford, 1996.

Davidson, Arnold Ira. *The Emergence of Sexuality: Historical Epistemology and the Formation of Concepts.* Cambridge: Harvard University Press, 2001.

Davidson, Cathy, and Jessamyn Hatcher. *No More Separate Spheres!* Durham: Duke University Press, 2002.

Deane, Herbert A. *The Political and Social Ideas of St. Augustine.* New York: Columbia University Press, 1963.

DeRogatis, Amy. "'Born Again is a Sexual Term': Demons, STDs, and God's Healing Sperm." *Journal of the American Academy of Religion* 77 (2009) 275–302.

Descarte, René. *Philosophical Writings.* Translated by John Cottingham et al. New York: Cambridge University Press, 1984.

Dever, Carolyn. *Death and the Mother from Dickens to Freud: Victorian Fiction and the Anxiety of Origins.* New York: Cambridge University Press, 1998.

Dickens, Charles. *David Copperfield.* Norton Critical Edition. New York: Norton, 1990

Dowling, Andrew. *Manliness and the Male Novelist in Victorian Literature.* Burlington, VT: Ashgate, 2001.

Dworkin, Andrea. *Pornography: Men Possessing Women.* New York: Putnam, 1981.

Edelman, Lee. *No Future.* Durham: Duke University Press, 2004.

Ellison, Marvin Mahan. *Erotic Justice: A Liberating Ethic of Sexuality.* Louisville: Westminster John Knox, 1996.

Empson, William. *Milton's God.* London: Chatto & Windus, 1961.

Estlund, David M., and Martha Craven Nussbaum. *Sex, Preference, and Family: Essays on Law and Nature.* New York: Oxford University Press, 1997.

Farley, Margaret. "An Ethic for Same-Sex Relations." In *Dialogue about Catholic Sexual Teaching,* edited by Charles E. Curran and Richard A. McCormick, 330–46. Readings in Moral Theology 8. New York: Paulist, 1993.

Farley, Margaret. *Just Love: A Framework for Christian Sexual Ethics.* New York: Continuum, 2006.

Fausto-Sterling, Anne. *Sexing the Body: Gender Politics and the Construction of Sexuality.* New York: Basic, 2000.

Flynn, Thomas R. "Partially Desacralized Spaces: The Religious Availability of Foucault's Thought." *Faith and Philosophy* 10 (1993) 471–85.

Forster, John. *The Life of Charles Dickens.* London: Chapman & Hall, 1872.

Foucault, Michel. *The Archaeology of Knowledge.* Translated by A. M. Sheridan Smith. New York: Pantheon, 1972.

———. *Discipline and Punish: The Birth of the Prison.* Translated by Alan Sheridan. New York: Vintage, 1995.

———. *The History of Sexuality.* Translated by Robert Hurley. New York: Vintage, 1980.

———. *The Order of Things; an Archaeology of the Human Sciences.* Translated by Alan Sheridan. New York: Vintage, 1973

———. *Politics, Philosophy, Culture: Interviews and Other Writings, 1977–1984.* Edited by Lawrence D. Kritzman. New York: Routledge, 1988.

———. *Power/Knowledge: Selected Interviews and Other Writings, 1972–1977.* Edited by Colin Gordon. New York: Pantheon, 1980.

Fraser, Nancy. "Recognition without Ethics?" In *The Turn to Ethics,* edited by Marjorie Garber et al., 95–126. New York: Routledge, 2000

Fraser, Nancy. *Unruly Practices: Power, Discourse, and Gender in Contemporary Social Theory.* Minneapolis: University of Minnesota Press, 1989.

Freud, Sigmund. *Civilization and Its Discontents.* Translated by James Strachey. New York: Norton, 1962

————. *Jokes and Their Relation to the Unconscious*. Translated by James Strachey. New York: Norton, 1960

————. *Three Essays on the Theory of Sexuality*. Translated by James Strachey. New York: Basic, 2000.

Fried, Charles. "Terminating life support: Out of the Closet!" *New England Journal of Medicine* 295 (1976) 390–391.

Friedman, Stanley. "Heep and Powell: Dickensian Revenge." *The Dickensian* 90/1:432 (1994) 36–43.

Gardella, Peter. *Innocent Ecstasy: How Christianity Gave America an Ethic of Sexual Pleasure*. New York: Oxford University Press, 1985.

Gaskell, Elizabeth. *North and South*. New York: Oxford University Press, 1998

Geroulanos, Stefanos. "Theoscopy: Transparency, Omnipotence, and Modernity." In *Political Theologies: Public Religions in a Post-Secular World*, edited by de Vries and Sullivan, 633–51. New York: Fordham University Press, 2006.

Gillis, John R. *For Better, for Worse: British Marriages, 1600 to the Present*. New York: Oxford University Press, 1985.

Glaser, Chris. *Coming out as Sacrament*. Louisville, KY: Westminster John Knox, 1998.

Goss, Robert E. "Challenging Procreative Privilege: Equal Rites." *Theology and Sexuality* 6 (1997) 33–55.

Gould, Deborah. *Moving Politics*. Chicago: University of Chicago Press, 2009.

Gregory, Eric. *Politics and the Order of Love: An Augustinian Ethics of Democratic Citizenship*. Chicago: University of Chicago Press, 2008.

Guest, P. Deryn. "Battling for the Bible: Academy, Church, and the Gay Agenda." *Theology and Sexuality* 15 (2001) 66–93.

Hackett, David G. "Gender and Religion in American Culture, 1870–1930." *Religion and American Culture* 5 (1995) 127–57.

Hall, Amy Laura. *Conceiving Parenthood: American Protestantism and the Spirit of Reproduction*. Grand Rapids: Eerdmans, 2008.

Halperin, David M. *One Hundred Years of Homosexuality*. New York: Routledge, 1990.

————. *Saint Foucault: Towards a Gay Hagiography*. New York: Oxford University Press, 1995.

Halperin, David, and Valerie Traub. *Gay Shame*. Chicago: University of Chicago Press, 2010.

Hampshire, Stuart. *Innocence and Experience*. Cambridge: Harvard University Press, 1989.

Haraway, Donna Jeanne. *Modest_Witness@Second_Millennium.Femaleman_Meets_Oncomouse: Feminism and Technoscience*. New York: Routledge, 1997.

Haraway, Donna Jeanne. *Simians, Cyborgs, and Women: The Reinvention of Nature*. London: Free Association, 1991.

Harcourt, Bernard E. "Foreword: 'You are Entering a Gay and Lesbian-Free Zone': On the Radical Dissents of Justice Scalia and Other (Post-)Queers." *Journal of Criminal Law and Criminology* 94 (2004) 503–49.

Hardy, Barbara. "The Moral Art of Dickens: David Copperfield." In *Charles Dickens's David Copperfield*, edited by Harold Bloom, 9–19. New York: Chelsea, 1987.

Harrison, Carol. *Augustine: Christian Truth and Fractured Humanity*. New York: Oxford University Press, 2000.

Hartle, Ann. "Augustine and Rousseau." In *The Augustinian Tradition*, edited by Gareth B. Matthews, 263–85. Philosophical Traditions 8. Berkeley: University of California Press, 1999.

Hartog, Hendrik. *Man and Wife in America*. Cambridge: Harvard University Press, 2000.

Hays, Richard. "Relations Natural and Unnatural." *Journal of Religious Ethics* 14 (1986) 184–215.

Herbert, T. Walter. *Sexual Violence and American Manhood*. Cambridge: Harvard University Press, 2002.

Herman, Judith Lewis. *Trauma and Recovery*. New York: Basic, 1992.

Heyward, Carter. *Touching Our Strength*. San Francisco: Harper & Row, 1989.

Hill, Susan E. "(Dis) Inheriting Augustine: Constructing the Alienated Self in the Autobiographical Works of Paul Monette and Mary Daly." *Literature and Theology* 13 (1999) 149–65.

Hoy, David Couzens. *Foucault: A Critical Reader*. New York: Blackwell, 1986.

Hunter, David G. "Augustinian Pessimism? A New Look at Augustine's Teaching on Sex, Marriage and Celibacy." *Augustinian Studies* 25 (1994) 153–77.

Irigaray, Luce. *Speculum of the Other Woman*. Ithaca, NY: Cornell University Press, 1985.

———. *This Sex Which Is Not One*. Ithaca, NY: Cornell University Press, 1985.

Jackson, Timothy P. *The Priority of Love: Christian Charity and Social Justice*. Princeton: Princeton University Press, 2003.

Jakobsen, Janet R. "Why Sexual Regulation?: Family Values and Social Moverments." In *God Forbid: Religion and Sex in American Public Life*, edited by Kathleen M. Sands, 104–23. New York: Oxford University Press, 2000

Jantzen, Grace M. *Becoming Divine: Towards a Feminist Philosophy of Religion*. Bloomington: Indiana University Press, 1999.

Johnson, Edgar. *Charles Dickens, His Tragedy and Triumph*. New York: Simon & Schuster, 1952.

Johnson, James Turner. *A Society Ordained by God*. Nashville: Abingdon, 1970.

Jordan, Mark. "Flesh in Confession: Alcibiades Beside Augustine." In *Toward a Theology of Eros*, edited by Burrus and Keller, 27–37. New York: Fordham University Press, 2006.

Juster, Susan, et al. "Forum: Religion and American Autobiographical Writing." *Religion and American Culture* 9 (1999) 1–29.

Kaeser, Gigi, and Peggy Gillespie. *Love Makes a Family: Portraits of Lesbian, Gay, Bisexual, and Transgender Parents and Their Families*. Amherst, MA.: University of Massachusetts Press, 1999.

Kamitsuka, Margaret D. "Toward a Feminist Postmodern and Postcolonial Interpretation of Sin." *The Journal of Religion* 84 (2004) 179–211.

Kaplan, Fred. *Dickens: A Biography*. New York: Morrow, 1988.

Kass, Leon. *Toward a More Natural Science: Biology and Human Affairs*. New York: Free Press, 1985.

Kasujja, Augustine. *Polygenism and the Theology of Original Sin Today*. Rome: Urbaniana University Press, 1986.

Katz, Jonathan Ned. *Gay American History*. New York: Harper & Row, 1985.

———. *The Invention of Heterosexuality*. New York: Dutton, 1995.

Kelly, David F. "Sexuality and Concupiscence in Augustine." *The Annual of the Society of Christian Ethics* (1983) 81–116.

Kelsey, David H. "Whatever Happened to the Doctrine of Sin?" *Theology Today* 50 (1993) 169–78.

Kierkegaard, Søren. *The Concept of Anxiety: A Simple Psychologically Orienting Deliberation on the Dogmatic Issue of Hereditary Sin*. Translated by Reidar Thomte and Albert Anderson. Princeton: Princeton University Press, 1980.

———. *Fear and Trembling*. Translated by Alastair Hannay. London: Penguin, 1985.

Kiki and Herb. "Do You Hear What We Hear?" Mr. Lady Records, 2000.

Kincaid, James. *Erotic Innocence: The Culture of Child Molesting*. Durham: Duke University Press, 1998.

Kottman, Paul A. "Translator's Introduction." In *Relating Narratives: Storytelling and Selfhood* by Adriana Cavarero. London: Routledge, 2000.

Krondorfer, Bjorn. "The Confines of Male Confessions: On Religion, Bodies, and Mirrors." In *Men's Bodies, Men's Gods: Male Identities in a (Post-) Christian Culture*, edited by Bjorn Krondorfer, 205–34. New York: New York University Press, 1996

Kvam, Kristen E., et al. *Eve and Adam: Jewish, Christian, and Muslim Readings on Genesis and Gender*. Bloomington: Indiana University Press, 1999.

Lamberigts, Mathijs. "A Critical Evaluation of Critiques of Augustine's View of Sexuality." In *Augustine and His Critics*, edited by R. Dodaro, and George Lawless, 176–97. New York: Routledge, 1997.

Laqueur, Thomas Walter. *Solitary Sex: A Cultural History of Masturbation*. New York: Zone Books, 2003.

Larson, Janet L. *Dickens and the Broken Scripture*. Athens: University of Georgia Press, 1985.

Lassen, Eva Marie. "The Roman Family: Ideal and Metaphor." In *Constructing Early Christian Families: Family as Social Reality and Metaphor*, edited by Halvor Moxnes, 103–120. New York: Routledge, 1997.

Lawler, Ronald, et al. "Masturbation." In *Dialogue about Catholic Sexual Teaching*, edited by Charles E. Curran and Richard A. McCormick, 361–71. Readings in Moral Theology 8. New York: Paulist, 1993.

Lear, Jonathan. *Happiness, Death, and the Remainder of Life*. Cambridge: Harvard University Press, 2000.

Lerner, Gerda. *The Creation of Patriarchy*. New York: Oxford University Press, 1986.

Levine, Judith. *Harmful to Minors: The Perils of Protecting Children from Sex*. Cambridge: Da Capo, 2003.

Lewis, R. W. B. *The American Adam: Innocence, Tragedy and Tradition in the Ninteenth Century*. Chicago: University of Chicago Press, 1955.

Linton, Eliza Lynn. *The Rebel of the Family*. Peterborough: Broadview, 2002

Lorde, Audre. *Sister Outsider: Essays and Speeches*. Crossing Press Feminist Series. Trumansburg, NY: Crossing, 1984

Lunn, Pam. "Anatomy and Theology of Marriage: Is Gay Marriage an Oxymoron?" *Theology and Sexuality* 7 (1997) 10–26.

Luther, Martin. *Martin Luther, Selections from His Writings*. Edited by John Dillenberger. Garden City, NY: Doubleday, 1961.

MacDonald, Scott. "Primal Sin." In *The Augustinian Tradition*, edited by G. B. Matthews, 110–139. Berkeley: University of California Press, 1999.

MacIntyre, Alasdair C. *Dependent Rational Animals: Why Human Beings Need the Virtues*. Chicago: Open Court, 1999.

———. *Three Rival Versions of Moral Enquiry: Encyclopaedia, Genealogy, and Tradition*. London: Duckworth, 1990.

Mackendrick, Karmen. "Carthage Didn't Burn Hot Enough: Saint Augustine's Divine Seduction." In *Toward a Theology of Eros*, edited by Virginia Burrus and Catherine Keller, 205–17. Transdisciplinary Theological Colloquia. New York: Fordham University Press, 2006.

MacKinnon, Catharine A. "Does Sexuality Have a History?" In *Discourses of Sexuality: From Aristotle to AIDS*, edited by Domna C. Stanton, 117–27. Ratio. Ann Arbor: University of Michigan Press, 1992.

———. "Pornography Left and Right." In *Sex, Preference, and Family: Essays on Law and Nature*, edited by David M. Estlund and Martha C. Nussbaum, 102–25. New York: Oxford University Press, 1997.

MacKinnon, Catharine A., and Andrea Dworkin. *In Harm's Way: The Pornography Civil Rights Hearings*. Cambridge: Harvard University Press, 1997.

Marcus, Sharon. *Between Women: Friendship, Desire, and Marriage in Victorian England*. Princeton: Princeton University Press, 2007.

Marion, Jean Luc. *God Without Being*. Translated by Thomas A. Carlson. Chicago: University of Chicago Press, 1991.

Markus, R. A. *Saeculum: History and Society in the Theology of St. Augustine*. Cambridge: Cambridge University Press, 1970.

Marlowe, Christopher. *Doctor Faustus*. New York: Oxford University Press, 1995.

Martin, Dale B. "Heterosexism and the Interpretation of Romans 1:18–32." *Biblical Interpretation* 3 (1995) 332–55.

Martinez, German. "Marriage as Worship: A Theological Analogy." In *Christian Perspectives on Sexuality and Gender*, edited by Elizabeth Stuart and Elizabeth Thatcher, 182–98. Grand Rapids: Eerdmans, 1996.

Masuzawa, Tomoko. *In Search of Dreamtime: The Quest for the Origin of Religion*. Chicago: University of Chicago Press, 1993.

Mathewes, Charles T. "Augustinian Anthropology: Interior Intimo Meo." *Journal of Religious Ethics* 27 (1999) 195–221.

———. "The Liberation of Questioning in Augustine's *Confessions*." *Journal of the American Academy of Religion* 70 (2002) 539–60.

———. "Original Sin and the Hermeneutics of Charity: A Response to Gilbert Meilaender." *Journal of Relgious Ethics* 29 (2001) 35–42.

Matter, E. Ann. "Christ, God and Woman in the Thought of St. Augustine." In *Augustine and His Critics: Essays in Honour of Gerald Bonner*, edited by Robert Dodaro, and George Lawless, 164–75. New York: Routledge, 1997.

Maturin, Charles Robert. *Melmoth the Wanderer*. New York: Oxford University Press, 1998.

Matzko, David. "The Relationship of Bodies: A Nuptial Hermeneutics of Same-Sex Unions." *Theology and Sexuality* 8 (1998) 96–112.

May, Todd. *Between Genealogy and Epistemology: Psychology, Politics, and Knowledge in the Thought of Michel Foucault*. University Park: Pennsylvania State University Press, 1993.

McFadyen, Alistair I. *Bound to Sin: Abuse, Holocaust, and the Christian Doctrine of Sin*. Cambridge Studies in Christian Doctrine 6. Cambridge: Cambridge University Press, 2000.

McWhorter, Ladelle. *Bodies and Pleasures: Foucault and the Politics of Sexual Normalization*. Bloomington: Indiana University Press, 1999.

Megill, Allan. *Prophets of Extremity: Nietzsche, Heidegger, Foucault, Derrida*. Berkeley: University of California Press, 1985.

Meilaender, Gilbert. "The First of Institutions: Theology of Marriage as Context for Interpreting Homosexuality." *Pro Ecclesia* 6 (1997) 444–55.

————. *Friendship: A Study in Theological Ethics.* Notre Dame: University of Notre Dame Press, 1981.

————. *The Limits of Love: Some Theological Explorations.* University Park: Pennsylvania State University Press, 1981.

————. "Sweet Necessities: Food, Sex, and Saint Augustine." *Journal of Religious Ethics* 29 (2001) 3–18.

————. *Things That Count: Essays Moral and Theological.* Wilmington, DE: ISI, 2000.

————. "What Sex Is—and Is For." *First Things* 102 (2000) 44–49.

Mendieta, Eduardo. *Take Care of Freedom and Truth Will Take Care of Itself: Interviews with Richard Rorty.* Stanford: Stanford University Press, 2006.

Midgley, Mary. "Philosophy and the Body." In *Religion and the Body*, edited by Sarah Coakley, 53–68. Cambridge Studies in Religious Traditions 8. New York: Cambridge University Press, 1997.

Milbank, John. *The Word Made Strange: Theology, Language, and Culture.* Cambridge: Blackwell, 1997.

Miles, Margaret R. *Carnal Knowing: Female Nakedness and Religious Meaning in the Christian West.* Boston: Beacon, 1989.

————. "Sex and the City (of God): Is Sex Forfeited or Fulfilled in Augustine's Resurrection of Body?" *Journal of the American Academy of Religion* 73 (2005) 307–27.

Miles, Steven H., and Allison August. "Courts, Gender, and the 'Right to Die.'" *Law, Medicine, and Health Care* 18/1–2 (1990) 85–95.

Miller, D. A. *The Novel and the Police.* Berkeley: University of California Press, 1988.

Miller, James. *The Passion of Michel Foucault.* New York: Simon & Schuster, 1993.

Milton, John. *Complete Poems and Major Prose.* Edited by Merritt Y. Hughes. Upper Saddle River, NJ: Prentice Hall, 1957.

Moberly, Elizabeth R. *Homosexuality: A New Christian Ethic.* Cambridge: James Clarke, 1983.

Moberly, Elizabeth R. *Psychogenesis, the Early Development of Gender Identity.* Boston: Routledge, 1983.

Mohr, Richard D. "The Pedophilia of Everyday Life." In *Curioser: On the Queerness of Children*, edited by Bruhm and Hurley, 17–30. Minneapolis: University of Minnesota Press, 2004.

Mollenkott, Virginia Ramey. *Women, Men, and the Bible.* New York: Crossroad, 1988.

Moretti, Franco. *The Way of the World: The Bildungsroman in European Culture.* Translated by Albert Sbragia. London: Verso, 2000.

Murdoch, Iris. *Metaphysics as a Guide to Morals.* London: Penguin, 1993.

Newey, Vincent. *The Scriptures of Charles Dickens: Novels of Ideology.* Burlington, VT: Ashgate, 2004.

Ngai, Sianne. "The Cuteness of the Avant-Garde." *Critical Inquiry* 31 (2005) 811–47.

Niebuhr, Reinhold. *The Nature and Destiny of Man.* New York: Scribner, 1941.

Novak, David. *Natural Law in Judaism.* Cambridge: Cambridge University Press, 1998.

Nussbaum, Martha C. "The Professor of Parody." *New Republic* 220/8 (1999) 37–45.

————. "Steerforth's Arm: Love and the Moral Point of View." In *Love's Knowledge: Essays on Philosophy and Literature*, 335–64. New York: Oxford University Press, 1990.

O'Connell, Robert J. "Sexuality in Saint Augustine." In *Augustine Today.* Edited by Ernest L. Fortin et al. Grand Rapids: Eerdmans, 1993.

Ohi, Kevin. "Autobiography and *David Copperfield*'s Temporalities of Loss." *Victorian Literature and Culture* (2005) 435–49.

O'Malley, Suzanne. *"Are You There Alone?" The Unspeakable Crime of Andrea Yates*. New York: Simon & Schuster, 2004.

Ortner, Sherry B. "Is Female as to Male as Nature Is to Culture?" In *Woman, Culture, and Society*, edited by Michelle Zimbalist Rosaldo and Louise Lamphere, 67–87. Stanford: Stanford University Press, 1974.

Outka, Gene. "Faith." In *Oxford Handbook of Theological Ethics*, edited by Gilbert Meilaender and William Werpehowski, 273–90. Oxford Handbooks. New York: Oxford University Press, 2005.

———. "The Particularist Turn in Theological and Philosophical Ethics." In *Christian Ethics: Problems and Prospects*, edited by Lisa Sowle Cahill, and James F. Childress, 93–118. Cleveland: Pilgrim, 1996.

———. "Theocentric Love and the Augustinian Legacy: Honoring Differences and Likenesses between God and Ourselves." *Journal of the Society of Christian Ethics* 22 (2002) 97–114.

Pagels, Elaine H. *Adam, Eve, and the Serpent*. New York: Random House, 1988.

Paglia, Camille. *Vamps and Tramps: New Essays*. New York: Vintage, 1994.

Pagliarini, Marie Anne. "The Pure American Woman and the Wicked Catholic Priest: An Analysis of Anti-Catholic Literature in Antebellum America." *Religion and American Culture* 9 (1999) 97–128.

Pascal, Blaise. *Pensées*. Translated by A. J. Krailsheimer. London: Penguin, 1995.

Peters, Pete. *Death Penalty for Homosexuals Is Prescribed in the Bible*. Laporte, CO: Scriptures for America, 1992.

Piper, John, and Wayne A. Grudem. *Recovering Biblical Manhood and Womanhood: A Response to Evangelical Feminism*. Wheaton, IL: Crossway, 1991.

Possidius. *The Life of Saint Augustine*. Edited by John E. Rotelle. Villanova: Augustinian, 1988.

Power, Kim. *Veiled Desire*. New York: Continuum, 1995.

Pranger, M. B. "Politics and Finitude: The Temporal Status of Augustine's *Civitas Permixta*." In *Political Theologies: Public Religions in a Post-Secular World*, edited by Hent de Vries and Lawrence E. Sullivan, 113–21. New York: Fordham University Press, 2006.

Quinn, Philip. "Disputing the Augustinian Legacy." In *The Augustinian Tradition*, edited by Gareth B. Matthews, 233–50. Philosophical Traditions 8. Berkeley: University of California Press, 1999.

Radcliffe, Ann Ward. *The Italian; or, the Confessional of the Black Penitents: A Romance*. New York: Oxford University Press, 1998.

Rahner, Karl. *Foundations of Christian Faith: An Introduction to the Idea of Christianity*. Translated by William V. Dych. New York: Seabury, 1978.

Ramsey Colloquium. "The Homosexual Movement." *First Things* 41 (1994) 15–20.

Ramsey, Paul. *Ethics at the Edges of Life: Medical and Legal Intersections*. New Haven: Yale University Press, 1978.

Ramsey, Paul. "Human Sexuality in the History of Redemption." In *The Ethics of St Augustine*, William S. Babcock, 115–45. JRE Studies in Religion 3. Atlanta: Scholars, 1991.

Ranke-Heinemann, Uta. *Eunuchs for the Kingdom of Heaven: Women, Sexuality, and the Catholic Church*. New York: Doubleday, 1990.

Reade, Charles. *Griffith Gaunt; or, Jealousy*. London: Chapman & Hall, 1866.

Reed, Rebecca Theresa, and Maria Monk. *A Veil of Fear: Nineteenth Century Convent Tales*. West Lafayette, IN: Notabell, 1999.

Rees, Geoffrey. "The Anxiety of Inheritance: Reinhold Niebuhr and the Literal Truth of Original Sin." *Journal of Relgious Ethics* 31 (2003) 75–99.

———. "'In the Sight of God': Gender Complementarity and the Male Homosocial Signification of Male-Female Difference." *Theology and Sexuality* 9 (2002) 19–47.

———. "Original Sin in the Original Position: A Kierkegaardian Reading of John Rawls's Writings on Justice." *Journal of the Society of Christian Ethics* 28 (2006) 61–91.

Rekers, George Alan. "Psychological Foundations for Rearing Masculine Boys and Feminine Girls." In *Recovering Biblical Manhood and Womanhood*, edited by Piper and Grudem, 294–311. Wheaton, IL: Crossway, 1991

Reyonds, Philip Lyndon. *Marriage in the Western Church: The Christianization of Marriage During the Patristic and Early Medieval Periods*. Supplements to Vigilae Christianae 24. Leiden: Brill, 1994.

Rich, Adrienne. "Compulsory Heterosexuality." In *Blood, Bread, and Poetry: Selected Prose, 1979–1985*. New York: Norton, 1986.

Ricoeur, Paul. *The Symbolism of Evil*. Translated by Emerson Buchanan. Boston: Beacon, 1969.

Rigby, Paul. *Original Sin in Augustine's Confessions*. Ottawa: University of Ottawa Press, 1987.

Riley, Patrick. *Civilizing Sex*. Edinburgh: T. & T. Clark, 2000.

Rist, John M. *Augustine: Ancient Thought Baptized*. Cambridge: Cambridge University Press, 1994.

Roberts, Christopher C. *Creation and Covenant: The Significance of Sexual Difference in the Moral Theology of Marriage*. New York: T. & T. Clark, 2007.

Rogers, Eugene F., Jr. *Sexuality and the Christian Body: Their Way into the Triune God*. Challenges in Contemporary Theology. Malden, MA: Blackwell, 1999.

Roscoe, Will. *Jesus and the Shamanic Tradition of Same-Sex Love*. San Francisco: Suspect Thoughts, 2004

Rose, Nikolas S. *Governing the Soul: The Shaping of the Private Self*. New York: Routledge, 1990.

Rose, Nikolas S. *The Politics of Life Itself: Biomedicine, Power, and Subjectivity in the Twenty-first Century*. Information Series. Princeton: Princeton University Press, 2006.

Rose, Phyllis. *Parallel Lives: Five Victorian Marriages*. New York: Knopf, 1983.

Rubin, Gayle. "Thinking Sex." In *Pleasure and Danger: Exploring Female Sexuality* edited by Carol Vance, 267–319. Boston: Routledge, 1984.

Rudy, Kathy. "'Where Two or More Are Gathered': Using Gay Communities as a Model for Christian Sexual Ethics." *Theology and Sexuality* 4 (1996) 81–99.

Ruether, Rosemary Radford. *Christianity and the Making of the Modern Family*. Boston: Beacon, 2000.

Russell, Letty M. *Church in the Round: Feminist Interpretation of the Church*. Louisville: Westminster John Knox, 1993.

———. *Just Hospitality*. Louisville: Westminster John Knox, 2009.

Sager, Mike. "Mr. Pitt and his Magical Mistress." *Esquire* 146/4 (2006) 164–69.

Schmitt, Carl. *Political Theology*. Translated by George Schwab. Chicago: University of Chicago Press, 2005.

Schreiner, Susan E. "Eve, the Mother of History: Reaching for the Reality of History in Augustine's Later Exegesis of Genesis." In *Genesis 1–3 in the History of Exegesis*, 135–86. Lewiston, NY: Mellen, 1988.

Schuld, J. Joyce. *Foucault and Augustine: Reconsidering Power and Love*. Notre Dame: University of Notre Dame Press, 2003.

Sedgwick, Eve Kosofsky. *Between Men: English Literature and Male Homosocial Desire.* New York: Columbia University Press, 1985.

———. *Epistemology of the Closet.* Berkeley: University of California Press, 1990.

———. "How to Bring up Your Kids Gay: The War on Effeminate Boys." In *Tendencies,* 154–64. Durham: Duke University Press, 1993.

Smith, Jonathan Z. "The Bare Facts of Ritual." In *Imagining Religion: From Babylon to Jonestown,* 53–65. Chicago Studies in the History of Judaism. Chicago: University of Chicago Press, 1982.

Soble, Alan. "Philosophy, Medicine, and Healthy Sexuality." In *Sexuality and Medicine,* edited by E. E. Shelp. Norwell: D. Reidel, 1987.

Stark, Judith Chelius. *Feminist Interpretations of Augustine.* University Park: Pennsylvania State University Press, 2007.

Stengers, Jean, and Anne van Neck. *Masturbation: The History of a Great Terror.* New York: Palgrave, 2001.

Stockton, Kathryn Bond. *Beautiful Bottom, Beautiful Shame: Where "Black" Meets "Queer."* Durham, NC: Duke University Press, 2006.

Stone, Ken. "Homosexuality and the Bible or Queer Reading? A Response to Martti Nissinen." *Theology and Sexuality* 14 (2001) 107–18.

———. *Practicing Safer Texts: Food, Sex, and the Bible.* New York: Continuum, 2005.

Stout, Jeffrey. "How Charity Transcends the Culture Wars: Eugene Rogers and Others on Same-Sex Marriage." *Journal of Religious Ethics* 31 (2003) 169–80.

Strenski, Ivan. "Religion, Power, and Final Foucault." *Journal of the American Academy of Religion* 66 (1998) 345–67.

Suchocki, Marjorie. "The Symbolic Structure of Augustine's *Confessions.*" *Journal of the American Academy of Religion* 50 (1982) 365–78.

Suffredini, Kara S. "Pride and Prejudice: The Homosexual Panic Defense." *Boston College Third World Law Journal* 21 (2001) 279–314.

Sullivan, Andrew. *Same-Sex Marriage, Pro and Con: A Reader.* New York: Vintage, 1997.

———. *Virtually Normal: An Argument About Homosexuality.* New York: Knopf, 1995.

Swancutt, Diana M. "Sexing the Pauline Body of Christ: Scriptural Sex in the Context of the American Christian Cultural War." In *Toward a Theology of Eros,* edited by Burrus and Keller, 65–98. New York: Fordham University Press, 2006.

Swift, Jonathan. *Gulliver's Travels.* Norton Critical Edition. New York: Norton, 1961.

Tambling, Jeremy. *Becoming Posthumous: Life and Death in Literary and Cultural Studies.* Edinburgh: Edinburgh University Press, 2001.

Tanner, John S. *Anxiety in Eden: A Kierkegaardian Reading of Paradise Lost.* New York: Oxford University Press, 1992.

Tanner, Kathryn E. *Theories of Culture: A New Agenda for Theology.* Guides to Theological Inquiry. Minneapolis: Fortress, 1997.

Taylor, Charles. *Sources of the Self: The Making of Modern Identity.* Cambridge: Harvard University Press, 1989.

Tennant, F. R. *The Sources of the Doctrines of the Fall and Original Sin.* Cambridge: Cambridge University Press, 1903.

Terry, Jennifer. *An American Obsession: Science, Medicine, and Homosexuality in Modern Society.* Chicago: University of Chicago Press, 1999.

Thatcher, Adrian. "'Crying out for Discernment'—Premodern Marriage in Postmodern Times." *Theology and Sexuality* 8 (1998) 73–95.

Thurber, James, and E. B. White. *Is Sex Necessary? Or, Why You Feel the Way You Do.* New York: Harper & Row, 1975.

Ticciati, Susanah. "The Castration of Signs: Conversing with Augustine on Creation, Language, and Truth." *Modern Theology* 23 (2007) 161–79.

Tillich, Paul. *The Courage to Be*. New Haven: Yale University Press, 1952.

———. *The Dynamics of Faith*. New York: Harper & Row, 1957.

Tisdale, Sally. "Talk Dirty to Me." In *The Philosophy of Sex: Contemporay Readings*, edited by A. Soble, 271–81. Lanham, MD: Rowman & Littlefield, 1997.

Trible, Phyllis. *Texts of Terror: Literary-Feminist Readings of Biblical Narratives*. Overtures to Biblical Theology. Philadelphia: Fortress, 1984.

Trollope, Anthony. *Sir Harry Hotspur of Humblethwaite*. London: Penguin, 1993.

Trollope, Frances Milton. *Father Eustace: A Tale of the Jesuits*. London: Colburn, 1846.

Trudgill, Eric. *Madonnas and Magdalens: The Origins and Development of Victorian Sexual Attitudes*. New York: Holmes & Meier, 1976.

Vance, Norman. *The Sinews of the Spirit: The Ideal of Christian Manliness in Victorian Literature and Religious Thought*. New York: Cambridge University Press, 1985.

Vernon, Mark. "Following Foucault: The Strategies of Sexuality and the Struggle to Be Different." *Theology and Sexuality* 5 (1996) 76–96.

Volf, Miroslav. *Exclusion and Embrace: A Theological Exploration of Identity, Otherness, and Reconciliation*. Nashville: Abingdon, 1996.

Walder, Dennis. *Dickens and Religion*. New York: Routledge, 1981.

Ware, Vron. "The Power of Recall: Writing against Racial Identity." In *Racialization: Studies in Theory and Practice*, edited by Karim Murji, and John Solomos, 123–39. New York: Oxford University Press, 2005.

Warner, Michael. *The Trouble with Normal: Sex, Politics and the Ethics of Queer Life*. New York: Free Press, 1999.

Warren, Charles E. *Original Sin Explained? Revelations from Human Genetic Science*. Lanham, MD: University Press of America, 2002.

Watt, David Harrington. "The Private Hopes of American Fundamentalists and Evangelicals, 1925–1975." *Religion and American Culture* 1 (1991) 155–75.

Weeks, Jeffrey. "Capitalism and the Organisation of Sex." In *Homosexuality: Power and Politics*, edited by Gay Left Collective, 11–20. London: Alison & Busby, 1980.

Weil, Simone. *Gravity and Grace*. Translated by Emma Crawford and Mario von der Ruhr. New York: Routledge, 2002.

West, Cornel. *Prophesy Deliverance! An Afro-American Revolutionary Christianity*. Louisville: Westminster John Knox, 2002.

Wetzel, James. *Augustine and the Limits of Virtue*. Cambridge: Cambridge University Press, 1992.

Williams, Rowan. "Insubstantial Evil." In *Augustine and His Critics: Essays in Honour of Gerald Bonner*, edited by Robert Dodaro and George Lawless, 105–23. New York: Routledge, 1997.

Wolterstorff, Nicholas. *Divine Discourse: Philosophical Reflections on the Claim That God Speaks*. New York: Cambridge University Press, 1995.

Wood, Mrs. Henry. *Lord Oakburn's Daughters*. London: Bentley, 1897.

Ziolkowski, Eric J. "St. Augustine: Aeneas' Antitype, Monica's Boy." In *Literature and Theology* 9 (1995) 1–23.

Subject and Name Index

confession, 4, 99, 144, 150, 155,
 165n63, 170, 178, 226, 238, 270,
 273, 281, 289
confessor, 52n52
Connolly, William, 17n27
constructivism, 151n30, 173
concupiscence, 181n3, 192, 206
contamination, 27n5, 29n9, 101
continence, 94, 185n8
conversion, 120, 163, 280
Copjec, Joan, 207
corruptibility, 138, 160
Cott, Nancy F., 26n2
Council on Biblical Manhood and
 Womanhood, 76–77, 81, 83, 112,
 125n62
Countryman, Louis William, 224n56
covenant, 26n2, 116
coverture, 129
creation *ex nihilo*, 164, 173
creator, xiv, 19–20, 36, 41, 56, 146, 155,
 160, 163, 168, 170, 172, 176, 180,
 187, 226, 229, 238, 274–75
criminal conversation, 129, 255
crisis, 22–23, 40, 57, 59, 60–61, 63, 66,
 82–83, 100–101, 132
Cross, Anthony J., 239n35
culture wars, 125n60
Cunningham, Valerie, 239n35
cuteness, 74
cyborg, 9n12

Da Silva, Stephen, 255n58
Daly, Mary, 27n5, 130n69, 147n24
Dames, Nicholas, 222n8
David Copperfield, 128, 227n4, 229–30,
 243, 245, 249–53, 261–68, 278
Davidson, Arnold, 40n31
Davidson, Cathy, and Jessamyn Hatcher,
 204n35
death: as punishment for sin, 11, 14–15,
 56, 99, 111–12, 174, 280; of a child,
 72, 87
death instinct, 15, 17, 68–69, 259
Deceased Wife's Sister's Bill, 231n20
defilement, 27, 29n9, 94, 248

degradation, 190, 209, 248, 281, 283
déjà vu, 264
democracy, 6n5, 278, 282–83
denial: of child sexuality, 73n33; of
 God, 146, 218; of homosexual
 child, 78–81, 111; of hospitality,
 252, 280; of intelligibility, 53, 126,
 200; of origins, 142, 234–35, 249,
 262; of responsibility for sin,
 149–50, 250, 269–70, 274, 281–82;
 of a wedding feast, 128
dependency, 152–54, 152n32, 156–57,
 162, 167, 229, 249, 264
depravity, 47
DeRogatis, Amy, 27n5
Descarte, René, 10n14
desire: for unity, 30–31, 33–34, 42–43,
 45–47, 50n50, 53, 67, 71, 94–95,
 100, 125–26, 129–30, 137, 149, 192,
 229, 233, 280–81; same sex, 26,
 62, 75, 77, 128–29; sexual, x, 2–4,
 29–30, 35, 41–42, 94, 107, 127, 132,
 135–36, 180, 192, 196, 232, 244,
 247–48, 248n52, 250, 253, 264,
 267, 280
Dever, Carolyn, 163n58
devil, 14, 203, 206–8, 242n41, 267–68,
Dickens, Catherine, 231n19
Dickens, Charles, 72, 226, 230; *David
 Copperfield*, 226–27, 229–31, 233–
 34, 237–38, 239–40, 258–59, 262,
 278; *The Old Curiosity Shop*, 72
dignity, 2
disbelief, suspension of, 69, 82
discernment, 39, 41, 82–83, 86, 116,
 185, 193, 199, 204, 218, 220
discourse: "more" of, 18–19; theology
 as, 17–24. *See also* theological
 discourse on sexuality
disgrace, 8, 15, 89, 93–95, 98–100,
 100–102, 110, 123, 126, 129, 136,
 171, 192, 195, 201, 212. *See also*
 Fall; grace
disintegration, of self, 36, 81, 101, 195,
 227

history (*continued*)
    of sexuality, 49, 132, 137, 138, 143,
    147, 188, 193, 195, 206, 286n13; of
    social relationship, 173
HIV, 111,
Hobbes, Thomas, 98n25
Hogarth, Catherine and Georgina, 231
home, 66n23, 76n42, 79, 88–89, 94,
    95, 100, 163n57, 204–6, 204n37,
    241–42, 246n50, 257–58
homicide, 127, 129
homo/heterosexual definition, 55, 57–
    63, 65–66, 66n22, 77n45, 82–84,
    100–103, 106, 112, 114, 116, 120,
    124, 126, 140, 144n22, 182, 184,
    187, 191, 199, 224n56, 280, 287
homosexual panic, 62–64, 67–68, 80,
    83, 101, 108, 109, 123, 126, 129n68,
    184–85, 187, 245, 267
homosociality, 62, 68, 83, 126, 144n22
homunculus, 48, 52, 102
honesty (and consistency), 141–43,
    150, 172, 249
honor, 96–97
hope, 10, 66n23, 81, 154, 175, 202, 217,
    218, 284, 287
hospitality, 11, 12, 20, 67, 124, 128,
    194, 201, 207, 252, 263, 265, 266,
    271, 278–81, 278n4 , 284, 288
humility, 142n19, 155, 214, 251, 266
humor: mature, 11, 16–17, 23–24, 54,
    69–70, 113, 120, 141, 177–78, 183,
    193, 201, 233, 283, 287; pagan, 12;
    faithful, 12
humorlessness, 23,68n26, 69, 187, 193,
    199, 201, 217, 239, 249,
Hunter, David G., 135n2
husband and wife, 27n5, 101, 199, 204,
    206

idolatry, 46, 122
ignorance, 20, 53, 57–58, 136, 209, 238
illumination, 136, 233, 259–60, 264,
    277
imagination: fallen, 35, 37, 69, 86, 198,
    208, 216, 282–83, 286; human,

16–17, 32, 42, 46, 51, 56, 202, 216,
    285–86; present, xiii, 284; romantic,
    137, 149, 224, 249; theological,
    xiii, 86
imago-dei, 60,
immortality, 10n16, 11n20
imperfectability, 10, 137, 196, 220, 221,
    283
incoherence, 59, 60, 198, 273
incompleteness, 141, 175
infanticide, 87n5
infection, 101, 111, 211, 212n46
infertility, 121, 122n57
inheritance, of sin, xii, 11, 22, 137, 143,
    171–74, 177, 201, 208, 211, 220,
    221, 275, 278, 284, 288
inhospitality, 278–80, 281, 289
injustice, ix, 12, 47, 54, 56, 60, 218, 249,
    254, 261, 262, 265, 268, 287
innocence, x–xi, 4, 9, 11–12, 13, 35,
    66–68, 66n22, 71, 74–76, 80–81,
    84, 124, 204, 209n43, 212, 215, 218,
    236–38, 242–43, 246–47, 249–53,
    255, 269, 275, 281, 281
intellect, 156, 157, 10n14
intention, 41, 73, 86, 103, 106, 153
intentionality, 35n22
intercourse, 8, 108, 140, 183–85, 197,
    222–23
invisibility, 53, 65–67, 100–104, 108,
    110–11, 116, 117, 122, 234, 241,
    246–47, 249, 253, 260, 270, 275,
    276, 281
Irigaray, Luce, 51n51
irony, 12

Jackson, Timothy, 202n29
Jakobsen, Janet R., 205n40
Jantzen, Grace, 132, 146n24
Jepthah, 98n25
Johnson, Edgar, 231n19
Johnson, James Turner, 26n2
Judaism, 106
judgment, 5, 15, 66, 70, 191, 196, 218,
    231n20, 244, 253, 279, 280
Julian, 135n2, 221, 223

Scripture Index